—FAVORITE—

KNITTING AND CROCHET PATTERNS

—FAVORITE—

KNITTING AND CROCHET PATTERNS

SEDGEWOOD PRESS

Published by Sedgewood Press

For Sedgewood Press
Editorial Director: Jane Ross
Supervising Editor: Gale Kremer
Production Manager: Bill Rose

Produced for Sedgewood Press by
Marshall Cavendish House
58 Old Compton Street
London W1V 5PA

For Marshall Cavendish
Consultant Editor: Virginia Colton
American Editors: Sally Harding
Eleanor Van Zandt
House Editor: Frances Jones
Designer: Val Wright

First printing 1982

LCCN 81-71014

Distributed in the Trade by:
Van Nostrand Reinhold Company

ISBN 0-442-28090-4

Printed in the United States of America

INTRODUCTION

FAVORITE KNITTING AND CROCHET PATTERNS brings together a wide range of designs, the best of the traditional and most glamorous of the fashionable. Whether you want to crochet a bikini in an evening or linger over a delicate set of knitted baby clothes, there's a pattern timed to your tastes. Whatever inspires you – matching Scandinavian ski sweaters or play overalls for the kids, a smoking jacket for grandad or a casual country sweater for yourself – it's all here in this comprehensive book of everyone's favorites.

FAVORITE KNITTING AND CROCHET PATTERNS is easy to follow, and extra helpful with its illustrated step-by-step guide to basic stitches and techniques. Aimed at beginners and experts alike, this book will be especially valuable to those who were taught by a relative or friend and may not be familiar with the common names of stitches and methods.

Every pattern is shown in full color and includes a black-and-white illustration of the garment showing measurements for each individual size. At the back of the book, you'll find such generally useful information as knitting and crochet abbreviations, a glossary of terms and a carefully detailed index.

This voluminous book of knitting and crochet contains over 100 exciting and imaginative patterns, enough to keep you and your growing family happy for many years.

CONTENTS

KNITTING

CROCHET

CROCHET INTRODUCTION

Crochet takes its name from the French word *croc* – meaning hook. Unlike knitting, in which rows of loops are worked back and forth on two needles, crochet is made with a single hook that forms one stitch at a time onto the fabric below. Despite the differences between the two crafts, crochet is probably an offshoot of knitting. There is evidence that knitting pre-dates crochet and this, along with the fact that knitting needles in the past sometimes had hooks on the ends, does support the hypothesis that a skilled knitter invented the first crochet loops. Probably the strongest link, however, between crochet and knitting is Tunisian (or Afghan) crochet in which loops are worked onto and off a long hook making it a perfect combination of the two techniques.
In sixteenth century Europe, when lace-making was one of the largest textile industries, crochet was used to imitate the more difficult to produce needle-made lace. But it was never restricted to fine work and we know that by the beginning of the nineteenth century, when numerous patterns were printed, it was widely used to make warm woolen clothing, just as it is today.

Types of crochet
With a tool as simple as a crochet hook and varying types of yarns, it is hard to believe that the same technique can be used to create so many different textures. At first glance it seems impossible that the fine intricate European lace, the smooth geometric patterned African skull caps, and the bright woolly medallions of American afghans could all have been produced with the same basic loops. The patterns in this book give some idea of the versatility of crochet. These include examples of crochet medallions, fine filet crochet, colorwork crochet and embossed crochet.

Reading the crochet patterns
Both the crochet and the knitting patterns in this book are written as simply and yet as comprehensively as possible, which should be welcomed by both beginners and experienced needleworkers alike. Each pattern begins with a section on *sizes*. This gives the relevant measurements of the finished garment, and lists the sizes that it can be made for.
The next section comprises a list of all of the necessary *materials* including yarns, hook (or needle) sizes and any extras required such as buttons, zippers, ribbons, etc. Where more than one color yarn is used, the colors are coded by letters (A, B, C, etc) for easy reference in the directions. Note that only the general type of yarn is given rather than a brand name. This allows you to choose from the wide range of yarns available in most needlework shops and saves you from the sometimes fruitless task of trying to find a particular brand which in the end does not offer the colors you want.
By checking your stitch *gauge* carefully and matching it to that given in the pattern directions, you will have no trouble fitting the yarn you have chosen to the pattern. The gauge refers to the size of the stitches. Before starting any crochet (or knitting) pattern, you should make a square sample swatch of the fabric using the yarn you have chosen, the hook (or needle) size and the type of stitch listed in the gauge directions. Make the first row of the sample slightly longer than the number of stitches specified to make up 4in.
When you have completed the sample, smooth it out on a flat surface, but do not stretch it. Then measure how many stitches there are per 4in. If the number does not match the number given in the patterns, you should change your hook (or needle) size and make another sample. A smaller hook will give more stitches per inch and a larger one will give fewer.
The *row-by-row* directions of the pattern give the details for making the crochet pieces. Be sure to follow them methodically and in the order specified.
The *finishing* directions tell you how to make any seams required. If pressing is called for, check the label on your yarn before proceeding. You may find that your yarn will be damaged by pressing or can only withstand a very low temperature. Yarn labels also give valuable information for cleaning, so it is wise to put one of them aside for future reference.

Symbols and abbreviations
If you are a beginner, you may not be familiar with the symbols and abbreviations employed to shorten crochet directions. Symbols used include asterisks, parentheses and brackets. *Asterisks* and *parentheses* indicate that a section of a pattern needs to be repeated. *Brackets* are used to separate the instructions when they vary for different sizes. The figure for the smallest size appears first and those for larger sizes follow inside the brackets.
A full list of crochet (and knitting) abbreviations is given at the back of the book along with a glossary.

BASIC TECHNIQUES

The following step-by-step instructions are meant for beginners, but may also be a useful guide for those who have been taught to crochet by a mother or grandmother and who are proficient in working the loops but are not familiar with the common names of the stitches.

All you need to try your hand at crochet is a hook and some yarn. Hooks come in more than 20 sizes, starting as fine as a No. 14 hook in steel. It is handy to keep several of the middle range sizes if you crochet frequently, as you will need them for altering stitch gauge (see previous page).

The only other items necessary for crochet are common sewing tools such as a tape measure, pins, blunt-ended needles and a pair of scissors.

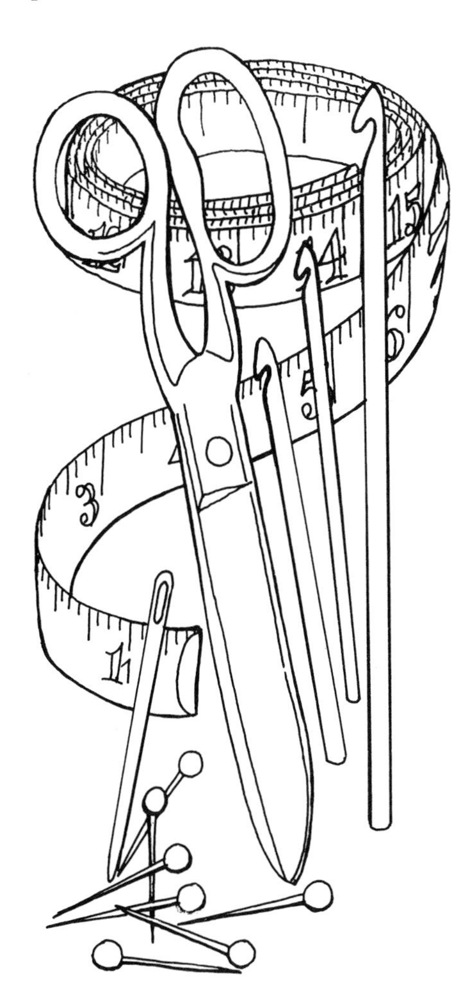

Slip knot

Crochet is a very easy craft to learn. Even if you have a friend or relative willing to teach you the basics, you will find that learning from a book has its advantages. First, the detailed drawings of the loops give you a clearer visual picture of the structure of the loops than you may be able to see with a woolly yarn. Also you can read the instructions as often as you like without feeling rushed. The slip knot creates the first loop on the hook required for both crochet and knitting.

1. Begin by making a circle of yarn as above.

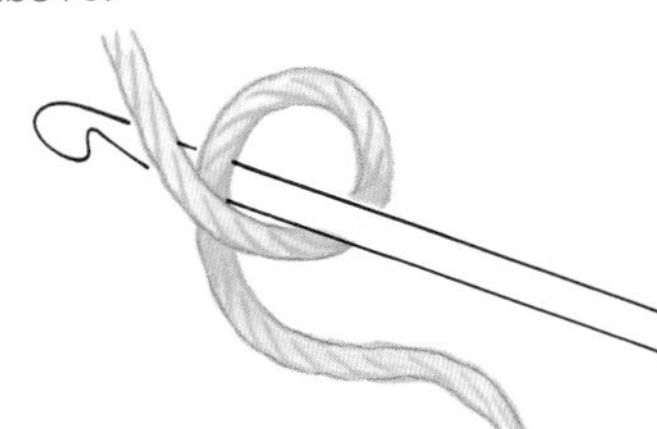

2. Then insert your hook through the ring and catch the yarn end.

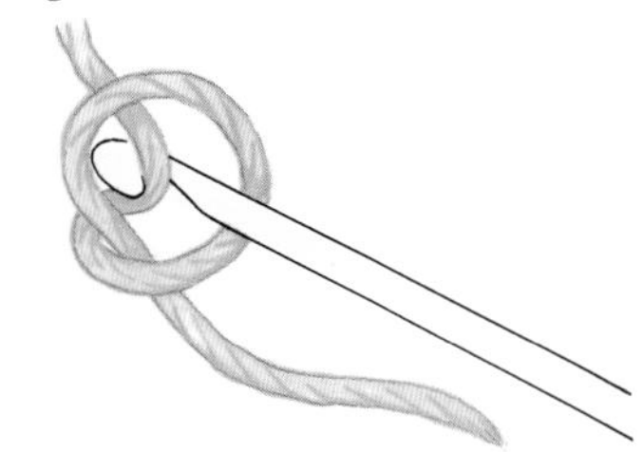

3. Draw a loop of the yarn through the ring.

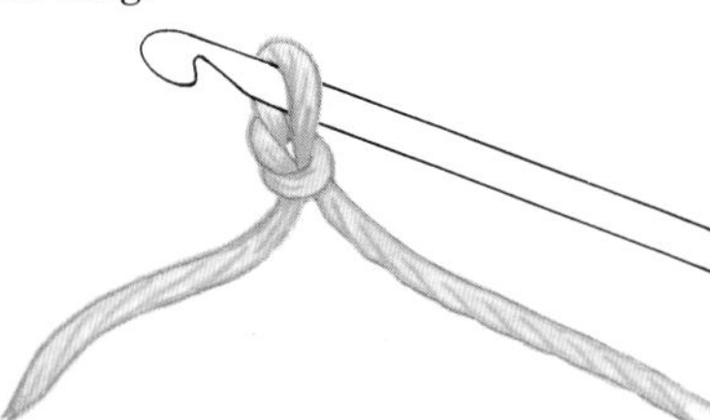

4. Pull the ends of the yarn to tighten the loop on the hook.

Chain stitch (ch)

The first row of crochet stitches is worked onto a length of chain loops called the *foundation chain*. The positions shown here for holding the yarn and the hook are merely suggestions. You might find it more comfortable to hold the hook in the "knife" position. Try both methods and choose the one that gives you the most control. Threading the yarn around the fingers regulates the flow of yarn and variations are endless. What is important is that the tension placed on the yarn is even so that consistently sized loops are formed.

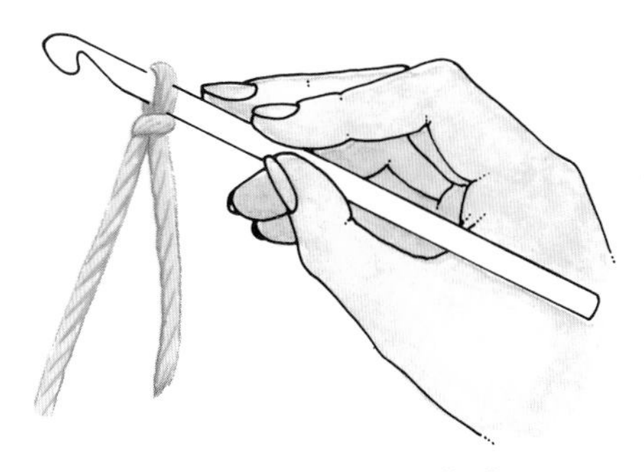

1. Hold the hook with a slip knot on it in the right hand, as if you were holding a pencil.

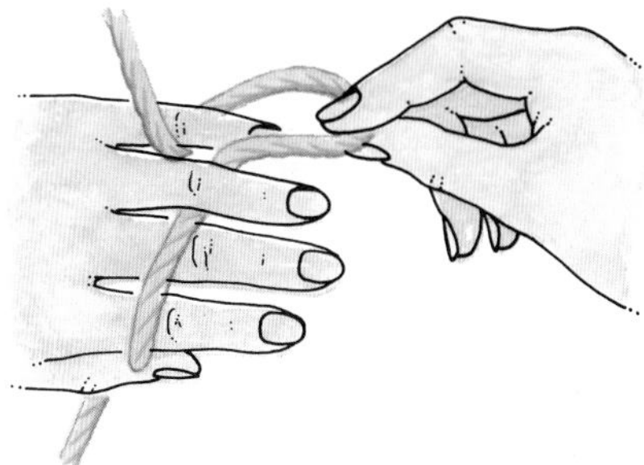

2. Lace the yarn around the fingers of the left hand as shown above.

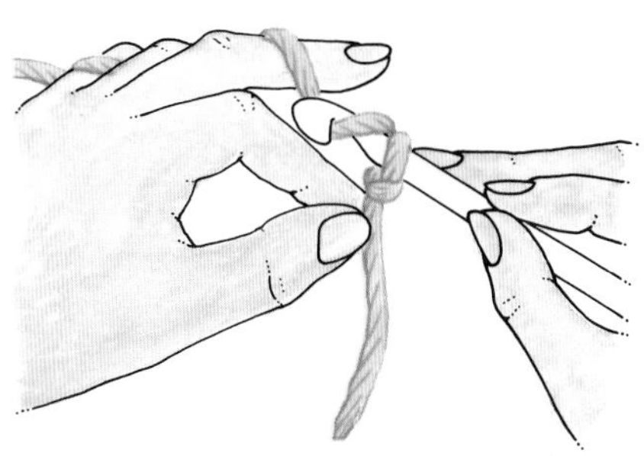

3. To make a chain, wrap the yarn over the hook and draw a loop through the slip knot. This completes the first chain. Continue making the required number of chains in the same way.

Slip stitch (sl st)

A slip stitch forms a flat chain onto the stitch below. It is rarely used to form a fabric on its own but is commonly used in shaping and for joining one part of the crochet to another. It is also useful for making crochet seams.

1. To work slip stitch on a foundation chain, first insert the hook into the second chain from the hook. Wrap the yarn over the hook as shown. Draw the yarn through the chain and the loop on the hook. One loop is now on the hook. This completes the first slip stitch. Continue in the same way to the end, working a slip stitch into each chain.

2. When decreasing stitches, for instance at an armhole, slip stitch over the stitches to be decreased in the row below. Then work chains (called turning chains) to bring the hook up to the correct height for the following stitches. Here two chains have been worked for the following half double stitch.

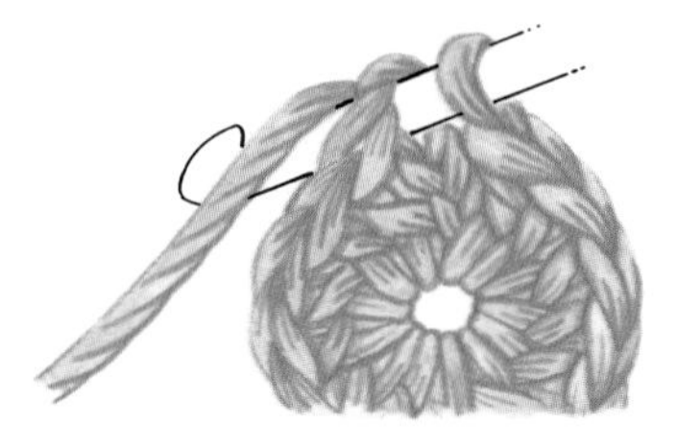

3. A slip stitch is also used when working in rounds to join the last stitch of the round to the first before beginning the next round. When the last stitch has been worked, insert the hook into the top of the turning chain at the beginning of the round and work a slip stitch.

Single crochet (sc)

Single, double, half double and triple crochet are the basic stitches used to produce crochet fabrics.

1. First make a foundation chain. Then insert the hook into the second chain from the hook. Wrap the yarn over the hook and draw a loop through the chain. Two loops are now on the hook.

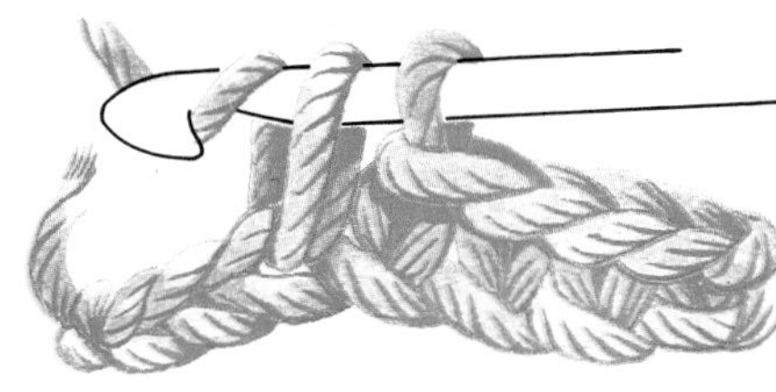

2. Wrap the yarn over the hook and draw it through both loops on the hook. This completes the first single crochet. Make a single crochet into each chain in the same way. Then turn the work so that the yarn is at the top right.

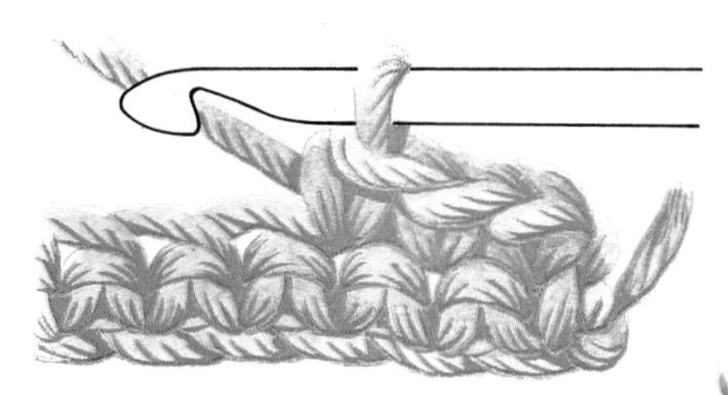

3. To begin the next row, first make one chain (the turning chain). This counts as the first stitch. Skip the first single crochet in the row below, insert the hook through both loops of the top of the next stitch and make a single crochet. Work into each stitch to the end of the row. Then make the last single crochet into the turning chain of the first row. Turn and work the next row in the same way.

Half double crochet (hdc)

1. Wrap the yarn from back to front over the hook. Then insert the hook into the third chain from the hook. Wrap the yarn over the hook and draw a loop through the chain. There are now three loops on the hooks.

2. Wrap the yarn over the hook and draw it through all three loops on the hook. This completes the first half double. Wrap the yarn over the hook and make a half double into the next chain in the same way. Continue working into each chain to the end. Then turn the work.

3. Make two chains to count as the first half double. Skip the first stitch in the row below and work into the next stitch.

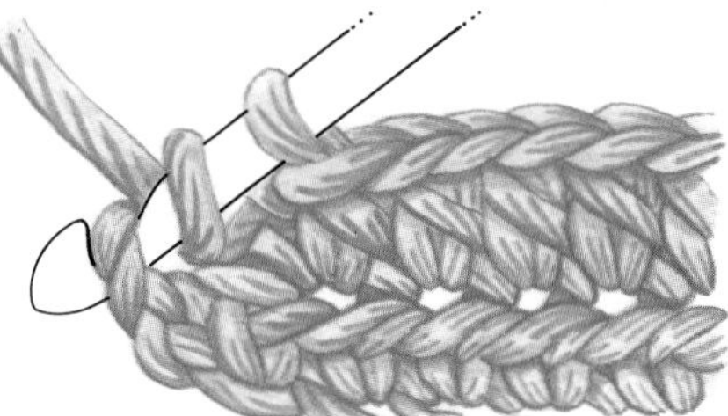

4. Make half doubles into each stitch to the end of the row. Then work the last stitch into the turning chain. Turn and begin the next row.

Double crochet (dc)

1. Wrap the yarn over the hook and insert the hook into the fourth chain from the hook. This counts as the first stitch.

2. Wrap the yarn over the hook and draw a loop through the chain. Three loops are now on the hook.

3. Wrap the yarn over the hook and draw it through the first two loops on the hook. Two loops remain on the hook.

4. Wrap the yarn over the hook and draw it through both remaining loops. This completes the double. Make doubles into each chain. Then turn the work. Work three chains to count as the first double. Skip the first stitch in the row below and make doubles into the next and each following stitch to the end. Work the last double into the turning chain. Turn and work the next row in the same way.

Triple crochet (tr)

1. Wrap the yarn over the hook twice and insert the hook into the fifth chain from the hook. The first four chains count as the first stitch. Wrap the yarn over the hook and draw it through the chain. There are now four loops on the hook.

2. *Wrap the yarn over the hook and draw it through the first two loops on the hook. Repeat from * twice more. This completes the first triple crochet. Work a triple into each chain in the same way. Then turn the work.

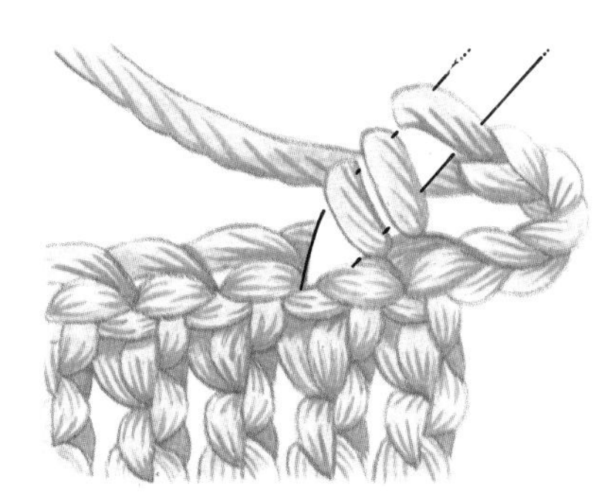

3. Make four turning chains to count as the first stitch. Skip the first stitch in the row below and make a triple into the next and all following stitches to the end. Work the last triple into the turning chain. Turn and work the next and all following rows in the same way.

Joining in a new yarn

It is easiest to join in a new yarn at the end of a row just before the work is turned. This is the method for changing colors for stripes; it is also suitable for starting a new ball of yarn when the old one is finished.
The new yarn is brought in while working the last loop of the last stitch of a row. For instance, if you are working single crochet, insert the hook into the turning chain. Then begin the last sc. Wrap the yarn over the hook and draw it through the chain. There are now two loops on the hook. Drop the old yarn and, using the new yarn, wrap the yarn over the hook and draw it through both loops. Then turn the work and, leaving the old yarn aside, begin the next row, making the turning chains with the new yarn. Adding the new yarn when working doubles is done in the same way. While making the last double of the row, introduce the new yarn when there are only two loops remaining on the hook. Draw the new yarn through both loops to close the double. Continue with the new yarn.

Splicing yarn

When finishing a ball of yarn it is sometimes necessary to join in a new yarn in the middle of a row. For instance, if you are using an expensive yarn, you may not want to waste it. Or, it may be important not to have joins showing at the edge of certain items such as scarves. In such cases it is best to splice together the ends of the old and the new yarns.
Continue crocheting until there are only a few inches of yarn left. Then untwist about 3in of the ends of both the old and new yarns. Lay them together so that they overlap up to the point where they were untwisted. Carefully retwist half of the thickness of each yarn together. Then clip the strands that were left aside to half their length and wind them in turn around the newly twisted yarn so that they meet but do not overlap at the center.

Decreasing

Decreases, for shaping garments, are usually worked one stitch in from the edge to produce a neat selvage. The principle is the same for all stitches but the working methods differ.

1. To decrease one single crochet, insert the hook into the next stitch, wrap the yarn over the hook (called *yo*) and draw a loop through. There are now 3 loops on the hook. Yo and draw through all 3 loops. One single crochet has been decreased.

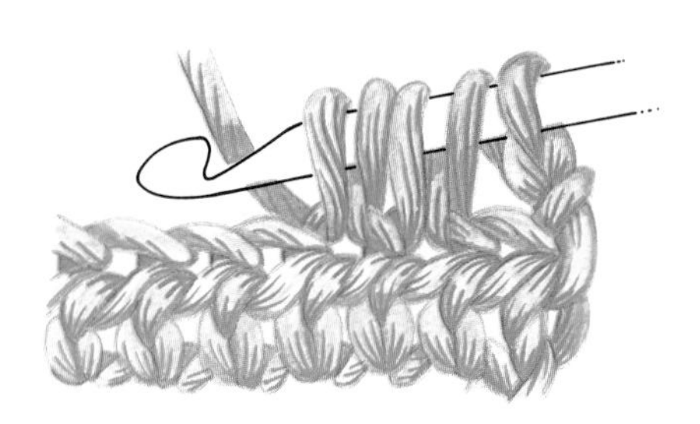

2. To decrease one half double, *yo, insert the hook into the next stitch, yo and draw a loop through. Repeat from * once more. There are now 5 loops on the hook. Yo and draw through all 5 loops. One half double has been decreased.

3. To decrease one double, *yo, insert the hook into the next stitch and draw a loop through. Yo and draw through the first 2 loops on the hook. Repeat from * once more. There are now 3 loops on the hook. Yo and draw through all 3 loops. One double has been decreased.

Increasing

When used for shaping, increases, like decreases, are usually made at the edges of the work.

1. You can increase a stitch at the beginning of a row by working into the first stitch in the row below after making the turning chain. (This is the stitch that is usually skipped.)

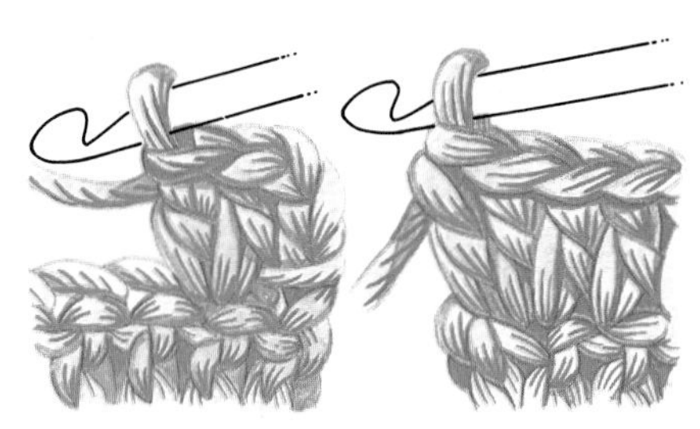

2. To achieve a neater edge when increasing, however, it is best to work the extra stitch one stitch in from each edge. At the beginning of the row, work the turning chain. Then skip the first stitch in the row below and make two stitches into the next stitch. At the end of the row, work two stitches into the last stitch below and work the next stitch into the top of the turning chain as usual.

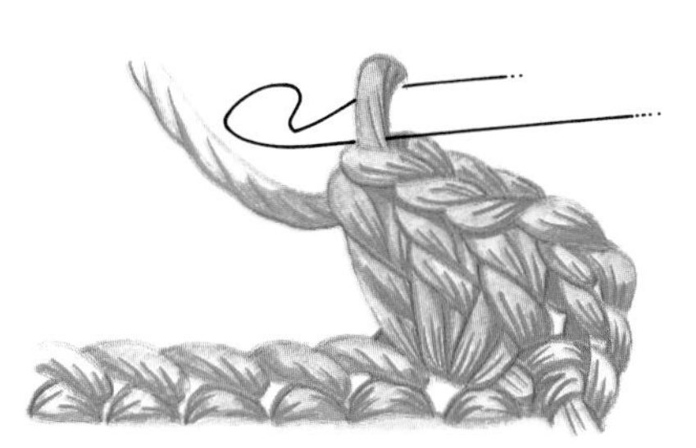

3. To increase two stitches, just work three stitches in all into the same stitch in the row below.

Working Afghan Squares

The steps below show how a simple granny square is made. The same basic principle applies to all crochet medallions.

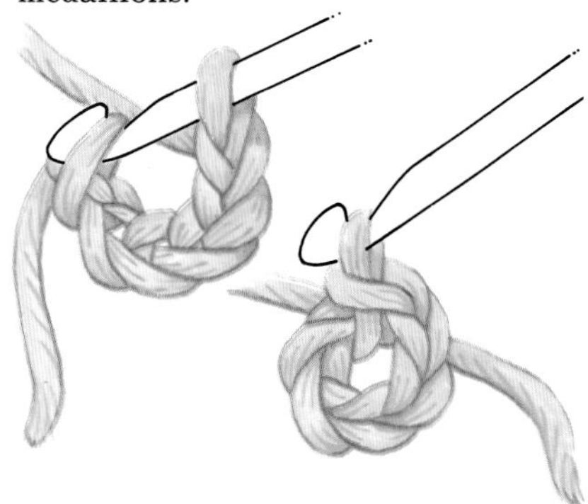

1. First a small number of chains are worked and joined into a circle with a slip stitch.

2. On the first round, four groups of doubles, separated by a chain stitch at each corner, are made into the circle. The yarn is then fastened off.

3. When adding a new color, the new yarn is joined to a chain space at a corner and three chains are worked to count as the first double. On this round two double groups, separated by a chain space, are made at each corner. On following rounds two double groups, separated by a chain space, are worked at each corner and one group is worked between each group along the edges.

CHRISTENING ROBE

Size
To fit 18in chest.
Length, 43in.

Materials
14oz sport yarn
Sizes C and E crochet hooks
4 skeins stranded embroidery floss in random pink
2 skeins in random green
Embroidery needle
2¼yd of ½in-wide ribbon
5 buttons

Gauge
22sts and 20 rows in 4in over bodice patt on size C hook.

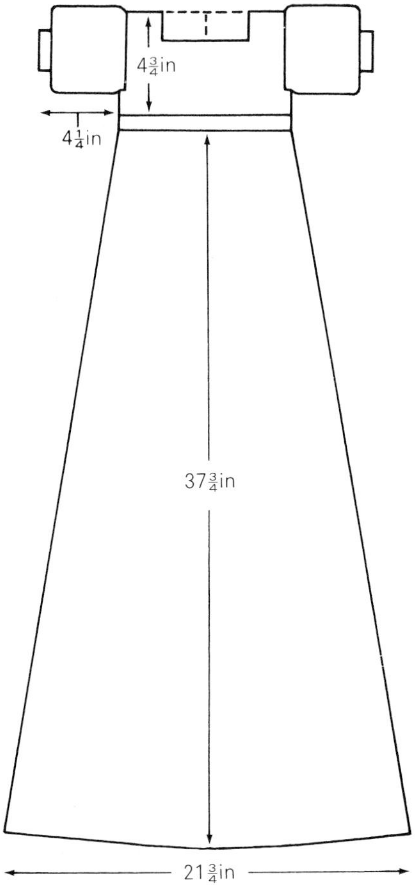

Bodice
Using size C hook make 28ch for center right back edge.
Base row 1sc into 2nd ch from hook, 1sc into each ch to end. Turn. 27sc.
Next row 1ch, 1sc into each sc to end. Turn.
Beg patt
1st row 4ch, skip first 2sc, *1dc into next sc, 1ch, skip next sc, rep from * to within last sc, 1dc into last sc. Turn. 13sps.
2nd row 1ch, 1sc into first dc, *1sc into next sp, 1sc into next dc, rep from * to within last 4ch, 1sc into last sp, 1sc into 3rd of 4ch. Turn.
3rd-5th rows 1ch, 1sc into each sc to end. Turn.
These 5 rows form the patt. Rep them twice more, then work the 1st to 3rd rows again.
Shape right armhole
Next row Patt across first 7sc, turn.
Next row Patt to end. Turn.
Next row 4ch, skip first 2sc, 1dc into next sc, (1ch, skip next sc, 1dc into next sc) twice, turn. 3sps.
Patt 2 rows, do not turn at end of last row but make 21ch. Turn.
Next row 1sc into 2nd ch from hook, 1sc into each of next 19ch, 1sc into each of last 7sc. Turn. 27sc.
Patt 9 rows.
Fasten off.
Shape neck
Next row Skip first 10 sts, rejoin yarn to next sc, 1sc into same place as join, 1sc into each sc to end. Turn. 17sc. Patt 19 rows, do not turn at end of last row but make 11ch. Turn.
Next row 1sc into 2nd ch from hook, 1sc into each of next 9ch, 1sc into each sc to end. Turn. 27sc. Patt 9 rows. Fasten off.
Shape left armhole
Next row Skip first 20sc, rejoin yarn to next sc, 1sc into same place as join, 1sc into each of next 6sc. Turn. 7sc. Patt 4 rows. 3sps.
Using a separate ball of yarn make 20ch and leave aside.
Next row 1ch, 1sc into each of the 7sc, then work 1sc into each of the 20ch. Turn. 27sc.
Patt 19 rows.
Next row 4ch, skip first 2sc, 1sc into next sc, *1sc into each of next 3sc, 3ch, skip next sc, 1sc into next sc, rep from * 3 times more, 1sc into each of last 4sc, do not turn but work 1sc into same place as last sc, 1sc into each row end along lower edge of bodice, turn.
Eyelet hole row 4ch, skip first 2sc, *1dc into next sc, 1ch, skip next sc, rep from * to last sc, 1dc into last sc. Turn.
Next row 1ch, 1sc into first dc, *1sc into next sp, 1sc into next dc, rep from * to within last sp, 1sc into last sp, 1sc into 3rd of 4ch.
Fasten off.

Sleeves
Join shoulder seams. Rejoin yarn to center of underarm and work 51sc evenly all around armhole. Turn.
Next row 3ch, *1dc into next sc, 2dc into next sc, rep from * to end. Turn. 76 sts.
Next row 3ch, skip first dc, 1dc into each dc to end, 1dc into top of 3ch.
Rep last row 7 times more.
Next row 3ch, * work next 2dc tog – 1dc dec –, 1dc into next dc, rep from * to end. Turn. 51 sts.
Next row 1ch, *1sc into next dc, skip next dc, rep from * to end. Turn.
Next row 4ch, skip first 2sc, *1dc into next sc, 1ch, skip next sc, rep from * to last sc, finishing 1dc into last sc. Turn.
Next row 1ch, 1sc into each dc and sp to end. Turn.
Next row 1ch, *1sc into each of next 3sc, 3ch, sl st into last sc worked, rep from * to end.
Fasten off.
Join underarm seam.

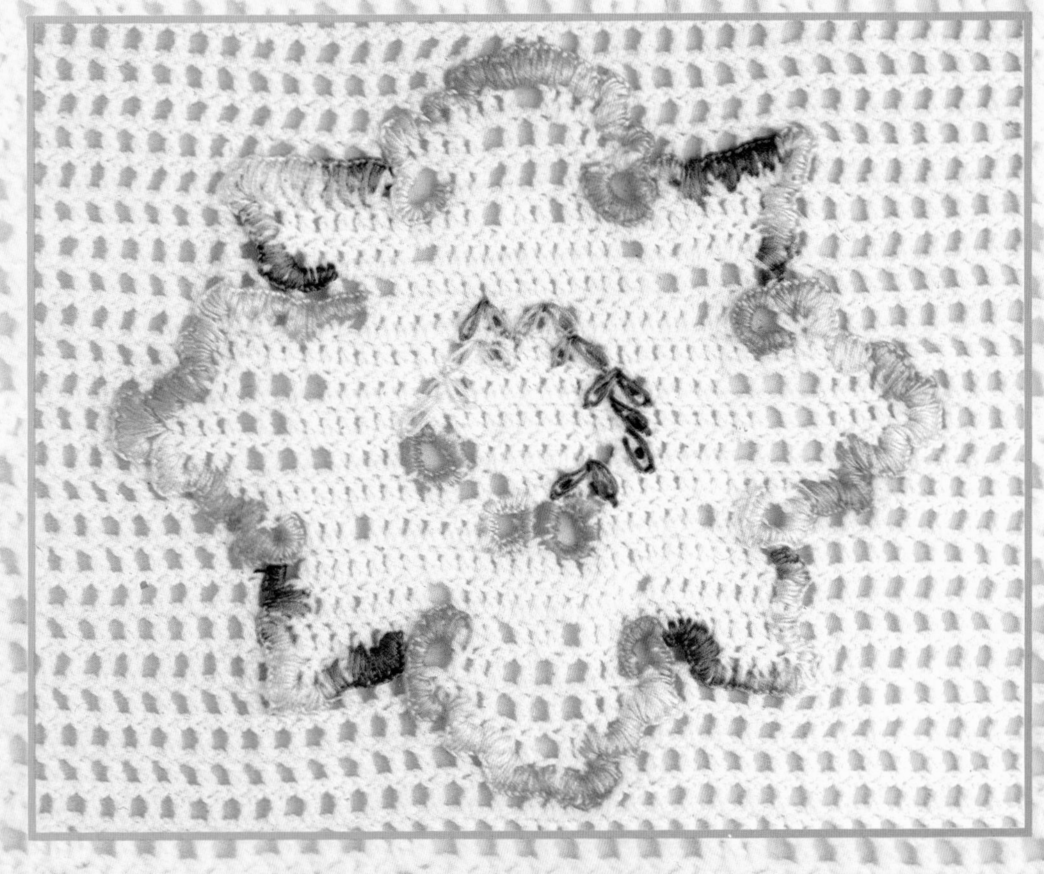

Skirt
Using size E hook make 230ch.
Base row 1dc into 6th ch from hook, *skip next ch, 1ch, 1dc into next ch, rep from * to end. Turn. 113sps.
Reading RS rows from right to left and WS rows from left to right, cont in patt from chart 1 until 24 rows have been worked (i.e. 3 rows of diamonds).
Now foll chart 2, beg motif.
25th row As chart 2 to within 49th sp, work in diamond patt to end. Turn.
26th–64th rows Work in diamond and motif patt as set. Fasten off.
Make another piece in the same way.

Embroidery
Using all 6 strands of pink stranded embroidery floss work a close blanket stitch around four petals of each flower, now work in same way around each petal. Work close blanket stitch around 3 of holes at center of each flower. Using green, work lazy daisy leaves to form a circle at center of each flower.
To finish
Join side seams of skirt. Work 1sc into each sp along top edge of skirt.
Next row 1ch, *1sc into each of next 2sc, skip next sc, rep from * all around. Fasten off.
Using needle and thread attach skirt to bodice, matching underarms and side seams.
Along lower edge of skirt work 1sc into each dc and 1sc into each sp. Turn.
Picot row *1sc into each of next 3sc, 3ch, sl st to last sc, rep from * all around. Fasten off.

Neck edging
Work a row of sc around neck edge, turn and work picot row as for lower edge of skirt. Thread ribbon through the slots on front bodice (or front and back bodice if desired). Thread ribbon through waist slots and tie in bow at center front. Press work very lightly with a warm iron and dry cloth.

CHART 1

CHART 2 DIAMOND PATTERN

Technique tip

Blanket stitch
This stitch can either be worked close together to create a solid line, or worked slightly apart as above.
Secure yarn on the wrong side of the work, bring needle and yarn to right side and insert needle in fabric for depth of stitch. Now make a straight downward stitch with the thread under the needle point. Pull up the stitch to form a loop. Continue in this way until the design is completed.

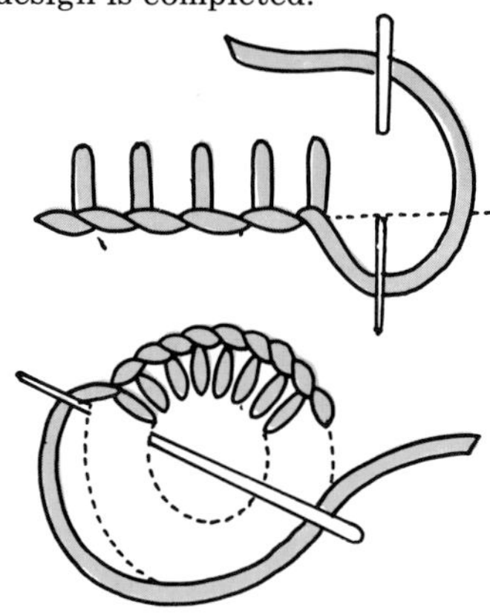

Lazy daisy stitch
Secure yarn on the wrong side of the work, bring needle and yarn to right side. Hold loop of yarn on right side with your thumb, then insert needle where it last emerged and bring out a short distance away from where it entered. Pull the yarn through, keeping the loop under the needle. Fasten the chain with a small stitch at the base of the loop. Continue in this way. Groups of lazy daisy stitches form the petals of flowers.

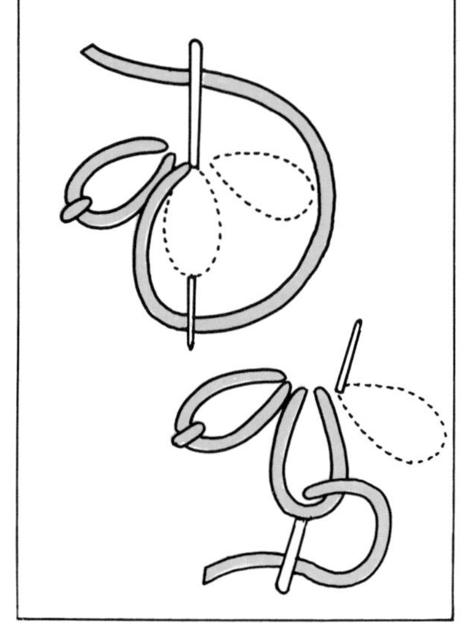

SLEEPING BAG AND BLANKET

Sizes
Blanket *34¾in × 26½in.*
Sleeping bag *To fit baby up to age six months*
Length, 25in.
Sleeve seam, 4¾in.

Materials
Sport yarn:
15oz in white
7oz in blue
6oz in green
5oz in yellow
4oz in pink
Sizes E and F crochet hooks
24in open-ended zipper
4 buttons

Gauge
Blanket *1 motif measures 4¾in square worked on size F hook.*
Sleeping bag *20dc and 11 rows to 4in worked on size E hook.*

Blanket

First strip

Motif Using size F hook and white, make 6ch. Join with a sl st into first ch to form a circle.
1st round Work 16sc into circle. Join with a sl st into first sc.
2nd round 6ch, *skip 1sc, 1dc into next sc, 3ch, rep from * 6 times. Join with a sl st to 3rd of first 6ch. Fasten off white. 8sps.
3rd round Join blue with a sl st to any sp, (1sc, 1hdc, 3dc, 1hdc, 1sc) all into same 3ch sp, *(1sc, 1hdc, 3dc, 1hdc, 1sc) all into next 3ch sp, rep from * 6 times. Join with a sl st to first sc. 8 petals.
4th round *5ch. 1sc around stem of next dc on 2nd row, keeping to back of work, rep from * 7 times more, catching up base of first 5ch of round on last sc to bring it in line with other 5ch loops.
5th round Into each 5ch loop work (1sc, 1hdc, 5dc, 1hdc, 1sc). Join with a sl st to first sc.
6th round *5ch, 1sc around next sc of 4th round, keeping the 5ch to back of work as on 4th round, rep from * 7 times, ending as for 4th round. Cut off blue.
7th round Join white with a sl st to any 5ch loop, 3ch, 5dc into same loop, *3ch, 6dc into next 5ch loop, 6dc into next 5ch loop, rep from * twice more, 3ch, 6dc into next 5ch loop. Join with a sl st to 3rd of first 3ch. 4 sets of 12dc separated with corner sp of 3ch.
8th round 3ch, 1dc into each of next 5dc, *(2dc, 2ch, 2dc) in corner sp. 1dc in each of next 12dc, rep from * twice more, (2dc, 2ch, 2dc) in next corner sp. 1dc in each of last 6dc. Join with a sl st to top of first 3ch.
9th round 3ch. 1dc into each of next 7dc, *(2dc, 2ch, 2dc) in corner sp. 1dc into each of next 16dc, rep from * twice more, (2dc, 2ch, 2dc) in corner sp, 1dc in each of last 8dc. Join with a sl st into top of first 3ch. Fasten off.
Make 5 more motifs in the same way, using blue for the petals of one more motif, pink for the petals of two motifs, then one green and one yellow.
Join motifs into a strip. Place WS of 2 motifs tog and using pink, work a row of sc across one edge (working through both thicknesses). Join in this order: blue to pink; green to blue; yellow to green; blue to yellow; pink to blue.

Edging of strip
1st row Using white and with RS of work facing, work along long edge of strip, sl st into corner sp of first motif, 3ch, *work 1dc into each of next 20dc, 1dc into next corner sp, 1dc into corner sp of next motif, rep from * along all 6 motifs, ending with 1dc in corner sp of last motif. Turn. 132sts.
2nd row Using pink, 3ch, skip first dc, 1dc into each dc, ending with 1dc into top of 3ch. Turn.
3rd row Using green, 3ch, skip first dc, *5dc in next dc, drop loop on hook, insert hook into first of these 5dc from front to back and draw dropped loop through – bobble made, 1dc into each of next 2dc, rep from * ending with 1 bobble, 1dc into top of 3ch. Turn.
4th row Using pink, 3ch, skip first dc, 1dc into each st to end. 132sts.
5th row Using white, 3ch, skip first dc, 1dc into each dc, ending with 1dc into top of 3ch. Turn.
6th row As 5th.
7th row Using yellow, as 3rd.
8th row Using white, as 6th.
9th row As 8th.
10th row Using blue, as 6th.
11th row As 10th. Fasten off.
Turn work and rep last 11 rows along other long edge of strip.

Second strip

Work as given for first strip.
Join strips tog. Place RS tog and using blue, work along one long side, working 1sc into each st

through both thicknesses.

Top and lower edging

With RS of work facing, join blue to first row end of strip edging along short edge of work, 3ch, *(2dc into next row end, 1dc into next row end) to corner sp of motif, 1dc into corner sp, 1dc into each of 20dc on motif, 1dc into next corner sp, rep from * once more, ending with (1dc into next row end, 2dc into next row end) to last row end, 1dc into last row end. Turn. 108sts.

Next row Using blue, 3ch, skip first dc, 1dc into each dc, ending with 1dc into top of 3ch. Fasten off.

Make a similar edging along other short edge.

Picot edging

With RS of work facing, join blue to first st on short edge of work, **work *1sc into each of next 3sts, 5ch, sl st into sc just worked (picot) *, rep from * to * to corner, turn corner, work 2sc in row end, 1sc in next row end, 5ch, sl st into last sc, then work from * to * to next corner, working 3sc into 2 row ends before corner, **, rep from ** to ** for other 2 sides of blanket. Join with a sl st to first sc. Fasten off.

Sleeping bag

Using size E hook throughout, make 6 motifs as given for blanket – 2 in blue, 2 in yellow, 1 in pink and 1 in green, but work a 10th round so that there are 20dc between corners.

Back

With RS of work facing and using pink, join 1 blue and 1 yellow motif tog with sc in same way as blanket.

With RS of work facing and using white, work across breadth of 2 motifs as foll: rejoin yarn to first corner sp on blue motif, 3ch, 1dc into each dc across this motif, 1dc into corner sp on this motif, 1dc into corner sp on yellow motif, 1dc into each dc of this motif, 1dc into corner sp. 52sts. Turn.

Next row Using pink, 3ch, skip first dc, 1dc into each st, ending with 1dc into top of 3ch. Turn.

Next row Using green, work a row of bobbles as given for blanket. Turn.

Next row Using pink, 3ch, skip first st, 1dc into each st, ending with 1dc into top of 3ch. Turn.

Cont working in dc and stripe sequence as foll: 2 rows white, 1 row yellow bobbles, 2 rows white, 1 row each of blue, white, pink, white, green, white, yellow, 7 rows white, 1 row each yellow, white,

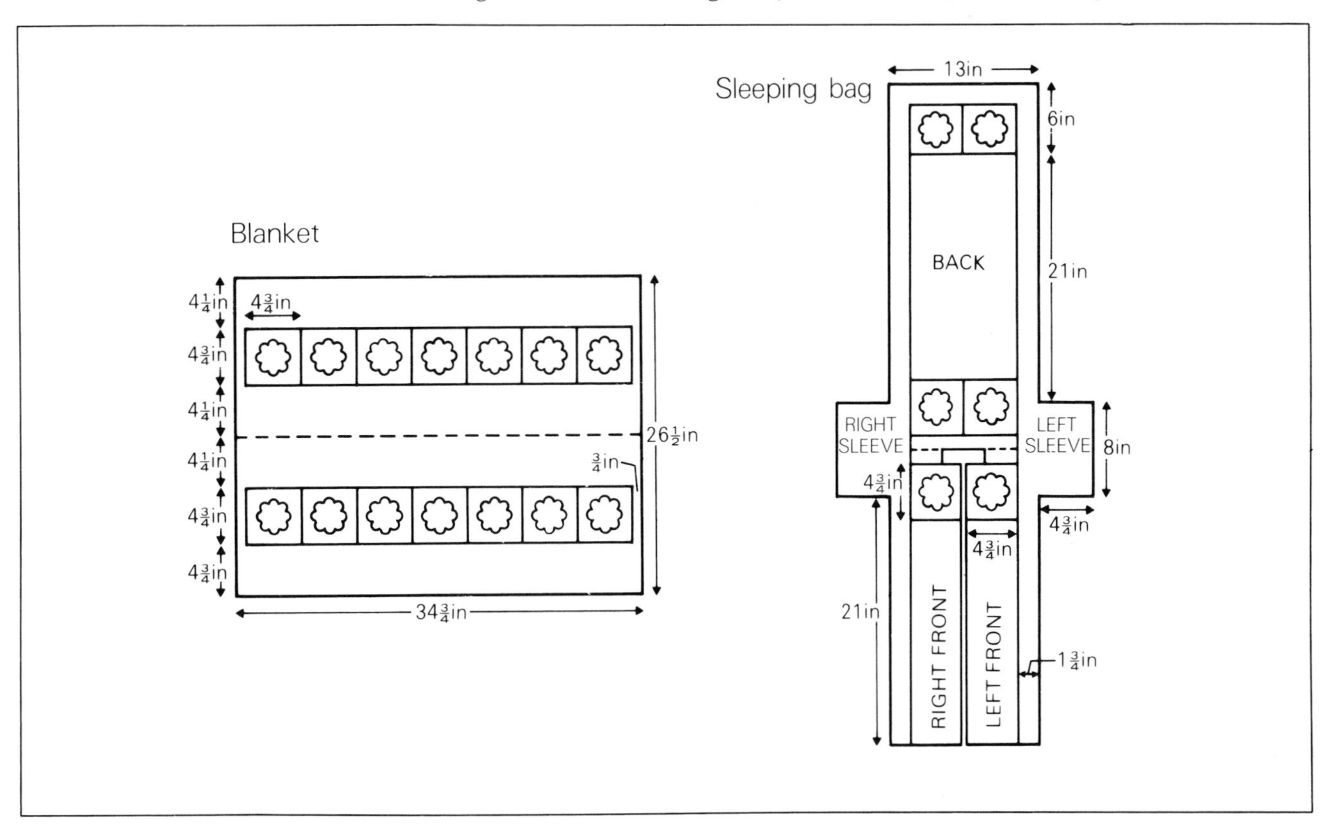

green, white, pink, white, blue, 2 rows white, 1 row yellow bobbles, 2 rows white, 1 row pink, 1 row green bobbles, 1 row pink, 7 rows white, 1 row each blue, white, pink, white, green, white, yellow, white.
Join tog 1 blue and 1 yellow motif with pink sc on RS of work. Using pink sc in same way, join 2 motifs to last row of back.

Shoulders
With RS of work facing and using blue, work 52dc across unworked edge of first 2 motifs of back. Turn. Work 2 rows in dc. Fasten off.

Left front
Along one edge of pink motif work 26dc in white. Now work as back from the first row of dc in pink to end, excluding the addition of the two motifs on lower edge.

Shoulder
With RS of work facing, join blue to right-hand corner of pink motif, 3ch, 1dc into each of next 17dc. Turn. Work 2 rows in dc.
Fasten off.

Right front
Work as left, but use green motif.

Shoulder
With RS of work facing skip corner space and first 2dc of green motif, rejoin blue to next dc, 3ch, 1dc into each dc to end and 1dc into corner sp. Turn.
Work 2 rows in dc. Fasten off.
Join shoulder seams.

Side edges and sleeves
With RS of work facing join blue to first row end on lower edge of left front.
1st row 3ch, 1dc into same place as join, *1dc into next row end, 2dc into next row end *, rep from * to * along side of left front to motif, 1dc into each dc of motif, then rep from * to * once more across shoulders, 1dc into each dc of motif on back, then rep from * to * down to motif at lower edge of back, 1dc into each dc (2dc, 2ch and 2dc) into corner space, 1dc into each dc across first motif, 1dc into each of next 2sp, 1dc into each dc across second motif on lower edge of back, (2dc, 2ch and 2dc) into corner space, now work up other side of back, across shoulders and down side edge to match. Turn.
2nd row 3ch, skip first dc, 1dc into each dc to end, working (2dc, 2ch and 2dc) into each of the corners on lower edge of back. Rep last row, working 1 row white, 1 row pink and 1 row white. Fasten off.

Left sleeve
With RS of work facing join green to 20th dc from shoulder seam on left front, 3ch, 1dc into each of next 19dc, then work 1dc into each of next 20dc on back. Turn. 40dc.
Now work 1 row white, 1 row yellow, 1 row white, 1 row pink, 1 row green bobbles, 1 row pink, 2 rows white, 1 row yellow bobbles, 1 row white, 2 rows blue and 1 row picot in blue.

Right sleeve
Work as given for left sleeve but join yarn to 20th dc on back.

To finish
With wrong sides together, match row ends, leaving the two motifs at lower edge of back free for flap. Join blue to lower edge of left side and working through the double thickness, work 1sc into each of first 3dc, *3ch, sl st into last sc worked, 1sc into each of next 3sts, rep from * along left side edge to sleeve, join sleeve seam by working (2sc into next row end, 1sc into next row end, 3ch, sl st into last sc worked) to end of sleeve. Fasten off. Join other sleeve seam and side seam in the same way but start at sleeve seam.

Front and neck edging
With RS of work facing join blue to first row end on right front and work *2sc into next row end, 1sc into next row end, 3ch, sl st into last sc worked, rep from * up to motif, **1sc into each of next 3dc, 3ch, sl st into last sc worked, rep from ** to shoulder, then rep from * across shoulder row ends, then from ** across back neck sts, from * across shoulder row ends and from ** down other motif, then from * down remainder of left front edge. Fasten off. Sew in zipper. Turn up lower flap, mark button positions, then sew on buttons using spaces in crochet for buttonholes. Work picot edging around flap in blue following Technique tip.

Technique tip

Picot edging
Picots form a simple but decorative edging for most garments and household items. A picot edging can be worked on to knitted or crochet fabrics.

Join on yarn and work 2 single crochets, now work 3 chains for the picot; the number of chains can vary according to the size of the picot required.

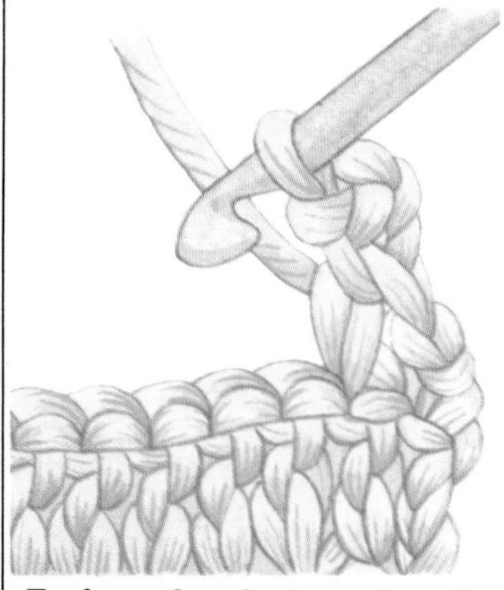
To form the picot, work a slip stitch into the top of the last single crochet worked. This completes the picot.

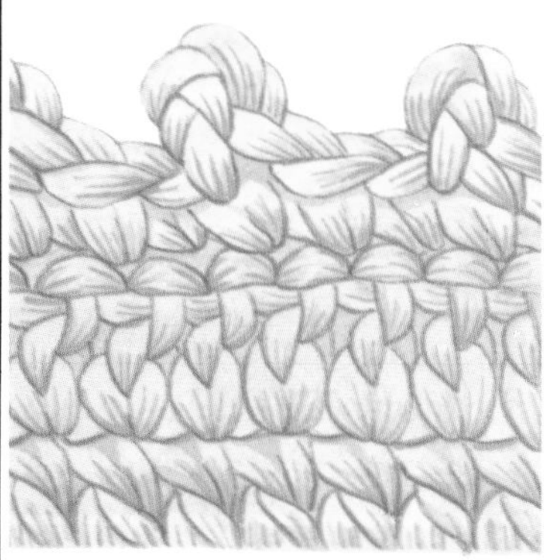
Work 3 single crochets and a picot along edge of work.

MADE TO MATCH

Quilt
Size
33 × 22in.

Materials
6oz sport yarn in each of pink, yellow, blue and green

Gauge
22hdc and 14 rows to 4in worked on size C hook.

Pillow
Size
13 × 16in.

Materials
2oz sport yarn in each of pink, yellow, blue and green

Gauge
22hdc and 14 rows to 4in worked on size C hook.

Sweater
Size
To fit 16–17in chest.
Length $10\frac{1}{4}$in.
Sleeve $5\frac{1}{2}$in.

Materials
2oz sport yarn in each of pink, yellow, blue and green
1 button

Gauge
22hdc and 14 rows to 4in worked on size C hook.

Pants
Size
Inner leg seam 10in.

Materials
6 oz sport yarn in yellow
Waist length of narrow elastic
Size C crochet hook
$4\frac{1}{2}$yd lightweight batting

Gauge
22hdc and 14 rows to 4in worked on size C hook.

Quilt
Using size C hook make 32ch.
Base row (WS) 1hdc into 3rd ch from hook, 1hdc into each ch to end. Turn. 31 sts.
Patt row 2ch, skip first hdc, 1hdc into each hdc to end, 1hdc into top of 2ch.
Turn. Rep patt row until work measures $5\frac{1}{2}$in. Fasten off. Work another piece in same color, do not fasten off. With wrong sides tog join pieces thus: working through double thickness work 31sc along 3 sides, leaving enough yarn to join 4th side, fasten off. Rep to make 6 pouches in each color.

To finish
Cut 24 pieces of batting $4\frac{3}{4}$in × $14\frac{1}{4}$in. Fold in three and insert one piece in each pouch. Join rem side of pouch. Sew pouches tog in color order as shown in diagram.

Pillow
Using size C hook and blue, make 89ch. Work base row and patt row as for quilt. 88sts. Cont in patt until work measures $3\frac{1}{4}$in from beg. Cut off blue. Join in pink and work a further $3\frac{1}{4}$in. Cut off pink. Join in green and work a further $3\frac{1}{4}$in. Cut off green. Join in yellow and work a further $6\frac{1}{4}$in. Cut off yellow. Join in green and work a further $3\frac{1}{4}$in. Cut off green. Join in pink and work a further $3\frac{1}{4}$in. Fasten off pink. Join in blue. Work a further $3\frac{1}{4}$in. Fasten off.

To finish
Cut a piece of batting 15in × 36in. Fold in three. Join side seams of pillow. Put batting in pillow. Join rem seam.

Sweater
Back
Using size C hook and blue, make 57ch.
Base row 1sc into 3rd ch from hook, 1sc into each ch to end. Turn. 56sts.
Work $\frac{3}{4}$in in sc. Cont in patt as on quilt until work measures $3\frac{1}{2}$in from beg. Cut off blue. Join in green.
Puff st row 3ch to count as first hdc and ch, *skip next hdc, yo, insert hook into next hdc and draw a loop through, (yo, insert hook into same hdc, yo, draw a loop through) twice, yo and draw through all loops on hook, 1ch, rep from * to end omitting 1ch on last rep and working 1hdc into last st. Cut off green. Join in pink.
Next row 2ch to count as first hdc, 1hdc into each st to end. Turn.
Cont in patt until work measures 6in from beg.
Shape armholes
Next row Sl st into each of first 8sts, patt to last 7sts. Turn. 42sts.
Cont in patt until work measures $6\frac{3}{4}$in from beg. Fasten off pink. Join in green and work puff st row. Join in yellow and cont in patt until work measures $10\frac{1}{4}$in from beg. Fasten off. Mark center 20sts for back neck.

Front
Work as given for back until 4 rows less than back to shoulder have been worked.
Shape neck
1st row Patt 13, dec one st (by working 2sts tog). Turn. Dec one st at neck edge on the next 3 rows. Fasten off. Skip center 12sts, attach yarn to next st, complete to match first side.

Sleeves
Using size C hook and blue make 33ch. Work base row as back. 32sts. Work 2in in sc.
Next row 2ch to count as first sc, 1sc into next sc, *2sc into next sc, 1sc into each of next 2sc, rep from * to end. 42sts. Cut off blue. Join in green and work puff st row. Cut off

green. Join in pink and cont in patt until sleeve measures 6¾in. Cut off pink. Join in green and work puff st row.
Next row 2ch to count as first sc, 1sc in each st to end. Fasten off.

Neckband
Join right shoulder seam. Using yellow work a row of sc around neck edge. Cut off yellow. Join in green and work puff st row.
Next row 2ch to count as first sc, 1sc into each st to end. Fasten off.

To finish
Catch edges of left shoulder seam together. Set in sleeves, sewing last 1¼in of sleeve seam to 7sts left at armhole shaping. Join side and sleeve seams. Sew button to left shoulder using space between dc as buttonhole.

Pants

Right leg Using size C hook and yellow make 37ch.
Base row 1sc into 2nd ch from hook, 1sc into each ch to end. Turn. 36sts.
Next row 2ch to count as first sc, skip first sc, 1sc into each sc to end, 1sc in top of 2ch. Turn.
Rep this row for 2in.
Inc row 2ch to count as first hdc, 1hdc into first sc, 2hdc into each sc to end, 2hdc into top of 2ch. Turn. 72sts.

Cont in patt as on quilt until work measures 10in from beg.

Crotch shaping

1st row Sl st to 6th hdc, patt to within last 5hdc. Turn. Dec 1hdc at each end of next 5 rows. 52sts. Cont until work measures 7in from beg of crotch shaping.

Shape back

1st row Sl st into each of first 4sts, 1sc into next st, 1hdc into each st to end. Turn.

2nd row Patt to within last 5sts, 1sc into next st, turn.

Rep the last 2 rows 3 times, then the first row again.

Next row Patt across all sts.

Patt a further 5 rows. Fasten off.

Left leg

Work as right leg reversing all shapings.

To finish

Join inside leg seams. Join crotch seam. Work a herringbone casing over elastic at waist.

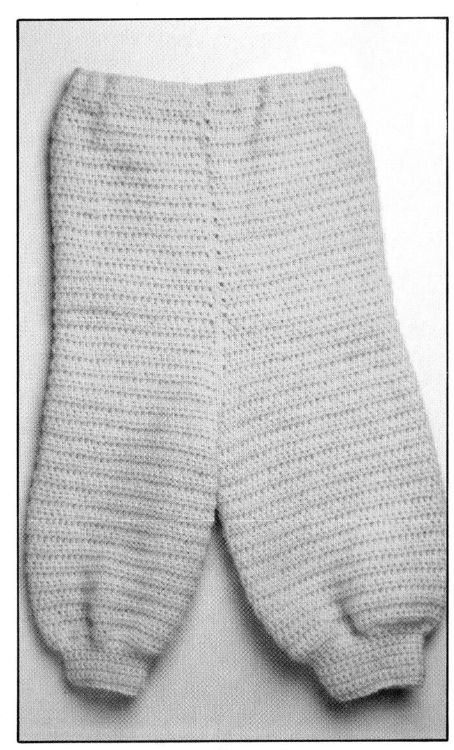

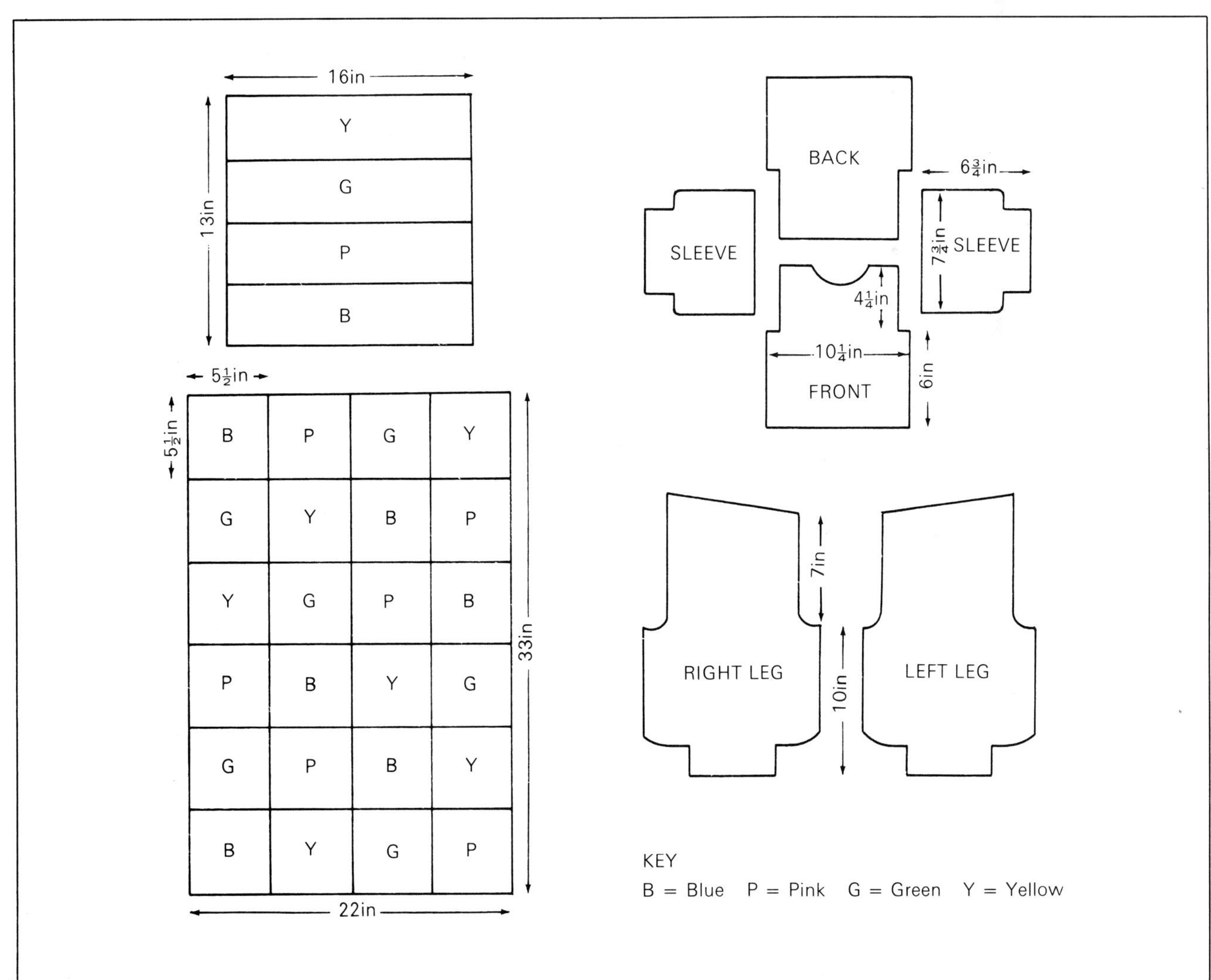

KIDS' COZY JACKETS

Sizes
To fit 20[22:24]in chest.
Length, 11[13:14]in.
Sleeve seam, 7[8:9]in.
Note *Directions for larger sizes are in brackets []; where there is only one set of figures it applies to all sizes.*

Materials
5[6:7] × 2oz balls of a heavy-weight bouclé yarn in main color
2oz of a sport yarn in contrasting color
Sizes E and I hooks
5[6:7] buttons for front and 2 buttons for sleeves

Gauge
10hdc and 8 rows to 4in with bouclé and size I hook.

Back

Using bouclé and size I hook make 31 [33:35]ch.
Base row 1hdc into 3rd ch from hook, 1hdc into each ch to end. Turn.
Beg patt.
Patt row 2ch to count as first hdc, 1hdc between last hdc of last row and next hdc, then work 1hdc into sp between each hdc to end. Turn. 30[32:34]hdc.
Rep patt row 8[11:12] times.
Place a marker at each end of last row, then work 8[9:10] rows more. Fasten off.

Right front

Work as given for left front, the work is reversible.

Left front

Using bouclé and size I hook, make 15[16:17]ch and work base row as for back. 14[15:16]hdc. Cont in patt until front measures as back to markers. Place marker on last row, cont in patt until front measures 3 rows less than back.
Shape neck
Work across first 10sts, turn. Work 2 rows without shaping. Fasten off.

Hood

Join shoulder seams, matching the 10sts of shoulders on fronts to the first 10sts at each end of row on back. With RS facing, using bouclé and size I hook, rejoin yarn to first st at right front neck, 2ch, now work 3[4:5]hdc along right front neck, 3hdc up side neck, 15[18:21]hdc along back neck (increasing to reach this number), 3hdc down side neck, then 4[5:6]hdc along left front neck. Turn. 29[34:39]hdc. Work in patt as for back for 5[6:7]in.
Shape top
Fasten off. Skip first 9[11:13]hdc, rejoin yarn to next hdc, 2ch, then work 1hdc over each of the next 10[11:12]hdc, turn.
Work on these 11[12:13]hdc until this section is equal in depth to the sts left unworked. Fasten off. Join hood seam.

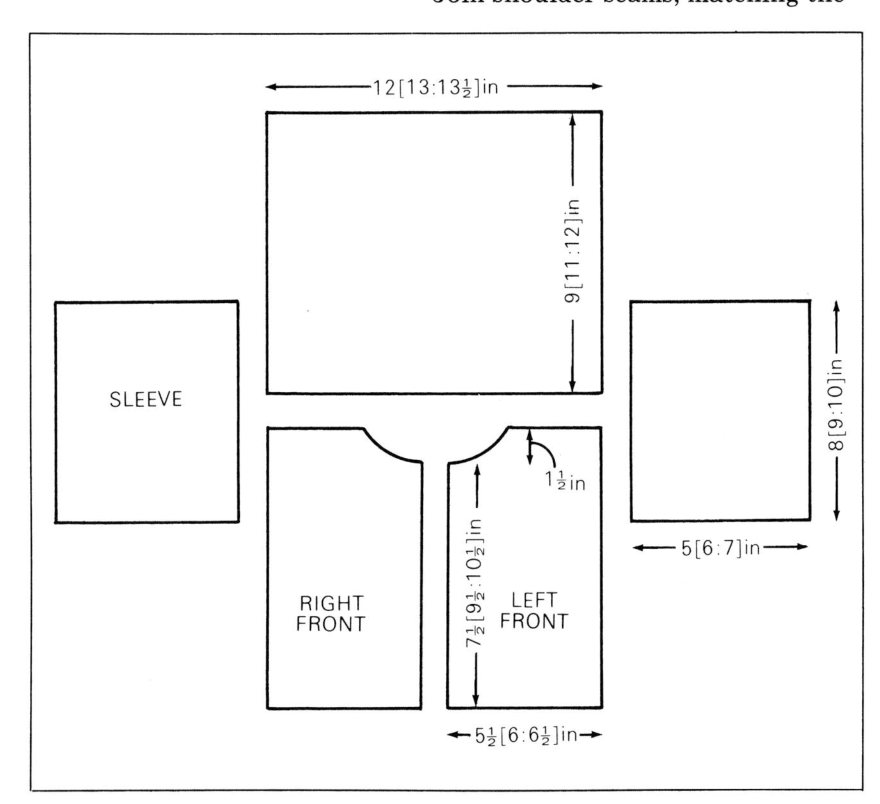

Sleeves

Using bouclé and size I hook, make 21[23:25]ch and work the base row as for back. Work the patt row of back 9[11:13] times. Fasten off.

Waistband

Join side seams to markers. With RS facing, using size E hook and sport yarn, join yarn to lower edge of left front and work 18[20:22]sc along left front, 40[44:50]sc along back and 18[20:22]sc along right front.
Turn. 76[84:94]sc.
Work 6 rows sc. Fasten off.

The border

Boy's version **With RS facing, using sport yarn and size E hook, join yarn to first row end of waistband on right front, 1sc into this row end, then work 1sc into every other row end along waistband, then work 2sc into each row end along front edge to hood, work 2sc into each row end of hood to seam, then work (1sc into next hdc, 2sc into next hdc) to other seam, then work down other side to match, ending with 1sc into each alternate row end of waistband. Turn.
Work 2 rows sc.**
1st buttonhole row 1ch, 1sc into each of first 3sc, (2ch, skip next 2sc, 1sc into each of next 5sc) 5[6:7] times, 1sc into each sc to end. Turn.

2nd buttonhole row 1ch, (1sc into each sc, 2sc into each sp) to end. Turn. Work 2 more rows sc. Fasten off.

Girl's version Work as given for boy's version from ** to **.

1st buttonhole row Work in sc to within last 38[45:52]sc, (2ch, skip next 2sc, 1sc into each of next 5sc) 5[6:7] times, 1sc into each of the last 3sc. Turn.

2nd buttonhole row 1ch, (1sc into each sc, 2sc into each sp) to end. Turn. Work 2 more rows sc. Fasten off.

Cuffs (alike)
Using size E hook and sport yarn, work 1sc into each rem loop along foundation edge of sleeve. Turn.

Next row 1ch, 1sc into each sc to end. Turn.

Rep last row 5 times more. Fasten off.

Sleeve tops (alike)
Using size E hook and sport yarn, work along top edge of sleeve working 2sc into each sp between hdc to end. Turn.

Now work 4 rows sc. Fasten off.

Placing center top of sleeve to shoulder seam, set in sleeves. Join underarm seams, excluding cuff.

Cuff fastening
Working 1sc into each row end, work a row of sc along back edge of cuff. Turn.

Next row 1ch, 1sc into each of first 2sc, 3ch, skip next 3sc, 1sc into each of last 2sc. Fasten off.

Work 2 rows of sc along front edge of cuff, then sew on buttons.

To finish
Do not press.

Sew buttons onto the border to correspond with buttonholes.

BABY'S OVERALLS

Sizes
Overalls *Crotch to waist, 8¼in. Inside leg, 9in.*
Jacket *To fit 20in chest. Length, 11in. Sleeve length, 6in with cuff turned back.*

Materials
Overalls *4oz sport weight yarn in main color A*
2oz each of 3 contrasting colors B, C and D.
Jacket *6oz in main color A and 2oz in contrasting color C*
Note *If you are making the set you will need 9oz in main color A and 2oz in each of 3 contrasting colors B, C and D*
Sizes B and E hooks
2 buttons and a length of elastic for back of overalls

Gauge
18sc and 22 rows to 4in on size E hook.

Overalls

Back
Using size E hook and A, chain 50 for top edge. Cut off A, join on B.
Base row 2ch to count as first sc, 1sc into each ch to end. Turn.
Next row 2ch, 1sc into each to end. Change to C.
Turn.
Shape back
1st row 2ch, 1sc into each sc to within last 6sc. Turn.
2nd row As first row, change to D.
3rd row As first row.
4th row As first row, change to A.
5th row As first row.
6th row As first row, change to B.
Next row 2ch, 1sc into each st in A and into the first 3sts in D. Turn.
Next row 2ch, 1sc into each st in B and into the first 3sts in A, change to C.
Next row 2ch, 1sc into each st. Turn.
Next row 2ch, 1sc into each st to end. Turn. 50sc. Change to D.
Next row 2ch, 1sc into each sc. Turn.
Next row 2ch, 1sc into each sc to end. Change to A. Turn.
Cont in sc working in stripes of 2 rows A, 2 rows B, 2 rows C and 2 rows D until 6th stripe in A has been completed.
Shape crotch
Next row Using B work across first 25sc for first leg, make 6ch, turn.
Next row 1sc into 3rd ch from hook, 1sc into each ch, then 1sc into each sc to end. Turn. 30sc.
Cont in stripe sequence on these 30sc until 6th stripe in A from beg of crotch has been completed. Work a further 3 rows in A. Fasten off.
Second leg
Using B, make 5ch, then work 1sc into each sc across back. Turn.
Next row 2ch, 1sc into each sc to end, 1sc into each of the 5ch. Turn. 30sc. Now work to match first leg.

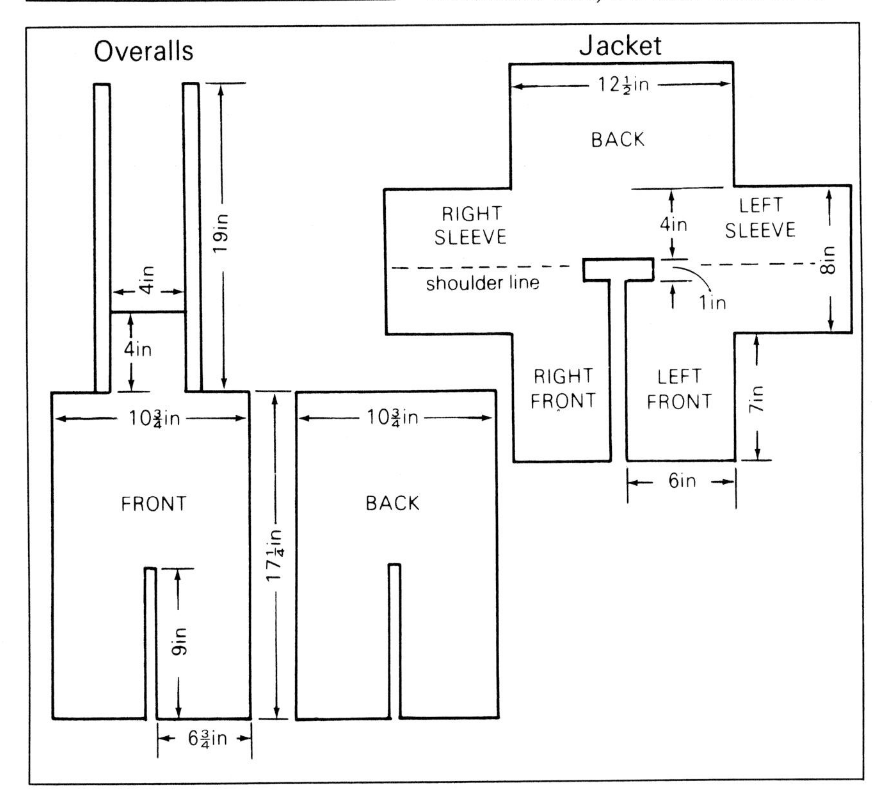

Front
Using size E hook and B, make 22ch for top edge of bib.
Base row 1sc into 3rd ch from hook, 1sc into each ch to end. Turn.
Next row 2ch. 1sc into each sc to end. Change to C. Turn.
Cont in stripe sequence as for back until 22 rows have been worked, so ending with 2 rows in D. Change to A and work 1 row. Cut off yarns.
Next row Using A, make 15ch, then work 1sc into each sc to end, make 15ch. Change to B. Turn.
Next row 1sc into 3rd ch from hook, 1sc into each of next 14ch, 1sc into each sc across bib, 1sc into each of last 15ch. Turn. 50sts.
Work 1 row in B. Cont in stripe sequence until body measures same as back to crotch, then complete as for back.
First strap
With RS facing and using size E hook, join A to bib at waist edge and work 1sc into each row end to

top of bib. Do not turn but make 71ch for strap.
Next row 1sc into 3rd ch from hook, 1sc into each ch, 1sc into each sc. Turn.
1st buttonhole row 2ch, 1sc into each sc to within last 25sts, (3ch, skip next 3sc, 1sc into each of next 5sc) 3 times, 1sc into top of ch. Turn.
2nd buttonhole row 2ch, (1sc into each of next 5sc, 3sc into next loop) 3 times, now work 1sc into each sc. Turn.
Next row 2ch, 1sc into each sc to end. Fasten off.
Second strap
Make 70ch; then, working from top edge of bib, work 1sc into each row end. Turn.
Next row 2ch, 1sc into each sc, 1sc into each ch to end. Turn.
1st buttonhole row 2ch, (1sc into each of next 5sc, 3ch skip next 3sc) 3 times, now work 1sc into each sc to end. Turn.
2nd buttonhole row 2ch, 1sc into each sc to within first buttonhole, (3sc into next loops, 1sc into each of next 5sc) 3 times, 1sc into top of ch. Turn.
Next row 2ch, 1sc into each sc to end. Fasten off.
Patches (make 2)
Using size E hook and A, make 12ch.
Base row 1sc into 3rd ch from hook, 1sc into each ch to end. Turn. Work 9 rows in sc.
Edging
Next row 2ch, work 3sc all into first sc, 1sc into each sc to within last sc, 3sc all into last sc; do not turn but cont along side edge working 1sc into each row end to corner, work 3sc all into first foundation ch, then 1sc into each ch to within last ch, 3sc all into last ch, 1sc into each row end to corner, sl st into top of the 2ch. Fasten off.
To finish
Join side and inner leg seams. Work herringbone st casing over elastic on wrong side of back at waist. Sew buttons to top edge of back. Sew on patches.

Jacket (one piece)

Using size E hook and A, make 58ch for lower edge of back.
Base row 1sc into 3rd ch from hook, 1sc into each ch to end. Turn.
Next row 2ch, 1sc into each sc. Turn.
Cont in sc work 2 rows C, 2 rows A, 2 rows C, 4 rows A, 2 rows C, 6 rows A and 2 rows C. Cont with A only, work in sc until work measures 7in from beg. Fasten off.
Make 34ch for first sleeve, then work across sts of back, make 35ch for 2nd sleeve. Turn.
Next row 1sc into 3rd ch from hook, 1sc into each ch to end, 1sc into each sc, then 1sc into each ch. 125sts. Cont in sc until sleeve measures 4in in depth, ending at sleeve edge.

Shape neck

Next row Work across first 53sts, turn.

Work 4 rows straight on these 53sts.

Next row Make 9ch for front neck, 1sc into 3rd ch from hook, 1sc into each of next 6ch,1sc into each sc to end. Turn. 61 sts.

Cont without shaping until sleeve measures 8in in depth, ending at front edge.

Next row Work across first 27sts. Turn. Work on these 27sts for right front, until front measures same as back to top of last colored stripe. Now work 2 rows C, 6 rows A, 2 rows C, 4 rows A, (2 rows C, 2 rows A) twice. Fasten off. Skip center 19sc for back neck, rejoin yarn to next sc and work to end. Turn.

Work 3 rows straight. Fasten off.

Next row Make 8ch for front neck, then work 1sc into each sc to end. Turn.

Next row Work to end, then work 1sc into each of the 8ch. Turn. 61sts. Cont without shaping until sleeve measures 8in in depth, ending at side edge. Fasten off. Skip first 34sts, rejoin yarn and work to end. Now complete to match right front.

Edging

Join side and underarm seams. With RS facing and using size B hook, join A to lower edge of right front and work (1sc into each of next 2 row ends, skip next row end) along right front to neck, 1sc into each st across front neck, 1sc into each row end up side neck, 1sc into each st across back neck, 1sc into each row end on other side of neck, 1sc into each st across front neck and (1sc into each of next 2 row ends, skip next row end) to lower edge. Fasten off.

Join C to last sc worked and work a row of crab stitch (sc worked from left to right) all around outer edge of jacket. Fasten off.

Sleeve edgings

With WS facing and using size B hook, join on A and work 1sc into each row end, sl st into first sc. Now work a round of crab stitch. Fasten off.

Turn work to RS, turn back first 6 rows of sleeve; then, using C and working into fold, work a row of crab stitch. Fasten off.

Ties (make 4)

Using size E hook and 2 strands of C tog make a ch approx 12½in long. Fasten off.

Sew one tie to each side of neck and other two approx 3¼in below.

RAGLAN JACKETS

Sizes
To fit 20[22:24]in chest.
Length, 13[15:16¾]in.
Sleeve seam, 7[8:9]in.
Note *Directions for larger sizes are in brackets []; where there is only one set of figures it applies to all sizes.*

Materials
Sport yarn:
Plain jacket *8[9:9]oz*
Two-color jacket *8[9:9]oz 2oz in main color (A) and in contrasting color (B)*
Textured jacket *8[9:9]oz 2oz in main color (A) and in each of 3 contrasting colors (B, C and D)*
Size E crochet hook

Gauge
20dc and 12 rows to 4in worked on size E hook.

Plain jacket

Back

Using size E hook make 57[62:67]ch.

Base row 1dc into 4th ch from hook, 1dc into each ch to end. Turn. 55[60:65]sts.

***Patt row** 3ch to count as first dc, 1dc into each dc to end, working last dc into turning ch. Turn. This row forms patt. Cont in patt until work measures 9[10¼:11½]in from beg.*

Shape raglan armholes

Next row Sl st into first 6[6:7]dc, 3ch, patt to within last 5[5:6]dc, turn. 45[50:53]dc.

Next row Patt to end. Turn.

Next row 3ch, 1dc into next dc, work next 3dc tog to decrease 2dc, 1dc into each dc to within last 5dc, dec 2dc, 1dc into each of last 2dc. Turn.

Rep last 2 rows until 21[22:25]dc rem. Patt 1 row. Fasten off.

Left front

Using size E hook make 37[40:42]ch. Work base row as for back. 35[48:40]sts. Work as for back from * to *.

Shape raglan armhole

Next row Sl st into first 6[6:7]dc,

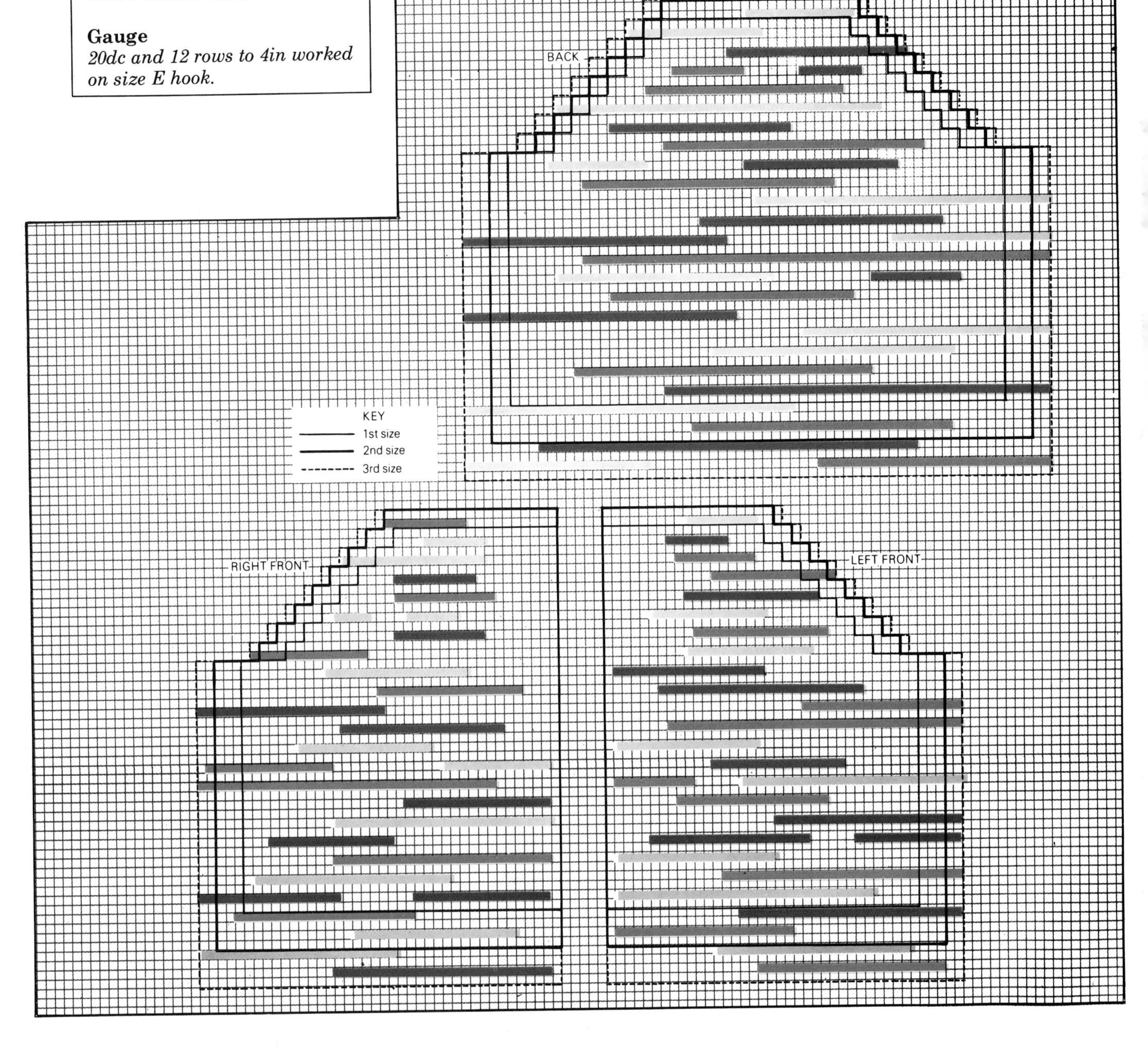

3ch, 1dc into each dc to end. Turn.
Next row Patt to end. Turn.
Next row 3ch, 1dc into next dc, dec 2dc, patt to end. Turn.
Rep last 2 rows until 18[19:20]dc rem. Patt 1 row. Fasten off.

Right front
Work as for left front, reversing raglan shaping.

Sleeves
Using size E hook make 34[36:38]ch. Work base row and patt row as for back. 32[34:36]sts. Cont in patt, but inc 1dc at each end of next row (by working 2dc into first and last dc) and every foll 4th[3rd:3rd] row until there are 42[46:50]dc. Cont straight until work measures 7[8:9]in from beg.
Shape raglan armholes
Work back raglan shaping rows until 8[8:10]dc rem. Patt 1 row. Fasten off.

Belt
Using size E hook make 8[10:10]ch. Work base row and patt row as for back, then cont in patt for 38[40:42]in. Fasten off.

To finish
All seams are joined by working sc on RS of fabric. Work 1sc into each st and 2sc into each row end. Join raglan, side and sleeve seams. With RS facing join yarn to right front at lower edge and work row of sc evenly along right front, around neck and along left front; do not turn but work row of crab st (sc worked from left to right). Fasten off. Fold back lapels and catch in place. Make a belt loop on each side seam at waist level. Thread belt through loops.

Two-color jacket
Work as for plain jacket but work sc on seams and front edging in contrasting color.

Textured jacket
Follow directions for plain jacket but work into back loop only of each st to be bound with crab st, as indicated on charts.

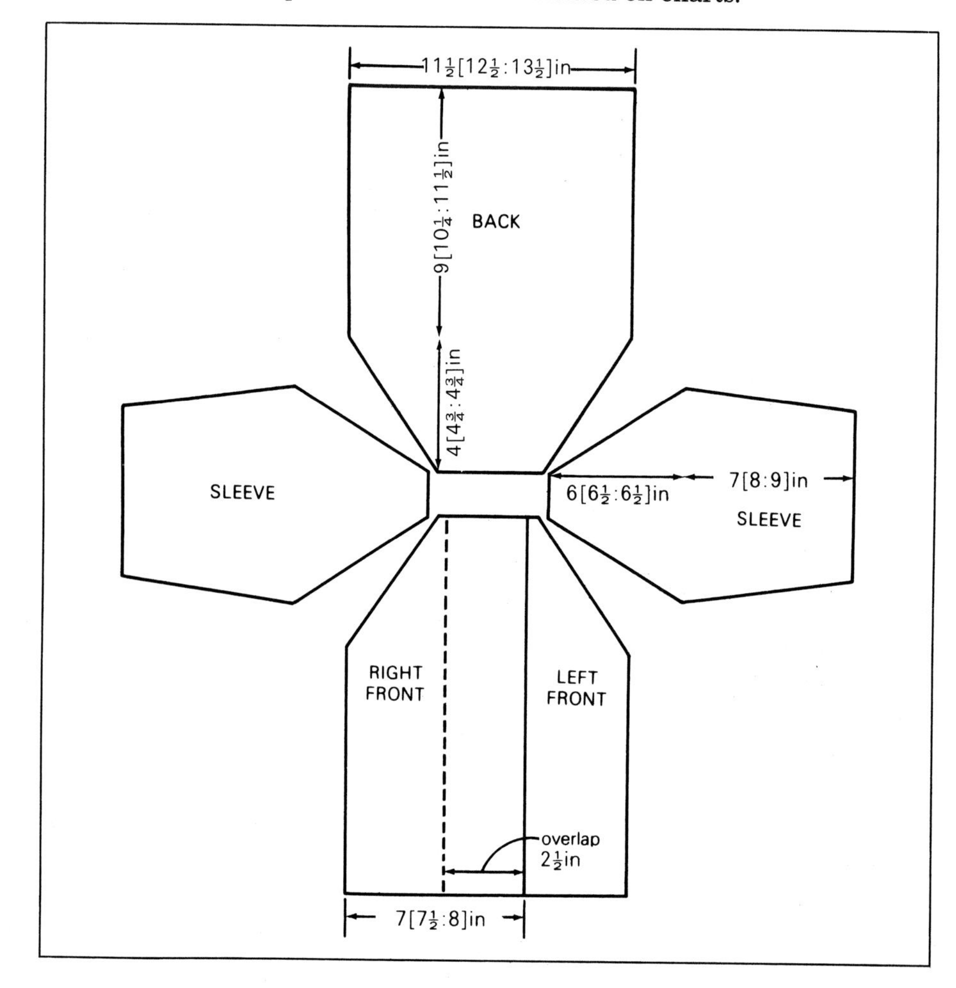

Technique tip
Working the textured effect
To work the textured effect on this pattern you need to leave the front loop of stitches free when working the background fabric. The texture is formed by working crab stitch into the free loops. The stitches that are not to be edged with crab stitch are worked into in the normal way, through both loops.

Following the charts for the position of texture, work a double crochet into back loop only of each double crochet shown in one of contrasting colors.

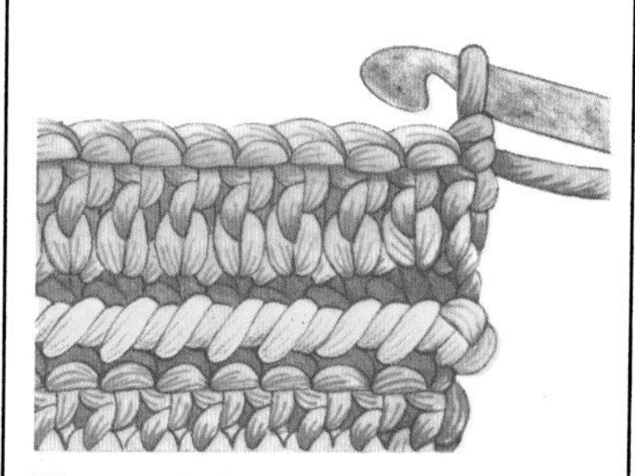

The crab stitch can either be worked after completing every few rows or after completing each piece of the garment. Join the contrasting yarn to the first loop at the left and work crab stitch into each loop to end. Fasten off. Darn in all ends on the wrong side of the fabric.

CLOWN CARDIGANS

Sizes
To fit 20[22:24]in chest.
Length to shoulder, 10¼[11½:13]in.
Sleeve seam, 7¾[9¼:10¾]in.
Note *Directions for the larger sizes are in brackets []; where there is only one set of figures it applies to all sizes.*

Materials
Knitting worsted:
V-neck cardigan *5[6:7]oz in main shade (A)*
1oz in each of 2 contrast colors for motif
4 buttons
Round-neck cardigan *4[5:6]oz in main shade (A)*
2oz in contrasting color (B)
1oz in each of 2 contrasting colors for motif
7 buttons
Size F crochet hook
1 pair No. 2 knitting needles

Gauge
18sts and 13 rows to 4in in hdc worked on size F hook.

V-neck cardigan

Back

Using size F hook and A, make 51[55:59]ch.
Base row 1hdc into 3rd ch from hook, 1hdc into each ch to end. Turn. 50[54:58]sts.
Patt row 2ch to count as first hdc, 1hdc into each hdc, ending with last hdc into top of 2ch. Turn.
Rep last row until work measures 5[6:7]in.

Shape raglan
1st row Sl st into each of first 5sts, 2ch, patt to last 4sts, turn.
2nd row 3ch, yo, insert hook into next st and draw a loop through, yo, insert hook into next st and draw a loop through, yo and draw through all loops on hook – called dec 1 –, patt to last 3sts, dec 1, 1hdc into top of 2ch. Turn.
3rd row 3ch, dec 1, patt to last 3sts, dec 1, 1hdc into top of 3ch. Turn.
Rep 3rd row until 12[14:16]sts rem. Fasten off.

Left front

Using size F hook and A, make 23[25:27]ch. Work base row as for back. 22[24:26]sts.
Cont in patt as given for back until front measures same as back to underarm.

Shape raglan and V-neck
1st row Sl st into each of first 5sts, 2ch, patt to end. Turn.
2nd row 2ch, dec 1 (neck edge), patt to last 3sts, dec 1, 1hdc into top of 2ch. Turn.
3rd row 3ch, dec 1, patt to end. Turn. Cont to dec one st at armhole edge on every row, *at same time* dec one st at neck edge on every 4th[3rd:3rd] row until 3[4:5]sts in all have been dec at neck edge. Keeping neck edge straight, cont to dec at armhole edge only until one st rem.

Right front

Work as given for left front to underarm.

Shape raglan and V-neck
1st row Patt to last 4sts, turn.
2nd row 3ch, dec 1, patt to last 3 sts, dec 1, 1hdc into top of 2ch. Turn.
Cont shaping as given for left front until 3[4:5] decs have been worked at front neck edge. Cont to dec at armhole edge only until one st rem. Fasten off.

Waistband

Join side seams. Using No. 2 needles, A and with RS facing, pick up and K one st from each foundation ch along lower edge of left front, back and right front. Work 12 rows K1, P1 ribbing. Bind off in ribbing.

Sleeves

Using size F hook and A, make 32[33:34]ch. Work base row as for back. Work 2[3:4] rows patt as for back.
Next row (inc row) 2ch, 2hdc into next hdc, patt to last 2sts, 2hdc into next st, 1hdc into top of 2ch. Turn.
Work 3[4:5] rows without shaping. Rep last 4[5:6] rows until there are 41[42:45]sts. Cont straight until sleeve measures 6½[8:9½]in.

Shape raglan top
Work as given for back raglan shaping until 3[4:5]sts rem. Work 0[1:1] rows. Fasten off.

Cuffs
Using No. 2 needles, A and with RS facing, pick up and K one st from each foundation ch. Work 12 rows K1, P1 ribbing. Bind off in ribbing.

Front band

Using No. 2 needles and A, cast on 7sts. Work 4 rows K1, P1 ribbing.
Next row (buttonhole row) Rib 3, bind off one st, rib to end.
Next row Rib to end, casting on one st over that bound off in previous row. Rib 14 rows. Rep last 16 rows until 4 buttonholes have

been completed. Cont in ribbing until band, when slightly stretched, fits around front edges and neck. Bind off in ribbing.

Motif

Face

Using size F hook and first contrasting color, make 3ch. Join with a sl st into first ch to form a circle.

1st round Work 8sc into circle.
2nd round Work 2sc into each sc.
3rd round (1sc into next sc, 2sc into next sc) to end. 24sts.
4th round 1sc into each sc to end.
5th round Using 2nd contrasting color, 1sc into each sc to end. Fasten off.

Hat

Using size F hook and first contrasting color, make 9ch.

1st row 1sc into 2nd ch from hook, 1sc into each of next 6ch, 3sc into last ch, cont around and work into other side of ch, 1sc into each of next 7ch. Turn.
2nd round 2ch, 1hdc into each of next 3sc, 1sc into each of next 4sc, 3sc into top sc, 1sc into each of next 4sc, 1hdc into each of last 4sc, change to 2nd contrasting color.
Next row 1sc into each st around,

then 1sc into each sp along straight edge. Join with sl st into first sc. Fasten off.

Bow tie
Using size F hook and first contrasting color, make 9ch.
1st row 1sc into 2nd ch from hook, 1sc into each ch to end. Turn. 8sc.
2nd row 1ch, 1sc into each sc to end. Turn. Rep last row again. Fasten off.
Using 2nd contrasting color, work 1sc into each st all around. Fasten off. Tie a length of 2nd contrasting color around center and draw up tightly. Embroider details – face, spots on tie and pompons on hat. Make 2 more motifs in same way.

To finish
Sew face to each sleeve and to one front. Sew on hat, stuffing lightly with cotton wool to give raised effect. Sew on bow tie, stuffing as well. Join raglan seams, then sleeve seams. Sew front band in position. Sew on buttons.

Round-neck cardigan

Back
Work as given for V-neck cardigan.

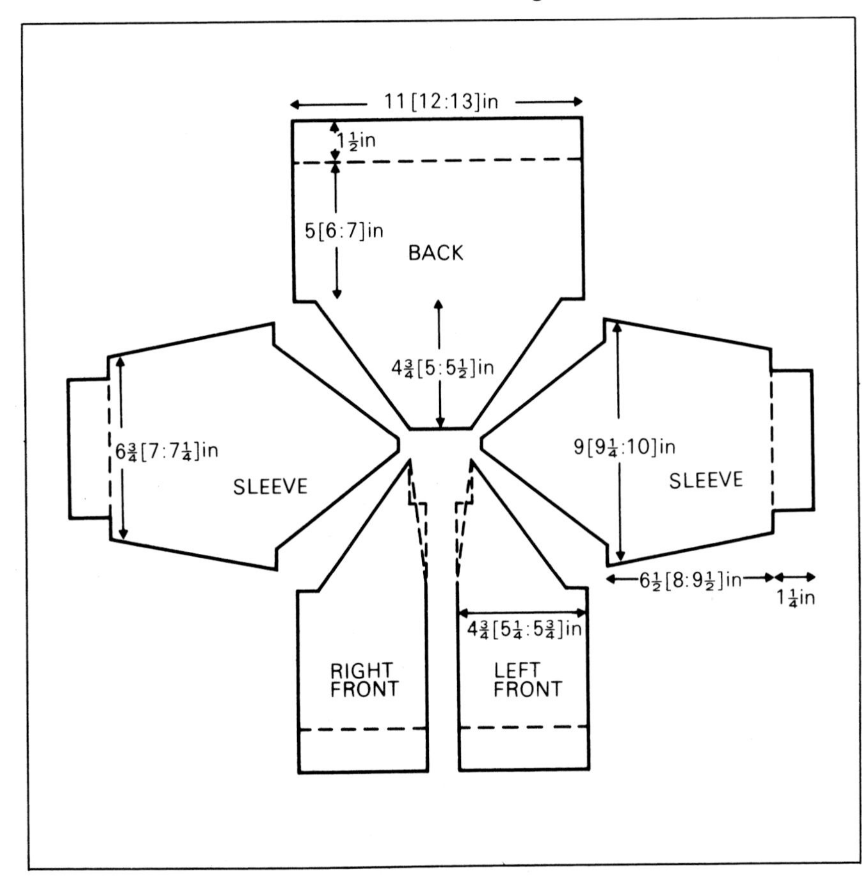

Left front
Work as given for left front of V-neck cardigan to underarm.
Shape raglan
1st row Sl st into each of first 5sts, 2ch, patt to end. Turn.
2nd row Patt to last 3sts, dec 1, 1hdc into top of ch. Turn.
3rd row 3ch, dec 1, patt to end. Turn. Rep last 2 rows until 9[9:11]sts rem, ending at neck edge.
Shape neck
Next row Sl st into each of first 4[5:6]sts, 2ch, patt to last 3sts, dec 1, 1hdc into top of ch. Turn.
Cont to dec at armhole edge only until one st rem. Fasten off.

Right front
As left front, reversing shaping.

Waistband
Work as given for V-neck cardigan using color B.

Buttonhole band
Using No. 2 needles and B, cast on 7sts. Work as for V-neck cardigan front band, making buttonholes on 5th and every foll 14th row until there are 6 buttonholes in all. Cont in ribbing until band fits from lower edge to neck. Leave sts on safety pin.
Button band
Work to match buttonhole band, omitting buttonholes.

Sleeves
Work as given for V-neck cardigan, working cuff in color B.

Motif
Make 3 motifs as given for V-neck cardigan.

To finish
Finish as given for V-neck cardigan from ** to **.

Neckband
Using No. 2 needles, B and with RS facing, rib across sts of right front band, pick up and K 8[9:10]sts up side of neck, 3[4:5]sts across sleeve top, 12[14:16]sts across back neck, 3[4:5]sts across sleeve top, 8[9:10]sts down other side neck, then rib across other front band. Rib 6 rows, making a buttonhole in line with other buttonholes on 3rd row. Sew front bands in position. Sew on buttons.

POPCORN PULLOVERS

Sizes
To fit 26[28:30]in chest.
Length, 13¾[16:19]in.
Sleeve seam, 12½[13¾:15]in.
Note *Directions for larger sizes are in brackets; one set of figures applied to all sizes.*

Materials
23[25:27]oz of a bulky yarn
Size H crochet hook
1 pair No. 7 knitting needles

Gauge
11dc to 4in on size H hook.

Front
**Using size H Hook chain 41[43:45].
Base row 1dc into 4th ch from hook, 1dc into each ch to end, turn.
Next row Ch 3 to count as first dc, now work 1dc into each dc to end, working last dc into top of the 3ch, turn. (39[41:43]dc). Begin patt.
1st row (RS) Ch 3, *work 4dc all into next dc, remove hook from loop and insert it into first of the 4dc worked, replace dropped loop on hook and draw through loop of first dc – popcorn formed, 1dc into next dc, rep from * to end of row. Turn. 19[20:21] popcorns.
2nd row Ch 3, 1dc into first popcorn, * work a popcorn into next dc, 1dc into next popcorn, rep from * to within last dc, 1dc into last dc. Turn.
3rd row Ch 3, into next dc, *1dc into next popcorn, 1dc into next dc, rep from * to end. Turn. 39[41:43]dc.
4th-8th rows Ch 3, 1dc into each dc to end. Turn. These 8 rows form the patt. ** Cont in patt, work 6[10:13] rows more.

Shape neck
Patt over first 13[14:15]dc, work next 2dc tog, turn and work on these dc for first side of neck. Work 2dc tog at neck edge on next 1[2:2] rows. Fasten off.
Skip center 9dc for neck, join yarn to next dc, work 2dc tog, then patt to end of row. Complete to match first side.

Waistband
With RS facing join yarn and using No. 7 needle pick up and K39[41:43]sts along lower edge.
1st rib row P1, (K1, P1) to end.
2nd rib row K1, (P1, K1) to end.
Rep these 2 rows for 2in. Bind off loosely in rib.

Back
Work as given for front from ** to

Technique tip

How to make a popcorn

Popcorn is the name given to the type of bobble used in this pattern. The idea is to work a number of stitches into one stitch and then draw them together, so making the bobble protrude from the background fabric.

This popcorn is made of four treble worked into one stitch. After working the four treble, remove the hook from the loop and insert it into the first of the four treble.

Keeping the hook in the first treble, insert it into the dropped loop. Draw this loop through the first treble, so gathering the four treble closely together to form the popcorn.

The popcorns are spaced across the row to prevent the fabric from spreading – as it would if they were placed close together.

**. Continue in patt, work until back is same length as front. Fasten off. Mark the 13th[13th:14th]st from each side edge to denote shoulders.

Waistband

Work as given for front waistband.

Sleeves

Using size H hook ch 21[23:25]. Work base row and next row as for front then proceed in patt but inc 1dc at each end of 3rd and every following 4th row by working 2dc into dc at each end of row, until 27[29:33]dc remain. Fasten off.

Cuffs

With RS facing join yarn and, using No. 7 needles, pick up and K27[29:31]sts evenly along lower edge. Work the 2 rib rows of waistband for 1½in. Bind off in rib.

Turtleneck

Join right shoulder seam. With RS facing join yarn to top of left front neck and using No. 7 needles pick up and K10[11:12]sts along left front neck. 13sts across center front neck. 10[11:12]sts along right front neck and 22[24:26]sts across back neck to marker, 55[59:63]sts. Work the 2 rib rows of waistband for 5in; end rib row 1. Bind off in rib.

To finish

Do not block. Join left shoulder and collar seam. Mark depth of armholes 5[5½:6]in from shoulder seams on back and front. Sew the sleeves to the armholes between markers. Join side and sleeve seams. Fold collar to right side.

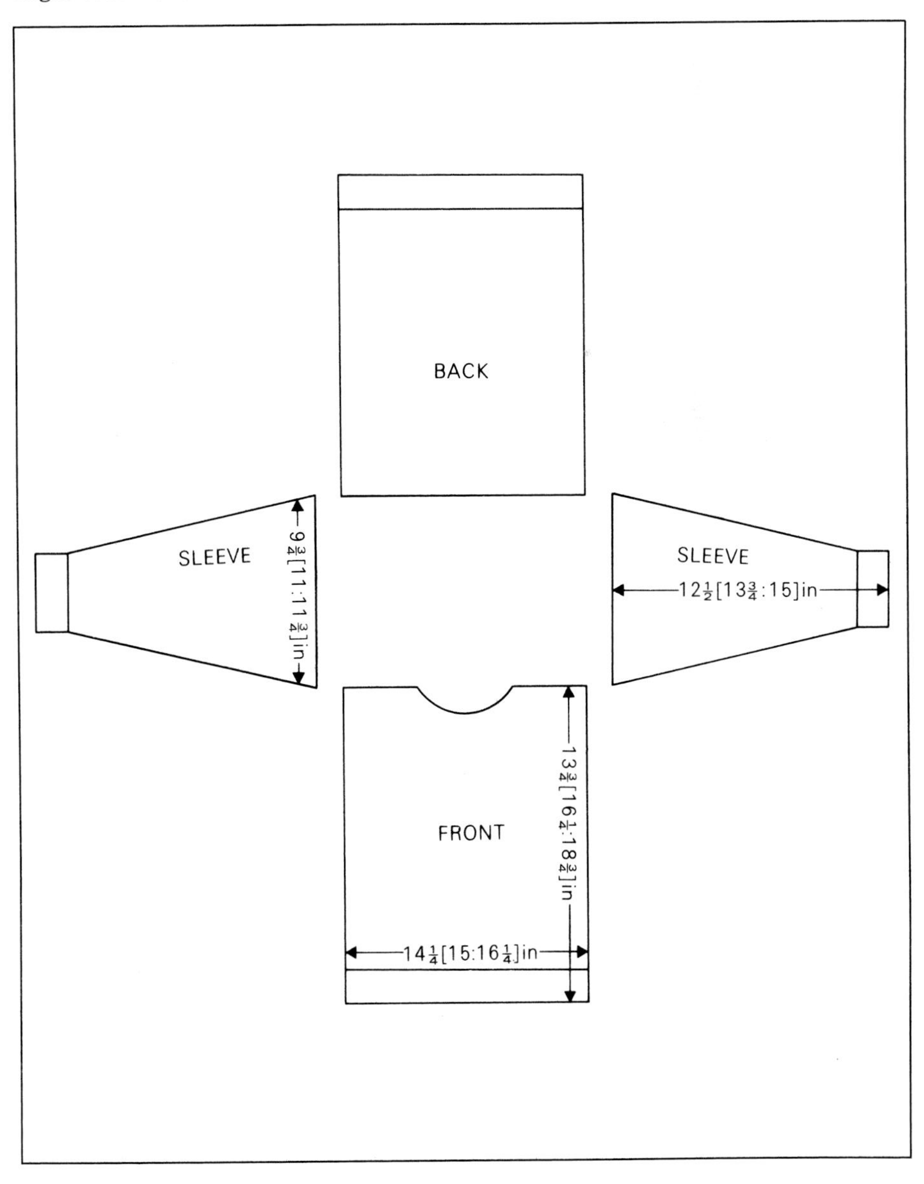

TWO IN COTTON

Sizes
To fit 22[24:26:28]in chest.
Dress *Length,*
18½[19½:21:22¼]in.
Sleeve seam, 2¼[2¼:2¾:2¾]in.
T-shirt *Length, 13[14:15½:17]in.*
Sleeve seam, as for dress.
Note *Directions for larger sizes are in brackets []; where there is only one set of figures it applies to all sizes.*

Materials
Dress *6[7:7:8]oz of a lightweight mercerized crochet cotton*
T-shirt *5[6:6:7]oz*
No. 0 and size B hooks
3 small buttons

Gauge
13sps and 14 rows to 4in worked on size B hook.

Dress

Back

Using size B hook make 112[116:120:124]ch.
Base row 1dc into 6th ch from hook, *1ch, skip next ch, 1dc into next ch, rep from * to end. Turn. 54[56:58:60]sps. Beg patt.
1st row 4ch, 1dc into next dc, *1ch, 1dc into next dc, rep from * to end, working last dc into 2nd of 6ch. Turn.
2nd row 4ch, (1dc into next dc, 1ch) 3[4:5:6] times, *(yo, insert hook around dc just worked, yo and draw a loop through) 6 times, yo and draw through all loops on hook – 1 puff st worked –, 1dc into next dc, (1ch, 1dc into next dc) 5 times, 1ch, rep from * to last 3[4:5:6]sps, work a puff st, patt to end. Turn.
3rd-5th rows As 1st row.
6th row 4ch, (1dc into next dc, 1ch) 6[1:2:3] times, *work a puff st, 1 dc into next dc, (1ch, 1dc into next dc) 5 times, 1ch, rep from * to last 6[1:2:3]sps, work a puff st, patt to end.
7th and 8th rows As 1st.
These 8 rows form patt.
Cont in patt until work measures 3¼in from beg.

Shape for side vents
Next 2 rows 7ch, 1dc into 6th ch from hook, 1ch, skip next ch, 1dc into next dc, patt to end. Turn. 58[60:62:64]sps. Working extra sps into patt, work 2 rows without shaping.
Next row 3ch, 1dc into next dc – 1sp decreased –, patt to within last dc and 4ch, 1ch, leaving last loop of each on hook work 1dc into next dc, 1dc into 3rd of the 4ch, yo and draw through all loops on hook – 1sp decreased. Turn.
Work 4 rows straight. Rep last 5 rows until 44[46:48:50]sps rem.
Cont straight until work measures 13¾[14½:15½:16¼]in.

Shape armholes
Next row Sl st over first 3sps, patt to within last 3sps, turn.
Dec one sp at each end of next 2 rows. 34[36:38:40]sps. Cont straight until armhole measures 4¾[5:5½:6]in.

Shape shoulders
Next row Sl st over first 6sps, patt to within last 5sps, turn.
Next row Sl st over first 4[5:5:5]sps, patt to within last 4[5:5:5]sps. Fasten off.

Lower edging
With RS of work facing join on yarn and, using No. 0 hook, work a row of sc evenly along side vents and lower edge, working 1sc into each sp and dc and 3sc at each corner. Turn. Work 4 rows in sc working 3sc at each corner. Fasten off.

Front

Work as back to beg of armhole shaping.

Shape armhole and divide for opening
Next row Sl st across first 3sps, patt across next 18[19:20:21]sps, turn.
Keeping neck edge straight, dec one sp at armhole edge on next 2 rows. 16[17:18:19]sps. Cont straight until armhole measures 3¼[3½:3½:4]in; end at neck edge.

Shape neck
Next row Sl st across first 3sps, patt to end. Turn.
Dec one sp at neck edge on next 4[4:5:6] rows. 9[10:10:10]sps. Cont straight until work measures 18¾[19¾:21¼:22½]in; end at armhole edge.

Shape shoulder
Next row Sl st over first 5sps, patt to end. Fasten off.
Skip 2sps at center front neck, join yarn to next dc and patt across next 18[19:20:21]sps, turn.
Work as first side reversing shaping.

Lower edging
Work as for lower edging of back.

Sleeves

With size B hook make 68[68:72:72]ch.
Base row 1dc into 6th ch from hook, *1ch, skip next ch, 1dc into next ch, rep from * to end. Turn. 32[32:34:34]sps. Cont in patt as for back for 2nd[2nd:3rd:3rd] sizes, until work measures 2¼[2¼:2¾:2¾]in.

Shape top
Next row Sl st over first 3 sps, patt to within last 3sps, turn.
Dec one sp at beg of every row until 14sps rem.
Next row Sl st over first 3sps, patt to within last 3sps. Fasten off.

Edging

With RS facing, join yarn to lower

edge of sleeve and with No. 0 hook work a row of sc along this edge, working 1sc into each sp and 1sc into base of each dc. Turn. Work 4 rows in sc. Fasten off.

Buttonhole band
With RS facing, join yarn to beg of right front opening and with No. 0 hook work 23sc along opening. Turn. Work 1 row in sc.
1st buttonhole row 1sc into each of first 4sc, (2ch, skip next 2sc, 1sc into each of next 6sc) twice, 2ch, skip next 2sc, 1sc into last sc. Turn.
2nd buttonhole row Work 1sc into each sc and 2sc into each sp to end. Turn. Work 1 row in sc. Fasten off.

Button band
With RS facing, join yarn to left front opening and with No. 0 hook work 23sc along opening. Turn. Work 4 rows in sc. Fasten off.

Collar
Join shoulder seams. With RS facing, join yarn to beg of right front neck and with No. 0 hook work 20[22:24:28]sc along right front neck. 33[33:37:41]sc along back neck and 20[22:24:28]sc along left front neck.
Turn. Work in sc for 3¼in. Fasten off. With RS facing, rejoin yarn at base of collar and work a row of sc evenly around outer edge of collar. Fasten off.

To finish
Do not press. Set in sleeves. Join side and sleeve seams. Sew on buttons.

T-shirt

Back
With size B hook make 84[88:92:96]ch.
Base row 1dc into 6th ch from hook, *1ch, skip next ch, 1dc into next ch, rep from * to end. Turn. 40[42:44:46]sps. Work in patt as given for back of dress of 3rd[4th:1st:2nd] sizes, until work measures 3¼in from beg.
Shape for side vents
Next 2 rows 7ch, 1dc into 6th ch from hook, 1ch, skip next ch, 1dc into next dc, patt to end. Turn. 44[46:48:50]sps. Cont straight until work measures 8¼[9:10:11]in. Shape armholes as for dress back.

Front
Work as back to beg of armhole. Shape armhole and divide for neck as dress front. Work sleeves, bands and collar and finish as for dress.

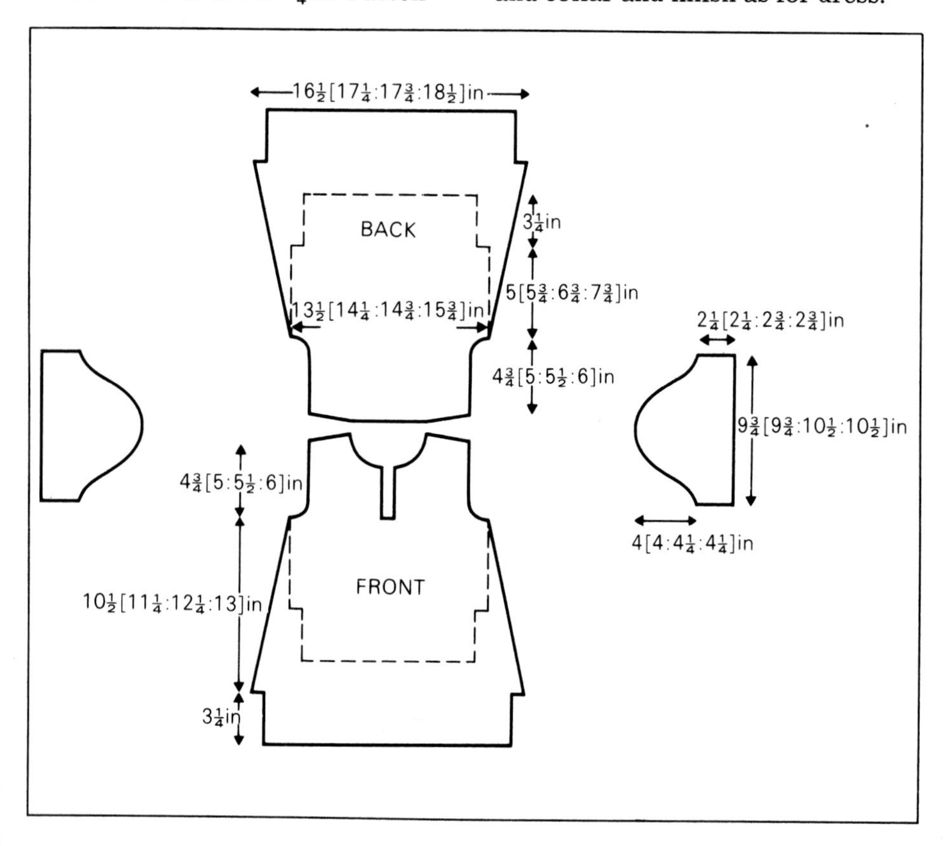

FRUIT POPOVERS

Dress

Back

Using size E hook and A, make 79[85:91:95]ch.

Base row 1hdc into 3rd ch from hook, 1 hdc into each ch to end. Turn.

Patt row 2ch to count as first hdc, 1 hdc into each hdc to end. Turn.

Rep patt row 3[3:5:6] times more.

Dec row Patt across first 20hdc, (yo, insert hook into next st and draw a loop through) twice, yo and draw through all loops on hook – called dec 1 –, 1hdc into each st to within last 22sts, dec 1, work to end. Turn.

Work 4[4:6:6] rows straight. Rep last 5[5:7:7] rows until 64[68:74:78]sts rem. Cont straight until 40[46:58:66] rows have been worked from beg. Mark each end of last row. **Work a further 16[18:20:22] rows.

Shape shoulders

Next row Sl st across first 7[8:8:9]sts, 2ch, 1hdc into each hdc to within last 6[7:7:8]sts, turn. Rep last row once.

Next row Sl st across first 8[7:9:8]sts, 2ch, patt to within last 7[6:8:7]sts. Fasten off.**

Front

Work as for back to position of markers.

*****Divide for neck**

Next row Patt across first 32[34:37:39]sts, turn.

Next row 2ch, 1hdc into next hdc, 2hdc into next hdc, patt to end. Turn.

Next row Patt to end. Turn.

Rep last 2 rows until 16[18:20:22] rows have been worked from marker.

Shape shoulder

Next row Sl st across first 7[8:8:9]sts, 2ch, patt to end. Turn.

Next row 2ch, 1hdc into next hdc, 2hdc into next hdc, patt to within last 6[7:7:8]sts, turn.

Next row Sl st across first 8[7:9:8]sts, 2ch, patt to end. Fasten off.

Rejoin yarn to next st at neck edge, 2ch, patt to end. Turn.

Next row Patt to within last 3sts, 2hdc into next st, patt to end. Turn.

Next row Patt to end. Turn.

Rep last 2 rows until 16[18:20:22] rows have been worked from marker.

Shape shoulder

Next row Patt to within last 6[7:7:8] sts, turn.

Next row Sl st across first 7[8:8:9]sts, 2 ch, work to within last 3sts, 2hdc into next st, patt to end. Turn.

Next row Patt to within last 7[6:8:7]sts. Fasten off.***

Sleeve edgings (alike)

Join shoulder seams. With RS of work facing and using size E hook join A to row end above marker and work 1sc into this row end, then work (2sc into next row end, 1sc into next row end) along armhole edge to next marker. Turn. 48[54:60:66]sc.

Next row 1sc into each sc to end. Turn. Join on B. (Do not cut off A.)

Picot row Working into front loop only on each st work (1sc into each of next 3sc, 3ch, sl st into last sc worked) all along sleeve edge. Fasten off B. Without turning work, pick up A and work along the back of the last row, working into the back loops only, 2ch, 1hdc into each st to end. Turn.

Next row 2ch, 1hdc into each st to end. Turn.

Rep last row twice. Fasten off.

Collar and neck edging

With RS of work facing and using size C hook join A to first row end on right front neck edge, work 1sc into same place as join, (2sc into next row end, 1sc into next row end) to corner, 3sc into corner, then 1sc into each st around neck, 3sc into corner, (1sc into next row end, 2sc into next row end) down left front edge. Turn. Join on B.

Next row With B, 1ch, 1sc into each sc all around, working 3sc into each corner. Turn.

Next row With A, 1ch, 1sc into each sc all around, working 3sc into each corner. Turn.

Next row With B, 1ch, (1sc into each of next 3sc, 3ch, sl st into last sc worked) all around. Fasten off.

Join edges of collar at center front. Fold back collar.

Lower edging

Join side and sleeve seams. With RS facing and using size C hook, join B to lower edge and working into rem

---

Sizes

To fit 22[24:26:28]in chest.

Dress *Length, 16[18:22:25]in.*

Smock *Length 14[15½:17½:20]in.*

Note *Directions for larger sizes are in brackets []; where there is only one set of figures it applies to all sizes.*

Materials

Dress *6[7:9:10] × 1oz balls sport yarn in main color (A)*

1 ball in contrasting color (B)

Smock *5[6:8:9] × 1oz balls sport yarn in main color (A)*

1 ball in contrasting color (B)

Apple motif 1 ball each in light green and dark green

Small quantity in brown for stalk

Strawberry motif 1 ball each in red and bottle green

Small quantity in yellow for embroidery

Sizes C and E crochet hooks

Gauge

21hdc to 4in on size E hook.

loop of foundation ch work (1sc into each of next 3sts, 3ch, sl st into last sc worked) all around, sl st into first sc. Fasten off.

Smock

Back

Using size E hook and A, make 75[79:85:89]ch.

Base row 1hdc into 3rd ch from hook, 1hdc into each ch to end. Turn.

Patt row 2ch to count as first hdc, 1hdc into each hdc to end. Turn.

Rep the patt row 3[3:5:6] times.

Dec row Patt across first 20sts, dec 1 (see dress dec row), work to within last 22sts, dec 1, patt to end. Turn.

Work 4[4:6:7] rows straight. Rep last 5[5:7:8] rows until 64[68:74:78]sts rem. Cont straight until 32[36:42:48] rows have been worked from beg. Mark each end of last row. Now work as for dress from ** to **.

Front

Work as for front to markers, then complete as for dress from *** to ***.

Sleeve edgings, collar and neck edging and lower edging

Work as given for dress.

Apple motif

Using size C hook and dark green, make 3ch, sl st into first ch to form ring.

1st round Work 8sc into ring.

2nd round 2sc into each sc all around. 16sc.

3rd round 1sc into each sc all around.

4th round (1sc into next sc, 2sc into next sc) 8 times. 24sc.

5th round (2sc into next sc, 1sc into each of next 2sc) 8 times. 32sc.

6th round (1sc into each of next 3sc, 2sc into next sc) 8 times. 40sc.

7th round (2sc into next sc, 1sc into each of next 4sc) 8 times. 48sc.

8th round 1sc into each sc all around.

Cont to inc in this way, inc 8sts evening on 3 rounds then work 1 round without shaping until there are 160sc in a round. Fasten off.

Using light green and working in cross stitch, embroider the "shine" onto the apple in a half moon shape.

Stalk

Using size C hook and brown make 21ch.

Base row 1sc into 2nd ch from hook, 1sc into each ch to end. Turn.

Next row 1ch, 1sc into each of first 15sc, turn.

Next row Sl st across first 5sts, 1sc into each sc to end. Turn.

Next row 1ch, 1sc into each st to end. 20sc. Fasten off.

Press motif and attach to garment, leaving a small opening at side edge for pocket.

Embroider flowers at lower edge and on one side of collar as shown.

Strawberry motif

Using size C hook and red make 2ch.

1st row 2sc into 2nd ch from hook. Turn.

2nd row 1ch, 2sc into each of the 2sc. Turn. 4sc.

3rd row 1ch, 2sc into first sc, 1sc into each of next 2sc, 2sc into last sc. Turn. 6sc.

4th row 1ch, 2sc into first sc, 1sc into each sc to within last sc, 2sc into last sc. Turn.

5th-8th rows As 4th row. 16sc.

9th row 1ch, 1sc into each sc to end. Turn.

10th and 11th rows 1ch, 2sc into first sc, work to within last sc, 2sc into last sc. Turn.

12th-20th rows Rep 9th-11th rows 3 times 32sc.

21st row 1ch, work to end. Turn.

22nd row 1ch, 2sc into first sc, work to within last sc, 2sc into last sc. Turn.

23rd-32nd rows Rep 21st and 22nd rows 5 times. 44sc.

33rd and 34th rows 1ch, work to end. Turn.

35th row 1ch, 2sc into first sc, work to within last sc, 2sc into last sc. Turn. 46sc.

36th-38th rows Rep 33rd-35th rows. 48sc.

39th and 40th rows 1ch, work to end. Turn.

41st row 1ch, (insert hook into next sc, draw yarn through) twice, yo and draw through all loops on hook – called decrease one or dec 1 –, 1sc into each sc to within last 2sc, dec 1. Turn.

42nd and 43rd rows 1ch, work to end. Turn. 46sc.

44th-46th rows Rep last 3 rows

once.
47th row 1ch, dec 1, work to within last 2sts, dec 1. Turn. 42sc.
48th row 1ch, work to end. Turn.
49th-52nd rows Rep last 2 rows twice. 38sc.
53rd row Sl st across first 3sts, work to within last 3sts, turn.
54th-57th rows Rep last row 4 times. Fasten off.
Using size C hook and red, work a row of sc evenly all around outer edge, sl st into first sc.
Fasten off.
Using yellow, work small V's over motif for "seeds".

Leaves
Using size C hook and bottle green, make 8ch for leaf.
Base row 1sc into 2nd ch from hook, 1sc into each of next 5ch, 3sc into last ch, without turning the work, work along other side of ch working 1sc into each of next 6ch. Turn.
1st row 1ch, 1sc into each of first 7sc, 3sc into top, then 1sc into each of the 7sc on other side. Turn.
2nd row 1ch, 1sc into each of first 8sc, 3sc into top, then 1sc into each of the 8sc on other side. Fasten off.
Make 3 more leaves in the same way.

Stalk
Work 7sc across flat edge of one leaf, then cont across the next leaf in the same manner until all leaves are in a line. Turn. 28sc.
Next row 1ch, 1sc into each sc to end. Turn.
Next row 1ch, (dec 1) to end. Turn. 14sc.
Next row 1ch, 1sc into each sc to end. Turn.
Next row 1ch, (dec 1) to end. Turn. 7sc.
Next row 1ch, 1sc into each sc to end. Turn.
Next row 1ch, 1sc into first sc, (dec 1) to end. Turn. 4sc.
Next row 1ch, (dec 1) twice. Turn. 2sc. Work 3 rows in sc.
Fasten off.
Press motif and attach to garment, leaving a small opening at side edge for pocket. Sew on stalk and leaves. Embroider flowers at lower edge and on one side of collar as shown.

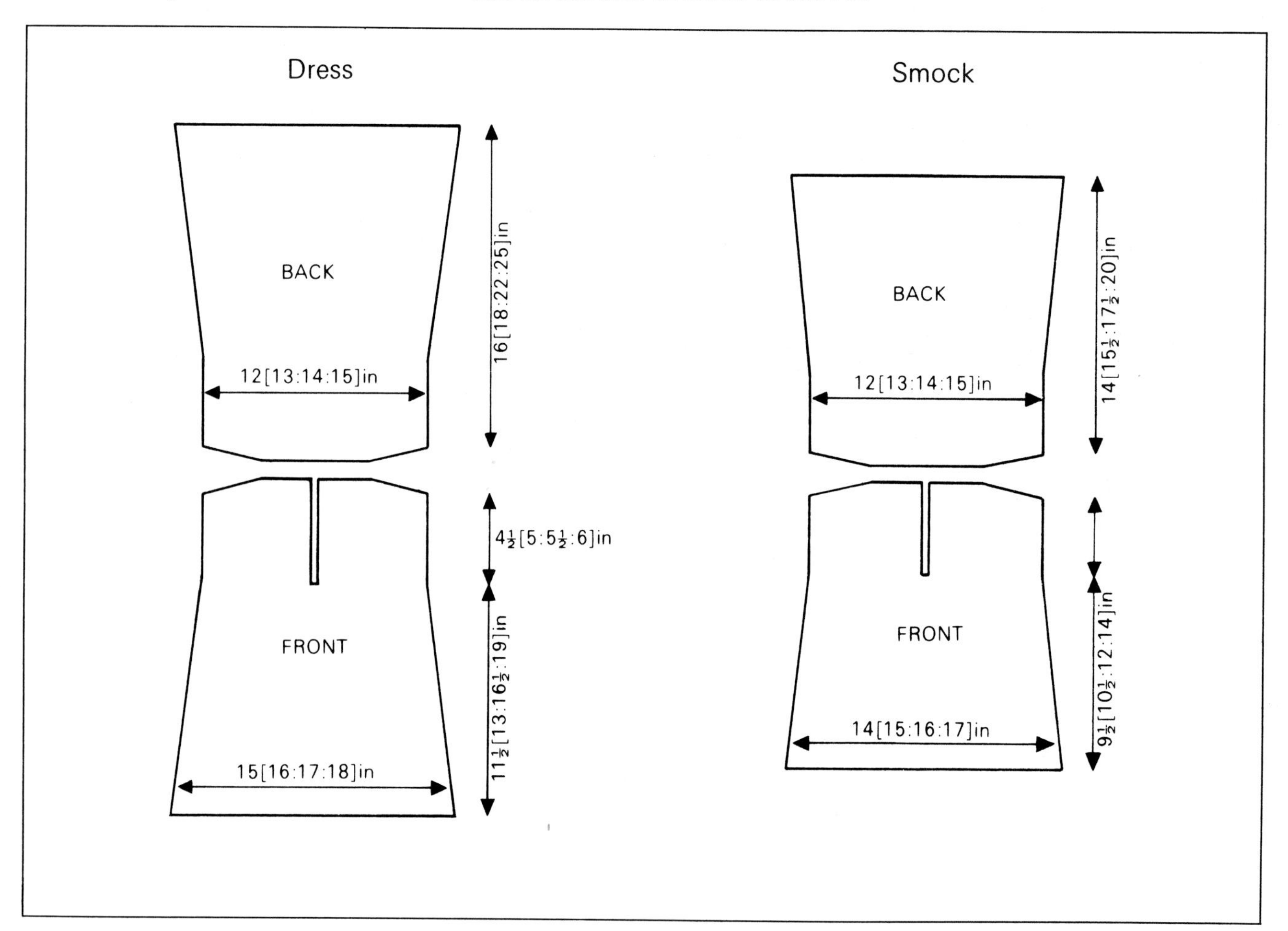

BELTED BATHROBES

Sizes
To fit 24[26:28:30]in chest.
Boy's robe
Length, 26¾[28½:30½:32½]in.
Girl's robe *Length,*
30¼[33½:34½:36½]in.
Sleeve seam, 10[12:14:16]in.
Note *Directions for larger sizes are in brackets []; where there is only one set of figures it applies to all sizes.*

Materials
Boy's *32[36:39:43]oz of a bulky yarn in main color (A) and 9[9:11:11]oz in contrasting color (B)*
Girl's *41[44:48:42]oz of a bulky yarn in main color (A) and 11[11:13:13]oz in contrasting color (B)*
Sizes F, H and I hooks
For knitted belt, a pair of No. 6 needles

Gauge
11dc and 7 rows to 4in worked on size I hook.

Back
Using size I hook and A, make 48[51:54:57]ch.
Base row 1dc into 4th ch from hook, 1dc into each ch to end. Turn. 46[49:52:55]sts.
1st row 3ch, skip first dc, 1dc into each dc to end, 1dc into top of turning ch. Turn. Rep last row 5[7:9:9] times.
Dec row 3ch, skip first dc, 1dc into each of next 14[15:16:17]dc, leaving last loop of each on hook, work 1dc into each of next 2dc, yo and draw through all loops on hook (1dc decreased), 1dc into each dc to within last 17[18:19:20]sts, dec 1dc, 1dc into each dc to end, 1dc into top of turning ch. Turn.
Work 7[9:11:11] rows without shaping. Rep last 8[10:12:12] rows once, then work the dec row again. 40[43:46:49]sts.
Cont without shaping until work measures 20[21:22½:24]in from beg for boy's robe or 23½[25:26½:28]in from beg for girl's.
Shape raglan armholes
1st row Sl st into first 3sts, 3ch, 1dc into each dc to within last 2sts. Turn.
2nd row 3ch, skip first dc, dec 1dc, 1dc into each dc to within last 3sts, dec 1dc, 1dc into top of the turning ch. Turn.
Rep the last row until 16[17:18:19]sts rem. Fasten off.

Left front
Using size I hook and A, make 29[31:33:35]ch and work base row as for back. 27[29:31:33]sts. Work 6[8:10:10] rows. Dec 1dc at center of next row. Work 7[9:11:11] rows without shaping. Rep last 8[10:12:12] rows once, then work the dec row again; 24[26:28:30]dc. Cont without shaping until work is same length as back up to beg of raglan shaping.
Shape raglan armhole and front edge
1st row Sl st across first 3sts, 3ch, 1dc into each dc to within last 3sts, dec 1dc, 1dc into top of turning ch. Turn.
2nd row 3ch, skip first dc, dec 1dc, 1dc into each dc to within last 3sts, dec 1dc, 1dc into top of turning ch. Turn. Rep last row until one st rem. Fasten off.

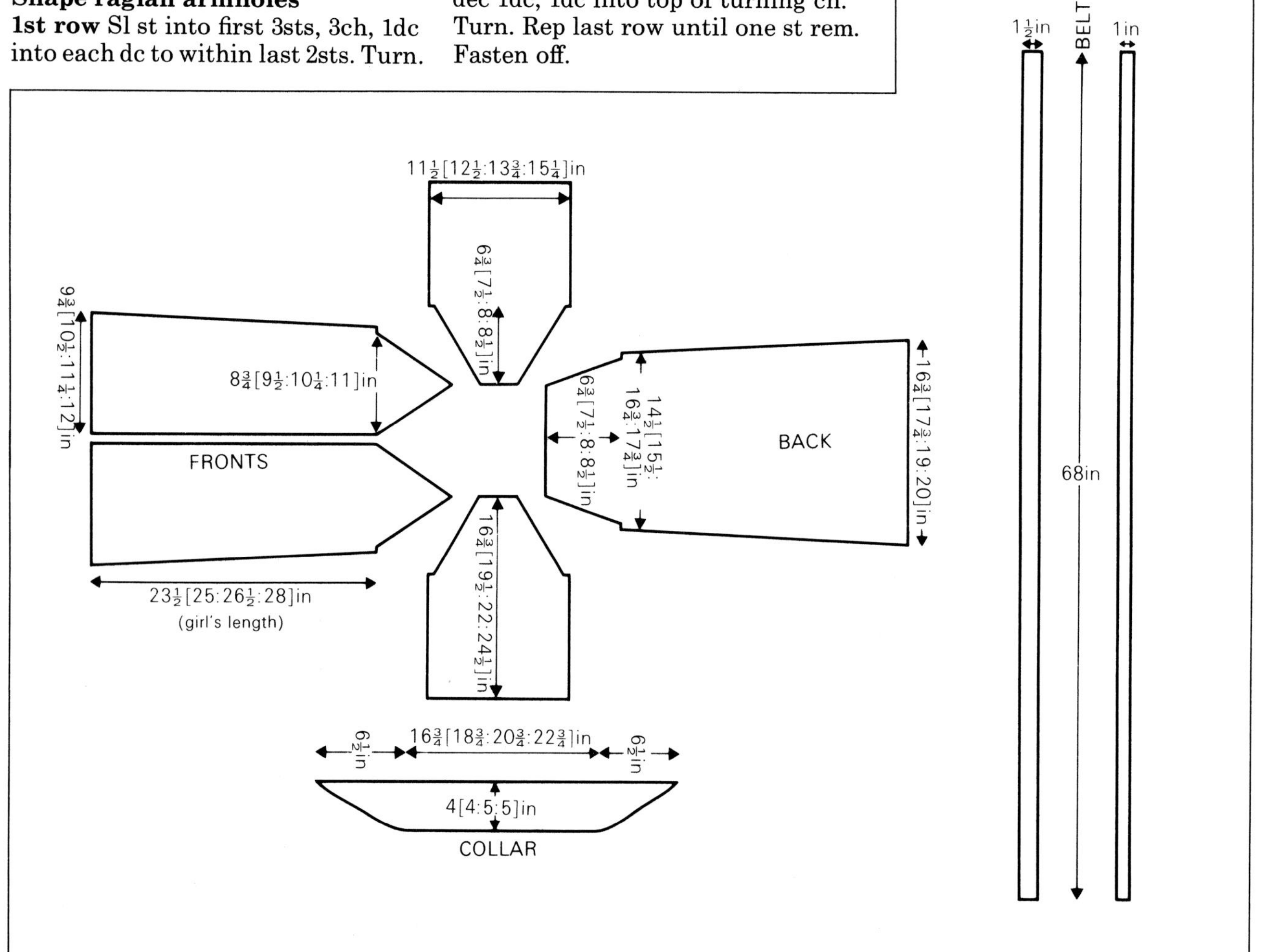

Technique tip

Crab stitch edging

Crab stitch is a single crochet edging that is worked in reverse – that is, from left to right instead of right to left – to produce the effects of a textured, bound edge.

Begin by working a row of single crochet along the side of the fabric to be edged. Do not cut off yarn.

Make one chain, then insert the hook into the previous single crochet to the right.

Take yarn around hook and draw a loop through, so having 2 loops on hook. Take yarn around hook again and draw it through both loops on hook.

Work in this way into each single crochet.

Right front
Work as for left front up to beg of raglan shaping.

Shape raglan armhole and front edge

1st row 3ch, skip first dc, dec 1dc, 1dc into each dc to within last 2sts, turn.

2nd row 3ch, skip first dc, dec 1dc, 1dc into each dc to within last 3sts, dec 1dc, 1dc into top of turning ch. Turn. Rep last row until one st rem. Fasten off.

Sleeves
Using size I hook and A, chain 34[36:40:44] and work base row as for back. Cont in dc until sleeve measures 10[12:14:16]in from beg.

Shape raglan armhole
Work as for back raglan armhole shaping until 8[8:10:12]sts rem. Fasten off.

Edging
Join raglan and side seams.
Using size H hook and with RS facing, join A to lower edge at center back and work 1sc into each foundation ch along this edge to corner of right front, work 3sc into first row end, then 2sc into each row end along front edge to top of first sleeve, 1sc into each st along top of sleeve, back neck and second sleeve, then 2sc into each row end along left front edge to within last row end, 3sc into last row end, then 1sc into each foundation ch along lower edge of back, sl st into first sc. Fasten off.

Collar
Using size H hook and B, make 2ch.
Base row 1sc into 2nd ch from hook. Turn.
1st row 1ch, 1sc into sc. Turn.
2nd row 1ch, 2sc into sc. Turn.
3rd row 1ch, 1sc into each of the 2sc. Turn.
4th row 1ch, 2sc into first sc, 1sc into next sc. Turn.
5th row 1ch, 1sc into each sc. Turn.
6th row 1ch, 2sc into first sc, 1sc into each sc to end. Turn.
7th row 1ch, 1sc into each sc to end. Turn.
Rep last 2 rows until there are 10[10:14:14]sts.
Next row 1ch, 1sc into each sc to end. Turn.
Rep last row 51[57:64:69] times.
Next row 1ch, leaving loop of each on hook work 1sc into each of next 2sc, yo and draw a loop through all loops on hook (1sc decreased), 1sc into each sc to end. Turn.
Next row 1ch, 1sc into each sc to end. Turn.
Rep last 2 rows until one st rem.
Work 1 row. Fasten off.

Edging
Using size H hook and with RS facing join B to first sc on right lower front edge, work 1sc into each sc along front edge to collar, 1sc into each row end all around collar, then 1sc into each sc along left front edge; do not turn. Change to size F hook and work a row of crab st (sc worked from left to right) along left front, around collar and along right front. Fasten off.

Cuffs (alike)
Using size H hook and B and with RS facing, work 1sc into each foundation ch along lower edge of sleeve. Now work 8[10:12:12] rows in sc; do not turn on last row but work a row of crab st.
Fasten off. Join seam and turn back cuff.

Pocket
Using size H hook and B, make 17[17:19:19]ch.
Base row 1sc into 2nd ch from hook, 1sc into each ch to end. Turn.
Next row 1ch, skip first sc, 1sc into each sc to end, 1sc into turning ch. Turn.
Rep last row 14[14:20:20] times more; do not turn on last row but work a row of crab st. Fasten off.
Sew pocket to left or right front.

Belts
Using size I hook and 2 strands of B tog throughout, make 3ch, work 1hdc into 3rd ch from hook. Turn.
Next row 2ch, 1hdc into hdc. Turn.
Rep last row until belt measures 68in or required length. Fasten off.
For alternative belt, knit as foll: using No. 6 needles and B, cast on 10sts and work in K1, P1 ribbing until belt measures 68in or required length. Bind off in ribbing.

To finish
Make a belt loop on each side seam at waist level and thread belt through. Press lightly with a warm iron over a damp cloth.

MOHAIR CAPE

Sizes
To suit 26–28[28–30]in chest.
Length at center back, 23½in.
Note *Directions for larger size are in brackets []; where there is only one set of figures it applies to both sizes.*

Materials
12oz of a medium-weight mohair in main color (A)
7oz of a knitting worsted (B)
Sizes E and F crochet hooks

Gauge
16sc to 4in with size E hook.
17sc to 4in with size F hook.

To make
Using size E (size F) hook and B, make 61ch.
1st row 1sc into 2nd ch from hook, 1sc into each ch to end. Turn. 60sc.
2nd-4th rows 1sc into each sc. Turn.
5th row *1sc into each of next 5sc, 2sc into next sc, rep from * to end. Turn. 70sc.
6th-9th rows Work in sc.
10th row *1sc into each of next 6sc, 2sc into next sc, rep from * to end. Turn. 80sc. Cut off B, Join on A.
For 1st size only, change to size F hook. For both sizes, work patt as follows:
11th row 4ch, 2tr into next sc, *skip 1sc, 3tr all into next sc, rep from * to end. Turn.
12th row 5ch, *skip next 2tr, leaving last loop of each on hook work 3tr all into next tr, yo and draw a loop through all loops on hook – bobble made or MB –, 5ch, skip next 2tr, 1sc into next tr, 5ch, rep from * to end, omitting 5ch at end of last rep and working last sc into top of 4ch.
13th row 8ch, *1sc into next bobble, 7ch, rep from * to end, finishing 3ch, 1tr into last st. Turn.
14th row Work 1sc into each ch and sc to end. Turn.
15th row 5ch, skip first 4sc, MB into next sc, *5ch, skip next 3sc, 1sc into next sc, 5ch, skip next 3sc, MB into next sc, rep from * to end, finishing 5ch, 1sc into last sc. Turn.
16th row 8ch, *1sc into next bobble, 7ch, rep from * to end, finishing 3ch, 1tr into last st. Turn.
17th row 4ch, 2tr into base of ch, 1ch, skip next 2ch, *3tr into next ch, 1ch, skip next 2ch, rep from * to end, finishing 3tr into last st. Turn.
Cut off A. Join on B. For 1st size only, change to size E hook. For both sizes, work in sc as follows:
18th row 1ch, *1sc into each of next 2sts, skip next st, rep from * to end, finishing 1sc into last st. Turn.
19th-23rd rows Work in sc.
Cut off B. Join on A.
24th row 5ch, 2tr into base of ch, *3tr into next sc, 1ch, skip 1sc, rep from * to end, finishing 3tr into last sc. Turn.
25th row *5ch, skip next 3tr, 1sc into next tr, 5ch, skip next 3tr, MB into next tr, rep from *, finishing 5ch, 1sc into last st. Turn.
26th row 8ch, 1sc into bobble, *7ch, 1sc into bobble, rep from *, finishing 3ch, 1tr into last st. Turn.
27th row As 14th.
28th row As 25th.
29th row As 26th.
30th row As 27th.
31st row As 25th.
32nd row As 26th.
33rd row 4ch, 2tr into base of ch, *skip next 2 sts, 3tr into next sc, rep from * to end, finishing 3tr into last st. Turn.
Cut off A. Join on B.
Change to size E hook.
34th row 2ch, 1sc into next st, skip next st, 1sc into each of next 2 sts, rep from * to end, finishing 1sc into last st. Turn.
35th-39th rows Work in sc.
Cut off B. Join on A.
Change to size F hook.
40th row 4ch, 2tr into base of ch, *1ch, skip next sc, 3tr into next sc, 1ch, skip next 2sc, 3tr into next sc, rep from * to end, finishing 3tr into last sc. Turn.
41st-56th rows As 24th-39th.
Fasten off.

Front borders (alike)
Using size E (size F) hook and B, work 6 rows of sc evenly along front edge. Fasten off.

Collar
Join B to neck edge and using size E (size F) hook work 5sc over front border, *1sc into each of next 2sts, skip next st, rep from * to front border, work 5sc over front border. Turn.
Next 2 rows Work in sc to end. Turn.
Next row *1sc into each of next 2sc, 2ch, skip next 2sc, rep from * to end, finishing 1sc into each of last 3sc. Turn.
Next row Work 1sc into each sc and 2sc into each sp to end. Turn.
Next row 1sc into each sc to end. Fasten off.
Working over the center 19sc only, rejoin B and work 1sc into each of next 19sc, sl st into next sc, turn.
Next row 1sc into each of next 19sc, sl st into next sc, 1sc into each of next 3sc, sl st into next sc, turn.
Rep last row until all sts are worked into the collar and outside edge of each side is reached. For 1st size only, change to size F hook.

Next row *1sc into each of next 9sc, 2sc into next sc, rep from * to end. Turn.
Next row 1 sc into each sc to within last 2sc, 2sc into next sc, 1sc into last sc. Turn. Rep last row once more.
Next row *1sc into each of next 9sc, 2sc into next sc, rep from * to within last 2sc, 2sc into next sc, 1sc into last sc. Turn.
Next row 1 sc into each sc to within last 2sc, 2sc into next sc, 1sc into last sc. Turn.
Rep last row twice more.
Next row *1sc into each of next 9sc, 2sc into next sc, rep from * to within last 2sc, 2sc into next sc, 1sc into last sc. Turn.
Next row 1sc into each sc to within last 2sc, 2sc into next sc, 1sc into last sc. Turn.
Rep last row 12 times. Fasten off.
Rejoin B to base of collar at left front and using size F hook work a row of sc evenly around outer edge of collar; do not turn but work a row of crab st (sc worked from left to right). Fasten off.

Tie
Using size F hook and B, make 2ch. Insert hook into first st, *yo and draw a loop through, yo and draw through both loops on hook, rep from *, always inserting hook into the left loop, until tie measures 47in. Fasten off.

Flowers (make 2)
Using size F hook and B, make 3ch, sl st into first ch to form a circle, *4ch, 1tr, 4ch and 1sc all into circle, rep from * 4 times more. Fasten off.
Thread tie through holes at neck, then sew one flower to each end.
Using A, work a few sts at center of each flower.

BUTTERFLY TOP

Back
Using No. 0 hook make 138[146:154]ch.
Base row 1dc into 4th ch from hook, 1dc into each ch to end. Turn 136[144:152]sts.
Beg pattern
1st row 3ch, skip first 2dc, 1dc into next dc, keeping hook at front of work – work 1dc into dc just skipped – called cross 2dc front or Cr2F, (Cr2F) to end, finishing with 1dc into top of 3ch. Turn.
2nd row 3ch, skip first dc, 1dc into next dc, (Cr2F) to last dc and turning ch, 1dc into last dc, 1dc into top of the 3ch. Turn.
These 2 rows form the patt. Cont in patt until work measures 18in from beg. Fasten off.

Front side panels (make 2)
Using No. 0 hook make 40[44:48]ch. Work base row as for back. 38[42:46]sts. Cont in patt until work measures same as back. Fasten off.

Center front filet panel
Using No. 0 hook make 63ch. Work base row as for back. 61sts.
Beg filet pattern
Next row 4ch, skip first 2dc, *1dc into next dc, 1ch, skip next dc, rep from * to end, finishing with 1dc into top of 3ch. Turn. 30sps. Beg working from chart reading uneven numbered rows (RS) from right to left and even numbered rows (WS) from left to right, until panel measures same as back, working same number of rows. Fasten off.

Joint front panels
With WS of center panel facing WS of left front panel and matching foundation chains on each piece, rejoin yarn to lower edge and crochet two pieces tog through double thickness as foll:
Next row 1ch, 1sc into same row end as join, *1sc into next row end, 2sc into next row end, rep from * to

end, working last sc through edge of both pieces. Turn.
Picot row 1ch, *1sc into each of next 3sc, 3ch, sl st into top of last sc worked – picot formed – rep from * to end, finishing with 1sc into turning ch. Fasten off. Join right front panel to center panel in same way. Join shoulder seams on WS, working 1sc into each st along top edge to center panel.

Cap sleeves

Mark 22nd[24th:26th] row from shoulder seams on back and front. With RS of work facing, join yarn to marked row with sl st, work 2sc into same row end as join, *1sc into next row end, 2sc into next row end, rep from * around armhole to marker. Turn. 66[72:78]sc.
Next row 3ch, skip first 2sc, (Cr2F) to end, finishing with 1dc into last sc. Turn. Beg row 2 of back, patt 5 rows.
Next row 1ch, 1sc into each st to end. Turn.
Picot row 1ch, *1sc into each of next 3sc, 3ch, as into top of last sc worked – picot formed – rep from * to end, finishing 1sc into turning ch. Fasten off.

To finish

Join side seams on WS with sc.
Neck edging
With RS of work facing join yarn to center of back neck and work 1sc into each st around neck edge, sl st into first sc; do not turn but work a row of picots as before, sl st into first sc. Fasten off.
Lower edging
With RS of work facing join yarn to one side seam and work *1sc into each of next 3ch, skip next ch, rep from * around lower edge, sl st into first sc; do not turn but work a row of picots as before, sl st into first sc. Fasten off.

Sizes
To fit 32[34:36]in bust.
Length, 18in.
Note *Directions for larger sizes are in brackets []; where there is only one set of figures it applies to all sizes.*

Materials
10 × 150yd or 8oz of a lightweight mercerized crochet cotton
No. 0 crochet hook

Gauge
32sts and 14 rows to 4in measured over crossed doubles on No. 0 hook.
Note *1 block consists of 3 doubles with 2 doubles for each additional block worked.*

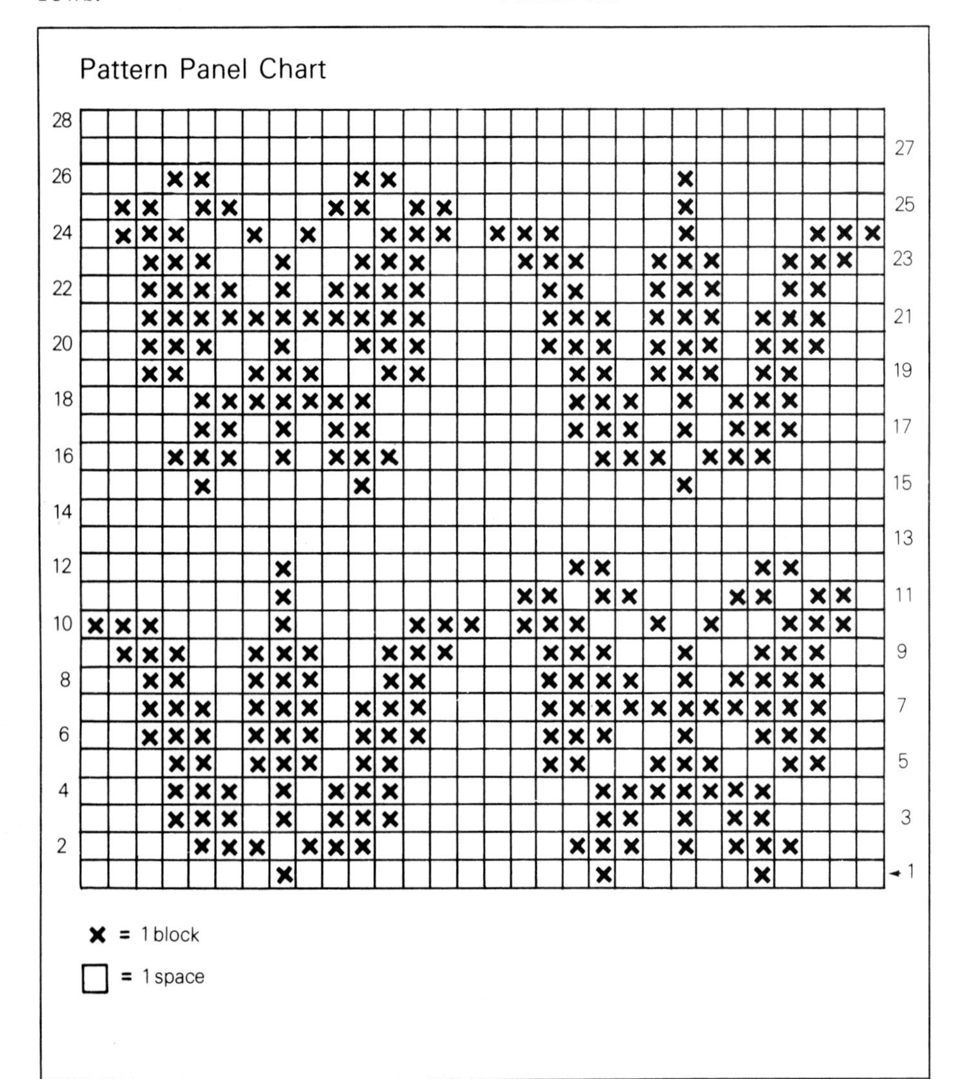

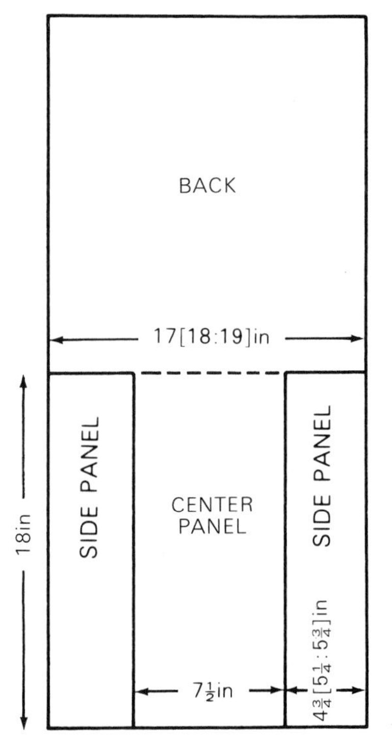

LACY LOOK

Sizes
To fit 32-34 [36-38]in bust.
Length, 23½in.
Sleeve length, 20in.
Note *Directions for larger sizes are given in brackets [ ]; where there is only one set of figures given it applies to both sizes.*

Materials
34[38]oz cotton sport-weight yarn
Size C crochet hook

Gauge
1 patt rep (12sts) and 6 rows to 2¼in on size C hook.

Back
With size C hook ch 113[125].
Base row 1dc into 4th ch from hook, 1dc into each ch to end. Turn.
1st patt row (RS) 3ch to count as first dc, 1dc into each of next 3sts, work 5dc all into next st, remove hook from loop and insert it from *front to back* into first of the 5dc worked, replace dropped loop on hook and draw through loop of first dc – called front bobble (FB); now work *1dc into each of next 11sts, FB into next dc, rep from * to within last 10sts, 1dc into each of last 10sts. Turn. 9[10] FB.
2nd patt row 3ch, *1dc into each of next 7dc, work 5dc all into next st, remove hook from loop and insert it from *back to front* into first of the 5dc worked, replace dropped loop on hook and draw through loop of first dc – called back bobble (BB); 1dc into next dc, 1dc into top of next bobble, 1dc into next dc, BB into next dc, rep from * to within last 2dc, 1dc into each of last 2dc. Turn. 18[20]BB.
3rd patt row As first patt row.
4th patt row 4ch to count as 1dc and 1ch, skip next dc, 1dc into next dc, *1ch, skip next dc, BB into next dc, (1ch, skip next st, 1dc into next dc) twice, 1ch, skip next dc, 1dc into top of next bobble, (1ch, skip next dc, 1dc into next dc) twice, rep from * to end. Turn. 9[10]BB.
5th patt row 4ch, 1dc into next dc, (1ch, 1dc into next dc) twice, 1ch, FB into next dc, 1ch, 1dc into top of next bobble, 1ch, FB into next dc, (1ch, 1dc into next dc) 3 times, FB into next dc, 1ch, 1dc into top of next bobble, 1ch, FB into next dc, rep from * to within last sp, 1ch, 1dc into last dc. Turn. 18[20]FB.
6th patt row 4ch, 1dc into top of next bobble, *1ch, BB into next dc, 1ch, 1dc into top of next bobble, (1ch, 1dc into next dc) 3 times, 1 ch, 1dc into top of next bobble, rep from * to end, but work last dc into 3rd of the 4ch. Turn.
7th patt row 3ch, 1dc into first sp, 1dc into next dc, 1dc into next sp. *FB into next dc, (1dc into next sp, 1dc into next st) 5 times, 1dc into next sp, rep from * to end, working last dc into 3rd of the 4ch. Turn.
8th patt row As 2nd patt row.
9th patt row As first patt row.
Rows 4 to 9 form the patt. Rep them twice more, then work rows 4 to 6 again. Using a separate ball of yarn work 84ch for second sleeve and leave aside.
Next row Work 86ch for first sleeve, 1dc into 4th ch from hook, 1dc into each of next 2ch, *FB into next ch, 1dc into each of next 11ch *, rep from * to * to within last 8ch, FB into next ch, 1dc into each of last 7ch, patt across back, then work across ch of second sleeve working 1dc into first ch; rep from * to * to within last 10ch, 1dc into each of last 10ch, turn. 23[24]FB.
Cont in patt until the 8th patt from beg has been completed. Fasten off.

Waistband
Using size C hook ch 22.
Base row 1sc into 3rd ch from hook, 1sc into each ch to end. Turn. 20sc.
Patt row 2ch to count as first sc, working into back loop only work 1sc into each sc to end. Turn.
Rep the patt row 78[84] times.
Do not turn but work 1sc into each row end along edge. Fasten off.

Front
Work as given for back until the 6th row of the 5th patt from beg has been worked.
Divide for opening
Next row Work across first 69[72]sps, turn and work on first set of sps until the 7th patt from beg has been completed.
Shape neck
Next row Work to within last 22[24]sts, turn. Cont in patt until front is same length as back. Fasten off. With RS facing skip center sp, join yarn to next dc and work as given for first side, reversing shaping at neck.

Waistband
Work as given for back waistband.

Cuffs (make 2)
Work as for back waistband but rep the patt row 39 times in all.

To finish
With RS facing, join yarn to lower edge of back and work 80[86]sc evenly along edge, turn. With waistband at back of work and working through the double thickness, work 1sc into each sc to

Technique tip

Working into one loop only

When you work a basic stitch, such as single, half double or double crochet, you will see that a chain is formed at the top of the stitch.

Usually the stitches on the following row are worked into both loops of the chain, but you can, instead, work a stitch into either the front or back loop only.

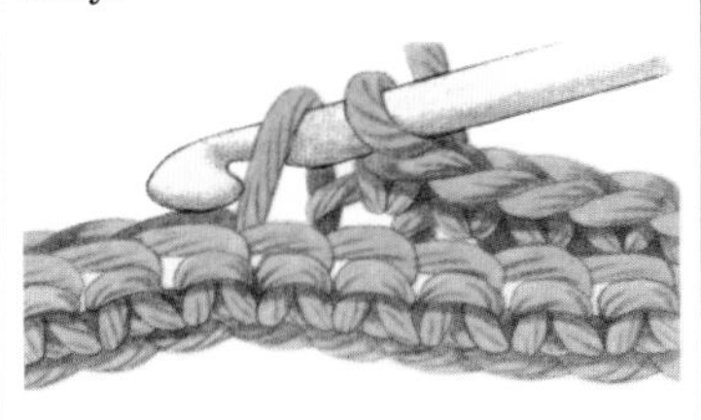

When you do this, you produce a different effect: the remaining loops on the previous row make a ridge on the fabric.

This ridge effect is not only decorative but also useful for waistbands and cuffs – as on our evening sweater – for it serves as a kind of mock ribbing.

end, so joining waistband to back. Fasten off. Join waistband to edge of front in the same way.
Join upper sleeve and shoulder seams. With RS facing join yarn to sleeve edge and work 1sc into each row end along this edge, turn. Join cuff to lower edge of sleeve as for back waistband but decrease 14sc evenly across the sleeve edge. Fasten off. Join other cuff same way. Join side and sleeve seams.

Neck edging
With RS facing join yarn to base of opening and work 1sc into each row end along right side of opening to neck, 4ch, skip next 2sts, *1dc into next st, 1ch, skip next st, rep from * all around neck, then work 1sc into each row end along left side of opening, turn.
Next row 1ch, work 1sc into each sc and 1sc into each dc and sp all around neck and opening. Fasten off.

Neck tie
Using yarn double, work a length of ch approximately 61in. Fasten off.

Tie trims (make 2)
Using yarn single, 4ch, sl st into first ch to form a circle.
Next round 3ch, 15dc into circle, sl st into top of the 3ch. Fasten off.
Thread tie through holes at neck, then attach a tie trim to each end.

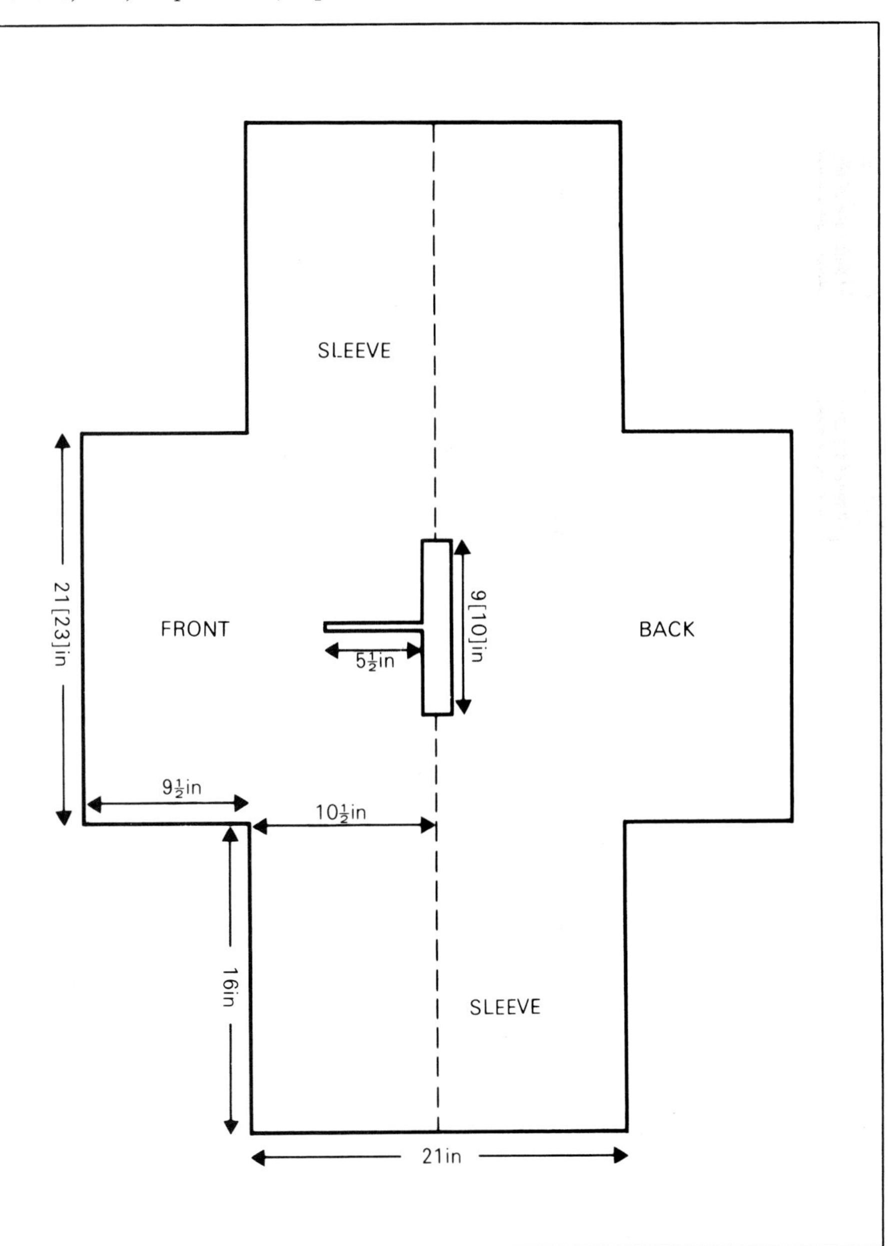

STRIPED FOR COMFORT

Sizes
Child's version *To fit 24[26:28:30]in chest.*
Length to shoulder, 19[21:23:25]in.
Sleeve seam, 10[12:14:16]in excluding cuff.
Mother's version *To fit 32[34:36:38]in bust.*
Length to shoulder, 27[28:28:29]in.
Sleeve seam, 17½[18:18½:19]in, excluding cuff.
Note *Directions for larger sizes are in brackets []; where there is only one set of figures it applies to all sizes.*

Materials
Sport yarn:
Child's version *2 × 2oz balls in main color (A)*
1[2:2:2] balls each in contrasting colors (B and C)
1 ball in contrasting color (D)
Mother's version *3 × 2oz balls in main color (A)*
2[2:3:3] balls each in contrasting colors (B and C)
2[3:3:3] balls in contrasting color (D)
Sizes E and F crochet hooks

Gauge
8V sts and 14 rows to 4in in patt worked on size F hook.

Child's version

Back

Using size F hook and A, make 119[131:143:155]ch for side seam.
Base row Into 5th ch from hook work (1hdc, 1ch, 1hdc – called V st). *skip 2ch, V st into next ch, rep from * to last 3ch, skip 2ch, 1hdc into last ch. Turn. 38[42:46:50]V sts.
Patt row 2ch to count as first hdc, *V st into 1ch sp of V in previous row, rep from *, ending with 1hdc into top of turning ch. Turn.
Cont in patt, work in stripe sequence of 1 row A, 3 rows B, 1 row each C, D and C, 3 rows each A and D, 1 row each C, B and C, 3 rows each A and B, 1 row C[4 rows C, 2 rows C, 1 row D, 2 rows C, 2 rows C, 1 row D, 2 rows C, 1 row A, 2 rows C, 1 row D, 2 rows C]. Rep first 24 rows in reverse order, beg with 3 rows B. Fasten off.

Front

Work as given for back.

Sleeves

Using size F hook and A, make 65[77:89:101]ch. Work base row as for back.
Work in stripe sequence of 2 more rows A, **3 rows B, 1 row each C, D and C, 3 rows each A, D, A and B **, 3 rows each C, A and C[3 rows each C and A, 1 row D, 3 rows each A and C, 4 rows each C and A, 2 rows D, 4 rows each A and C, 4 rows each C and A, 2 rows D, 4 rows each A and C].
Rep 18 rows from ** to ** in reverse order. Work 3 rows A. Fasten off.

To finish

Join shoulder seams, leaving 5[5½:6:6¼]in open for neck. Fold sleeve in half lengthwise and, matching center top of sleeve to shoulder seam, sew in position. Join side and sleeve seams.

Cuffs

Using size E hook, B and with RS facing, work 1sc into alternate row ends at sleeve edge. Turn.
Next row 1ch, 1sc to end. Turn.
Rep last row until cuff measures 1½in. Fasten off. Join cuff seam.
Neck edge Using size E hook, B and with RS facing, work *1sc into next row end, 2sc into next row end, rep from * all around neck edge. Turn. Work 1sc into each sc to end. Fasten off. Join neck seam.
Lower edge Using size E hook, B and with RS facing, work 1sc into each row end all around lower edge. Turn.
Next row 3ch, skip first sc, 1dc into each sc to end. Fasten off.

Tie

Using size E hook and 2 strands of B, make a chain approx 55in long. Thread through row of dc at lower edge.

Bobbles (make 2)

Using size E hook and B, make 3ch. Join with sl st to first ch to form circle. 3ch, work 1 1dc into circle. Join with sl st to first ch. Fasten off. Attach a bobble to each end of tie.

Mother's version

Back

**Using size F hook and A, make, 167[173:173:179]ch for side seam.
Base row Into 5th ch from hook work (1hdc, 1ch, 1hdc – called V st). *skip 2ch, V st into next ch, rep from * to last 3ch, skip 2ch, 1hdc into last ch. Turn. 54[56:56:58]V sts.
Patt row 2ch to count as first hdc, *V st into 1ch sp of V in previous row, rep from *, ending with 1hdc into top of turning ch. Turn.
Cont in patt, work in stripe sequence of 1 more row A, 3 rows B, 1 row each C, B and C, 3 rows each A and D, 1 row each C, B and C, 6 rows each D and A, 1 row C**, 1 row B[2 rows B, 1 row A, 2 rows B:4 rows B, 1 row A, 4 rows B:6 rows B, 1 row A, 6 rows B]. Rep 31 rows from ** to ** in reverse order. Fasten off.

Front

Work as for back until 21[22:23:24] rows have been completed from beg.
1st and 3rd sizes only
Shape neck
Next row Keeping stripe sequence same as back, patt across first 49[51]V sts, 1hdc into first hdc of next V, turn. Cont straight until 31[35] rows have been worked from beg; end at lower edge.
Divide for front opening
Next row Patt to last 16V sts, 1hdc

into first hdc of next V st. Fasten off.
Make 53ch and work base row across these ch until there are 16V sts, then cont in patt down front. Cont without shaping until 41[47] rows have been worked from beg. Fasten off.
Next row Make 19ch in correct color, patt to end. Turn.
Next row Patt to 19ch, (skip 2ch, V st into next ch) 4 times, skip 2ch, 1hdc into last ch. Turn. Finish to match back.
2nd and 4th sizes only
Shape neck
Next row Keeping stripe sequence same as back, sl st across first hdc and next 4V sts, sl st into first hdc of next V, 2ch, patt to end. Cont straight until 33[37] rows have been worked from beg; end at lower edge.

Divide for front opening
Next row Patt to last 16V sts, 1hdc into first hdc of next V st. Fasten off.
Make 50ch and work base row across these ch, then cont in patt down front. Cont without shaping until 44[48] rows have been worked from beg. Fasten off.
Next row Make 17ch in correct color, patt to end. Turn. Finish to match back.

Sleeves
Using size F hook and A, make 110[113:116:119]ch. Work base row as for back. Cont in patt, work stripe sequence as for first 29[31:31:31] rows of back, then 1[1:4:8] rows A. Rep first 29[31:31:31] rows in reverse order. Fasten off.

Cuffs
Using size E hook, B and with RS facing, work along row ends on one edge. *1sc into each of next 2 row ends, skip 1 row end, rep from * to end. Turn.
Next row 1ch, 1sc into each sc to end. Turn.
Rep last row until cuff measures 2¼in. Fasten off.

To finish
Join shoulder seams.
Neck edge Using size E hook, B and with RS facing, work in sc around neck edge, 1sc into each row end along straight part of front neck. 1sc into each sp along side neck, 1sc into each row end along back neck, 1sc into each sp along side neck, then 1sc into each row end along left front neck. Turn.
Next row 1ch, 1sc into each sc to end. Turn.
Rep last row 5 times. Fasten off.
Front opening Using size E hook, B and with RS facing, work a row of sc up front opening, around neck and down other side of front opening. Fasten off.
Fold sleeve in half lengthwise and, matching center top of sleeve to shoulder seam, sew sleeve in position. Join side and sleeve seams.
Lower edge Using size E hook, B and with RS facing, work 1sc into each sc around lower edge. Turn.
Next row 3ch, 1dc into each sc to end. Fasten off.

Tie
Using size E hook and 2 strands of B, make a chain approx 83in long. Thread through row of dc at lower edge.

Bobbles (make 2)
Using size E hook and B, make 3ch. Join with sl st to first ch to form circle, 3ch, 11dc into circle. Join with sl st to first ch. Fasten off. Attach one bobble to each end of tie. Press front neck very lightly.

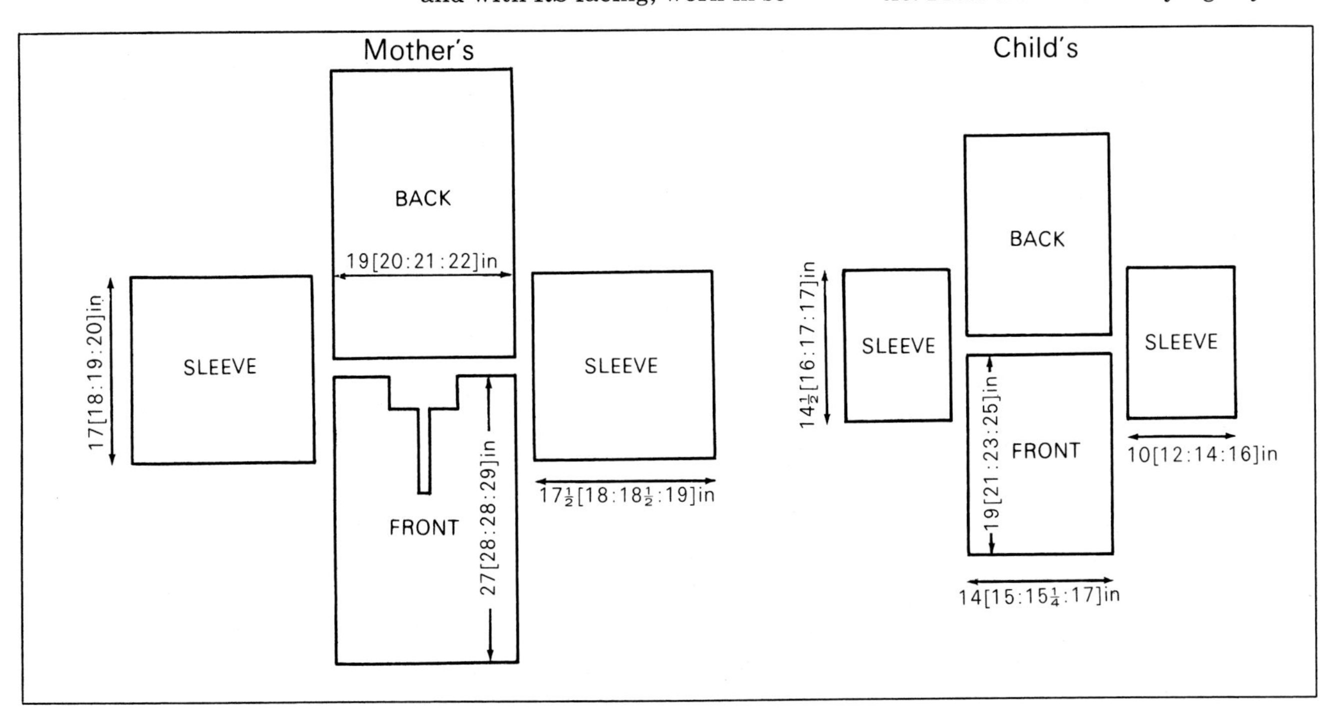

TOUCH OF TAPESTRY

Sizes
To fit 34[36:38]in bust.
Length, 21in.
Sleeve seam, 17½[17¾:16]in.
Note *Directions for larger sizes are in brackets []; where there is only one set of figures it applies to all sizes.*

Materials
7[8:8] × 2oz balls of a sport yarn in main color (A)
1 ball in each of 8 contrasting colors (see chart)
Size E crochet hook
1 pair No. 2 knitting needles

Gauge
20hdc and 16 rows to 4in worked with size E hook.
20sc and 24 rows to 4in worked with size E hook.

Front
Using size E hook and A, make 93[97:101]ch.
Base row 1sc into 2nd ch from hook, 1sc into each ch to end. Turn. 93[97:101]sc.
Next row 1ch to count as first sc, 1sc into each sc to end. Turn.
Cont in sc, working in patt from chart until the 106th row has been worked, then work 2 rows in A. Fasten off.

Waistband
Using No. 2 needles and A, with RS facing, pick up and K 93[97:101]sts evenly along foundation edge.
1st ribbing row K1, (P1, K1) to end.
2nd ribbing row P1, (K1, P1) to end. Rep these 2 rows for 2in. Bind off loosely in ribbing.

Neckband
Using No. 2 needles and A, with RS facing, pick up and K 135[139:143]sts evenly along top edge. Work 2 ribbing rows of waistband for ¾in. Bind off in ribbing.

Back
Using size E hook and A, make 94[98:102]ch.
Base row 1hdc into 3rd ch from hook, 1hdc into each ch to end. Turn. 93[97:101]hdc.
Next row 2ch to count as first hdc, 1hdc into each hdc to end. Turn.
Cont in hdc until work measures the same as front. Fasten off.

Waistband
Work as for front waistband.

Neckband
Work as for front neckband.

Sleeves
Using size E hook and A, make 63[67:71]ch. Work base row as for back, then cont in hdc inc 1hdc at each end of 7th and every foll 6th row until there are 80[84:88]hdc.
Cont straight until work measures 15½[15¾:16]in. Fasten off.

Cuffs
Using No. 2 needles and A, pick up and K 53[55:59]sts evenly along foundation edge. Work 2 rib rows for 2in. Bind off loosely in ribbing.
To finish
Press front lightly. Join shoulder seams, leaving 9in open at center for neck. Sew sleeves to back and front, then join side and sleeve seams.

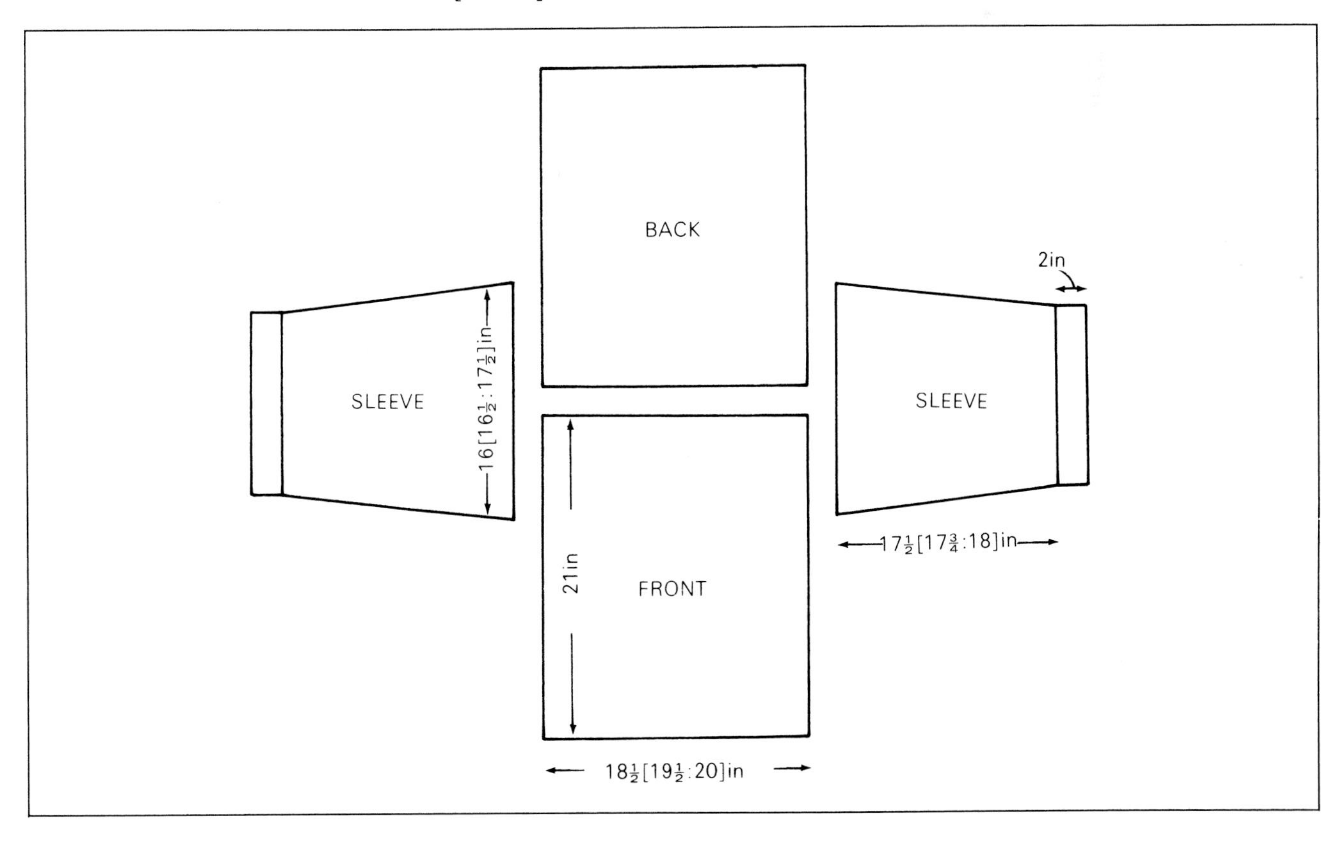

100
90
80
70
60
50
40
30
20
10
2nd
1st
1st
2nd
3rd
KEY
mauve
green
yellow
beige
brown
red
rose
pink
peach
cream

COMFORTABLE CABLE

Sizes
To fit 32-34[36-38]in bust.
Length from shoulder, 29½in including 3⅛in waistband (both sizes).
Sleeve seam, 18in including 3⅛in cuff (both sizes).

Materials
32oz bulky yarn
Size J crochet hook

Gauge
12sts and 8 rows to 4in in half doubles worked on a size J hook.

Note The main part of the garment is made in one piece starting at the lower edge of the right sleeve. Follow the figures in brackets for the 36-38in size.
Using size J hook chain 56.
Foundation row Work 1hdc into 3rd ch from hook. 1hdc into each ch to end. Turn. 55hdc.
Continue to work into back loop only of each st throughout.
1st row 2ch (counts as first hdc), skip first st, 1hdc into each st to end of row, working last st into the turning ch. Turn. This row forms main pattern. Rep the first row 4[6] times.
Fasten off. Do not turn work.

To work the mock cables
1st row With right side (RS) of work facing, rejoin yarn at right-hand edge of work, 1ch, 1sc into first st, **1hdc into each of next 8sts. Turn. Work on these 8sts for first mock cable.
2nd row 2ch, skip first st, 1hdc into each of next 7sts. Turn.
Rep 2nd row twice. Do not turn work.

To draw the mock cable together
Insert hook into the end of the 3rd row of cable, yo and pull it through, rep into the 2nd and 1st row. 4 loops on hook. Yarn over hook and draw through all loops to draw the mock cable together. Mock cable now has 9sts. Turn.
5th row 1ch, skip first st, 1sc into next st, 1hdc into each of next 6sts, 1 sc into turning ch. Do not turn.
Draw row ends together as before drawing 1 loop through 4th, 3rd, 2nd and 1st rows (5 loops on hook), yo and draw through all loops on hook. Mock cable now has 10sts.
Work 1sc into next st of last complete main patt row.
Rep from **5 times, working the last sc into turning ch of main patt row. 6 cables have been made. Turn.
6th row Wrong side 3cn, skip first st, 1dc into next st (which will count as dc 2 tog group), *1hdc into each of next 8sts, leaving last loop of each st on hook, work 1dc into each of next 3sts, working the center dc into the sc between cables and working under both loops of this stitch, yo and draw through all 4 loops on hook – called dc 3tog –, rep from *, ending last rep with dc 2 tog under top 2 loops of last sc. Turn. 55sts.
These 6 rows form mock cable patt.
Rep main patt row 9 times, 6 mock cable patt rows once more then main patt row 5[3] times more.
Note To lengthen or shorten the sleeve work 2 rows more or less for every 1in.

Shape back and front
Next row Ch 46 loosely. Turn and work 1hdc into 3rd from hook, 1hdc into each of next 43ch. Leave working loop on an extra hook.
Using another ball of yarn, ch 45. Join with a sl st to top of turning st at other side of sleeve. Fasten off.
Pick up the working loop on extra hook. Continue working in patt across sleeve and 45ch just worked. 145sts.
Rep main patt row 3[5] times more, then 6 mock cable patt rows once more, working 16 mock cables across row in all then rep main patt row 3 times.
Divide for neck opening
Back Work over first 64sts only for back, rep main patt row 6 times, mock cable rows once working 7 cables across row, and main patt 4 times more. Fasten off.
Front Return to last complete row worked, skip first 17sts at center for neck opening. Rejoin yarn to next stitch and complete front over last 64sts as given for back. Do not fasten off. Turn.
To complete back and front
Next row Work in main patt across

Technique tip

How to make the mock cable motifs

Make the motifs working over a block of eight stitches only for several rows at a given point in the pattern row. Shape them at each end by drawing a loop through the ends of each row and then pulling the yarn through all the loops on the hook. This has the effect of gathering each end of the motif together to make the scallop shape.

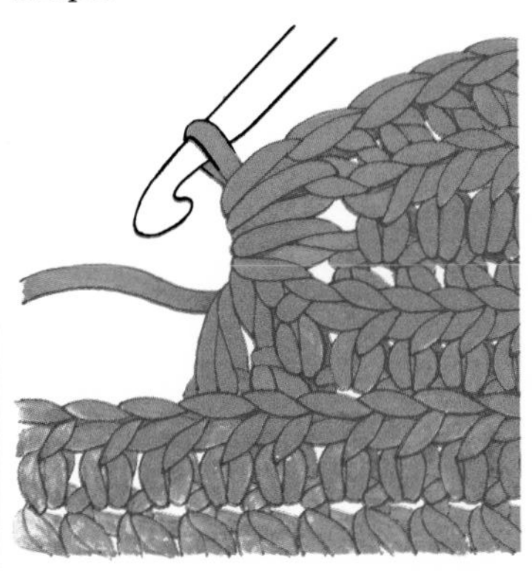

Work one stitch into the main pattern row before making the next scallop. Continue working the motifs all across the row in order to produce the cable effect.

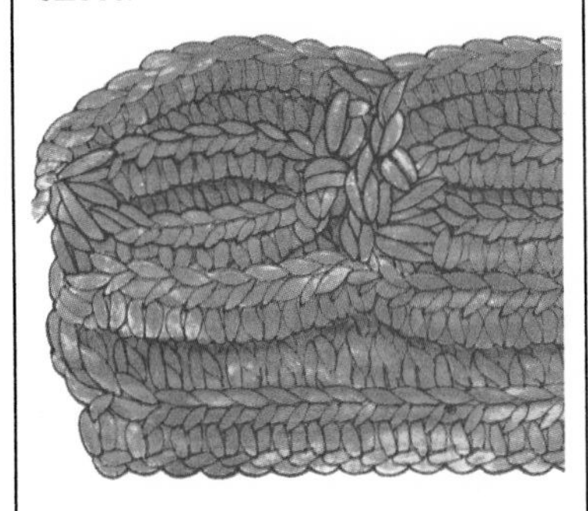

front sts, ch 17 loosely, continue in main patt over back sts to end. Turn.

Next row Rep main patt over back sts, across 17ch sts at center and across front sts. Turn. 145sts. Rep main patt row 3 times, 6 mock cable rows once working 16 cables across row, and main patt row 3[5] times more. Fasten off.

Shape sleeve

With right side of work facing, skip first 45sts. Rejoin yarn to next st. Work in main patt across next 55sts only for 2nd sleeve leaving last 45sts.

Rep main patt row 6[4] times, 6 mock cable rows once more working 6 cables across row, main patt row 9 times, 6 mock cable rows once and main patt row 5[7] times, or to adjusted length. Fasten off.

To finish

Do not press. With right sides of work tog, join side and sleeve seams using a flat seam.

Cuffs

With right side of work facing rejoin yarn at sleeve seam. Continue working in rounds.

Next round 3ch, *leaving last loop of each dc on hook, work 1dc into each of next 2sts of foundation row, yo and draw through all 3 loops on hook – called 2dc tog –, rep from * all around. Join with a sl st to top of 3ch, 27sts.

Next round 3ch, to count as first dc, *yo insert hook from front to back into space before next dc, bring hook around stem of this dc and out to the front, yo and complete dc in normal way – called raised dc front –, yo, insert hook from back of work through space before next dc to front, around stem of next dc and back through next space to back of work, yo and complete dc in normal way – called raised dc back –, rep from * to end of round. Join with a sl st to top of first 3ch.

Next round Work 1 raised dc front into raised dc at front of row below and 1 raised dc back into raised dc at back of row below, rep the last round until cuff measures 3in from beg. Fasten off. Work other cuff in the same way.

Lower Border

With right side of work facing, rejoin yarn at side seam.

Next round 3ch, work 1dc into each row end all around bottom of sweater, join with a sl st to top of first 3ch.

Work in rounds of raised doubles as given for cuff until lower border measures 3in. Fasten off.

Collar

With RS of work facing, rejoin yarn at center back.

Next round 3ch, *1dc into the next row end, rep from * to end of round working 2dc tog over inside corners of left and right shoulders.

Continue in rounds of raised doubles as for cuff until work measures 6in. Fasten off. Darn in all ends.

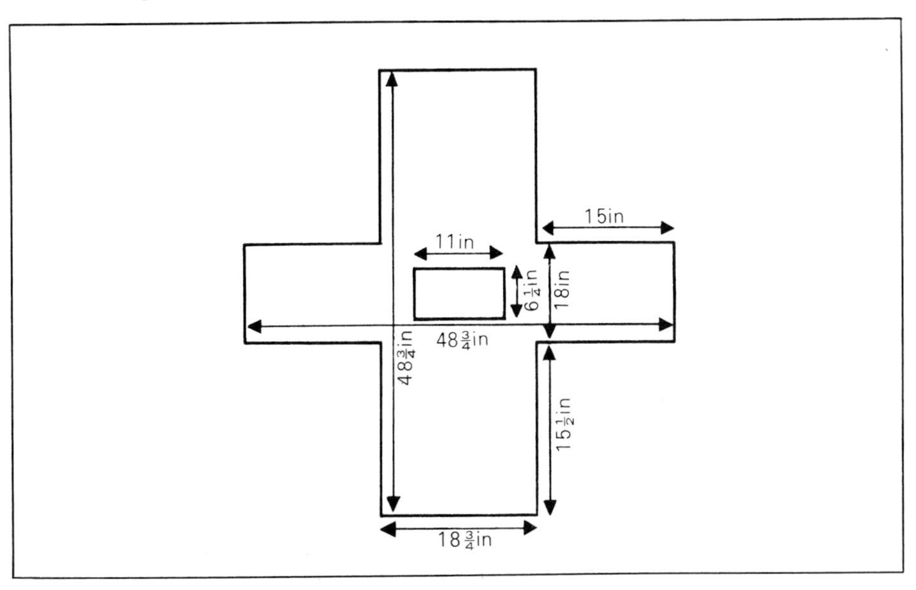

SOFT SUMMER SPECIAL

Sizes
To fit 32[34:36:38]in bust.
Length, 21¼in.
Sleeve seam, 17[17:17½:17½]in.
Note *Directions for larger sizes are in brackets []; where there is only one set of figures it applies to all sizes.*

Materials
9[9:10:10] × 2oz balls of a lightweight mohair
Scraps of a sport yarn for embroidery
Sizes F and H crochet hooks
1 pair No. 3 knitting needles
4 buttons

Gauge
10hdc to 3in using size H hook.

Technique tip

Stitches used in flower motifs

Stem stitch
Using yarn double, work from left to right, taking small stitches. The yarn always re-emerges on the left side of the previous stitch.

Satin stitch
Using yarn double, work straight stitches closely together across the shape as shown in diagram.

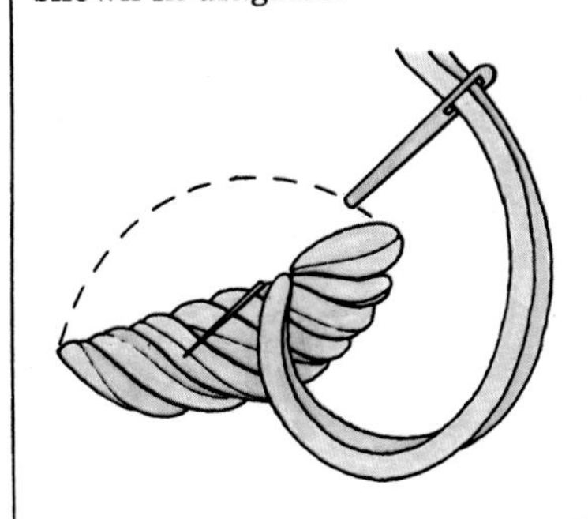

Back
Using size H hook make 83[86:89:92]ch.
Base row 1hdc into 3rd ch from hook, 1hdc into each ch to end. Turn. 82[85:88:91]sts.
Next row (eyelet-hole row) 2ch to count as first hdc, 1hdc into each of next 2 hdc, *1ch, skip 1hdc, 1hdc into each of next 2hdc, rep from *, ending with 1hdc in top of turning ch. Turn.
Next row 2ch, 1hdc into each hdc and 1ch sp to end. Turn.
Patt row 2ch, 1hdc into each hdc to end. Turn.
Cont in patt until work measures 10½in.
Shape armholes
Next row Sl st into 4th hdc, 2ch, 1hdc into next hdc, patt to last 3hdc, turn.
Cont in patt, dec 1hdc (by skipping first and last hdc of row) at each end of every row until 50[53:56:59]sts rem. Patt 7 rows without shaping.
Shape shoulders
Next row Sl st over first 5[5:6:7]hdc, 1sc into each of next 5hdc, patt to last 10[10:11:12]hdc, 1sc into each of next 5hdc. Fasten off.

Waistband
Using No. 3 needles and with RS facing, pick up and K 82[85:88:91]sts along other side of base row. Work 19 rows K1, P1 ribbing, beg alternate rows P1 for 2nd and 4th sizes. Bind off in ribbing.

Right front
Using size H hook make 59[61:63:64]ch. Work base row as for back. 58[60:62:63]sts.
Next row (eyelet-hole row) 2ch, 1hdc into each of next 2hdc, *1ch, skip 1hdc, 1hdc into each of next 2hdc, rep from * to last 1[0:2:0]hdc, 1hdc into each of last 1[0:2:0]hdc. Turn.
Next row 2ch, 1hdc into each hdc and 1ch sp to end. Turn.
Next row (1st buttonhole row) Patt to last 4hdc, 1ch, skip 1hdc, 1hdc into each of last 3hdc. Turn.
Next row Patt to end, working 1hdc into 1ch sp over buttonhole. Turn.
Patt 3 more rows.

Next row (2nd buttonhole row) 2ch, 1hdc into each of next 2hdc, 1ch, skip 1hdc, 1hdc into each hdc to end. Turn.
Next row Patt to end, working 1hdc into 1ch sp over buttonhole. Turn.
Patt 3 rows, then rep 1st buttonhole row again.
Next row Patt to end, working 1hdc into 1ch sp over buttonhole. Turn.
Shape front edge
Dec 1hdc at front edge on next and every other row until work

measures $10\frac{1}{2}$in from beg, ending at side edge.

Shape armhole

Next row Sl st into 4th hdc, 1hdc into next hdc, patt to last hdc, turn. Dec 1hdc at armhole edge on every row, at the same time cont to dec at front edge as before until 10[10:11:11]hdc have been decreased at front edge. Keeping front edge straight, cont to dec at armhole edge until 32[34:35:36]sts rem. Fasten off.

Waistband

Using No. 3 needles and with RS facing, pick up and K 48[50:52:54]sts along other side of base row. Work 9 rows K1, P1 ribbing.

Next row (buttonhole row) Rib to 1st 4sts, bind off 2sts, rib 2.

Next row Rib to end, casting on 2sts over those bound off in last row. Rib another 8 rows. Bind off in ribbing.

Left front

Work as for right front, omitting buttonholes.

Right yoke

Using size H hook make 16[16:17:18]ch. Work base row as for back. 15[15:16:17]hdc. Patt 7 rows.

Shape shoulder

Next row 2ch, 1hdc into each of next 4hdc, 1sc into each of next 5hdc. Fasten off.

Left yoke

Work as for right yoke to shoulder.

Shape shoulder

Next row Sl st over first 5[5:6:7]hdc, 1sc into each of next 5hdc, 1hdc into each of next 5hdc. Fasten off.

Sleeves

Using size H hook make 57ch. Work base row as for back, 56sts. Cont in patt until work measures $14\frac{1}{2}[14\frac{1}{2}:15:15]$in from beg.

Shape top

Work as for back armhole shaping until 24hdc rem. Fasten off.

Cuffs

Using No. 3 needles, RS facing, pick up and K 48sts along other side of base row. Work 19 rows K1, P1 ribbing. Bind off in ribbing.

To finish

Using sport yarn, embroider flower motif on left front and 4 small flowers on each yoke. Gather top part of fronts to fit along lower edge of yokes, then sew in position. Join shoulder seams. Join side and sleeve seams. Set in sleeves.

Edging Use size F hook and with RS facing, work a row of sc up right front edge, around neck edge and down left front edge. Turn and work a 2nd row. Fasten off.

Sew on buttons. Make a twisted cord, using 5 strands of yarn each 5yd long. Thread cord through eyelet holes above waistband.

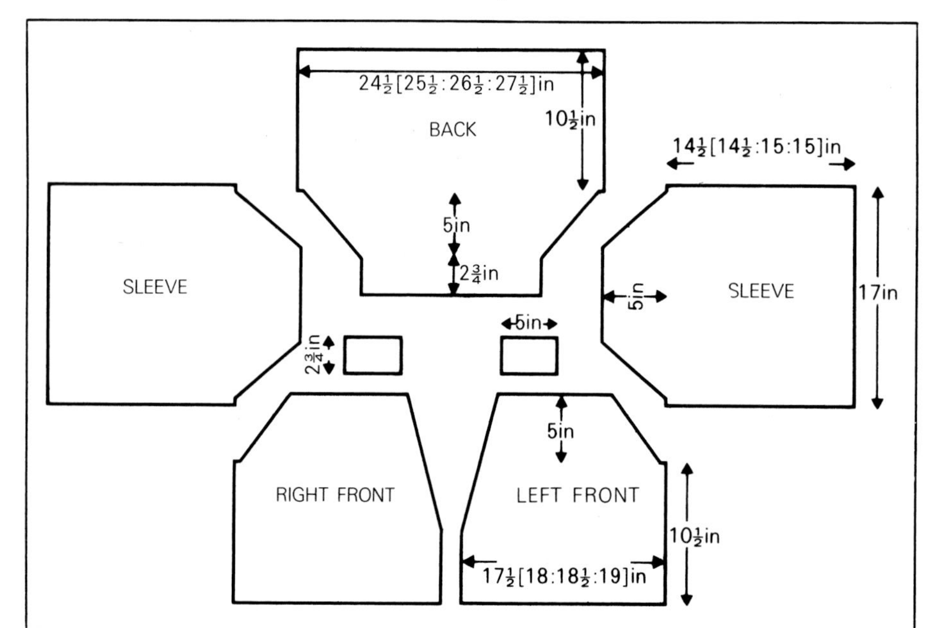

Daisy stitch

Using yarn double, work a chain (A), then fasten loop at outer edge with a small stitch (B). For the larger flower, work another round of petals outside the first.

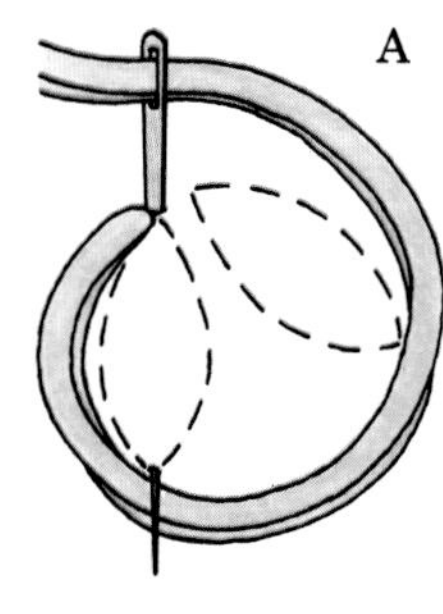

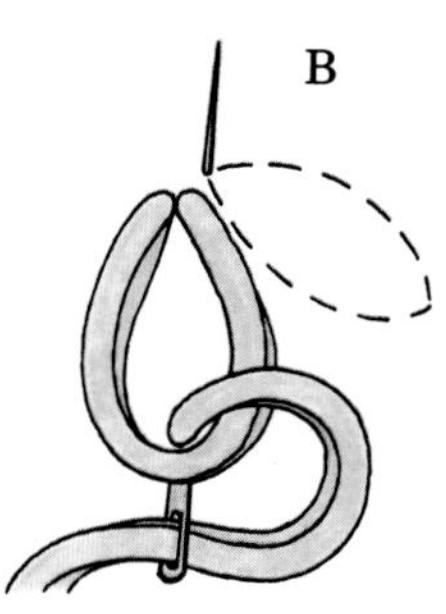

French knots

Bring the yarn through fabric from back to front, hold the yarn with the left thumb and wind the needle twice around the yarn. Still holding the yarn, twist the needle back to the starting point and insert it close to where the yarn first emerged (see arrow). This completes first French knot. Then bring needle through to front again at position for next knot. Continue in the same way.

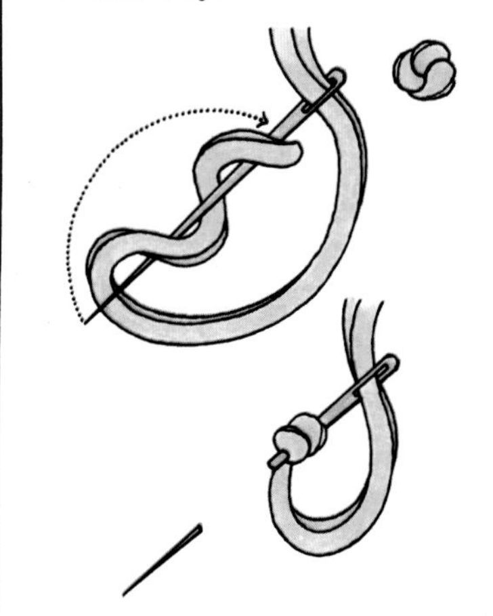

CARDIGAN WITH CLASS

Back
Using size 3 hook make 117[123:127]ch.
Base row 1sc into 3rd ch from hook, *1dc into next ch, 1sc into next ch, rep from * to last ch, 1sc into last ch. Turn. Begin patt.
1st row 3ch, skip first sc, *1sc into next dc, 1dc into next sc, rep from * to last sc, 1dc into last sc. Turn.
2nd row 1ch, sc into first dc, *dc into next sc, 1sc into next dc, rep from * to end of row, working last sc into top of 3 turning chains. Turn. 115[121:125]sts. These 2 rows form patt. Cont in patt until work measures 19[19¼:19¾]in from beg, ending with WS row.
Shape shoulders
Next row Sl st across first 13[13:14]sts. Patt to last 13[13:14]sts. Turn.
Rep last row once more.
Next row Sl st across first 13[15:13]sts, patt to last 13[15:13]sts. Leave these unworked, fasten off.
Waistband Using No. 2 needles and with RS of work facing, pick up and K 138[144:148]sts along lower edge. Work 50 rows K1, P1 ribbing. Bind off in ribbing.
Left front
Using size C hook make 53[56:58]ch.
Work base row and patt rows as for back. Cont in patt until work measures 7in, ending with 2nd patt row.
Shape front edge
Keeping patt correct, dec one st at beg of next and every foll 4th row until 39[41:42]sts rem. Continue without shaping until front measures same as back to shoulder, ending at armhole edge.
Shape shoulder
Sl st across first 13[13:14]sts on next row and across first 13[15:13]sts on foll row. Fasten off.

Waistband
Using No. 1 needles and with RS of work facing pick up and K 68[72:76]sts evenly along lower edge. Work 50 rows K1, P1 ribbing. Bind off in ribbing.

Right front
Work as given for left front until work measures 7in, ending with a 1st patt row. Complete as for left front.

Waistband
Work as for left front waistband.

Sleeves
Using Size C hook ch 83[85:87].

Sizes
To fit 34[36:38]in bust.
Length, 24½[24¾:25¼]in.
Sleeve seam, 18½in.
Note *The figures in brackets refer to the 2nd and 3rd sizes respectively.*

Materials
19[20:22]oz of 3-ply rayon twist thread
Size C crochet hook
1 pair No. 2 knitting needles
6 buttons

Gauge
24sts and 20 rows to 4in in patt worked on size C hook.

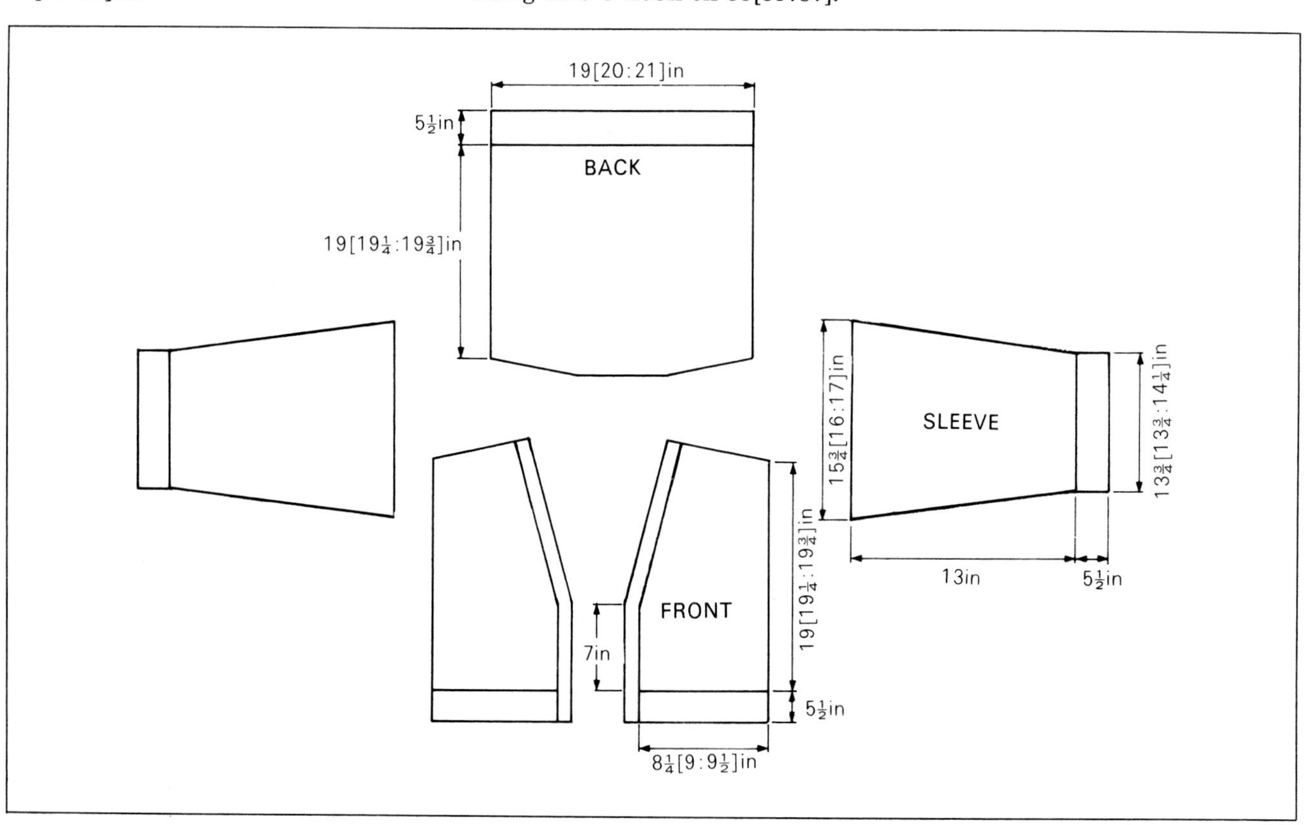

Technique tip

How to pick up stitches

Picking up stitches on the edge of the fabric to work a waistband or front edging is often more practical than working separate bands, which must then be sewn on to the garment. The waistband – usually it is in ribbing – is worked downward so that the bound-off edge forms the bottom of the garment or sleeve: there is no difference in the appearance of the ribbing when it is knitted in this way.

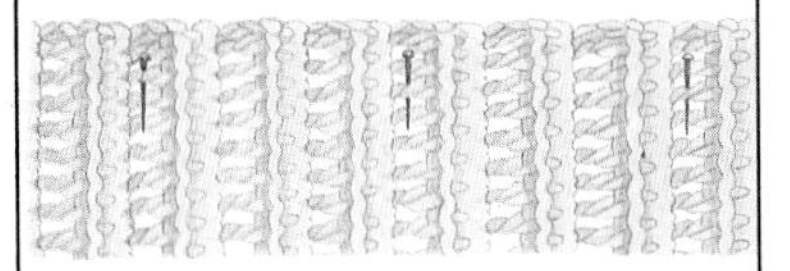

It's a good idea to begin by dividing the edge you are working on into sections; this helps you to pick up the stitches evenly across the garment. Fold the work in half and place a pin on the center fold, then divide each side in half again in the same way. Thus, if you are going to pick up 100 stitches altogether, you will know that you must pick up 25 stitches in each section.

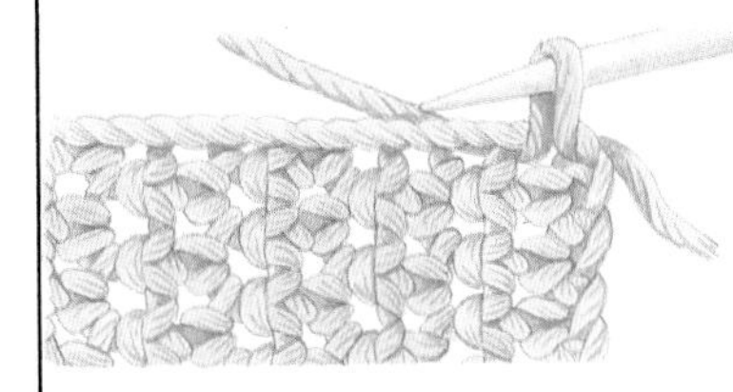

Hold the work with the right side facing and insert the needle into the edge of the fabric. Loop the yarn around the needle and draw it through for the first stitch. Make sure that the yarn is held to the left, so that it will be at the right end of the needle when you turn and begin knitting.

Continue along the edge, drawing a loop through in the same way of each stitch. You can then turn and begin knitting into these loops in the normal way for the edging.

When picking up stitches from worked stitches, insert the needle into the remaining loop of the stitch; when picking up stitches from the row ends, insert the needle into the loop at the end of the row.

Work the base row as given for back. Continue in patt as for back, inc one st at each end of every 8th row until there are 95[99:103]sts. Continue without shaping until sleeve measures 13in from beg. Fasten off.

Cuffs

Using No. 1 needles and with RS of work facing pick up 80[82:84]sts along lower edge. Work 50 rows K1, P1 ribbing. Bind off in ribbing.

Front band

Join shoulder seams. Using No. 1 needles cast on 18sts. Work 4 rows ribbing as for back.

Next row (buttonhole row) Rib 7, bind off 4sts, rib to end.

Work the next row in ribbing casting on 4sts above those bound off on previous row. Continue working in ribbing, working another buttonhole on every foll 23rd and 24th rows until 6 buttonholes have been made in all. Continue in ribbing, omitting buttonholes, until band is long enough to fit up left front, around neck and down right front when slightly stretched.

To finish

Mark depth of armholes $8\frac{1}{4}[8\frac{3}{4}:9]$in from shoulder seams on back and fronts and sew sleeves to armholes between markers. Join side and sleeve seams. Sew front band in place up left front, around neck and down right front. Sew on buttons.

COLD WEATHER FRIEND

Sizes
To fit 32-34[36-38]in bust.
Length when hanging, 35in.
Sleeve seam, 18in.

Note *Directions for the larger size are in brackets []; where there is only one set of figures it applies to both sizes.*

Materials
46[50]oz of a knitting worsted
Size I and wooden size 13 hooks
5 buttons

Gauge
10sts to 4¼in and 10 rows to 6in in patt on size 13 hook.

Right half
**Using size 13 hook chain 22 for lower edge of sleeve.
Base row 1dc into 3rd ch from hook, *1hdc into next ch, 1dc into next ch, rep from * to last ch, 1hdc into last ch. Turn. 21sts. Beg patt.
1st row (WS) 2ch to count as first hdc, *work around next dc by working yo, insert hook from back to front between next 2sts, around dc and through work from front to back, draw yarn through and complete dc in usual way – called double around back (dc around Bk), 1hdc into next hdc, rep from * to end, working last hdc into turning ch. Turn.
2nd row 2ch, work 1dc and 1hdc into first hdc for inc, *work around next dc by working yo, insert hook from front to back between next 2sts, around dc and through work from back to front, draw yarn through and complete dc in usual way – called double around front (dc around Ft), 1hdc into next hdc, rep from * to last dc, 1dc around Ft, 1hdc, 1dc and 1hdc all into last hdc for inc. Turn.
Rep last 2 rows until 24 rows in all have been worked and there are 65sts; end with patt row. This completes first sleeve. Using separate ball of yarn chain 48 loosely and leave aside.
Next row Chain 49 loosely, 1dc into 3rd ch from hook, (1hdc into next ch, 1dc into next ch) to end of ch, then work across sleeve, 1hdc into next hdc, *1dc round Ft, 1hdc into next hdc, rep from * to end, do not turn but work across 48ch, working (1dc into next ch, 1hdc into next ch) to end. Turn. 161sts.
Next row 2ch, *work 1dc around Bk, 1hdc into next hdc, rep from * to end. Turn.
Next row 2ch, *work, 1dc around Ft, 1hdc into next hdc, rep from * to end. Turn. Rep these 2 rows 5[6] times more.**
Divide for neck
Next row Patt across 79sts, turn. Patt 6 rows for right back. Fasten off. With WS facing, skip next 7sts for neck, rejoin yarn to next st, 2ch, patt to end. Turn. 75sts. Patt 6 rows for right front. Fasten off.

Left half
Work as for right half from ** to **.
Divide for neck
Next row Patt across first 75sts, turn. Patt 6 rows for left front. Fasten off. With WS facing, skip next 7sts for neck, rejoin yarn to next st, 2ch, patt to end. Turn. 79sts. Patt 6 rows for left back. Do not fasten off. Join backs placing WS tog, sl st into first st on last row of right back, 1ch, work row of crab st (sc worked from left to right) through double thickness to top of neck. Fasten off.

To finish
Join side and sleeve seams with crab st.

Collar
With WS facing, join yarn to top of left front neck and using size 13 hook work 1sc into each row end

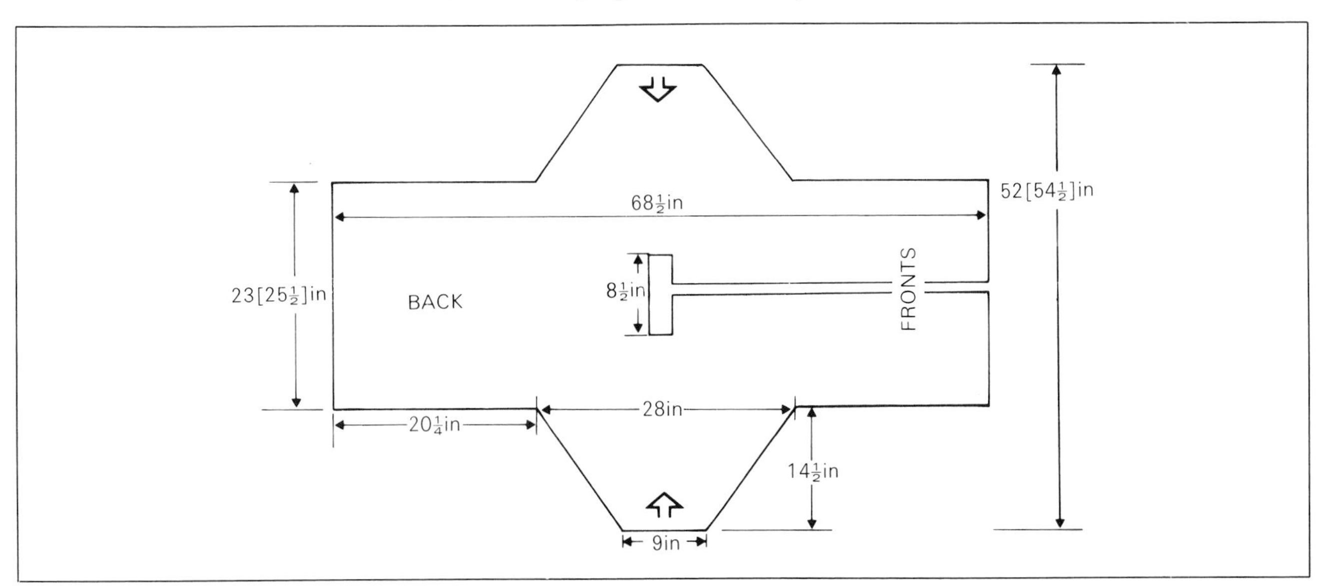

around neck, working 3sc tog at each corner. Turn. 39sc.
Next row 2ch, *1dc into next sc, 1hdc into next sc, rep from * to end. Turn. Work 2 rows patt as on back and fronts. Change to size I hook.
Edging
Work row of sc evenly along left front to lower edge, turn, 2 rows sc, so ending at lower edge, do not turn; change to size 13 hook, 1sc into each st along lower edge, do not turn; change to size I hook and work row of sc evenly along right front edge to top of collar, turn.
Buttonhole row 2ch, 1sc into each of next 23sc, 3ch, skip next 2sc, (1sc into each of next 9sc, 3ch, skip next 2sc) 4 times, 1sc into each sc to end. Turn.
Next row Work 1sc into each sc and 2sc into each buttonhole to end. Do not turn but work row of crab st all around outer edge working into each sc. Fasten off.

Cuffs (alike)
Join on yarn and using size I hook work 1sc into each ch around lower edge of sleeve, do not turn but work row of crab st. Fasten off. Sew on buttons.

Technique tip

Multiple increasing
When working several sections of a garment all in one piece you will often need to work a multiple increase when you begin a new section. In the coat you start at the cuff edge and work to the center back and the front edge, working a multiple increase when you begin the main sections.

To work a multiple increase at the beginning of the row, work a length of chain for the number of stitches you wish to add, plus extra chains for the first stitch. (The number of chains depends on the stitch being used.)

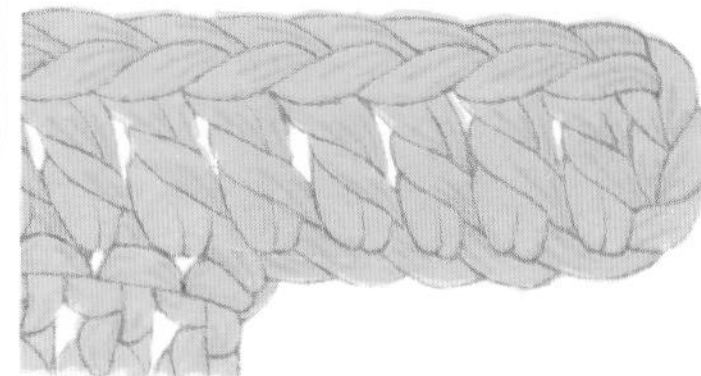

Pattern into the chain made, then pattern across the main section.

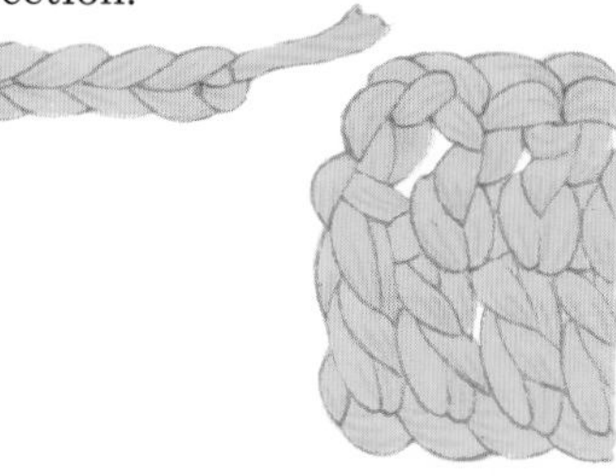

To work a multiple increase at the end of the row, join on a separate ball of yarn and work a length of chain for the number of stitches you wish to add. (You will not need any extra chains for the first stitch in this case.) Fasten off the yarn.

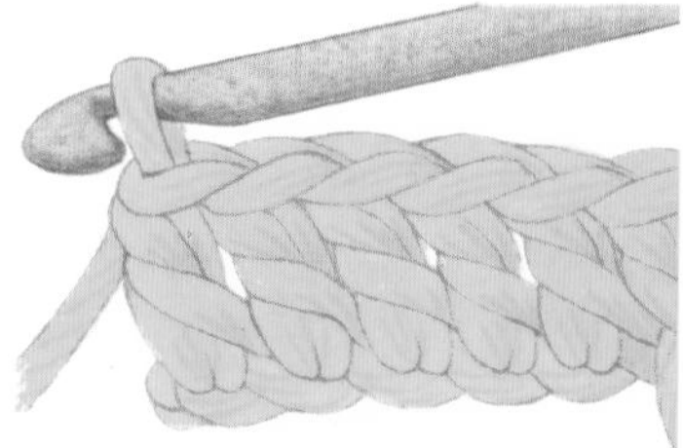

Pattern across the main section, then pattern into each chain you have made.

SUMMER BLAZER

Main body
Using No. 7 hook make 346[376]ch for entire lower edge.
Base row 1tr into 5th ch from hook, 1tr into each ch to end. Turn. 343[373]sts.
Next row 6ch, 1tr into 4th tr, (2ch, skip next 2tr, 1tr into next tr) to end, working last tr into top of the 4ch. Turn. 114[124]sps.
Next row 6ch, 1tr into 2nd tr, (2ch, 1tr into next tr) to end, working last tr into 3rd of the 6ch. Turn.
Reading RS rows from right to left and WS rows from left to right, following chart A for motifs, set patt as foll:
1st row 6ch, 1tr into 2nd tr, (2ch, 1tr into next tr) 13[15] times, *(2tr into next sp, 1tr into next tr) twice – 2 blocks made –, (2ch, 1tr into next tr) 26[28] times, rep from * twice more, (2tr into next sp, 1tr into next tr) twice, (2ch, 1tr into next tr) 14[16] times, working last tr into 3rd of the 6ch. Turn.
2nd row 6ch, 1tr into 2nd tr, (2ch, 1tr into next tr) 12[14] times, *2tr into next sp, 1tr into each of next 7tr, (2ch, 1tr into next tr) 25[27] times, rep from * twice more, 2tr into next sp, 1tr into each of next 7tr, (2ch, 1tr into next tr) 14[16] times, working last tr into 3rd of the 6ch. Turn.
3rd row 6ch, 1tr into 2nd tr, (2ch, 1tr into next tr) 2[4] times, *(2tr into next sp, 1tr into next tr) twice, (2ch, 1tr into next tr) 8 times, 2tr into next sp, 1tr into each of next 10tr, 2tr into next sp, 1tr into next tr, (2ch, 1tr into next tr) 13[15] times, rep from * to end, omitting last 2ch and tr on last rep. Turn.
4th row 6ch, 1tr into 2nd tr, (2ch, 1tr into next tr) 11[13] times, *1tr into each of next 7tr, 2ch, skip next 2tr – 1 space made over 1 block –, 1tr into each of next 7tr, (2ch, 1tr into next tr) twice, (2tr into next sp, 1tr into next tr) twice, (2ch, 1tr into next tr) 4 times, 2ch, skip next 2tr, 1tr into each of next 4tr, (2ch, 1tr into next tr) 13[15] times, rep from * to end, finishing last rep (2ch, 1tr into next tr) 3[5] times. Turn.
Cont working from chart until 20th row has been completed. Work 4 rows in sps. Reading RS rows from right to left and WS rows from left

Sizes
To fit 32–34[36–38]in bust.
Length, 24¾[25¼]in.
Sleeve seam, 18in.
Note *Directions for larger size are in brackets []; where there is only one set of figures it applies to both sizes.*

Materials
11[13] × 150yd balls of a lightweight mercerized crochet cotton
No. 7 steel crochet hook

Gauge
9sps and 8 rows to 3¼in on No. 7 hook.

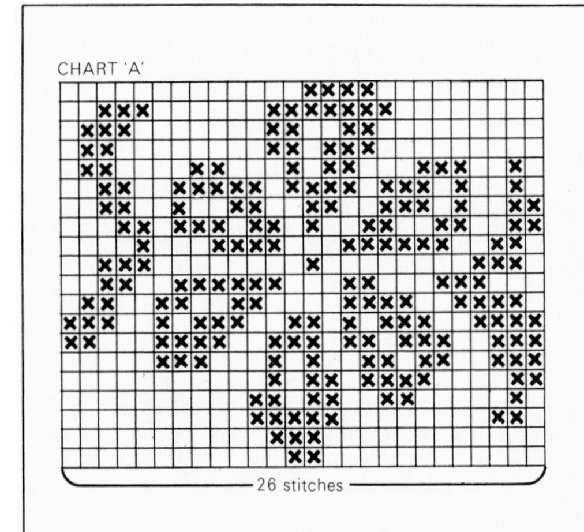

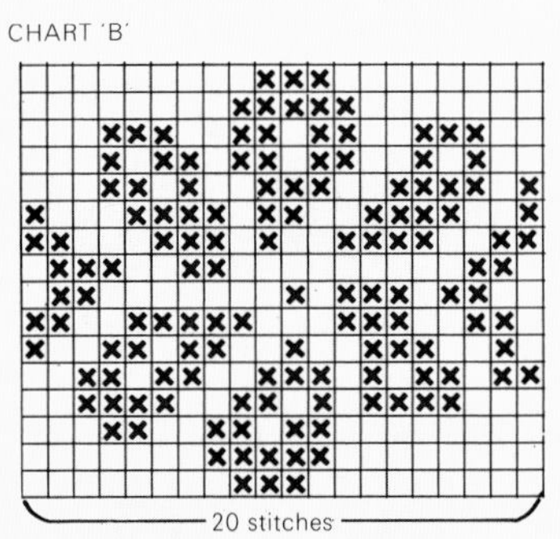

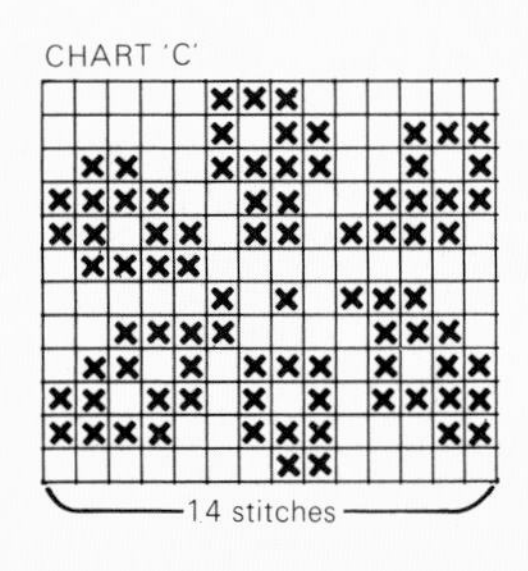

KEY □ ='1SP' – (2ch, 1dtr) × ='1 BLOCK' – (3 dtr)

to right, foll chart B for motifs, set patt as follows:
1st row 6ch, 1tr into 2nd tr, (2ch, 1tr into next tr) 12[14] times, *(2tr into next sp, 1tr into next tr) 3 times, (2ch, 1tr into next tr) 25[27] times, rep from * twice more, (2tr into next sp, 1tr into next tr) 3 times, (2ch, 1tr into next tr) 12[14] times. Turn. Cont working from chart until 16th row has been completed. Work 1 row in sps.

Divide for armholes

Next row (WS) 6ch, 1tr into 2nd tr, (2ch, 1tr into next tr) 28[31] times, turn. Work on these sts for left front. Work 2 rows in sps. Reading RS rows from right to left and WS rows from left to right, foll chart C for motifs, set patt as follows:
1st row 6ch, 1tr into 2nd tr, (2ch, 1tr into next tr) 11[12] times, (2tr into next sp, 1tr into next tr) twice, (2ch, 1tr into next tr) 15[17] times. Turn. Cont working from chart until the 12th row has been completed. Now cont in sps only until work measures $24\frac{3}{4}$[$25\frac{1}{4}$]in from beg. Fasten off.
With WS facing rejoin yarn to base of last tr before left front, turn.
Next row 6ch, 1tr into next tr, (2ch, 1tr into next tr) 55[59] times, turn. Work on these sts for back. Work 2 rows in sps.
Reading RS rows from right to left and WS rows from left to right, foll chart C for motifs, set patt as follows:
1st row 6ch, 1tr into 2nd tr, (2ch, 1tr into next tr) 11[12] times, (2tr into next sp, 1tr into next tr) twice, (2ch, 1tr into next tr) 26[28] times, (2tr into next sp. 1tr into next tr) twice, (2ch, 1tr into next tr) 14[15] times. Turn.
Cont working from chart until the 12th row has been completed. Now cont in sps only until work measures $24\frac{3}{4}$[$25\frac{1}{4}$]in from beg. Fasten off.
With WS facing rejoin yarn to base of last tr before back, turn.
Next row 6ch, 1tr into next tr, (2ch, 1tr into next tr) 28[31] times. Turn. Work on these sts for right front. Work 2 rows in sps.
Reading RS rows from right to left and WS rows from left to right, foll chart C for motifs, set patt as follows:
1st row 6ch, 1tr into 2nd tr, (2ch,

1tr into next tr) 12[14] times, (2tr into next sp, 1tr into next tr) twice, (2ch, 1tr into next tr) 14[15] times. Turn. Cont working from chart until the 12th row has been completed. Now cont in sps only until work measures 24¾[25¼]in from beg. Fasten off.

Border
Join 17[18] sps at each side of fronts and back for shoulder seams. With RS of work facing join yarn to right front at lower edge and work 3ch, 3dc into end of base row, now work 3dc into each sp along right front, across right front top edge, across back neck, left front top edge, and left front edge, ending with 3dc into edge of base row. Fasten off.

Sleeves
Using No. 7 hook make 136[142]ch.
Base row 1tr into 5th ch from hook, 1tr into each ch to end. Turn. 133[139]sts.
Next row 6ch, 1tr into 4th tr, (2ch, skip next 2tr, 1tr into next tr) to end, working last tr into top of the 4ch. Turn. 44[46]sps.
Next row 6ch, 1tr into 2nd tr, (2ch, 1tr into next tr) to end, working last tr into 3rd of the 6ch. Turn.
Reading RS rows from right to left and WS rows from left to right, foll chart A, setting patt as foll:
1st row 6ch, 1tr into 2nd tr, (2ch, 1tr into next tr) 20[21] times. (2tr into next sp, 1tr into next tr) twice, (2ch, 1tr into next tr) 21[22] times, working last tr into 3rd of the 6ch. Turn.
Cont working from chart until the 20th row has been completed. Work 4 rows in sps. Now set chart B as follows:
1st row 6ch, 1tr into 2nd tr, (2ch, 1tr into next tr) 20[21] times, (2tr into next sp, 1tr into next tr) 3 times, (2ch, 1tr into next tr) 20[21] times. Turn. Cont working from chart until the 16th row has been completed.
Now cont in sps only until work measures 18in from beg. Fasten off.

Collar
Using No. 7 hook make 144ch.
Base row 1tr into 9th ch from hook, (2ch, skip next 2ch, 1tr into next ch) to end. Turn. 46sps.
Next row 6ch, 1tr into 2nd tr, (2ch, 1tr into next tr) to end, working last tr into 3rd of the 6ch. Turn.
Rep last row 8 times.
Border
Next row 3ch, now work 3dc into each sp along side edge, lower edge and second side edge, working 10dc into each corner sp. Fasten off.

To finish
Join sleeve seams. Set in sleeves, matching sps, join rem of side seams. Sew on collar, leaving 2¾in of front edges for lapels. Press seams.

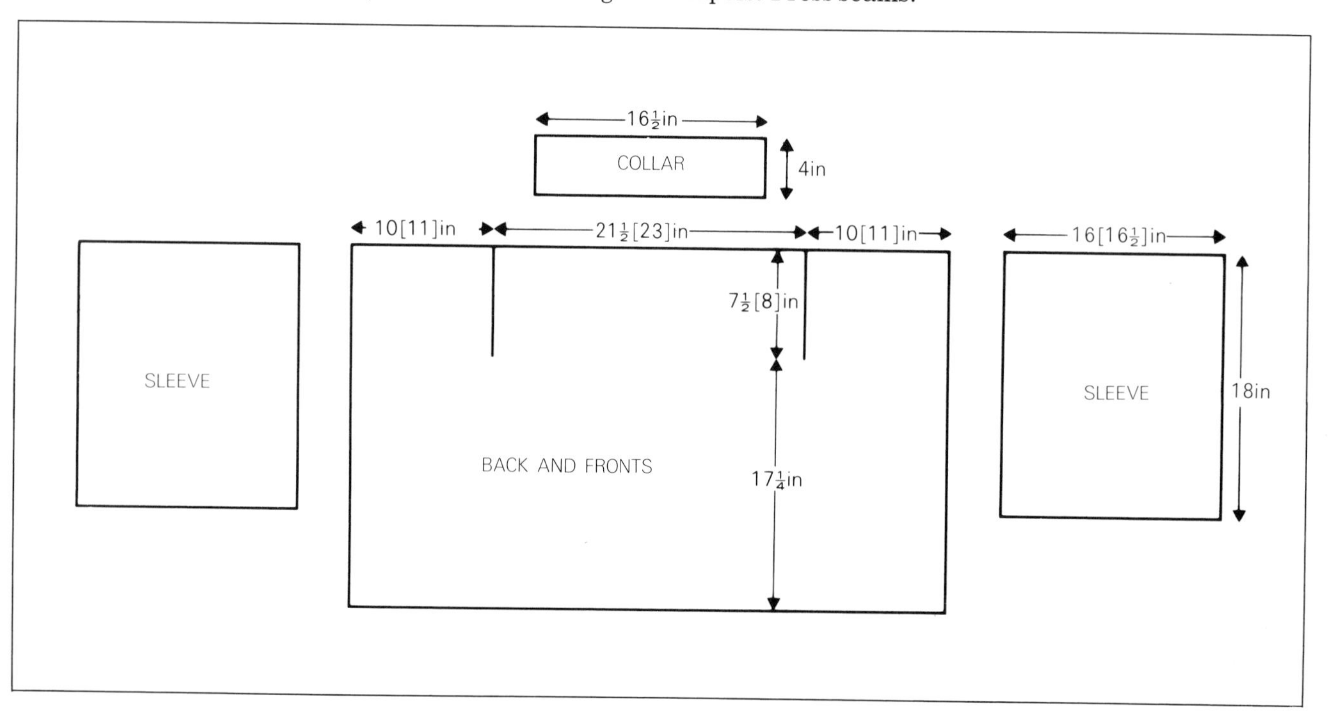

JET SET BIKINIS

Gold bikini

Briefs

Using No. 0 hook and A, make 111ch for top edge of back.

Base row 1sc into 3rd ch from hook, 1sc into each ch to end. Turn. 110sts.

Cont in sc decreasing 1sc at beg of every row, by skipping 1sc, until 12sts remain. Work 8 rows without shaping, then inc 1sc at beg of every row, by working 1sc into first sc, until there are 68sts.

Edging

Work a row of sc around outer edge of briefs, working 3sc at each corner and joining last sc to first with sl st. Join on B. Work 1sc into each sc around outer edge and at each corner work 90ch, sl st into each ch to form ties, join last sc to first with a sl st. Fasten off. Knot ends of ties.

Top

Using No. 0 hook and A, make 60ch.

Base row 1sc into 3rd ch from hook, 1sc into each ch to end. Turn. 59sts.

Cont in sc dec 1sc at beg of every row until one st remains. Work a row of sc evenly around outer edge, join last sc to first with a sl st. Fasten off. Make another piece in same way.

Edging

Using No. 0 hook and B, make 150ch, sl st into each ch to end for first tie, now work 1sc into each sc along lower edge of one triangle, 5ch, 1sc into each sc along lower edge of other triangle, make 150ch, sl st into each ch for 2nd tie, now work *1sc into each sc along side of triangle, make 150ch, sl st into each ch for neck tie. 1sc into each sc along other side of triangle *, sl st into each of the 15ch at center rep from * to *, sl st into first sc at lower edge. Fasten off.

Purse (made in one piece)

Using No. 0 hook and A, make 27ch.

Base row 1sc into 3rd ch from hook, 1sc into each ch to end. Turn.

Patt row 2ch to count as first sc, 1sc into each sc to end. Turn.

Rep patt row 98 times, chain 140, sl st into each ch to end for tie. Fold purse in half lengthwise and working through double thickness work 1sc into each row end along side edge, 3sc into corner, 1sc into each sc along fold, 3sc into corner, then 1sc into each row end along other side edge, work 140ch, sl st into each ch for tie. Fasten off.

Black bikini

Briefs

Using No. 0 hook and A, chain 187 for top edge of back and straps.

Gold bikini

Size

To fit 32-34in bust, 34-36in hips.

Materials

5oz of a medium-weight mercerized crochet cotton in main color (A)
1oz in contrasting color (B)
No. 0 crochet hook

Gauge

14sc and 16 rows to $1\frac{1}{2}$in.

Black bikini

Size

As gold bikini.

Materials

6oz of a medium-weight mercerized cotton in main color (A)
1oz in contrasting color (B)
No. 0 crochet hook
Elastic thread
3 hooks and eyes

Gauge

14sc and 16 rows to $1\frac{1}{2}$in.

Base row 1sc into 3rd ch from hook, 1sc into each ch to end. Turn. 186sts.
Next row 2ch to count as first sc, 1sc into each st to end. Turn. Rep last row once more. Cut off yarn. Skip first 38sc, for side strap, rejoin yarn to next sc, 2ch, 1sc into each sc to within last 38sc, turn.
Cont in sc decreasing 1sc at beg of every row, by skipping 1sc, until 12 sts remain. Work 8 rows without shaping, then inc 1sc at beg of every row, by working 1sc into first sc, until there are 68sts.
Work 3 rows without shaping. Fasten off. Join side bands to front. Join on A and work a row of sc evenly around outer edge. Cut off A; join B and work 1sc into each sc around outer edge. Fasten off. Run 2 rows of thread elastic around top.

Top
Using No. 0 hook and A, chain 27.
Base row 1sc into 3rd ch from hook, 1sc into each ch to end. Turn. 26sts.
Next row 2ch to count as first sc, 1sc into each sc to end. Turn. Rep last row 5 times.
Inc 1sc at each end of next and every foll 8th row until there are 44sts. Work 168 rows without shaping. Dec 1sc at each end of next and every foll 8th row until 26sc remain. Work 7 rows without shaping. Do not turn on last row but work a row of sc around outer edge working 3sc at each corner. Cut off A; join on B and work 1sc into each sc around outer edge. Fasten off.

Tie
Using No. 0 hook and B, chain 350, sl st into each ch to end. Fasten off. Sew 3 hooks and eyes to ends to fasten. Knot tie around center of band.

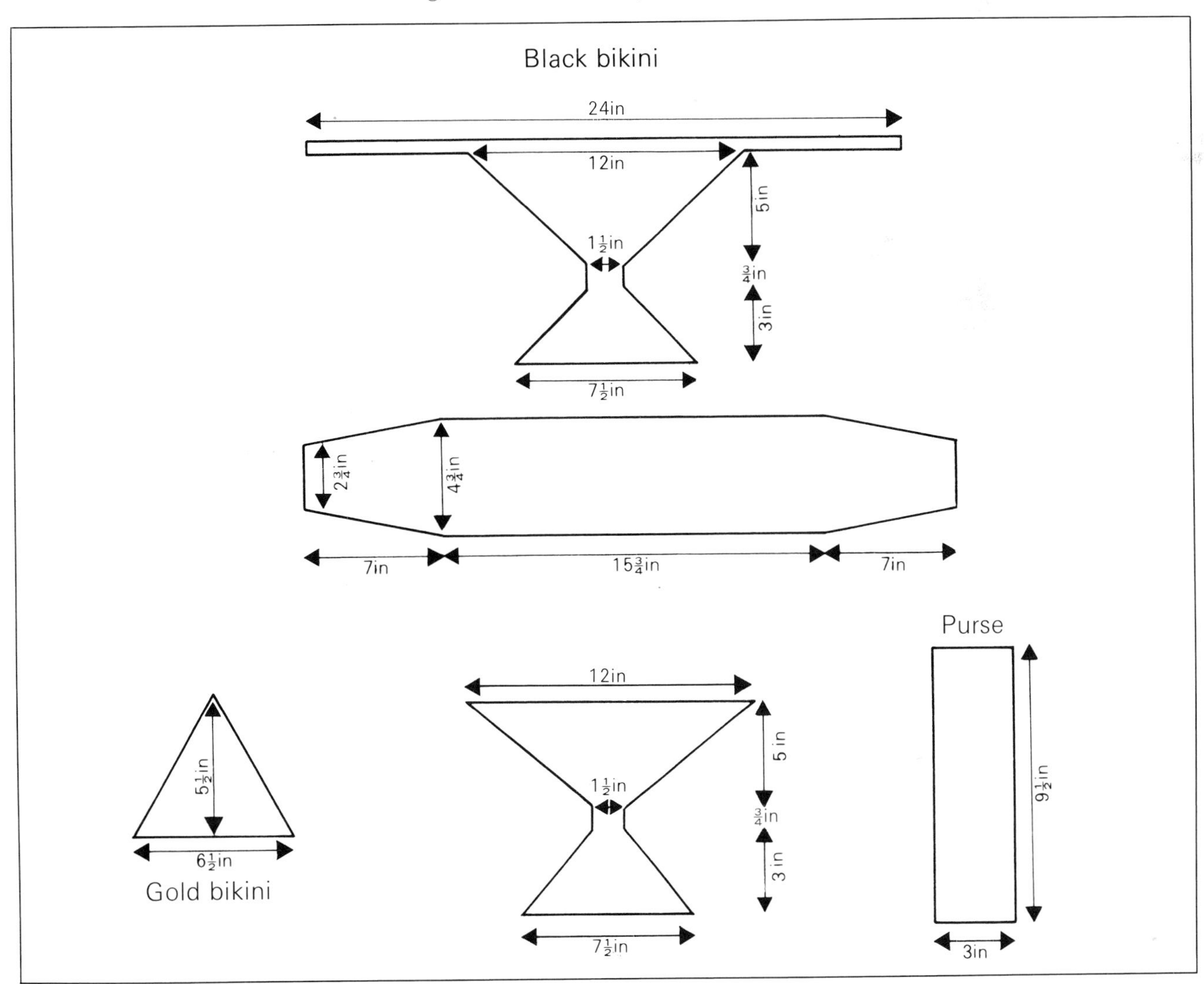

HOME COMFORT

Sizes
To fit 32[34:36]in bust.
Length to shoulder, 44in.
Sleeve seam, 13in.
Note *Directions for larger sizes are in brackets []; where there is only one set of figures it applies to all sizes.*

Materials
10[11:11]oz of a lightweight mohair in main color (A)
7[7:8]oz in contrasting color [B]
Size E crochet hook
7 buttons and a snap

Gauge
16dc and 8 rows to 4in in patt worked on size E hook.

Back
Using size E hook and A, make 21[23:25]ch for back neck.
Base row Into 4th ch from hook work 1dc, 1dc into each ch to last ch, 2dc into last ch. Turn. 20[22:24]dc.
Shape raglan
1st to 2nd rows 3ch to count as first dc, 1dc into st at base of ch, 2dc into next dc, 1dc into each dc to last 2sts, 2dc into next dc, 2dc into 3rd of 3ch. Turn. 4dc inc on each row.
3rd row 3ch, 1dc into st at base of ch, 1dc into each dc to last st, 2dc into 3rd of 3ch. Turn. 2dc inc.
Rep last 3 rows until there are 68[72:78]dc, noting that you should work throughout in stripe sequence of 10 rows A, 1 row B, 9 rows A, 2 rows B, 8 rows A, 3 rows B, 7 rows A, 4 rows B, 6 rows A, 5 rows B, 5 rows A, 6 rows B, 4 rows A, 7 rows B, 3 rows A and 8 rows B.
Shape waist
Keeping stripe sequence correct, work 7[6:5] rows in dc without shaping.
Next row (dec row) 3ch, 1dc into each of next 3[5:8]dc, *skip 1dc, 1dc into each of next 19dc, rep from * twice more, skip 1dc, 1dc into each dc to end. Turn. 4dc dec. Patt 5 rows without shaping.
Next row (dec row) 3ch, 1dc into each of next 2[4:7]dc, *skip 1dc, 1dc into each of next 18dc, rep from * twice, skip 1dc, 1dc into each dc to end. Turn. 4dc dec. Patt 11 rows without shaping. 60[64:70]tr.
Shape hips
Next row (inc row) 3ch, 1dc into each of next 1[3:6]dc, *2dc into next dc, 1dc into each of next 10dc, rep from * 4 times, 2dc into next dc, 1dc into each dc to end. Turn. 6dc inc. Patt 7 rows without shaping.
Next row (inc row) 3ch, 1dc into each of next 2[4:7]dc, *2dc into next dc, 1dc into each of next 11dc, rep from * 4 times, 2 dc into next dc, 1dc into each dc to end. Turn. 6dc inc.
Cont in this way, inc 6dc and working one more st between incs, on every foll 10th row until there are 90[94:100]dc. Cont without shaping until stripe sequence has been completed. Fasten off.

Left front
Using size E hook and A, make 5ch. Work throughout in same stripe sequence as given for back.
Shape neck and raglan
1st row Into 4th ch from hook work 1dc, 2dc into last ch. Turn 4dc.
2nd row 3ch, 2dc into each of next 2dc, 1dc into 3rd of 3ch. Turn. 6dc.
3rd row 3ch, 1dc into each of next 3dc, 2dc into next dc, 2dc into 3rd of 3ch. Turn. 8dc.
4th row 3ch, 1dc into st at base of ch, 1dc into each of next 6dc, 2dc into 3rd of 3ch. Turn. 10dc.
5th row 3ch, 1dc into st at base of ch, 2dc into next dc, 1dc into each of next 6dc, 2dc into next dc, 2dc into 3rd of 3ch. Turn. 14dc.
6th row 3ch, 1dc into st at base of ch, 2dc into next dc, 1dc into each of next 10dc, 2dc into next dc, 2dc into 3rd of 3ch. Turn. 18dc.
7th row 4[5:6]ch, turn and into 4th ch from hook work 1dc, 1dc into each of next 0[1:2]ch, 1dc into each of next 17dc, 2dc into 3rd of 3ch. Turn. 21[22:23]dc.
8th row 3ch, 1dc into st at base of ch, 2dc into next dc, 1dc into each dc to end. Turn.
9th row 3ch, 1dc into each dc to last 2dc, 2dc into next dc, 2dc into 3rd of 3 ch. Turn.
10th row 3ch, 1dc into st at base of ch, 1dc into each dc to end. Turn.
11th row As 9th.
12th row As 8th.
13th row 3ch, 1dc into each dc to last dc, 2dc into 3rd of 3ch. Turn.
14th row As 8th.
15th row As 9th. 35[36:37]dc.
2nd and 3rd sizes only
16th row As 10th. 37[38]dc.
3rd size only
17th row As 9th. 40dc.

All sizes
Shape waist
Patt 7[6:5] rows in dc without shaping.
Next row (dec row) 3ch, 1dc into each of next 7[8:10]dc, skip 1dc, 1dc into each of next 16dc, skip 1dc, 1dc into each dc to end. Turn. 2dc dec. Patt 5 rows without shaping.
Next row (dec row) 3ch, 1dc into each of next 7[8:10]dc, skip 1dc, 1dc into each of next 14dc, skip 1dc, 1dc into each dc to end. Turn. 2dc dec. Patt 11 rows without shaping.
Shape hips
Next row (inc row) 3ch, 1dc into each of next 3[4:5]dc, *2dc into next

dc, 1dc into each of next 10dc, rep from * once, 2dc into next dc, 1dc into each dc to end. Turn. 3dc inc.
Patt 7 rows without shaping.
Next row (inc row) 3ch, 1dc into each of next 3[4:5]dc, *2dc into next dc, 1dc into each of next 11dc, rep from * once more, 2dc into next dc, 1dc into each dc to end. Turn. 3dc inc.
Cont in this way, inc 3dc and working one more st between incs on every foll 10th row, until there are 46[49:51]dc. Cont without shaping until stripe sequence has been completed. Fasten off.

Right front
Work as for left front, reversing shaping.

Sleeves
Using size E hook and A, make 7[7:8]ch for top of sleeve. Work throughout in stripe sequence as given for back.
Base row Into 4th ch from hook work 1dc, 1dc into each of next 2[2:3]ch, 2dc into last ch. Turn. 6[6:7]dc.
Shape raglan
Work as for back raglan shaping until there are 54[56:57]dc.
Shape sleeve
Patt 5[4:3] rows without shaping.
Next row (dec row) 3ch, 1dc into each of next 0[1:2]dc, *skip 1dc, 1dc into each of next 16dc, rep from * twice more, skip next dc, 1dc into each dc to end. Turn. 4dc dec.
Patt 3 rows without shaping.
Next row (dec row) 3ch, 1dc into each of next 1[2:3]dc, *skip 1dc, 1dc into each of next 14dc, rep from * twice, skip next dc, 1dc into each dc to end. Turn. 4dc dec.
Patt 3 rows without shaping.
Next row (dec row) 3ch, 1dc into each of next 0[1:3]dc, *skip 1dc, 1dc into each of next 13dc, rep from * twice more, skip 1dc, 1dc into each dc to end. Turn. 42[44:45]dc. Patt 1 more row using A, then using B patt 6 rows.

Cuffs
Next row (inc row) Using A, 3ch, 1dc into each of next 0[1:3]dc, *2dc into next dc, 1dc into each of next 12dc, rep from * twice, 2dc into next dc, 1dc into each dc to end. Turn. 46[48:49]dc. Work 5 more rows using A.
Fasten off.

To finish
Do not press. Join raglan seams. Join side and sleeve seams, reversing seam at cuff.
Neck edging Using size E hook and A, work 6 rows sc around neck edge, working approx 2sc into each row end and 1sc into each dc.
Left front edging Using size E hook and color to match stripe, work 6 rows sc in each separate stripe section. Join seams neatly on WS of work.
Right front edging Work as for left front edging, leaving opening for buttonhole in seam at lower edge of each stripe in B.
Picot edging Using size E hook and matching color, work all around neck, cuffs and lower edge as foll: 1sc, *3ch, sl st into last sc worked, 1sc into each of next 3sc, rep from * to end. Fasten off.
Press seams under a dry cloth with a cool iron. Sew on buttons.
Sew the snap in position at the neck.

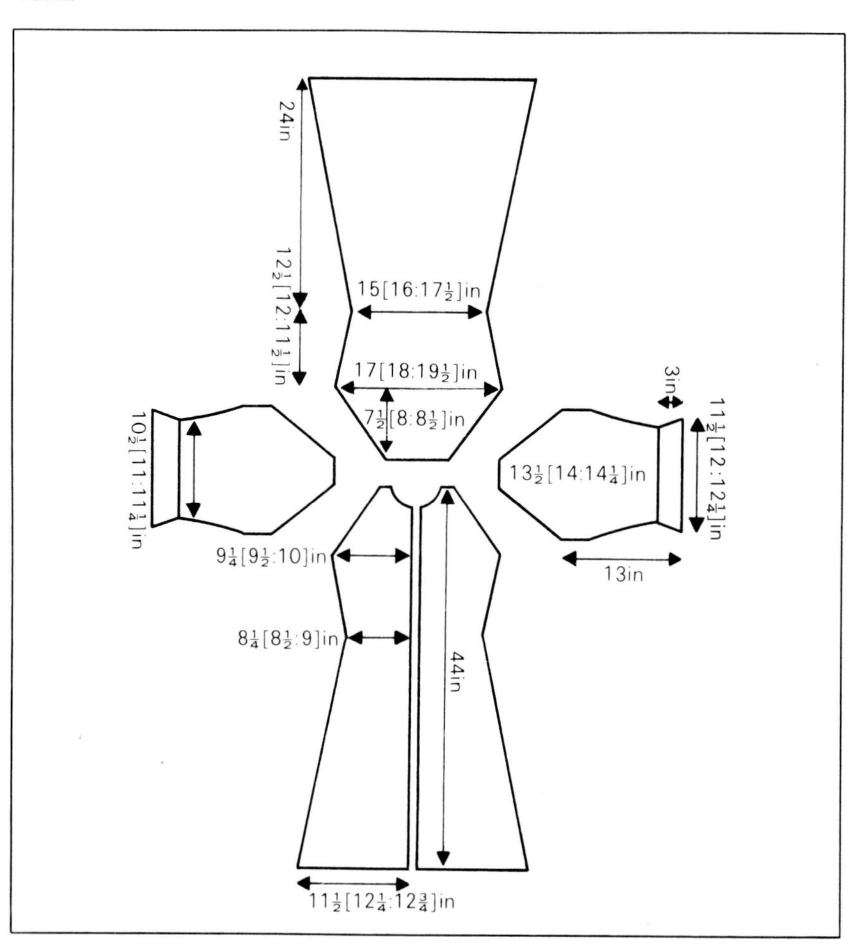

EVENING FRILLS

Size
45¾in in diameter.

Materials
Approx 24oz of a fingering yarn
Size C crochet hook

Gauge
First 4 rounds measure 5in in diameter.

To make
Using size C hook make 12ch, sl st into first ch to form a circle.
1st round 4ch to count as first tr, work 39tr into circle, sl st into top of 4ch.
2nd round 5ch, * 1tr into next tr, 1ch, rep from * all around, sl st into 4th of the 5ch.
3rd round Sl st into first sp, 1sc into same sp, *5ch, 1sc into next sp, rep from * all around, finishing 2ch, 1dc into first sc.
4th round *7ch, skip next loop, 1sc into next loop, (5ch, 1sc into next loop) twice, rep from * all around, finishing 2ch, 1dc into dc of previous round.
5th round *3ch, 3tr, 7ch and 3tr all into next loop, 3ch, 1sc into next loop, 5ch, 1sc into next loop, rep from * all around, finishing 2ch, 1dc into dc of previous round.
6th round 4ch, *15tr all into next 7ch loop, skip next 3ch sp, 1tr into next 5ch loop, rep from * all around, omitting 1tr at end of last rep, sl st into top of the 4ch.
7th round Sl st into next tr, 1sc into next tr, *(5ch, skip next tr, 1sc into next tr) 6 times, 3ch, skip first tr of next 15tr group, 1sc into next tr, rep from * all around, joining the last 3ch with a sl st to first sc.
8th round Sl st to center of first loop, 1sc into same loop, *(5ch, 1sc into next loop) 5 times, 3ch, skip next 3ch, 1sc into next 5ch loop, rep from * all around, omitting 1sc at end of last rep, sl st into first sc.
9th round Sl st to center of first loop, 1sc into same loop, *(5ch, 1sc into next loop) 4 times, 5ch, skip next 3ch, 1sc into next 5ch loop, rep from * omitting 1sc at end of last rep, sl st into first sc.
10th round Sl st to center of next loop, 1sc into same loop, *5ch, 1sc into next loop, rep from * all around omitting 1sc at end of last rep, sl st into first sc.
11th round Sl st to center of first loop, 1sc into same loop, *(5ch, 1sc into next loop) twice, 6ch, 2sc into next loop, 1sc into next sc, 2sc into next loop, 6ch, 1sc into next 5ch loop, rep from * omitting 1sc at end of last rep, sl st into first sc.
12th round Sl st to center of first loop, 1sc into same loop, *5ch, 1sc into next loop, 7ch, 2sc into next loop, 1sc into each of next 5sc, 2sc into next loop, 7ch, 1sc into next loop, rep from * all around omitting 1sc at end of last rep, sl st into first sc.
13th round Sl st into first loop, 1sc into same loop, *(7ch, 1sc into same loop) 3 times, 7ch, 3sc into next loop, 1sc into each of next 9sc, 3sc into next loop, 7ch, 1sc into next 5ch loop, rep from * all around, omitting 1sc at end of last rep, sl st into first sc.
14th round Sl st to center of first loop, 1sc into same loop, *5ch, 1sc into same loop (1ch, now work 1sc, 5ch and 1sc all into next loop) twice, 7ch, 1sc into next loop, 5ch, skip next sc, leaving last loop of each on hook work 1tr into next sc, skip next 2sc, 1tr into next sc, (skip next sc, 1tr into next sc) 3 times, skip next 2sc, 1tr into next sc, yo and draw through all loops on hook, 5ch, 1sc into next loop, 7ch, 1sc into next loop, rep from * all around, finishing 3ch, 1tr into first sc.
15th round 13ch, *miss next 5ch loop, 1sc into 5ch loop, 10ch, 1dc into next 7ch loop, 10ch, yo, (insert hook into next loop and draw a loop through) twice, (yo and draw through first 2 loops on hook) 3 times, 10ch, 1dc into next 7ch loop, 10ch, rep from * all around, sl st into 3rd of the 13ch.
16th round Sl st into first sp, 6ch, (1tr into first sp, 2ch) 3 times, * into next sp work (1tr and 2ch) 4 times, rep from * all around, sl st into 4th of the 6ch.
Rep rounds 3 to 16 inclusive twice more, then rounds 3 to 6 again. Fasten off.

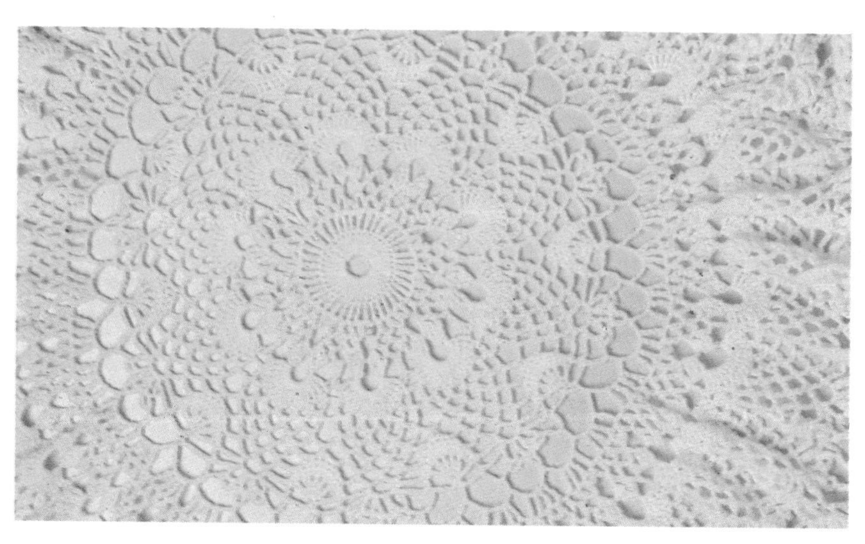

SCARVES WITH STYLE

Silky scarf

Size

7in wide by 72½in long, excluding fringe.

Materials

8oz of a medium-weight rayon yarn
No. 4 steel hook

Mohair scarf

Size

9½in wide by 88¼in long.

Materials

7oz of a lightweight mohair yarn
Size F hook

Silky scarf

To make
Using No. 4 steel hook chain 57.
1st row 1dc into 4th ch from hook, 1dc into each of next 7ch, *1ch, skip next ch. 1dc into each of next 17ch, rep from *once, 1ch, skip next ch, 1dc into each of last 9ch. Turn.
2nd row 3ch to count as first dc, 1dc into each of next 7dc, *1ch, skip next dc, 1dc into next sp, 1ch, skip next dc, 1dc into each of next 15dc, rep from *once, 1ch, skip dc, 1dc into next sp, 1ch, skip next dc, 1dc into each of last 7dc, 1dc into the turning ch. Turn. Beg row 3, cont in patt working from chart below until first row of 12th patt has been worked. Fasten off.

Fringe
Using three 18in lengths of yarn tog knot fringe (see Technique tip).

Mohair scarf

To make
Using size F hook chain 46.
Base row 1dtr into 8th ch from hook, *1ch, skip next ch, 1dtr into next ch, rep from * to end.
Turn.
Patt row 6ch to count as first dtr and 1ch, 1dtr into next dtr, *1ch, 1dtr into next dtr, rep from * to end, finishing 1ch, skip next ch, 1dtr into next ch.
Turn. 20sps.
Rep the patt row until work measures 87½ from beg.
Edging row *4ch, 1sc into next sp, rep from * to end.
Fasten off.
Join yarn to base row and work edging row along this edge.

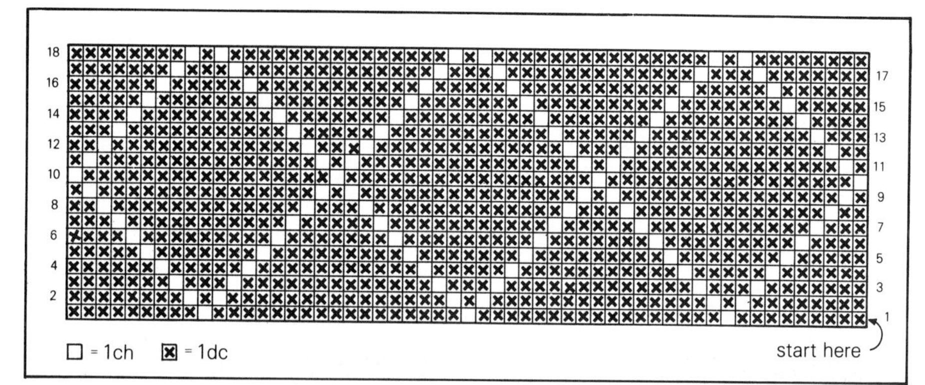

Technique tip

To make a knotted fringe
Cut the yarn into the required lengths. For the long, silky scarf you will need strands 18in long. Take three strands together at a time and knot fringe as follows.

Holding the right side of the edge to be fringed so that it is facing you, insert a crochet hook through the edge from back to front, fold the three strands in half and place the loop on the hook.

Pull the hook towards you, thus pulling the loop through the fabric.

Slide the hook upwards, around the six strands, and draw the ends of yarn through the loop. Pull the knot up tightly.

Knot each fringe in the same way at regular intervals along the edge.

Triangular scarf
Size
30½in wide by 19in deep.

Materials
2oz of a 3ply sport yarn
No. 0 steel hook

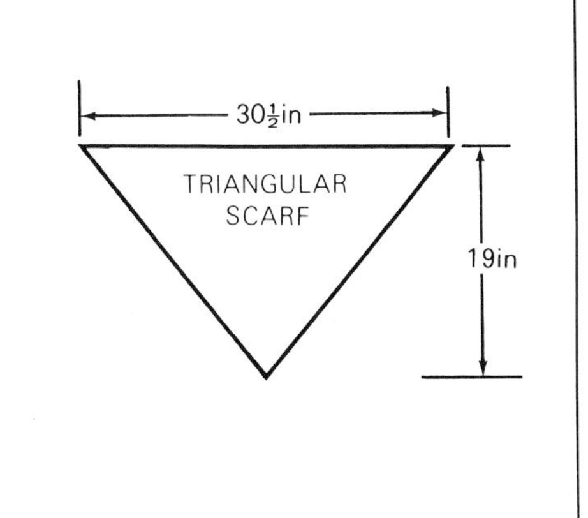

Triangular scarf

To make
Using No. 0 steel hook chain 6, join with sl st to first ch to form circle.
1st row 5ch to count as first tr and 1ch, work 1tr, 1ch and 1tr into circle. Turn. 2sps.
2nd row 5ch, 1tr into first sp, 1ch, 1tr into same sp, 1ch, 1tr into next sp, 1ch, 1tr into same sp. Turn. 4sps.
3rd row 5ch, 1tr, 1ch and 1tr all into first sp, (1ch, 1tr into next sp) 3 times, 1 ch, skip next ch, 1tr into next ch. Turn. 6sps.
4th row 5ch, 1tr, 1ch and 1tr all into first sp, now work 1ch and 1tr into each sp to end, finishing 1ch, 1tr into last tr. Turn.
Rep last row to 30½in width.
Now work edging this way:
Next round Work 3sc into each sp along the 3 sides and 6sc into each corner sp, finishing sl st into first sc.
Next round 3ch, work 5dc all into first sc, *skip next 2sc, sl st into next sc, skip next 2sc, 6dc all into next sc, rep from * all around, finishing sl st into top of the 3ch. Fasten off.

FAIR ISLE FAVORITE

Sizes
To fit 36–38[40–42]in chest.
Length, 25½[26¼]in.
Note *Directions for larger size are in brackets []; where there is only one set of figures it applies to both sizes.*

Materials
Sport yarn:
8[9]oz in main color (A)
3[4]oz contrasting color (B)
2oz contrasting color (C)
1[2]oz contrasting color (D)
1oz contrasting color (E)
Size F Tunisian crochet hook
Size C crochet hook

Gauge
20sts and 16 vertical loop rows to 4in worked on size F Tunisian hook.
Note *When working color patt, strand color not in use loosely across WS of work.*

Back
Using size F Tunisian hook and A, make 101[111]ch.
Work 10 rows in plain Tunisian crochet (i.e. 5 vertical loop rows).
Next row Work 1A, *1E, 1A, rep from * to end. Do not turn work.
Next row Work back in colors as set.
Next row Work 1E, *1A, 1E, rep from * to end. Do not turn work.
Next row Work back in colors as set. Beg with 8th row, cont in patt, working from chart until work measures 15in. Cut off B, C, D and E.
Cont with A only.
Shape armholes
Next row Sl st over first 5 loops, work to within last 4 loops. Do not turn work.
Next row Work to end.
Next row Sl st over first 3 loops, work to within last 2 loops. Do not turn work.
Next row Work to end.
Dec one st at each end of next 4[6] vertical loop rows. 81[87] vertical loops. Cont straight until armhole measures 8[8¾]in. Fasten off.

Front
Work as for back until work is 8 vertical loop rows less than back to armholes.
Divide for neck
Next row Work across first 50[55] loops. Do not turn work.
Next row Work to end.
Cont on these loops for first side of neck. Dec one loop at neck edge on next loop row and foll 3 alternate loop rows, ending at side edge. 46[51] loops.
Shape armhole
Next row Sl st over first 5 loops, work to end. Do not turn work.
Next row Work to end.
Next row Sl st over first 3 loops, work to within last 2 loops, dec one loop.
Do not turn work.
Next row Work to end.
Cont to dec one loop at neck edge on every foll alternate loop row, *at the same time* dec one loop at armhole edge on next 4[6] loop rows. 33[35] loops. Keeping armhole edge straight, cont to dec at neck edge on every alternate loop row until 21[23] loops rem. Cont without shaping until work measures same as back. Fasten off.
With RS of work facing, return to where sts were left, skip center loop, join yarn to next loop and work to end of row. Complete to match first side, reversing shaping.

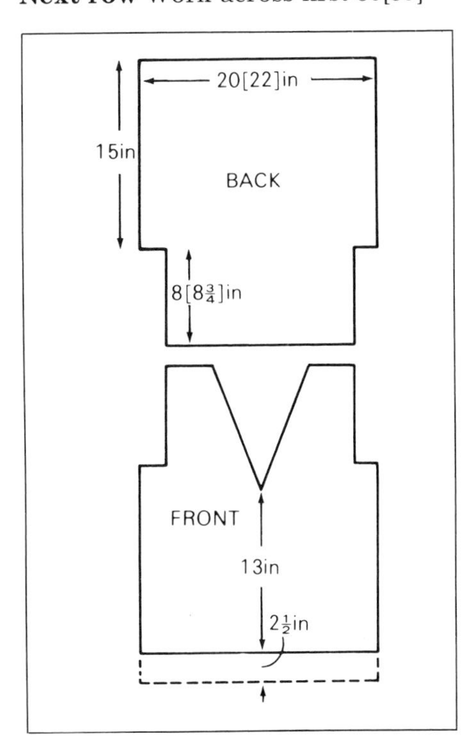

Neckband
Join shoulder seams. With RS of work facing, using size C crochet hook and A, join yarn to back neck and work 1sc into each st across back neck, 45[49]sc down left front neck, one st into center of V, 45[49]sc up right front neck, sl st into first sc. Turn.
Cont in rows of sc, turning after each row and dec one st at each side of center front st on every row for 1¼in. Fasten off.

Armhole borders
Using size C hook and A, work 86[94]sc around armhole. Cont in rows of sc for 1¼in. Fasten off.

Waistband
Join side seams. Using size C hook and A, make 15ch.
Base row 1sc into each ch to end. Turn. Working into back loop only, cont in sc until work, when slightly stretched, fits around lower edge. Fasten off. Join short ends.

To finish
Press lightly. Sew on waistband.

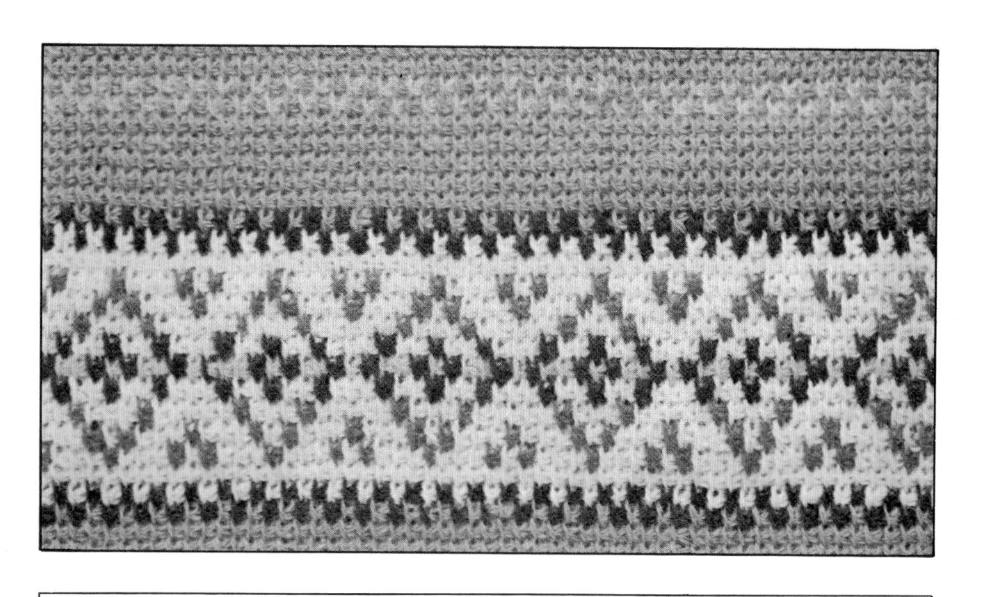

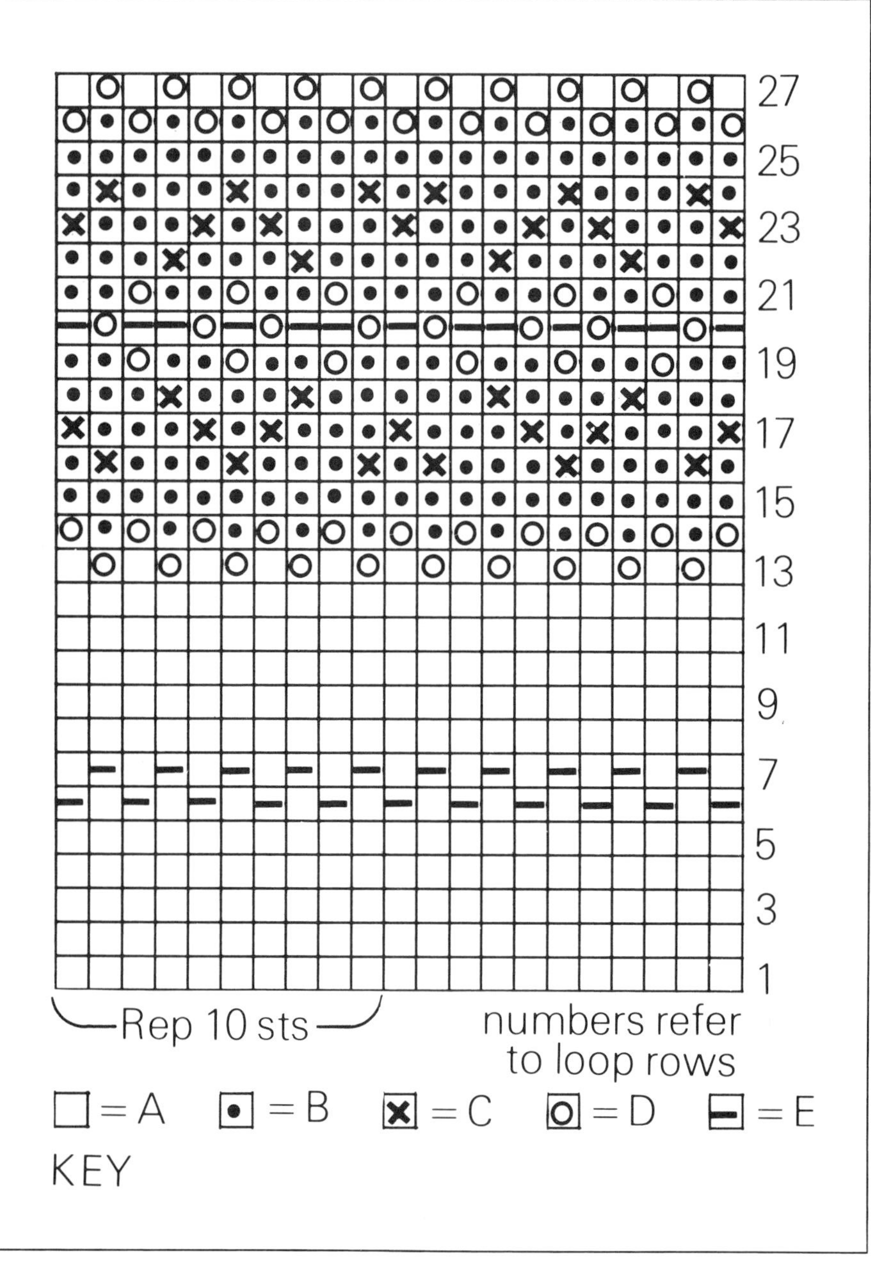
27
25
23
21
19
17
15
13
11
9
7
5
3
1
Rep 10 sts
numbers refer
to loop rows
= A
= B
= C
= D
= E
KEY

TUNISIAN VEST

Sizes
To fit 36[38:40]in chest.
Length, 20½[21:22]in.
Note *Directions for larger sizes are in brackets []; where there is only one set of figures it applies to all sizes.*

Materials
4 × 2oz balls of a knitting worsted in main color (A)
3[3:4] balls in each of 2 contrasting colors (B and C)
Size H Tunisian crochet hook
Size H crochet hook
5 buttons

Gauge
17sts and 34 rows to 4in worked on size H Tunisian hook.

Back
Using size H Tunisian hook and B, make 78[82:88]ch.
Base row Insert hook into one loop only of 2nd ch from hook, yo and draw a loop through, *insert hook into one loop only of next ch, yo and draw a loop through, rep from * to end. 78[82:88] loops on hook. Do not turn the work.
Next row Using C, yo and draw a loop through first loop on hook, *yo and draw through 2 loops on hook, rep from * to end. 1 loop rem on hook.
Cont in stripe sequence of 1 row B, 2 rows C, 2 rows B, 2 rows A, 2 rows C, 2 rows A and 1 row B, working in patt as follows:
1st row Insert hook from right to left under 2nd vertical bar, yo and draw a loop through, *insert hook from right to left under next vertical bar, yo and draw a loop through, rep from * to end. Do not turn work. 78[82:88] loops on hook.
2nd row Yo and draw a loop through first loop on hook, *yo and draw through next 2 loops on hook, rep from * to end. 1 loop rem on hook. These 2 rows form the patt.
Cont in patt until work measures 12½[12½:13]in; end with 2nd row.
Shape armholes
Next 2 rows Sl st across first 8[9:10]sts, patt to within last 8[9:10]sts, then work back.
Dec one st (by working under 2 vertical loops tog) at each end of next and foll 3 alternate rows. 54[56:60]sts. Cont straight until armhole measures 7½[8:8½]in; end with 2nd row.
Shape shoulders
Next 2 rows Sl st across first 9 sts, patt to within last 8[9:10]sts, then work back. Rep last 2 rows once more. Fasten off.

Right front
Using size H Tunisian hook and B, make 39[41:44]ch. Cut off yarn. Working in patt and stripe sequence to match back, shape as follows:
Rejoin yarn to 11th ch, (insert hook into one loop only of next ch, yo and draw a loop through) twice, so having 3 loops on hook, then work back.
Next row Remove hook from loop, insert hook into one loop only of the ch to the right of the loop, place loop back on hook and patt to end, then (insert hook into one loop only of next ch, yo and draw a loop through) twice, then work back.
Cont to pick up 1 loop at short side and 2 loops at long side on every other row until all ch are being worked on short side (front edge), pick up rem ch at long side and cont in patt on these 39[41:44]sts until front from end of shaping is same length as back to armholes, ending at front side.
Shape armhole and front edge
Next 2 rows Patt to within last 9sts, then work back. Dec one st at beg of next and every foll 4th row and at the same time dec one st at armhole edge on next and foll 3 alternate rows. 18sts. Cont without shaping until armhole is same depth as back armholes to shoulders, ending with a 2nd row.
Shape shoulder
Next 2 rows Patt across 8[9:10]sts, then work back. Fasten off.

Left front
Work as for right front, reversing all shaping and rejoin B to 27th[29th:32nd] ch for lower shaping.
Armhole edgings (alike)
Join shoulder seams.
Using size H crochet hook and A, work 3 rows of sc evenly along armhole edge. Fasten off.
The edging
Join side seams.

Technique tip

Tunisian crochet

Tunisian crochet is worked with a long hook which resembles both a knitting needle and a crochet hook. The reason for the hook being long is that all the loops are kept on the hook for the first row and worked off on the second row.

First make a length of chain. Now insert the hook into one loop only of the second chain from the hook, yarn over hook and draw a loop through – so having 2 loops on hook.
Work into each chain in this way, keeping each loop on the hook. Do not turn the work.

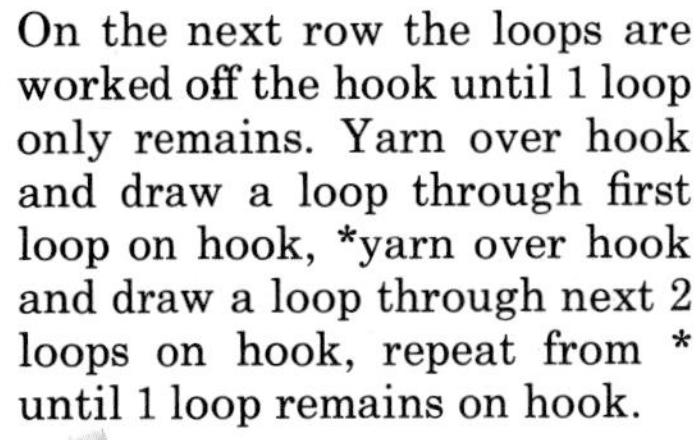

On the next row the loops are worked off the hook until 1 loop only remains. Yarn over hook and draw a loop through first loop on hook, *yarn over hook and draw a loop through next 2 loops on hook, repeat from * until 1 loop remains on hook.

On the next row the loops are picked up again by inserting the hook from right to left under the vertical loop, placing yarn over hook and drawing a loop through again; do not turn the work at the end of the row.
Work loops off hook again until 1 loop only remains on hook. The last 2 rows are repeated throughout.

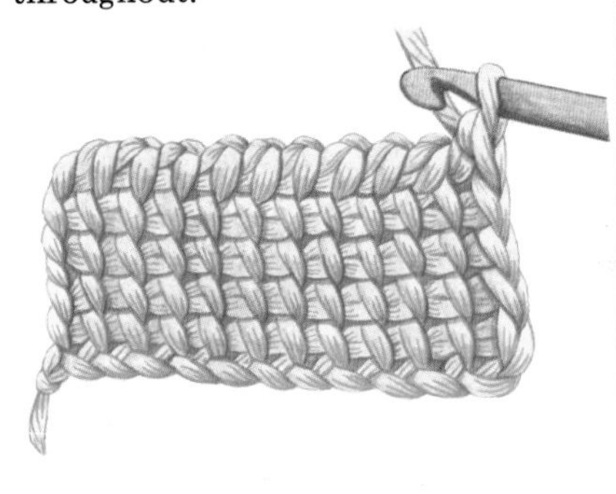

12¾[13:14]in
7½[8:8½]in
12½[12½:13]in
18¼[19¼:20¾]in
12½[12½:13]in
2¾in
9¼[9¾:10½]in
12½[12½:13]in

Using size H crochet hook, join A to right side seam and work a row of sc all around outer edge, sl st into first sc.
Work 2 more rounds of sc, working 2sc into each of the 2sc at points on the fronts.
1st buttonhole round Work in sc to beg of 11th stripe in A at lower edge of left front, (2ch, skip next 2sc, 1sc into each of next 10sc) 4 times, then work another buttonhole, work in sc to end, sl st into first sc.
2nd buttonhole round Work 1sc into each sc and 2sc into each buttonhole and point, sl st into first sc.
Work 1 more round, working 2sc at points. Fasten off.

To finish
Press according to directions on yarn label. Sew on buttons.

THREE FOR THE BEACH

Striped T-shirt

Sleeves and yoke section
(make 2)
1st size only Using size F hook and A make 45ch for sleeve edge.
Base row 1dc into 4th ch from hook, 1dc into each ch to end. Turn. 43sts.
Next row 3ch to count as first dc, 1dc into each dc to end, 1dc into top of turning ch leaving last 2 loops of last dc on hook, drop A and draw through B. Turn.
Next row 3ch, 1dc into each dc to end. Turn.
Next row 3ch, 1dc into each dc to end leaving last 2 loops of last dc on hook, drop B and draw through A. Turn. Cont in dc and changing yarns in this way on every other row, work 2 rows A and 2 C.
Beg stripe sequence.
Work 2 rows A, 2 rows B, 2 rows A and 2 rows C until a total of 94 rows has been worked, ending with 2 rows A.
Fasten off.
2nd size only Using size F hook and A, make 47ch for sleeve edge.
Base row Work 1dc into 4th ch from hook, 1dc into each ch to end leaving last 2 loops of last dc on hook, drop A and draw through B. Turn. 45sts.
Next row 3ch to count as first dc, 1dc into each dc to end, 1dc into top of 3ch. Turn.
Next row 3ch, 1dc into each dc to end leaving last 2 loops of last dc on hook, drop B and draw through A. Turn. Cont in dc and changing yarns in this way on every other row, work 2 rows A and 2 rows C.
Now work stripe sequence as for first size until a total of 96 rows has been worked, ending with 1 row A.
Fasten off.
3rd size only Using size F hook and C, make 49ch for sleeve edge.
Base row Work 1dc into 4th ch from hook, 1dc into each ch to end leaving last 2 loops of last dc on hook, drop C and draw through A. Turn. 47sts.
Next row 3ch to count as first dc, 1dc into each dc to end, 1dc into top of 3ch. Turn.
Next row 3ch, 1dc into each dc to end leaving last 2 loops of last dc on hook, drop A and draw through B. Turn.
Continuing in dc and changing yarns in this way on every other row, work 2 rows B, 2 rows A, 2 rows C.
Now work stripe sequence as for first size until a total of 98 rows has been worked, ending with 1 row C.
Fasten off.

Striped T-shirt

Sizes
To fit 38[40:42]in chest.
Length, 27[27½:28½]in.
Sleeve seam, 8½in.

Materials
13[13:14]oz of a medium-weight mercerized crochet cotton in main color (A)
7[7:9]oz in 1st contrasting color (B)
6[6:7]oz in 2nd contrasting color (C)
Sizes E and F crochet hooks

Gauge
18dc and 10 rows to 4in on size F hook.

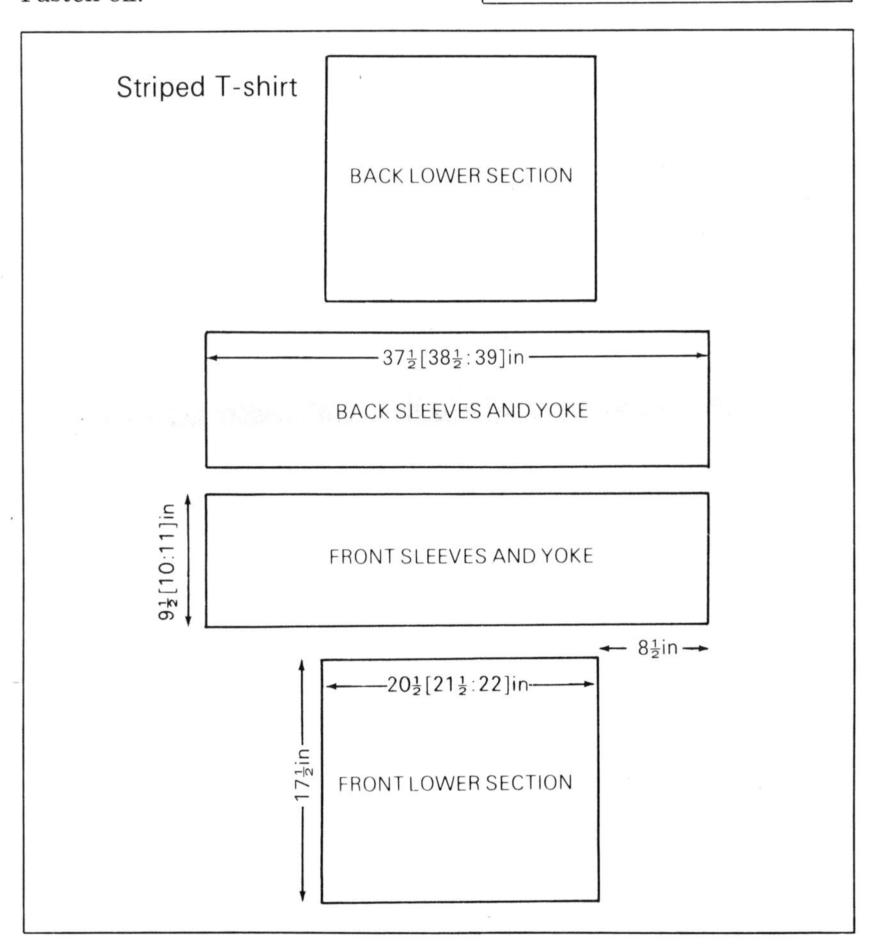

> ## Oatmeal T-shirt
> **Sizes**
> *To fit 38[40:42]in chest.*
> *Length, 25½[26:26½]in.*
> *Sleeve seam, 7½in.*
> **Note** *Directions for larger sizes are in brackets []; where there is only one set of figures it applies to all sizes.*
>
> **Materials**
> *15oz of a lightweight nubbly yarn*
> *Sizes E and F crochet hooks*
> *4 buttons*
>
> **Gauge**
> *18dc to 4¼in and 11 rows to 4in on size F hook.*

Lower sections (make 2)
All sizes Using size F hook and A, make 94[98:102]ch.
Base row Work 1dc into 4th ch from hook, 1dc into each ch to end. Turn.
Next row 3ch to count as first dc, 1 dc into each dc to end leaving last 2 loops of last dc on hook, drop A and draw through B. Turn.
Cont in dc and changing yarns in this way on every other row, work 2 rows B, 2 rows A, 2 rows C and 2 rows A until work measures 17½in from beg. Fasten off.

To finish
Mark top sections 8½in from each sleeve edge. Attach lower sections to top sections between markers. Join side and underarm seams. Join upper sleeve and shoulder seams for 13½in, so leaving an opening at center for neck. Using size E hook and B, work a row of sc evenly all around neck.
Using size E hook and B, work 1sc into each st around lower and sleeve edges.

Oatmeal T-shirt
Back
Using size F hook make 87[90:93]ch.
Base row Work 1dc into 4th ch from hook, 1dc into each ch to end. Turn. 85[88:91]sts.
Patt row 3ch to count as first dc,

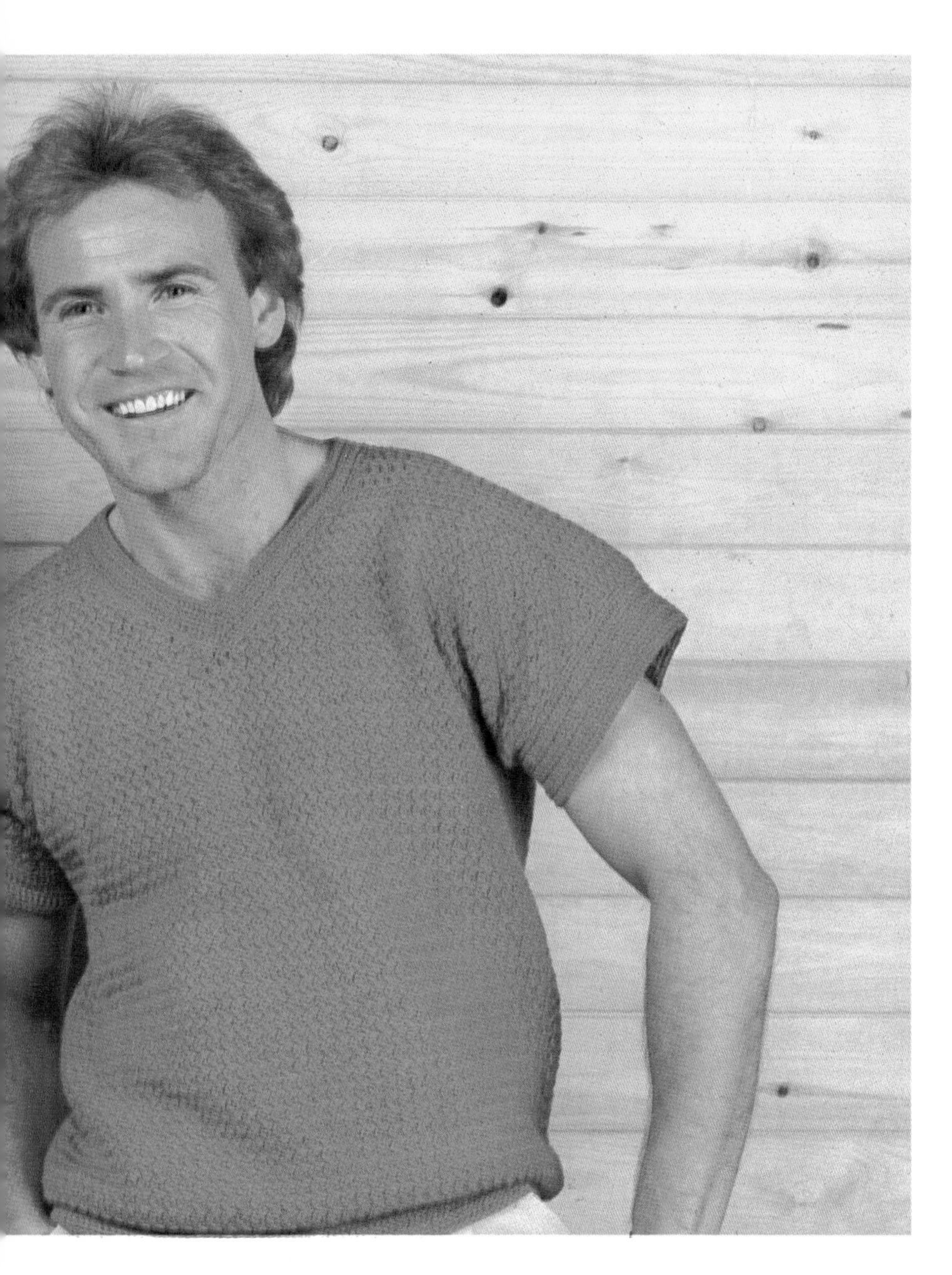

1dc into first sp between dc, *1dc into next sp between dc, rep from * to end. Turn.
Rep patt row until work measures 15½in from beg.

Shape armholes
Sl st over first 6dc, 3ch, patt to within last 5dc, turn. 75[78:81]dc.
Cont straight until armhole measures 8[8½:9]in. Change to size E hook.

Next row 1ch to count as first sc, working into the top of each dc work 1sc into each dc to end. Turn. 75[78:91]sc.

Next row 1ch, 1sc in each sc to end. Turn. Rep last row until armholes measure 10[10½:11]in.

Shape shoulders

1st row Sl st across first 8[9:9]sts, work to within last 7[8:8]sts, turn.
2nd row Sl st across first 8[8:9]sts, work to within last 7[7:8]sts, turn.
3rd row Sl st across first 8sts, work to within last 7sts. Fasten off.

Front
Work as for back until armhole shaping row has been completed. 75[78:81]dc. Work 1 row.

Divide for opening

Next row Work across the first 35[36:38]dc, turn. 34[35:37]sts. Cont in patt until work measures same as back to beg of sc panel, ending at front edge.

Shape neck
Change to size E hook.

Next row Sl st across first 8sts, 1sc in each st to end. Turn. Cont in sc, dec one st at neck edge on next 7[7:8] rows. Cont straight until front measures same as back to shoulder; end at front edge.

Shape shoulder

Work to within last 7[8:8]sts, turn.

Next row Sl st across first 8[8:9]sts, work to end. Fasten off. Skip 5[6:5]sts at center front, rejoin yarn to next st, then work in patt across the rem 34[35:37]sps, turn. 35[36:38]sts. Cont in patt until work measures as first side to sc panel; end at armhole edge.

Shape neck

Change to size E hook.

Next row Work 1sc in each st to within last 7sts. Cont in sc, dec one st at neck edge on next 7[7:8] rows. Cont straight until work measures as back to shoulder; end at armhole edge.

Shape shoulder

Sl st across first 8[9:9]sts, work to end. Turn.

Next row Work to within last 7[7:8]sts. Fasten off.

Sleeves

Using size F hook make 55[59:63]ch. Change to size E hook and work 1sc into 2nd ch from hook, 1sc into each ch to end. Turn. 54[58:62]sc.

Next row 1ch, 1sc in each sc to end. Turn.

Rep last row 4 times. Change to size F hook.

Next row 3ch, skip first sc, 1dc into each sc to end. Turn.

Patt row 3ch to count as first dc, 1dc into first sp between dc, *1dc into next sp between dc, rep from * to end. Turn.

Cont in patt, inc one st at each end of every foll 4th row until there are 62[66:70]sts. Cont without shaping until sleeve measures 7in from beg. Mark each end of last row with a colored thread.

Work 3 rows without shaping.

Shape top

Next row Sl st across first 4dc, 3ch, (1dc into next sp) to within last 3sps, turn.

Rep last row until 8[6:4]sts rem. Fasten off.

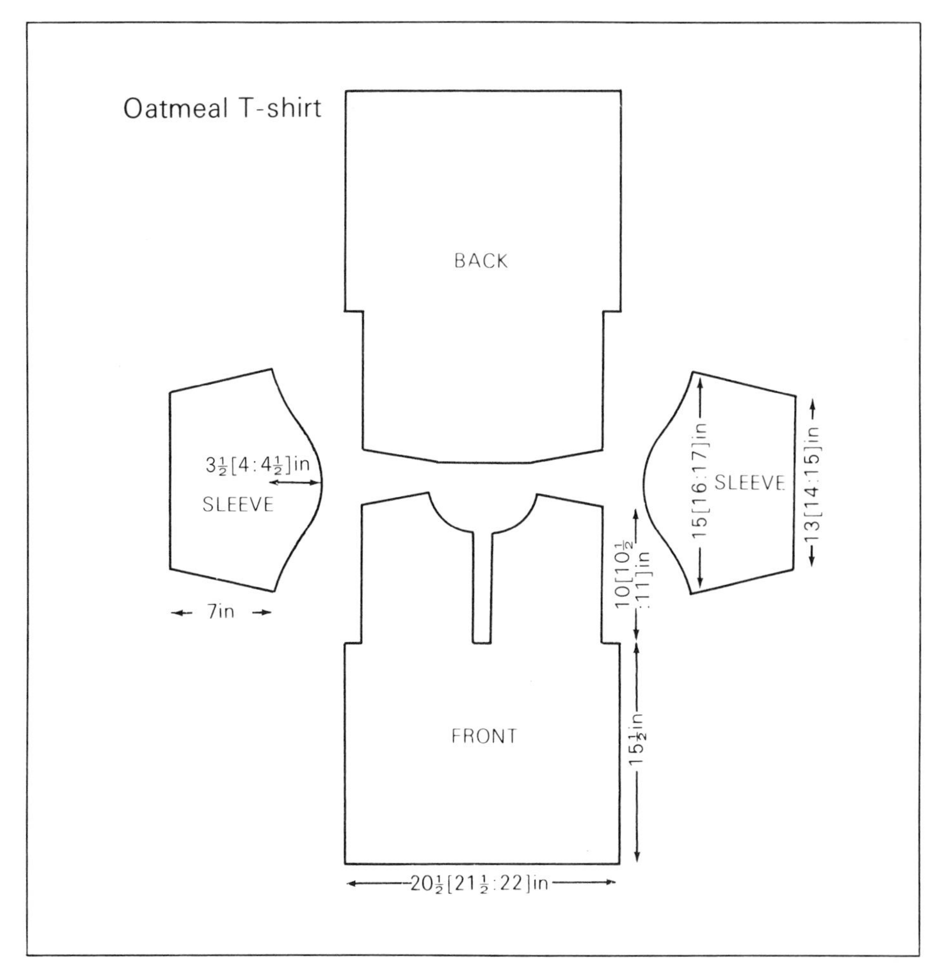

Button band
Join shoulder seams.
Using size E hook join on yarn and work 6sc along lower edge of front opening.
Next row 1ch, 1sc into each sc to end. Turn.
Rep last row until band fits along opening to beg of neck shaping, when slightly stretched, ending at front end. Fasten off. Mark 3 button positions on this band, the first $1\frac{1}{2}$in from base of opening, the last $1\frac{1}{2}$in from the top and the other one evenly spaced between.

Buttonhole band
Working in front of and on top of button band work a sc into each of same 6 places as 6sc of button band. Now cont in sc work to match button band, making buttonholes to correspond as follows:
1st buttonhole row 1ch, 1sc into each of the first 2sc, 2ch, skip next 2sc, 1sc into each of last 2sc. Turn.
2nd buttonhole row 1ch, 1sc into each of the first 2sc, 1sc into each of the 2ch, then work 1 sc into each of the last 2sc. Turn. Do not fasten off.

Neckband
Work across buttonhole band, then work 1sc into each of the sts of left front neck, 1sc into each row end up side neck, 1sc into each sp between dc on back neck, 1sc into each row end down right side neck, 1sc into each st along right front neck and 1sc into each of the 6sc of button band. Work 5 rows in sc, working a buttonhole over the 3rd and 4th rows. Fasten off.

To finish
Sew front bands in position. Join side and sleeve seams, leaving 3 rows above markers on sleeves open. Set in sleeves, placing 3 rows above markers to armhole shaping. Sew on buttons. Press very lightly with warm iron and dry cloth.

Rustic T-shirt

Back
Using size E hook make 101[105:109]ch.
Base row Work (1sc and 1dc) into 3rd ch from hook, *skip next ch, (1sc and 1dc) into next ch, rep from * to end. Turn. 50[52:54] patts.
Patt row 1ch, *skip next dc, (1sc and 1dc) into next sc, rep from * to end. The last row forms the patt and is rep throughout. Cont in patt until back measures $13\frac{1}{2}$in. Do not turn.
Shape sleeves
Make 13ch at end of last row. Turn.
Next row Work 1sc into 3rd ch from hook, 1dc into same ch, (skip 1ch, 1sc and 1dc into next ch) 5 times, patt across sts for back.
Using a separate ball of yarn, sl st into last st of previous row and make 12ch. Fasten off. Return to end of row just worked and cont to work across additional ch, (skip next ch, 1sc and 1dc into next ch) 6 times. 62[64:66] patts.**
Cont without shaping until sleeve measures $6\frac{1}{4}[6\frac{3}{4}:6\frac{3}{4}]$in; end with WS row.
Yoke detail
*** **Next row** 2ch, work 1hdc into each st to end. Turn.
Next row 2ch, working into front loop only of each st, work 1hdc into each st to end. Turn.***
Next row 1ch, *skip 1hdc, work (1sc and 1hdc) into next hdc, rep

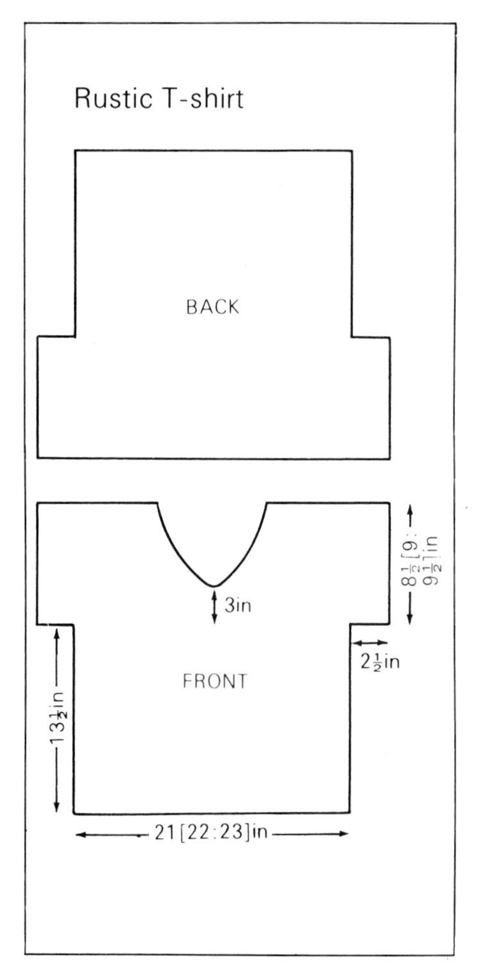

Rustic T-shirt

Sizes
To fit 38[40:42]in chest.
Length, 25[$25\frac{1}{2}$:26]in.
Sleeve seam, $4\frac{1}{2}$in.
Note *Directions for larger sizes are in brackets []; where there is only one set of figures it applies to all sizes.*

Materials
17[18:19] × 1oz balls of a sport yarn
Sizes C and E crochet hooks

Gauge
10 patterns measure $4\frac{1}{4}$in using size E hook.

from * to end. Turn. 62[64:66] patts. Cont without shaping until sleeve measures $8\frac{1}{2}$[9:$9\frac{1}{2}$]in. Fasten off.

Waistband
With RS facing and using size C hook, rejoin yarn at lower edge of back. Work 3ch, then work 1hdc into each remaining loop on foundation ch. Turn. 100[104:108]hdc.
Working into front loop only of each st, work 10 more rows hdc. Fasten off.

Front
Work as for back to **. Cont straight until sleeve measures 3in from beg, ending with a WS row.
Shape neck
Next row 1ch, work 30[31:32] patts, skip 1dc, 1sc into next sc, turn and leave rem 31[32:33] patts unworked.
Next row 1ch, skip first sc and next dc, work (1sc and 1dc) into next sc, patt to end. Turn.
Next row Work in patt until one patt rem unworked, skip next dc, 1sc into last sc. Turn.
****Rep last 2 rows until sleeve measures $6\frac{1}{4}$[$6\frac{3}{4}$:$6\frac{3}{4}$]in; end with WS row.
Work as given for back from *** to ***, dec 1hdc by skipping one st at neck edge on every row. Cont to shape neck as before, until 22[22:23] patts rem. Cont without shaping until sleeve measures same as sleeves of back. Fasten off. With RS of work facing, rejoin yarn to next dc at center front, work (1sc and 1dc) into next sc, patt to end. Turn.
Next row Work in patt until 1 patt remains unworked, skip next dc, work 1sc into last sc. Turn.
Next row 1ch, skip first sc and next dc, work (1sc and 1dc) into next sc, patt to end. Turn.
Rep last 2 rows. Now work as for first side from **** to end.

Waistband
Work as given for back.

To finish
Press work lightly as given on yarn labels. Join shoulder seams.
Neck border
With RS facing and using size C hook, rejoin yarn at left shoulder and work 44[47:50]sc down left side of front neck, place a marker after last sc for center front V, work 44[47:50]sc up right side of neck and 37[41:41]sc along back neck. Turn. 125[135:141]sc. Work 4 rows hdc as for waistband, working 2hdc tog at each side of marker on every row. Fasten off. Sew ends of neck border tog.
Sleeve borders
With RS facing and using size C hook, rejoin yarn to lower edge of sleeve and work 92[98:104]sc along this edge. Work 8 rows hdc as for waistband. Fasten off. Finish other sleeve in the same way. Join side and underarm seams. Press lightly.

COOL AND CASUAL

Sizes
To fit 36[38:40]in chest.
Length, 28[29:30]in.
Sleeve seam, 17½[18:18½]in, including cuff.
Note *Directions for larger sizes are in brackets []; where there is only one set of figures it applies to all sizes.*

Materials
23[25:27] × 2oz balls of a medium-weight cotton bouclé
Sizes E and G crochet hooks
Hip length of ½in-wide elastic

Gauge
30sts and 20 rows to 8in over hdc on size G hook.

Back
Using size G hook make 81[85:89]ch.
Base row 1hdc into 3rd ch from hook, 1hdc into each ch to end. Turn. 80[84:88]hdc.
Patt row 2ch to count as first hdc, skip first hdc, 1hdc into each hdc, ending with 1hdc into top of 2ch. Turn. Rep last row 68[70:72] times more. Fasten off.

Front
Work as given for back until 46 rows have been completed.
Divide for neck
Next row Patt across first 40[42:44]sts, turn.
Next row 2ch, skip first hdc, leaving last loop of each on hook, work 1hdc into each of next 2hdc, yo and draw through all loops on hook – called dec 1 – patt to end. Turn.
Next row Patt to end. Turn.
Rep last 2 rows until 28[29:30]sts rem. Fasten off.
Rejoin yarn to sts that were left at base of V, 2ch, patt to end. Turn.
Next row Patt to last 3sts, dec 1, 1hdc into top of 2ch. Turn.
Next row Patt to end. Turn.
Rep last 2 rows until 28[29:30]sts rem. Fasten off.

Sleeves
Using size G hook make 53[57:61]ch. Work base row as for back. 52[56:60]sts. Cont in patt as for back, inc one st at each end of every 5th row until there are 68[72:76]sts. Cont straight until sleeve measures 15[15½:16]in. Fasten off.

Neckband
Join shoulder seams. With RS of work facing and using size E hook, rejoin yarn to first row end on right front neck at base of V, work (1sc into next row end, 2sc into next row end) to shoulder, 1sc into each st across back neck, then (1sc into next row end, 2sc into next row end) down left front neck, turn.
Next row 1ch, 1sc into each sc all around neck edge. Turn.
Rep last row 3 times more. Fasten off.

Cuffs
Using size E hook work along foundation ch of sleeve by working (1sc into each of next 2ch, skip 1ch) to end. Turn.
Next row 1 ch, 1sc into each sc to end. Turn.
Rep last row 10 times. Fasten off.

To finish
Press lightly under damp cloth with warm iron. Sew sleeves in position. Join side and sleeve seams. Overlap right and left front neckbands at base of V and sew in position. Turn approx ½in to WS at lower edge to form casing for elastic. Thread elastic through casing.

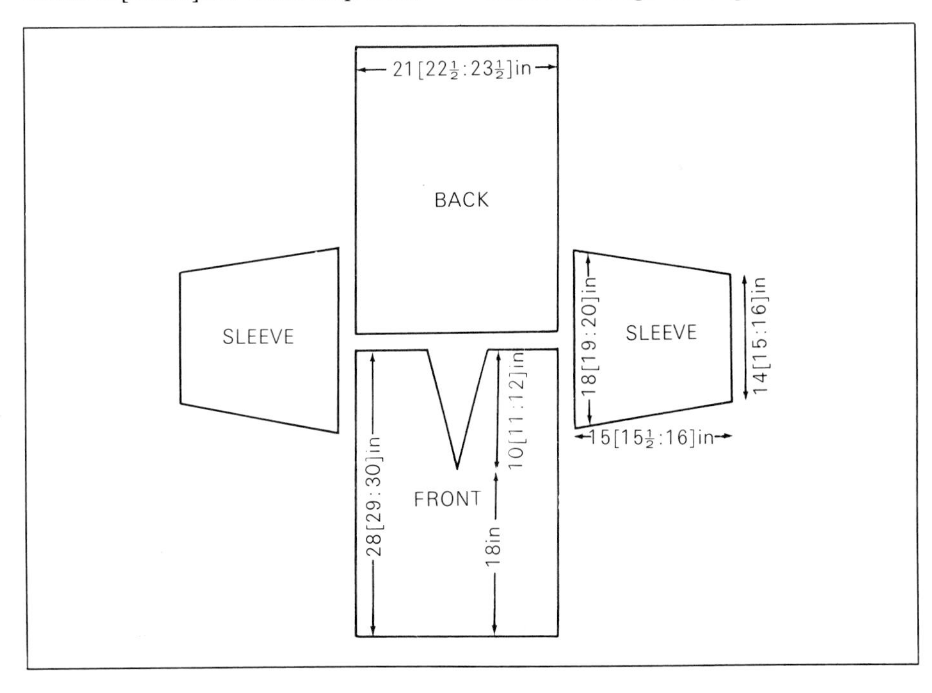

SPORTY SWEATER

Sizes
To fit 36[38:40]in chest.
Length, $29\frac{3}{4}$[30:31]in.
Sleeve seam, $18\frac{3}{4}$in.
Note *Directions for larger sizes are in brackets []; where there is only one set of figures it applies to all sizes.*

Materials
20[20:22]oz of a lightweight bouclé yarn
Size G Tunisian crochet hook
1 pair No. 5 knitting needles

Gauge
17sts and 16 rows (i.e. 8 vertical loops) to 4in worked on size G Tunisian crochet hook.

Back

Using size G Tunisian crochet hook, make 84[88:94]ch.
1st row Insert hook into 2nd ch from hook, yo and draw a loop through, *insert hook into next loop, yo and draw a loop through, rep from * to end. 84[88:94] loops on hook.
2nd row Yo and draw through first loop on hook, *yo and draw through next 2 loops on hook, rep from * to end.
3rd row *Insert hook from right to left through next vertical loop, yo and draw a loop through, insert hook from left to right through next vertical loop, yo and draw a loop through, rep from * to end, insert hook from right to left into end st, yo and draw a loop through. Do not turn work. 84[88:94] loops on hook.
The 2nd and 3rd rows form patt.
Cont in patt until work measures 16[16:$16\frac{1}{2}$]in; end with a 2nd row.

Shape raglan armholes
Next row Sl st across first 4 loops, patt to within last 4 loops, then work back. Dec one loop (by working 2 loops tog) at each end of next and every foll loop row until 32[34:38]sts rem; end with a 2nd row. Fasten off.

Front

Work as back to beg of armhole shaping.

Shape raglan armholes
Next row Sl st across first 4 loops, patt to within last 4 loops, then work back.

Divide for neck
1st row Dec 1 loop, work 36[38:41] loops, then work back.
2nd row Work 37[39:42] loops, then work back.
Dec 1 loop at armhole edge on next and every foll loop row, *at same time* dec 1 loop at neck edge on next and every foll alternate loop row until 16[17:19] dec have been worked at neck edge. Cont to dec at armhole edge only until one loop rem. Fasten off. Rejoin yarn to inner edge of sts that were left and work to match first side.

Sleeves

Using size G Tunisian hook, make 52[52:58]ch. Work 1st row as for back. 52[52:58] loops on hook. Cont in patt inc 1 loop (by working 1st into first loop and 2sts into last loop) at each end of every foll 9th loop row until there are 66[66:72] loops. Cont straight until work measures $16\frac{1}{2}$in; end with a 2nd row.

Shape raglan armhole
Work as for back raglan armhole until 14[12:16] loops rem.
Fasten off.

Cuffs

With RS facing and using No. 5 needles pick up and K 52[52:58]sts along lower edge. Work 18 rows K1, P1 ribbing. Bind off in ribbing.

Waistbands (alike)

With RS facing and using No. 5 needles pick up and K 84[88:94]sts along lower edge. Work 18 rows K1, P1 ribbing. Bind off in ribbing.

Neckband

Join raglan seams. With RS facing and using No. 5 needles, join yarn to center back neck and pick up and K 27sts along neck, 10[10:12]sts from top of sleeve and 62[62:64]sts along front neck to center. 99[99:103]sts. Work 8 rows K1, P1 ribbing, dec one st at center front edge on every other row. Bind off in ribbing. Work 2nd side to correspond with first.

To finish

Join side, sleeve and neckband.

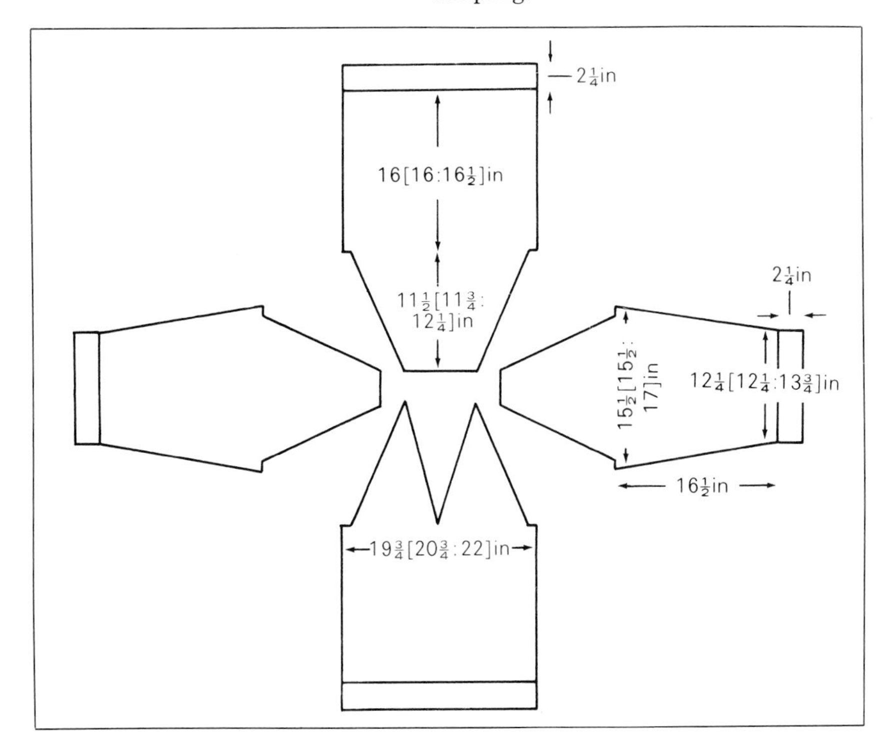

CHUNKY CHOICE

Sizes
To fit, 38[40:42]in chest.
Length, 29½[30¼:31]in.
Sleeve seam, 21[22:23]in.
Note *Directions for larger sizes are in brackets []; where there is only one set of figures it applies to all sizes.*

Materials
48[50:52]oz of a bulky knitting yarn
Sizes H and K crochet hooks
1 × 23½in open-ended zipper

Gauge
12sts and 10 rows to 4in in patt st on size K hook.

Back
Using size K hook chain 64[67:70].
Base row 1sc into 2nd ch from hook, 1sc into each ch to end. Turn. 63[66:69]sc.
Patt row (RS) 1ch, working into the back loop only, work 1sc into each sc to end. Turn.
Rep the patt row until work measures 15in from beg.
Fasten off.

Left front
Using size K hook chain 32[34:36].
Base row 1sc into 2nd ch from hook, 1sc into each ch to end. Turn. 31[33:35]sc.
Patt row (RS) 1ch, working into the back loop only, work 1sc into each sc to end. Turn.
Rep the patt row until work measures 15in from beg. Fasten off.

Right front
Work as given for left front.

Right yoke and sleeve
Using size K hook, chain 32[34:36] for back yoke. Work base row and patt row as for back. 31[33:35]sc.
Cont in patt until work measures 4[4:4¼]in from beg, ending at neck edge. Fasten off.
Using size K hook, chain 26[28:30] for right front yoke. Work base row and patt row as for back, then cont in patt until work is 1 row longer than back yoke, so ending at neck edge. Do not turn work but make 6ch, then patt across back yoke. 62[66:70]sc. Cont in patt on these 62[66:70]sc until yoke fits along top edge of front; mark the ends of last

row to denote end of yoke.
Shape for sleeve
Dec 1sc at each end of next row by working 2sc together.
Work 3 rows straight.
Rep last 4 rows 11 times.
38[42:46]sts rem. Cont without shaping until sleeve measures 18[19:20]in. Fasten off.

Left yoke and sleeve
Using size K hook chain 26[28:30] for left front yoke. Work base row as back then cont in patt for 4in. Fasten off. Using size K hook chain 32[34:36] for back yoke. Work base row and patt row as for back, then cont in patt until work is 1 row longer than front, so ending at neck edge. Do not turn work but make 6ch, then patt across front yoke. Cont in patt on these 62[66:70]sc to match right yoke and sleeve.

To finish
With WS of back yokes together and working through double thickness, work 1sc into each sc to end (seam edge will be on RS). Working sc on the RS of work join back and fronts to lower edge of yoke, between markers, then join side and sleeve seams in the same way.

Cuffs
Using size H hook chain 6, 1 sc into 2nd ch from hook, 1 sc into each ch to end. Turn.
Next row 1ch, working into the back loop only, inc as foll: work 1sc into first sc, 1sc into each sc to within last sc, 2sc into last sc. Turn. 7sc. Rep last row once. 9sc.
Cont in patt, without shaping, work

28[30:32] rows. Do not turn work but work 28[30:32]sc along the long edge, omitting shaped section. Fasten off.
Join cuff to sleeve by working 28[30:32] sc along lower edge of sleeve, then with WS facing join cuff to sleeve with sc, so that seam is on WS of work.

Collar
Using size K hook and with WS facing work 36[39:41]sc around neck edge, turn and work in patt for 7 rows.
Next row Work to end increasing 12sc evenly across this row. 47[50:52]sc. Cont without shaping, work 8 rows. Fasten off.

Waistband
Using size H hook chain 14.
Base row 1sc into 2nd ch from hook, 1sc into each ch to end. Turn. Cont in patt as for back work 98[102:106] rows. Dec 1sc at each end of next 4 rows by working 2sc tog. Fasten off. With RS facing join yarn to top right-hand corner and working along long edge work 98[102:106]sc, omitting shaped section at end. Fasten off. Join waistband to jacket on WS of work as for cuffs.

Edging
Using size H hook work a row of sc very firmly along edge of each front. Sew in zipper and press.

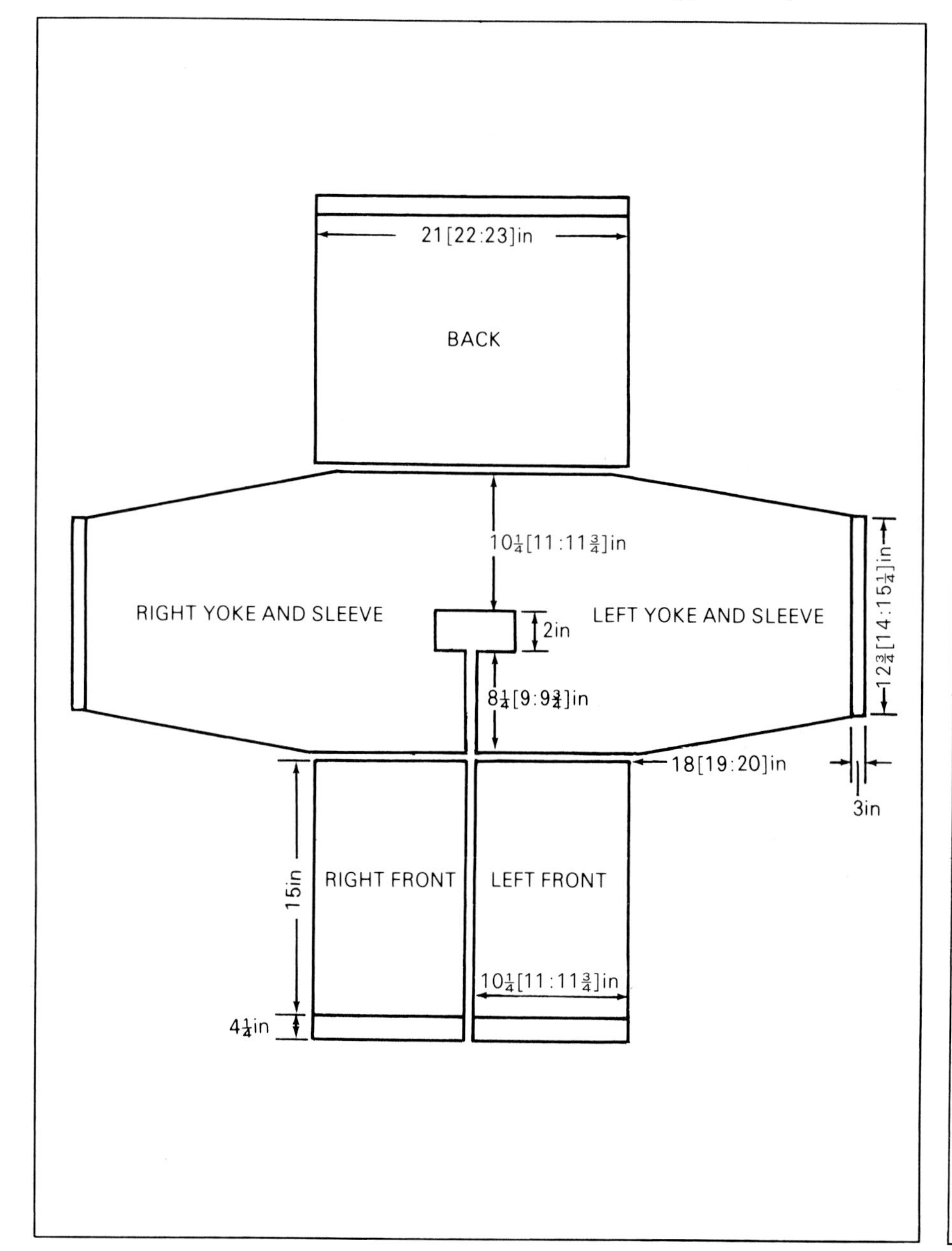

Technique tip

Joining the back yoke
The back yoke is worked in two pieces and should be joined so that the seam is not obvious. To do this you work the seam on the right side of the fabric, so forming a ridge which will blend in with the pattern of the jacket.
Place the wrong sides of both pieces together with the edges to be joined level. Insert the crochet hook into the first loop at right-hand edge of both pieces. Wind yarn around hook and draw a loop through, then work 1 chain.

Insert hook into next loop on first piece and corresponding loop on second piece and work 1 single crochet so joining the pieces.

Continue in this way all along the row. Fasten off. When the yoke is laid flat you will see the seam blends with the pattern.

ARAN SWEATERS

Sizes
To fit 28[30:32:34:36:38:40]in chest.
Length, 18[$19\frac{3}{4}$:21:$22\frac{1}{2}$:$23\frac{3}{4}$:25:26]in.
Sleeve seam, 14[16:17:$17\frac{3}{4}$:18:$18\frac{1}{2}$:19]in.
Note *Directions for larger sizes are in brackets []; where there is only one set of figures it applies to all sizes.*

Materials
20[22:23:27:29:30:34]oz of a knitting worsted
Sizes F and H crochet hooks

Gauge
14hdc to 4in on size H hook.

Back
Using size F hook make 55[59:63:67:71:75:79]ch.
Base row (RS) 1dc into 4th ch from hook, 1dc into each ch to end. Turn. 53[57:61:65:69:73:77]sts.
1st ribbing row 3ch to count as first dc, *insert hook from back of work around stem of next dc, yo and draw a loop through, complete as for a dc – called raised dc at back or RDB – insert hook from front of work around stem of next dc, yo and draw a loop through, complete as for a dc – called raised dc at front or RDF – rep from * to last 2sts, RDB around next dc, 1dc into turning ch. Turn.
2nd ribbing row 3ch. *RDF around next dc, RDB around next dc, rep from * to last 2sts, RDF around next dc, 1dc into turning ch. Turn. Rep these 2 rows until work measures $1\frac{1}{2}$[$1\frac{1}{2}$:2:2:2:$2\frac{1}{4}$:$2\frac{1}{4}$]in from beg; end with first row ** . Change to size H hook. Beg patt.
1st row 2ch to count as first hdc, 1hdc into each st to end. Turn. Cont in hdc until work measures 11[$12\frac{1}{4}$:13:$13\frac{3}{4}$:$14\frac{1}{4}$:15:$15\frac{1}{4}$]in from beg; end with WS row.
Shape armholes
Next row Sl st over first 3sts, patt to last 2sts, turn. Rep last row once. Dec one st at each end of next and foll 1[1:2:2:3:3:4] rows. 41[45:47:51:53:57:59]sts. Cont straight until armholes measure 7[$7\frac{1}{2}$:8:$8\frac{3}{4}$:$9\frac{1}{2}$:10:$10\frac{3}{4}$]in, end with WS row.
Shape shoulders
Next row Sl st over next 4[5:5:5:6:6:6]sts, patt to last 3[4:4:4:5:5:5]sts, turn. Rep last row once.
Next row Sl st over first 5[4:5:6:5:6:7]sts, patt to last 4[3:4:5:4:5:6]sts, turn. 21[23:23:25:25:27:27]sts rem for neck. Fasten off.

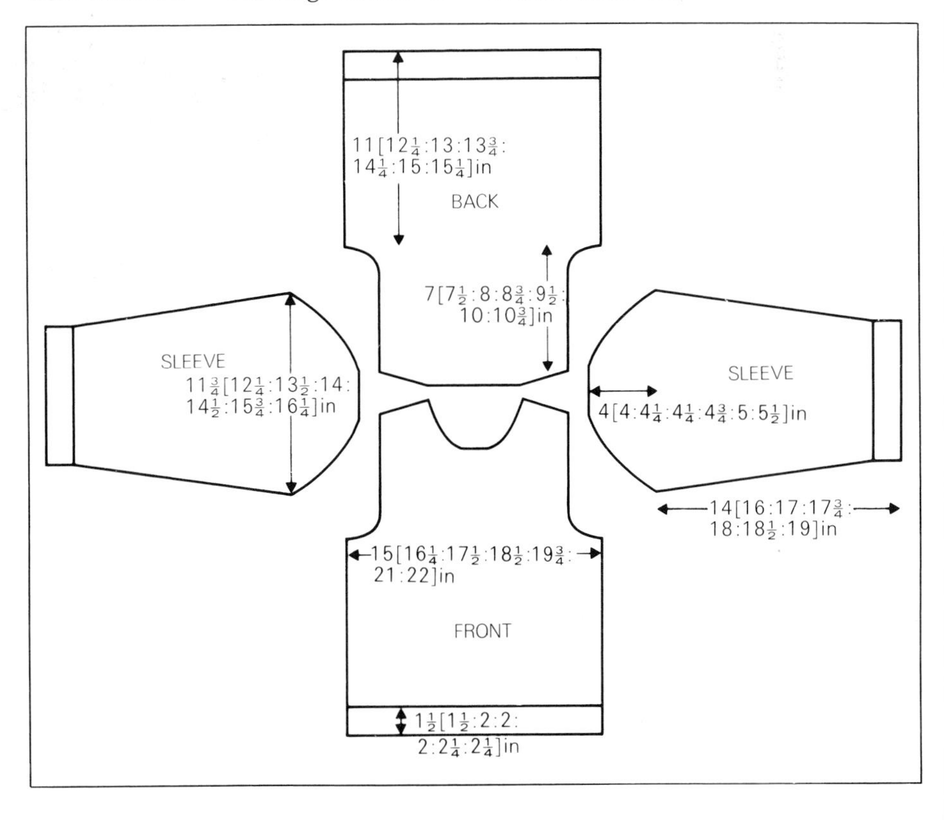

Front
Work as for back to **. Change to size H hook. Beg patt.
1st row 2ch, 1hdc into each of next 16[18:19:21:23:24:26]sts, RDF around each of next 4sts, 1hdc into each of next 11[11:13:13:13:15:15]sts, RDF around each of next 4sts, 1hdc into each of next 17[19:20:22:24:25:27]sts. Turn.
2nd row 2ch, 1hdc into each of next 15[17:18:20:22:23:25]sts, RDB around each of next 4sts, 1hdc into each of next 13[13:15:15:15:17:17]sts RDB around next 4sts, 1hdc into each st to end. Turn.
3rd row 2ch, 1hdc into each of next 14[16:17:19:21:22:24]sts, RDF around each of next 4sts, 1hdc into each of next 7[7:8:8:8:9:9]sts, (yo, insert hook into next st, yo and draw a loop through) 4 times into same st, yo and draw through all 9 loops on hook – called make bobble or MB – 1hdc into each of next

Technique tip

Working surface crochet

Surface crochet is, as the name suggests, worked onto the surface of the finished fabric. It is often used on Aran designs as you can produce a clear, three-dimensional effect. It has been used to outline the groups of bobbles on these sweaters, the first row forming a diamond pattern and the second row outlining the diamonds.

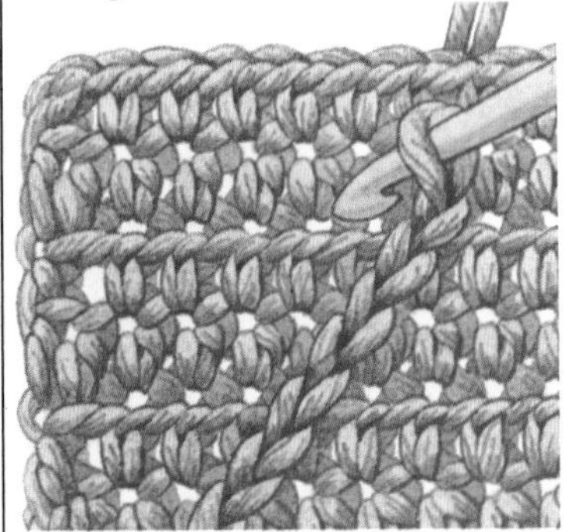

The way the yarn is held determines the direction in which the stitches will slope. To work the stitches sloping to the right, with the right side of the work toward you join yarn to lower edge of fabric with a slip stitch. Always keeping the yarn at the front of the work and to the right of the stitch to be worked, insert hook from front to back and under bar at top of stitch, then through fabric from back to front, yarn over hook and draw a loop through, yarn over hook and draw a loop through both loops on hook – so forming a single crochet. Continue to work single crochet in this way, moving stitches two stitches to the right on every row.

To work the stitches sloping to the left, work as for sloping stitches to the right, but keep yarn at left of the stitches to be worked and move the single crochet two stitches to the left on every row.

7[7:8:8:8:9:9]sts, RDF around each of next 4sts, 1hdc into each st to end. Turn.
4th row 2ch, 1hdc into each of next 13[15:16:18:20:21:23]sts, RDB around each of next 4sts, 1hdc into each of next 17[17:19:19:19:21:21]sts, RDB around next 4sts, 1 hdc into each st to end. Turn.
5th row 2ch, 1hdc into each of next 12[14:15:17:19:20:22]sts, RDF around each of next 4sts, 1hdc into each of next 6[6:7:7:7:8:8]sts. MB, 1hdc into each of next 5sts, MB, 1hdc into each of next 6[6:7:7:7:8:8]sts, RDF around each of next 4sts, 1hdc into each st to end. Turn.
6th row As 4th.
7th row As 3rd.
8th row As 2nd.
Rep these 8 rows until work is as long as back to underarm; end with WS row.

Shape armholes
Work as for back armhole shaping until 41[45:47:51:53:57:59]sts rem. Cont straight until armholes measure 4¾[5:5½:6:6¼:6¾:7]in from beg; end with WS row.

Shape neck
Next row Patt over first 15[17:18:19:20:22:23]sts, turn.
Next row Sl st over first 3sts, patt to end. Turn. ***Dec one st at neck edge on next 3[4:4:4:5:5:5] rows. 10[11:12:13:14:15:16]sts. Cont straight until armhole measures same as back to shoulder; end at armhole edge.

Shape shoulder
Next row Sl st over first 4[5:5:5:6:6:6]sts, patt to end. Turn.
Next row Patt to last 3[4:4:4:5:5:5]sts, turn. 4[3:4:5:4:5:6]sts rem.
Fasten off. Skip center 11[11:11:13:13:13:13]sts, rejoin yarn and patt to end.
Next row Patt to last 2sts, turn. Finish as for first side from *** to end.

Sleeves
Using size F hook make 23[25:25:27:29:31:31]ch. Work as for back to ** 21[23:23:25:27:29:29]sts. Change to size H hook. Work 2 rows hdc.
3rd row 2ch, 1hdc into edge st at base of ch, 1hdc into each of next 9[10:10:11:12:13:13]sts, MB, 1hdc into each st to last st, 2hdc into last st. Turn.
4th row 1hdc into each st to end. Turn.
5th row 2ch, 1hdc into each of next 7[8:8:9:10:11:11]sts, MB, 1hdc into each of next 5sts, MB, 1hdc into each st to end. Turn.
6th row 2ch, 1hdc into st at base of ch, 1hdc into each st to last st, 2hdc into last st. Turn.
7th row 2ch, 1hdc into each of next 11[12:12:13:14:15:15]sts, MB, 1hdc into each st to end. Turn.
8th row 2ch, 1hdc into each st to end. Turn. Cont in patt as set, working bobbles in center, inc one st at each end of next and every foll 3rd row until there are 41[43:47:49.51:55:57]sts. Cont straight until sleeve measures 14[16:17:17¾:18:18½:19]in from beg; end with WS row.

Shape top
Dec one st at each end of next 7[7:8:8:8:9:10] rows, then 2sts at each end of foll 4[4:4:4:5:5:5] rows. 11[13:15:17:15:17:19]sts rem. Fasten off.

Neckband
Join right shoulders. With size F hook and RS facing, work 12[13:13:14:14:15:15]sc down left front neck, 11[11:11:13:13:13:13]sc across front neck 13[14:14:15:15:16:16]sc up right front neck and 21[23:23:25:25:27:27]sc across back, 1 row in dc. Rep 2 ribbing rows as for waistband until neckband measures ¾[¾:1:1:1:1½:1½]in. Fasten off.

To finish
Surface crochet Outline bobble panels, using yarn double. Beg at 1st patt row on front and sleeves, join yarn to st under first bobble and work zig-zag lines, moving 2sts to left and right to enclose 4 bobbles in diamond shape. Lines cross on a 1st patt row immediately above and below 2 single bobbles. For man's sweater, outline each side of diamond shapes – with 2 background sts between – with separate zig-zag line. Join left shoulder and neckband seam. Set in sleeves. Join side and sleeve seams. Press seams.

DIAMOND DUO

Sizes
To fit 26–28[38–40]in chest.
Length, 18½[28]in.
Sleeve seam, 14½[20]in.
Note *Directions for larger size are in brackets []; where there is only one set of figures it applies to both sizes.*

Materials
Knitting worsted:
19[36] × 1oz balls in main color A
4 balls in contrasting color B
4[6] balls in contrasting color C
3[4] balls in contrasting color D
2[3] balls in contrasting color E
Size F crochet hook

Gauge
20sts and 24 rows to 4in in seed st worked with size F hook.

Double crochet diamonds
Using size F hook and D, make 2ch, work 1sc into 2nd ch from hook. Turn.
1st row 1ch, 2sc into the 1sc. Turn.
2nd row 1ch, 2sc into each of the 2sc. Turn.
3rd row 1ch, 1sc into each of the 4sc. Turn.
4th row 1ch, 2sc into first sc, 1sc into each of next 2sc, 2sc into last sc. Turn. 6sc.
5th row 1ch, 1sc into each sc to end. Turn.
6th row 1ch, 2sc into first sc, 1sc into each sc to within last sc, 2sc into last sc. Turn. 8sc.
7th row As 5th.
Cont in this way, inc one st at each end of every alternate row until diamond measures 4[5½]in across; end with straight row.
Next row 1ch, leaving loop of each on hook, work 1sc into each of next 2sc, yo and draw a loop through all loops on hook – 1sc dec –, 1sc into each sc to within last 2sc, dec 1sc. Turn.
Next row 1ch, 1sc into each sc to end. Turn.
Rep last 2 rows until 2sts rem. Work 2 tog. Fasten off. Make 7 more diamonds.

Bobble diamonds
Using size F hook and C make 2ch, 1sc into 2nd ch from hook. Turn.
1st row 1ch, 3sc into the 1sc. Turn.
2nd row 1ch, sl st into first sc, yo, insert hook into next st, yo and draw loop through, yo and draw loop through first loop on hook, yo, insert hook into same st, yo and draw loop through, yo and draw loop through 4 loops on hook, yo and draw through rem 2 loops –

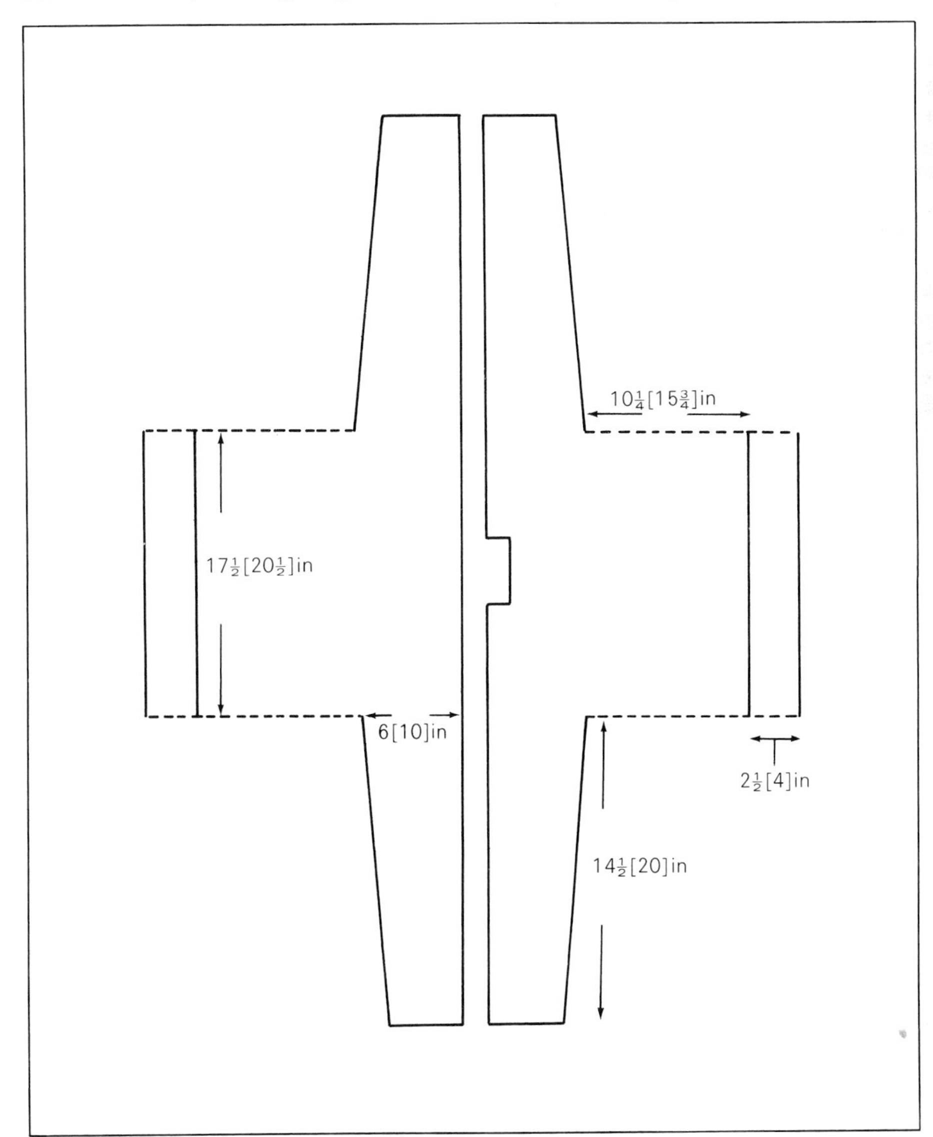

bobbles made or MB –, sl st into last sc. Turn.
3rd row 1ch, 2sc into first sl st, 1sc into bobble, 2sc into last sl st. Turn.
4th row 1ch, sl st into first sc, MB into next sc, sl st into next sc, MB into next sc, sl st into last sc. Turn.
5th row 1ch, 2sc into first sl st, (1sc into next bobble, 1sc into next sl st) to within last sl st, 2sc into last sl st. Turn.
6th row 1ch, sl st into first sc, (MB into next sc, sl st into next sc) to within last sc, sl st into last sc. Turn.
Rep last 2 rows until diamond measures 4[5½]in across; end with a bobble row.
Next row 1ch, dec 1sc, 1sc into each st to within last 2sts, dec 1sc. Turn.
Next row 1ch, sl st into first sc, (MB into next sc, sl st into next sc) to within last sc, sl st into last sc. Turn.
Rep last 2 rows until 3sts rem. Work 1 row bobbles, then work the 3sts tog. Fasten off. Make 7 more diamonds.

Half double diamonds
Using size F hook and B make 3ch, work 1hdc into 3rd ch from hook. Turn.
1st row 2ch, 1hdc into first hdc, 2hdc into top of turning ch. Turn.
2nd row 2ch, 1hdc into first hdc, 1hdc into each st to end, 1hdc into top of ch. Turn.
3rd row As 2nd.
4th row 2ch, 1hdc into first hdc, 1hdc into each st to end, 2 hdc into top of ch. Turn. Rep last 3 rows until work measures 4[5½]in across.
1st dec row 2ch, skip first hdc, leaving last loop of each on hook work 1hdc into each of next 2sts, yo and draw through all loops on hook – 1hdc dec –, 1hdc into each st to end. Turn.
2nd dec row As 1st dec row.
3rd dec row 2ch, skip first hdc, dec 1hdc, work to within last 3sts, dec 1hdc, 1hdc into top of 2ch. Turn.
Rep last 3 rows until 3sts rem, work 3 tog. Fasten off. Make 7 more diamonds.

Half diamond
Using size F hook and A, make 3ch.
1st row 1sc into 2nd ch from hook, 1sc into next ch. Turn.
2nd row 2ch, sl st into first sc, 1hdc into next sc, sl st into same sc. Turn. 4sts.
3rd row 2ch, skip first sl st, sl st into next hdc, 1hdc into next sl st, sl st into top of 2ch. Turn.
4th row 1ch, sl st into first sl st, 1hdc into same sl st, sl st into next hdc, 1hdc into next sl st, sl st and 1hdc into top of 2ch. Turn.
5th row 1ch, sl st into first hdc, 1hdc into next sl st, sl st into next hdc, 1hdc into next sl st, sl st into next hdc, 1 hdc into next sl st. Turn.
6th row 2ch, sl st into first hdc, (1hdc into next sl st, sl st into next hdc) to last sl st, 1hdc and sl st into last sl st. Turn.
7th row 2ch, skip first sl st, (sl st into next hdc, 1hdc, into next sl st) to last 2ch, sl st into top of 2ch. Turn.
8th row 1ch, sl st into first sl st, 1hdc into same sl st, (sl st into next hdc, 1hdc into next sl st) to last 2ch, sl st and 1hdc into top of 2ch. Turn.
9th row 1ch, sl st into first hdc, (1hdc into next sl st, sl st into next hdc) to last sl st, 1hdc into last sl st. Turn. Rep rows 6 to 9 inclusive until there are 19[25]sts and work measures 4[5½]in across. Fasten off. Make 7 more half diamonds in A, then work 8 half diamonds in E.

Sleeves and yoke sections
Back
Using size F hook and A, make 6ch, then starting at center of one half diamond in A work 1hdc into each sl st and sl st into each hdc to end of diamond, then work across 3 more half diamonds in A, now work to center of one more half diamond, 6ch. Fasten off.
Next row Make 6ch, then working in patt, work into the first 6ch of last row, work across top of diamonds, then work into the last 6ch of last row, 6ch. Fasten off.
Rep last row 11[15] times. 224[296]sts. Cont in patt until work measures 6[10]in from top of half diamonds.
Shape shoulders
Next row Fasten off. Skip the first 28[32]sts, rejoin yarn to next st and patt to within last 28[32]sts, turn. Rep last row 3 times. 32[38]sts rem for back neck. Fasten off.

Front
Rejoin A to other half of diamond

at underarm and work as for back to within 10[12] rows of completion of sleeve.
Shape neck Work across first 112[128]sts, turn. Work 9[11] rows on these sts.
Shape shoulder
Next row Fasten off. Skip first 28[32]sts, rejoin yarn to next st, work to end. Turn.
Next row Work to within last 28[32]sts, turn.
Next row Fasten off. Skip first 28[32]sts, work to end. Fasten off.
Skip center 32[38]sts for center front neck, rejoin yarn to next st and work to end. Turn.
Now work straight until sleeve measures same as first sleeve, ending at neck edge.
Shape shoulder
Next row Work to within last 28[32]sts, turn.
Next row Fasten off. Skip first 28[32]sts, work to end. Turn.
Next row Work to within last 28[32]sts. Fasten off.

Waistband
Using size F hook and A, make 17[21]ch.
Base row 1sc into 2nd ch from hook, 1sc into each ch to end. Turn.
Patt row 1ch, working into the *back* loop only of each st, work 1sc into each st to end. Turn. Rep last row until waistband measures 26[30]in, without stretching. Fasten off.

Cuffs
Using size F hook and A, make 15[17]ch and work base row as for waistband, then work patt row until cuff measures 6[8]in. Fasten off.

Collar
Using size F hook and A, make 31[41]ch and work base row as for waistband, then work patt row for 15[20]in. Fasten off.

To finish
Sew all diamonds tog, as shown in chart. Join upper sleeve and shoulder seams, then join underarm seams. Join short edges of collar. Seam collar to neck on outside. Turn back collar. Join short edges of cuffs, then sew cuffs to sleeves. Join short edges of waistband and sew to lower edge.
Press lightly with warm iron over damp cloth.

SMOKING JACKET

Sizes
To fit 38[40:42]in chest.
Length, $26\frac{3}{4}$[$26\frac{3}{4}$:28]in.
Sleeve, $18\frac{1}{2}$[19:19]in.
Note *Directions for larger sizes are in brackets []; where there is only one set of figures it applies to all sizes.*

Materials
40[42:43]oz of a knitting worsted
Size H crochet hook
2 buttons

Gauge
17sts and 20 rows to 4in on size H hook.

Back
Using size H hook make 85[89:93]ch.
Base row 1dc into 4th ch from hook, 1dc into each ch to end. Turn. 83[87:91]sts.
Next row 1ch, skip first dc, 1sc into each dc to end, 1dc into top of the 3ch. Turn. Beg patt.
1st row (RS) 2ch for first sc, *work *around* next sc by working yo, insert hook from front to back between next 2sc, around sc at left and through work from back to front, draw yarn through and complete dc in usual way – called double around front or dc around Ft –, 1sc into next sc, rep from * to end. Turn.
2nd row 1sc into each st to end. Turn. These 2 rows form the patt.*
Cont in patt until work measures $17\frac{3}{4}$[$17\frac{3}{4}$:18]in; end with a WS row.
Shape armholes
Next row Sl st across first 5sts, patt to within last 4sts, turn.
Dec one st at each end of foll 5[4:4] alternate rows. 65[71:75]sts. Cont straight until work measures $26\frac{3}{4}$[$26\frac{3}{4}$:28]in from beg; end with a WS row.
Shape shoulders
Next row Sl st across first 12[12:13]sts, work to within last 11[11:12]sts, turn.
Next row Sl st across first 12[13:15]sts, work to within last 11[12:14]sts. Fasten off.

Pocket linings (make 2)
Using size H hook make 25ch.
Base row 1sc into 3rd ch from hook, 1sc into each ch to end. Turn. 24sts.
Next row 1sc into each st to end. Turn. Rep last row until work measures 6in from beg. Fasten off.

Right front
Using size H hook make 55[59:63]ch. Work as for back for 8in; end with a RS row.
Pocket row 1sc into each of first 9sc, 1sc into each of the 24sc of one pocket lining, skip next 24sc on front, 1sc into each sc to end. Turn. Cont in patt until work measures 32 rows less than back; end with a RS row.
Shape front edge
Next row Work to within last st, turn. Work 3 rows straight. Rep last 4 rows until work measures same as back to armhole; end at side edge.
Shape armhole
Cont to dec at front edge on every 4th row at same time shape armhole as follows:
Next row Sl st across first 5sts, work to end. Turn.
Dec one st at armhole edge on foll 5[4:4]alternate rows. Cont to shape front edge until 34[36:38]sts rem, then on every alternate row until 22[23:26]sts rem. Cont straight until front measures same as back to shoulder; end at armhole edge.
Shape shoulder
Next row Sl st across first 12[12:13]sts, work to end. Fasten off.

Left front
Work as given for right front reversing shaping and placing pocket thus:
Pocket row 1sc into each of first 20[24:28]sc, 1sc into each of the 24sc of pocket lining, skip next 24sc on front, 1sc into each sc to end. Turn. When work measures $10\frac{3}{4}$in make 2 buttonholes on a WS row thus:
Next row 1sc into each of next 2sc, 4ch, skip next 4sc, 1sc into each of next 10sc, 4ch, skip next 4sc, 1sc into each sc to end. Turn.
Next row 1sc into each sc and 4sc into each buttonhole. Turn.

Sleeves
Using size H hook make 55[55:63]ch. Work base row and next row as for back. Cont in patt inc one st at each end of 8th and every foll 6th row until there are 77[77:81]sts. Cont straight until work measures $18\frac{1}{2}$[19:19]in; end with a WS row.
Shape top
Next row Sl st across first 5sts, work to within last 4sts, turn.
Dec one st at each end of every other row until 39[39:43]sts rem. Fasten off.

Collar
Join shoulder seams. Using size H hook make 6ch. Work base row and patt row as for back, then cont in patt inc one st at end of every sc row until there are 34sts. Cont straight until collar fits along front edge from beg of shaping to center back neck. Mark this row, then

work other half of collar to match, dec at beg of every sc row for shaping. Fasten off.

To finish

Press lightly. Set in sleeves. Join side and sleeve seams. Stitch down pocket linings. Placing marker at center back neck, attach collar. Roll back collar and stitch in place. Sew on buttons. Work a row of sc around front edge and pocket tops.

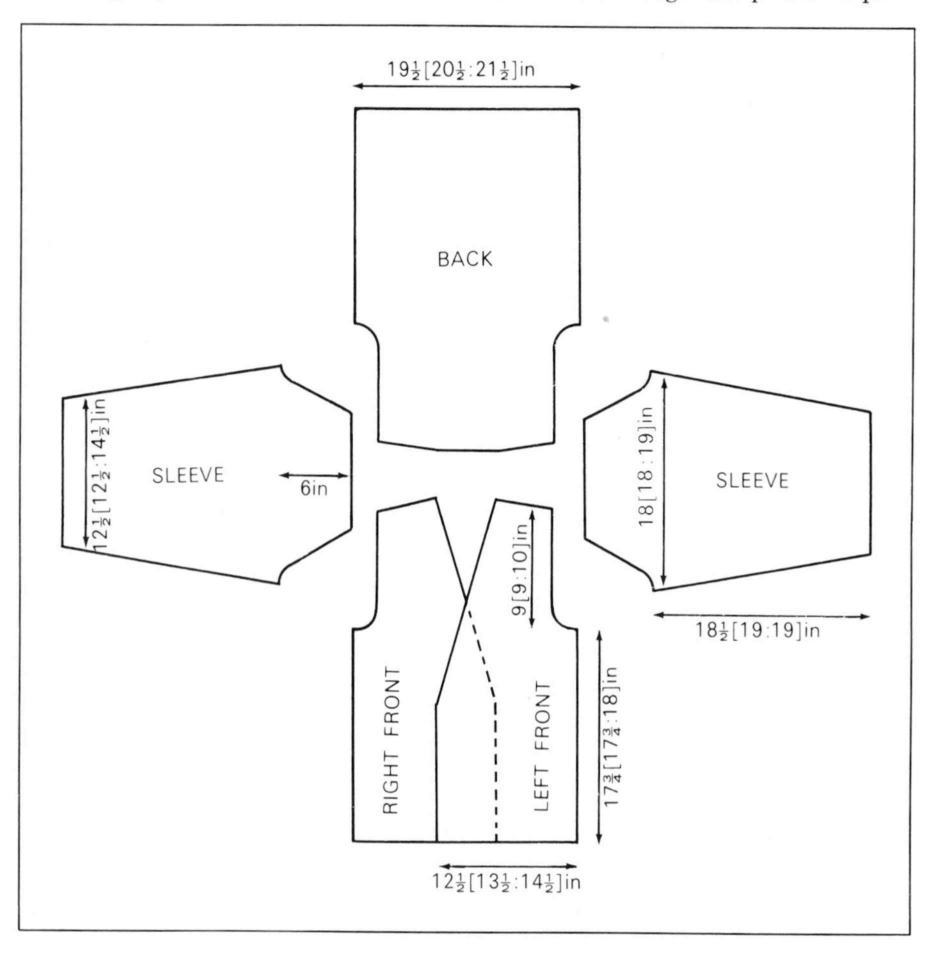

Technique tip

Neatening and reinforcing buttonholes

To give a professional finish to a garment the buttonholes can be finished off with buttonhole stitch. This will also strengthen the buttonhole and keep it in good shape during use.

This sketch shows the buttonhole on the man's jacket before it has been finished with buttonhole stitch.

To work buttonhole stitch, thread a blunt-ended yarn needle with same yarn as garment and join yarn to wrong side of fabric at lower edge of buttonhole. Insert needle through fabric from back to front, then insert needle from front to back through fabric approximately $\frac{3}{16}$in from lower edge of buttonhole, up through buttonhole making sure that yarn is under the needle point. Pull up the stitch to form a loop. Continue to corner of buttonhole. Work 3 straight stitches. Continue to work in buttonhole stitch along top edge of buttonhole, then finish remaining corner with 3 straight stitches. Fasten off thread with two backstitches. This sketch shows the buttonhole finished.

KNITTING
INTRODUCTION

It will probably never be possible to accurately date the origin of knitting, as the clues disappeared centuries ago along with the delicate textile fibers. The complexity of the structure of the earliest known knitted loops, however, strongly indicates that knitting was, more than likely, a fully developed craft before the birth of Christ, and must have taken centuries to reach such a level of sophistication. The myth from an ancient city in Yemen may come close to the truth. It claims that knitting has existed forever and that Eve knitted the pattern on the serpent's back. "Where" knitting originated is just as much a mystery as "when." Although Arabia is often given credit for being its birthplace, this is probably due to the fact that Arabian sailors spread the techniques as they traveled the ancient world. Early examples of knitting have been found as far apart as China and Peru. But no doubt every continent would like to lay claim to the invention of such an intricate and rewarding craft!

Wherever, whenever and however knitting first appeared on the scene, by the sixteenth century it was a fully-fledged industry in Western Europe. Not only widely used to produce everyday garments such as hats and stockings, knitting was also used to create very intricately patterned wall hangings and rugs. The fact that in 1527 a boy apprentice in Paris had to serve six years and pass a 13-week examination before becoming a master knitter, shows how much respect the skill must have commanded. Needless to say, women were excluded from the early textile guilds, but they too practised knitting, both in the home and in nunneries. Also, the tedious production, in later centuries, of fine knitted lace was left largely to women. It is only in very recent history that knitting has become an activity almost exclusively related to women; as late as the early twentieth century knitting was still a tradition among rural fishermen and shepherds in some European countries.

Unfortunately one rarely sees any knitting being produced today that is as fine and richly patterned as the early museum pieces, but recently there has been something of a revival. Let us hope that we will be able to witness the craft being carried even further with more striking use of color and more fascinating designs.

Needles

Knitted fabric has many advantages over woven fabric, one of which is that it can be produced with tools as simple as knitting needles. There are three types of knitting needles in common use today – the familiar needles that have a point at one end and a fixed stopper at the other; the needles that have points at both ends, called "double-pointed;" and the circular needles, which have two stiff points joined by a flexible wire center. They are all available in many sizes and are made of steel, wood or plastic. Both double-pointed needles and circular needles are used for knitting a seamless fabric in a circle or "in the round." Small items such as gloves or socks require the short double-pointed needles, whereas circular needles can hold all the loops of the bodice of a sweater. Actually circular needles can be used for knitting in flat rows as well as in rounds and they have many advantages over ordinary needles: they are easier to carry around because they fold up and will not poke out of your knitting bag; and there are no long ends, so that you can knit with them in confined spaces. Finally, with circular needles the weight of bulkier knitting will rest in your lap and the fabric will not be pulling down the needle points.

Types of knitting

It is amazing that with only two needles and a ball of yarn, innumerable knitting textures can be created. The patterns that follow cover many types of knitting, including openwork or lace stitches, colorwork and the highly embossed knitted fabric produced with bobbles and cables. Although it may appear complicated to the beginner, anyone can learn to knit. The basic techniques described on the following pages will come in handy for the beginner and will serve as a quick reminder to those who have not picked up their needles for a few years.

Reading the knitting patterns

Be sure to read the section in the crochet introduction that gives helpful hints for following pattern directions. Pay particular attention to the explanation of stitch gauge, as brand names of yarns are not given in this book. This means that you will have to check your gauge very carefully before beginning a pattern. But it does give you the advantage of not being restricted to a particular brand and its color range.

If you are in doubt about any knitting terms, refer to the glossary that appears at the back of the book along with a list of knitting abbreviations.

BASIC TECHNIQUES

The knitted fabric is produced by working a series of loops on and off the needles, either in rows using two needles, or in rounds using four needles. Shown here are the basic knitting techniques that you will need to master in order to follow a knitting pattern. If you are a beginner and are attempting to learn to knit from these instructions, use a knitting worsted and a pair of No. 5 needles, as these will be easiest for you to handle.
It is worthwhile collecting needles in several sizes as they come in handy when trying to alter stitch gauge. Also handy are knitting accessories, including stoppers for the ends of double-pointed needles, a row counter, a cable needle and a needle size gauge to measure unmarked needles.

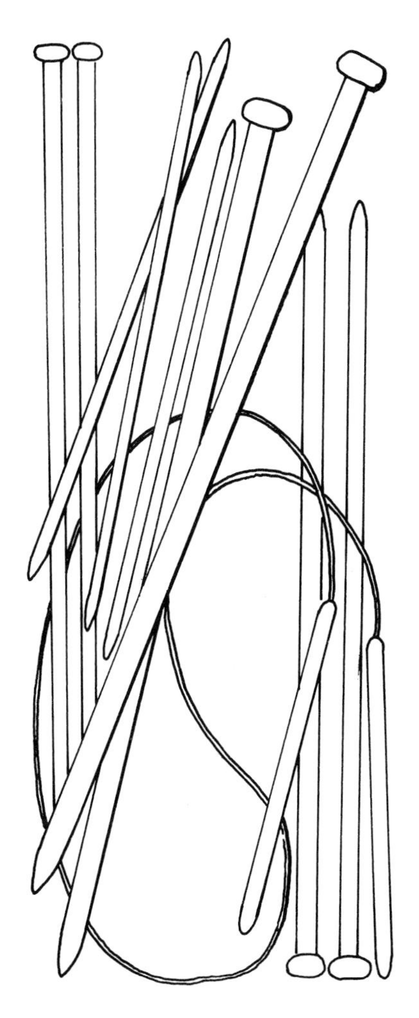

Holding the yarn and the needles

The positions shown below are only suggestions and as you begin to pick up the techniques you may alter these positions to suit you better. In continental Europe the yarn is generally held in the left hand. The point of the right needle then "catches" the yarn instead of the yarn having to be looped around the needle point as it is when it is held in the right hand. The European method is quicker, but it is probably easier to learn with the right-hand method.

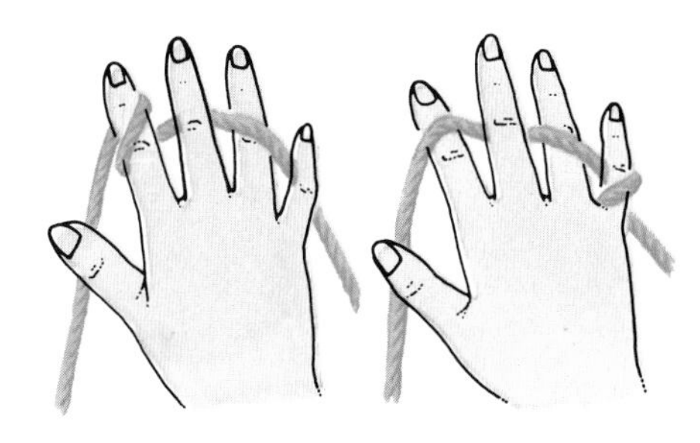

1. Threading the yarn between the fingers helps control both the speed and evenness of the knitting. You should choose a method for holding your yarn that will allow you to release it steadily as you make loops. Some knitters find they prefer a tight hold and others a loose hold. It is not important whether you knit loosely or tightly. What is important is that you feel you have a comfortable control over the flow of yarn so that you can produce even sized loops.

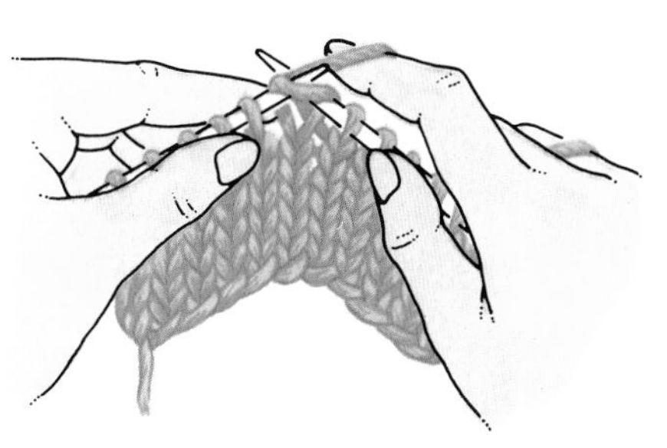

2. The way the needles are held above is popular as it provides a firm, but not rigid, hold with which the needles can be easily manipulated. The needle in the left hand is referred to in the following instructions as the left-hand needle and the needle in the right hand as the right-hand needle.

Single cast on

The first step in knitting is to make a base row of loops on the needle. This is called *casting on.* There are many methods of casting on. Some use two needles and others only one; one of each type is given here. Before beginning to cast on, you will have to make a slip knot on the needle. Step-by-step instructions for this appear in the crochet techniques section of the book.

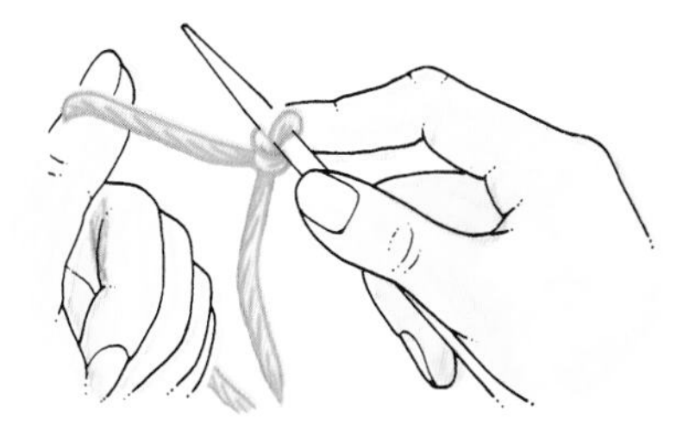

1. Make the slip knot onto the right-hand needle. Then wrap the yarn around the left thumb, as shown, and hold it firmly in the palm of the left hand.

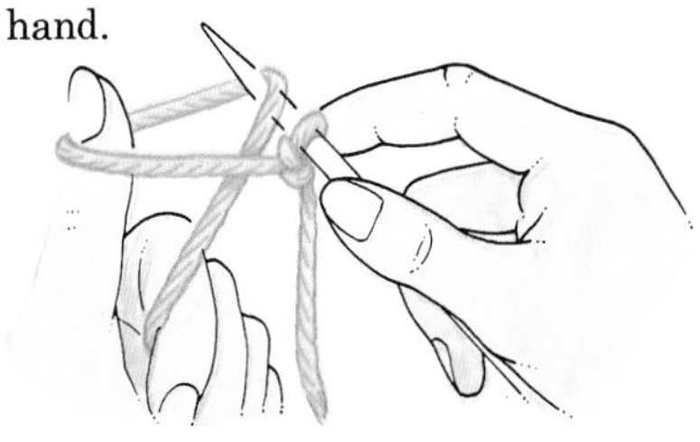

2. Insert the point of the needle from back to front through the loop on the thumb and lift the loop off the thumb.

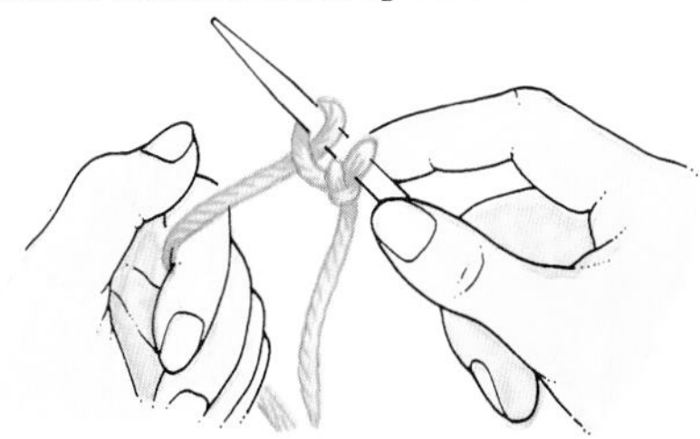

3. Pull the end of the loop to tighten it as you slide it into position next to the slip knot on the needle. This completes the new loop. Continue to cast on as many stitches as required in the same way. Try to keep an even tension for each loop and do not pull them too tightly or the first row will be difficult to knit. Once all of the new loops have been cast on, turn the needle so that the working yarn is at the right. You are now ready to begin the first row.

Cable cast on

The cable cast on produces a reinforced edge that is very elastic.

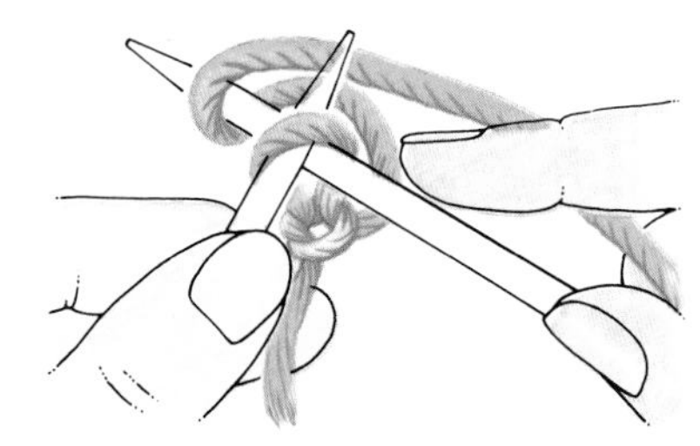

1. With a slip knot on the left-hand needle, insert the right-hand needle from the front to the back through the loop as shown. Then wrap the yarn under and over the point of the right-hand needle.

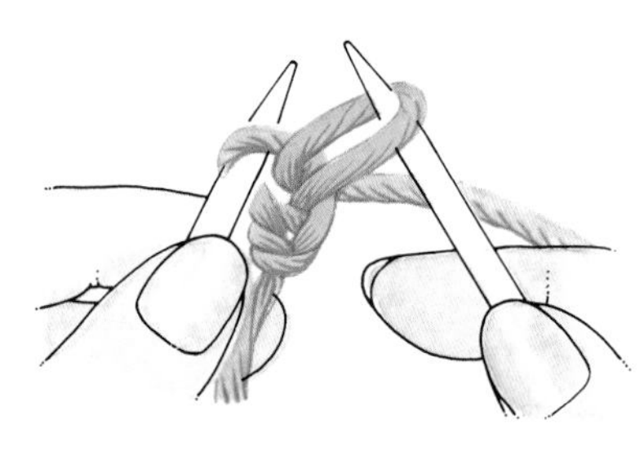

2. Draw the yarn through the loop. Then transfer the new loop from the right-hand to the left-hand needle.

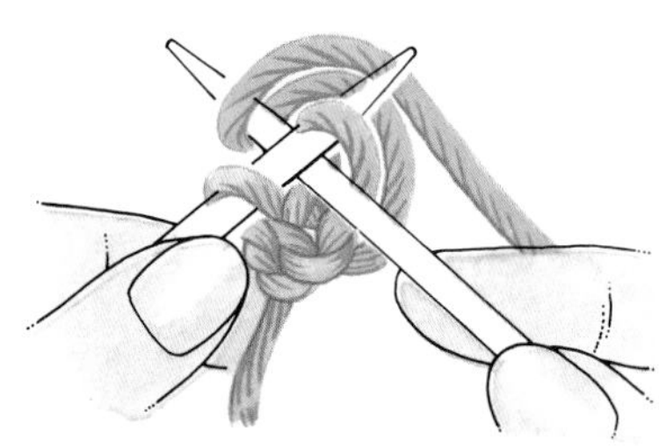

3. Insert the right-hand needle between the two loops and wrap the yarn around the point of the right-hand needle.

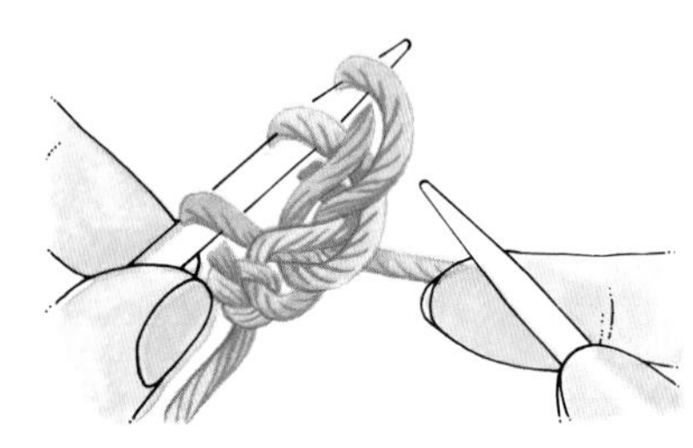

4. Draw the yarn through between the two loops. Place the new loop on the left-hand needle as before. Repeat steps 3 and 4 until you have cast on the required number of stitches.

The knit stitch (K)

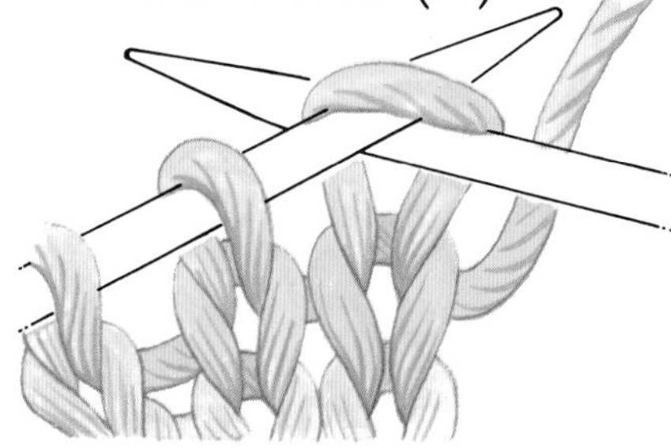

1. With the needle holding the stitches in the left hand, insert the right-hand needle through the first loop from front to back.

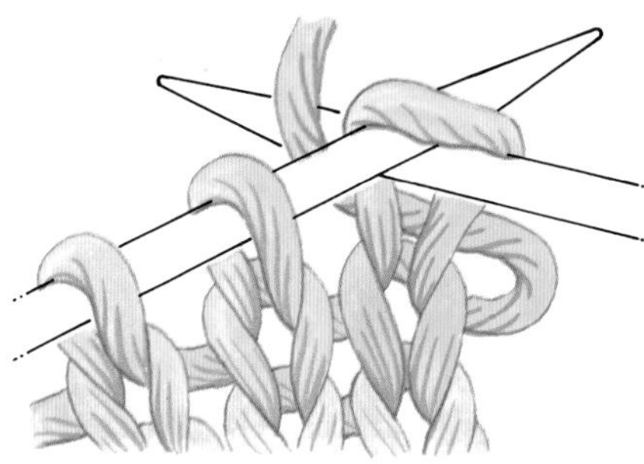

2. Wrap the yarn under and over the point of the right-hand needle.

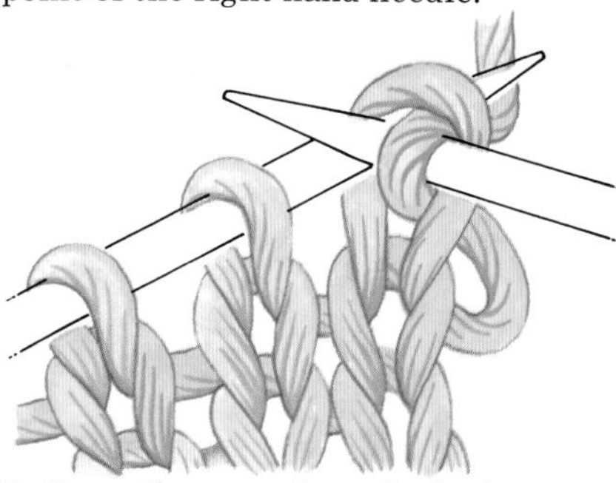

3. Draw the yarn through the loop with the point of the right-hand needle.

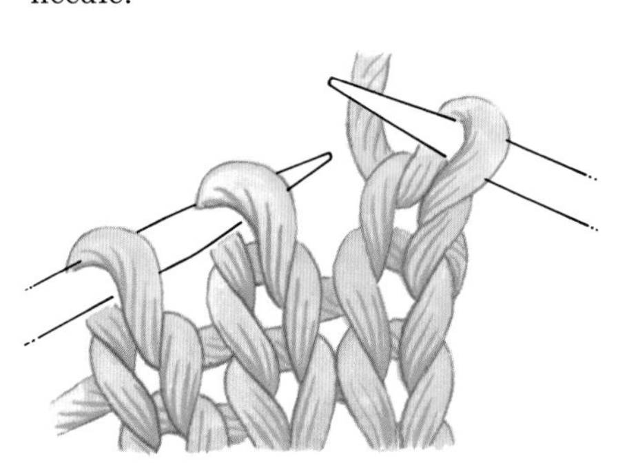

4. Now, with the new loop on the right-hand needle, slip the old loop off the left-hand needle. This completes the first knit stitch. Continue across the row in the same way, making new loops into the stitches on the left-hand needle. At the end of the row, turn the work and transfer the right-hand needle to the left hand to begin the next row.

The purl stitch (P)

1. If you want to create a *stockinette stitch* fabric, you must knit all of the stitches of the first row (the right side) and purl all of the stitches of the second row (the wrong side) and so on. To make a purl stitch, insert the right-hand needle through the loop on the left-hand needle from back to front.

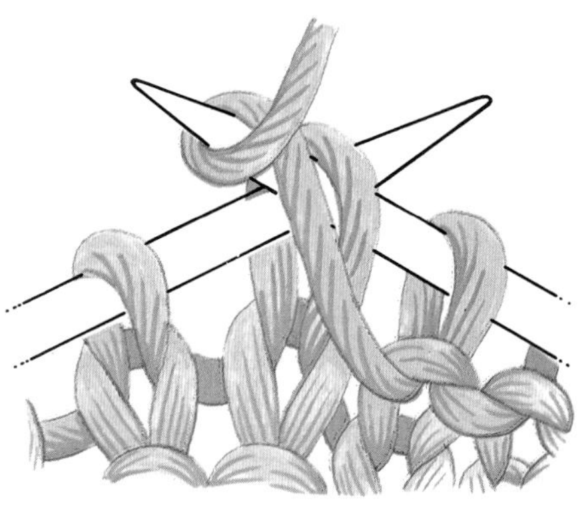

2. Wrap the yarn over and under the point of the right-hand needle.

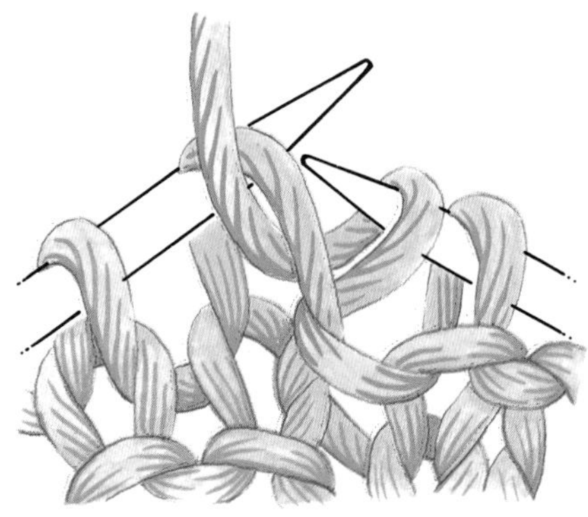

3. Draw the yarn through the loop. With the new loop on the right-hand needle, slip the old loop off the left-hand needle. This completes the purl stitch. Continue across the row making new loops into the stitches in the row below. If you purl (or knit) every row, a *garter stitch* fabric will result. The simple knit and purl stitches are the two basic components of all knitted fabric.

Binding off

When all the required rows of knitting have been completed, you will need to bind off the stitches.

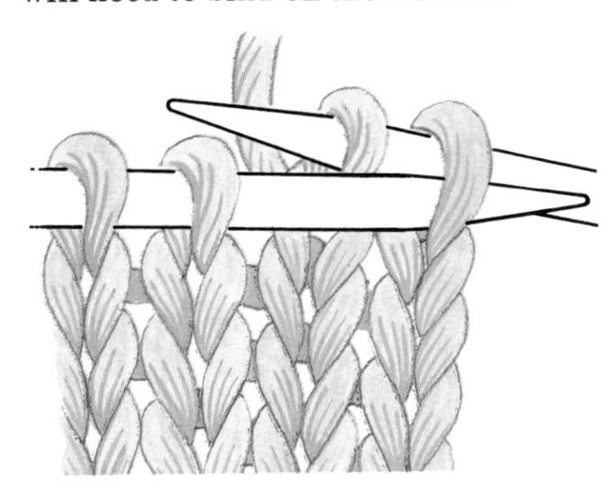

1. Knit the first two stitches in the usual way. Then insert the point of the left-hand needle through the first stitch on the right-hand needle. Lift the first stitch over the second stitch and off the needle. One stitch has now been bound off.

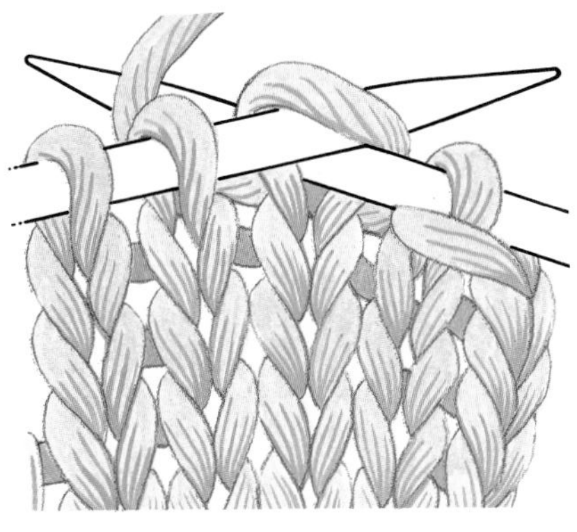

2. Knit the next stitch on the left-hand needle in the usual way. Then again lift the first loop on the right-hand needle over the second and off the needle.

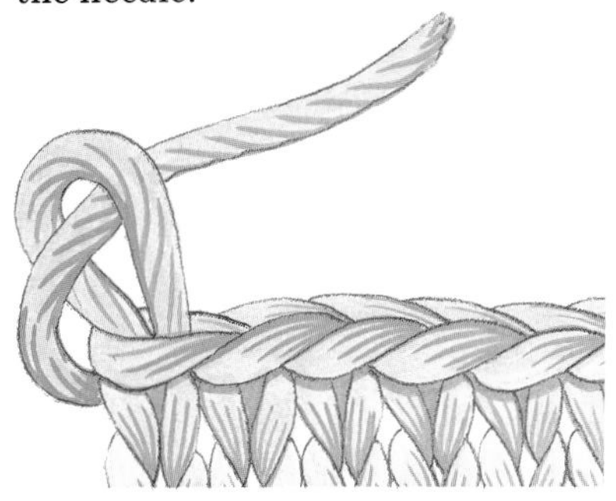

3. Repeat this process across the entire row. Then break off the yarn, draw the yarn end through the last loop and pull to tighten. To bind off purl stitches, purl into each stitch instead of knitting into them. Bind off the stitches, lifting each stitch over the following stitch as above. For ribbing, knit all knit stitches and purl all purl stitches while binding off.

Decreasing

Decreasing is used to shape fabric and, when combined with yarn over increases, to form decorative textures.

Knit 2 stitches together (K2tog)
1. The simplest way to decrease the number of stitches is to work two loops off the needle together. To knit two stitches together, insert the right-hand needle through the second and then the first stitch on the left-hand needle. Wrap the yarn around the point of the right-hand needle.

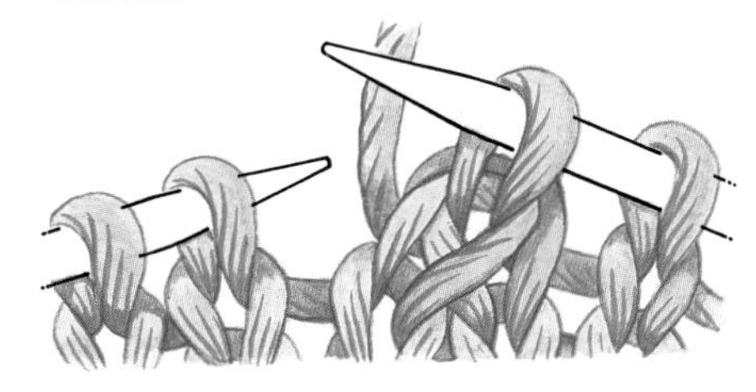

2. Draw a new loop through both stitches at the same time, thus making one new stitch.

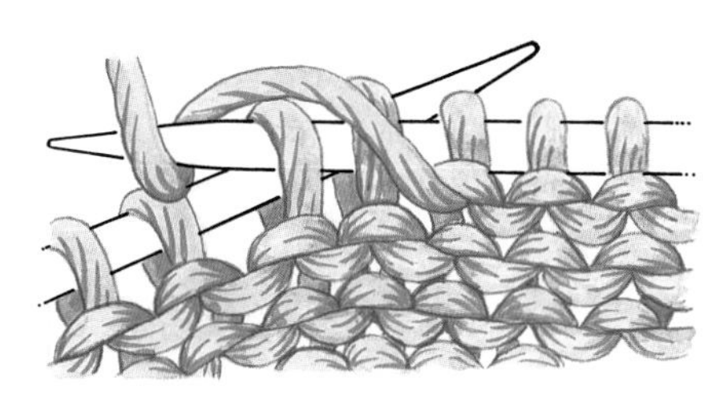

Purl 2 stitches together (P2tog)
1. Purl stitches can be decreased in the same way. First insert the right-hand needle purlwise through the first and then the second stitch on the left-hand needle. Wrap the yarn around the point of the right-hand needle.

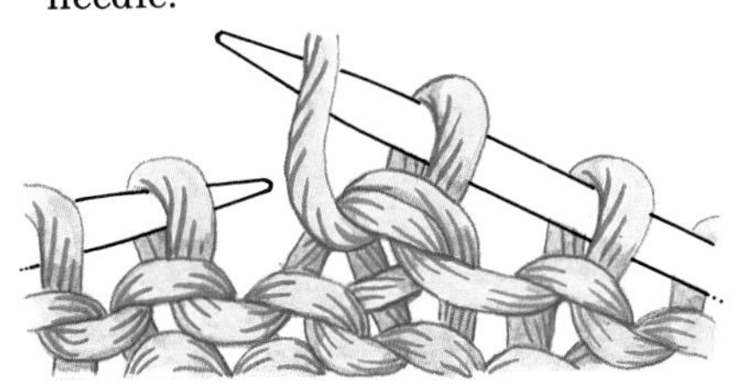

2. Then draw a new loop through both stitches at the same time.

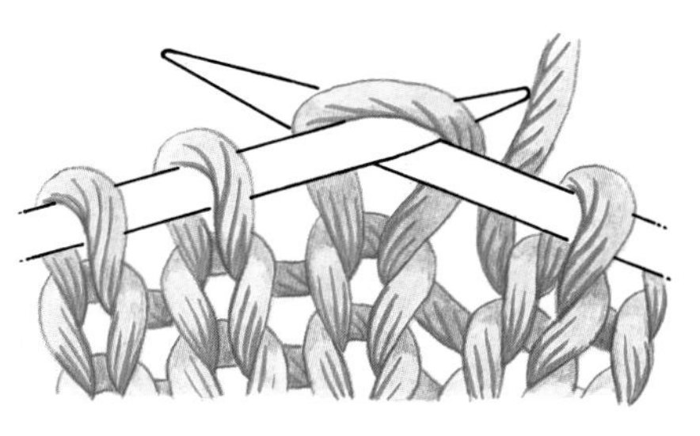

Slip 1, knit 1, pass slipped stitch over (sl 1, K1, psso)
1. Another method of decreasing is similar to binding off. First insert the right-hand needle knitwise into the first stitch on the left-hand needle and slip it onto the right-hand needle without knitting it.

2. Knit the next stitch on the left-hand needle in the usual way. With the point of the left-hand needle, lift the slipped stitch over the stitch just knitted and off the needle.

Twisting stitches

In order to twist stitches, sometimes called for in stitch directions, you must knit through the back loop of the stitch (*K tbl*). First insert the right-hand needle through the back of the next stitch on the left-hand needle as shown above. Then knit the stitch off in the usual way. A purl stitch is twisted in the same way, by purling through the back of the loop instead of the front (*P tbl*).

Increase

Increasing stitches, like decreasing stitches, is used both to shape fabric and form textured patterns. Shaping commonly calls for the simple bar increase given below. Yarn overs (right) are decorative increases which, when matched with decreases, form openwork lace stitches.

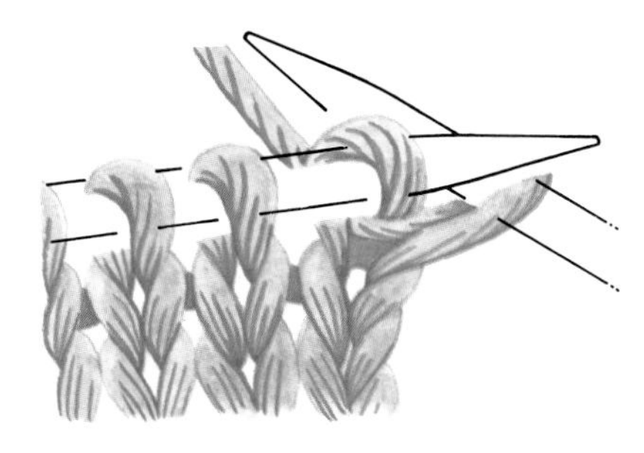

Bar increase (inc 1)
1. For shaping, the bar increase is usually made at the beginning or at the end of a row. Begin by knitting into the first stitch as usual, but without dropping the old loop from the left-hand needle.

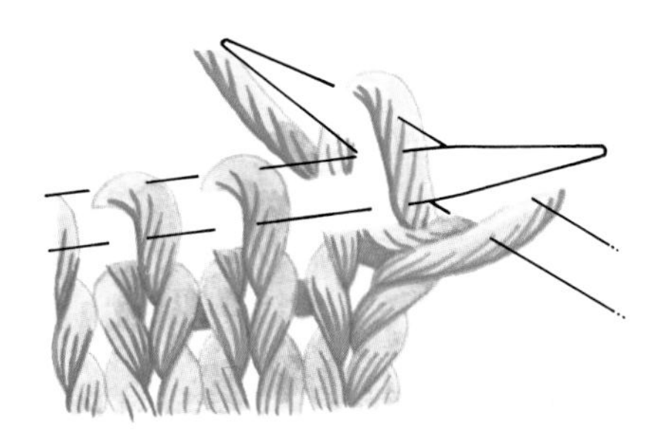

2. Then insert the right-hand needle into the back of the same stitch. Wrap the yarn under and over the point of the right-hand needle.

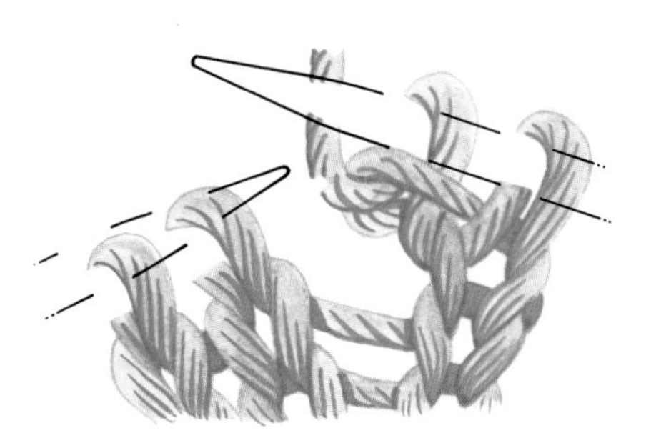

3. Draw the yarn through to form a second loop. Finally slip the old stitch off the left-hand needle. You have now made two stitches out of one. This is also called *"knitting into the front and back of the same stitch."*

Yarn over (yo)
Yarn overs are formed by merely looping the yarn over the right-hand needle to make a new stitch, under which a hole is created.

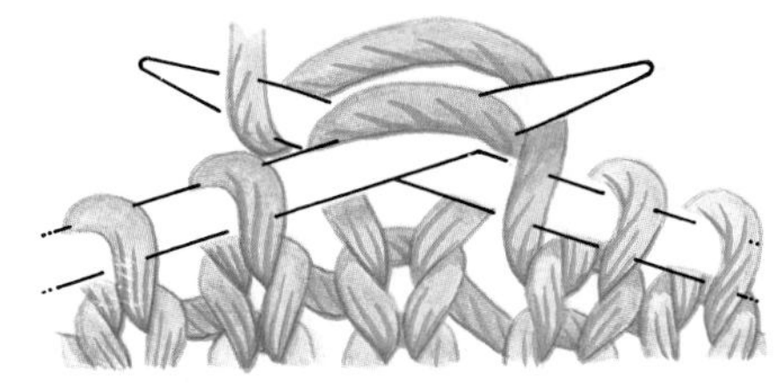

Before a knit stitch
1. To make a yarn over between two knit stitches, bring the yarn to the front of the work between the two needles. Then take the yarn over the top of the right-hand needle and knit the next stitch in the usual way.

2. Before a knit stitch and after a purl stitch, simply take the yarn over the top of the right-hand needle and knit the next stitch in the usual way.

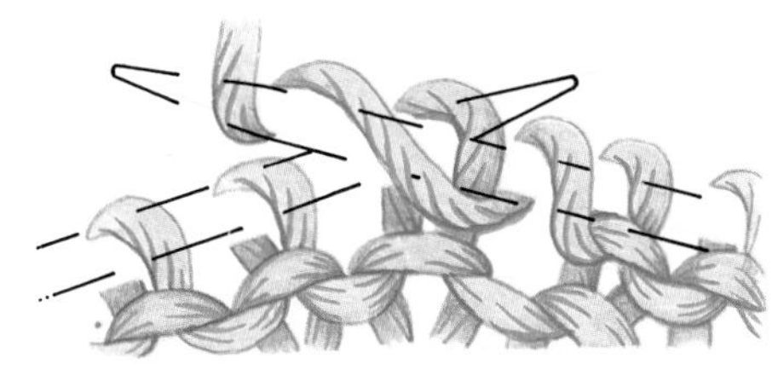

Before a purl stitch
1. Between two purl stitches, take the yarn over and under the right-hand needle and purl the next stitch in the usual way.

2. After a knit stitch, bring the yarn to the front of the work and then over and under the right-hand needle before purling the next stitch.

Picking up stitches along a selvage

When making the borders around edges of the knitted fabric, as for neck or armhole ribbing, you will have to pick up stitches along the selvage. This is called *"pick up and K"* or *"pick up and P"* in the directions. You may be able to do this by picking up just one stitch into each loop which forms a row end along the edge. This is not always possible, however, and it may be necessary to work an extra stitch into every few loops. The main point to remember is that you should pick up stitches evenly along the edge. If you do not, the fabric edge will pucker in some places and stretch out in others. It is best to unravel an unevenly picked up edge and try again until you get it right.

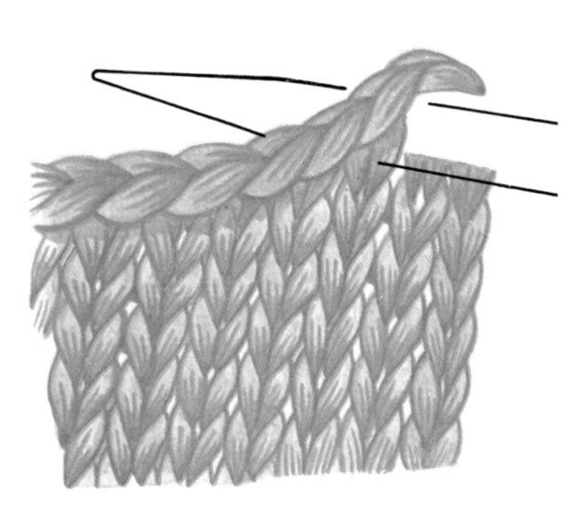

1. To knit up stitches along a selvage, first insert the right-hand needle from *front to back* through the selvage loop.

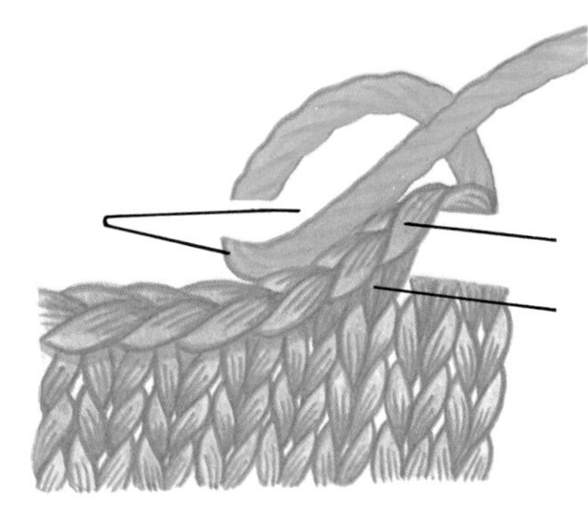

2. Then wrap the yarn around the point of the right-hand needle and draw a knit stitch through it. To pick up and purl a stitch, start by inserting the needle from *back to front* through the selvage and then purl in the usual way.

BABY WARDROBE

Size
To fit a baby from 3 to 6 months.
Gauge
30sts to 4in in patt worked on No. 3 needles.

Leggings
Materials
4oz sport yarn
1 pair each Nos. 2 and 3 knitting needles
Elastic cord

Shirt
Materials
4oz sport yarn
1 pair each Nos. 2 and 3 knitting needles
1¾yd narrow ribbon

Bonnet, bootees and mittens
Materials
2oz sport yarn
1 pair each Nos. 2 and 3 knitting needles
2¼yd of 1in-wide ribbon

Blanket
Materials
15oz sport yarn
1 pair No. 6 knitting needles

Dress
Materials
4oz sport yarn
1 pair each Nos. 1, 2 and 3 knitting needles
3 small buttons

Angel top
Materials
4oz sport yarn
1 pair each Nos. 1, 2 and 3 knitting needles
3 small buttons

Jacket
Materials
4oz sport yarn
1 pair each Nos. 1, 2 and 3 knitting needles
4 small buttons

Leggings

Right leg
**Using No. 2 needles cast on 73sts.
1st row K1, (P1, K1) to end.
2nd row P1, (K1, P1) to end.
Rep these 2 rows 4 times.
Change to No. 3 needles.
Shape back
Next 2 rows Work 16, turn, sl 1, work to end.
Next 2 rows Work 24, turn, sl 1, work to end.
Next 2 rows Work 32, turn, sl 1, work to end.
Cont shaping in this way until the row "work 56, turn, sl 1, work to end" has been worked. Cont in stockinette st but inc one st at each end of 3rd and every following 10th row until there are 81sts in all.
Cont without shaping until work measures 8in from beg, ending with a P row.
Shape leg
Bind off 3sts at beg of next 2 rows, then dec one st at each end of next and every foll 3rd row until 39sts rem.
Cont without shaping until work measures 8in from beg of leg shaping (measured on the straight), ending with a P row.**
Shape instep
1st row K29, K2 tog, turn.
2nd row P13, turn.
Work 28 rows stockinette st on these 13sts for instep, dec one st at end of last row. 12sts.
Cut off yarn. With RS of work facing, pick up and K 14sts along side of instep.
K across instep sts, pick up and K 14sts along other side of instep and K across sts on left-hand needle. 65sts.
Work 15 rows garter st.
Shape foot
1st row K2, K2 tog, K1, K2 tog, K27, K2 tog, K2, K2 tog, K25.
2nd row K to end.
3rd row K1, K2 tog, K1, K2 tog, K25, K2 tog, K2, K2 tog, K24.
4th row K to end.
5th row K28, K2 tog, K2, K2 tog, K23.
6th row K to end. Bind off loosely.

Left leg
Work as given for right leg from ** to ** but reverse shaping by knitting one row before shaping back.
Shape instep
1st row K20, K2 tog, turn.
2nd row P13, turn.
Work 28 rows stockinette st on these 13sts for instep, dec one st at end of last row. 12sts.
Cut off yarn. With RS of work facing, pick up and K 14sts along side of instep. K across instep sts, pick up 14 stockinette st along other side of instep and K across 17sts on left-hand needle, 65sts.
Work 15 rows garter st.
Shape foot
1st row K25, K2 tog, K2, K2 tog, K27, K2 tog, K1, K2 tog, K2.
2nd row K to end.
3rd row K24, K2 tog, K2, K2 tog, K25, K2 tog, K1, K2 tog, K1.
4th row K to end.
5th row K23, K2 tog, K2, K2 tog, K28.
6th row K to end. Bind off loosely.

To finish
Block according to yarn used, pressing lightly. Join front, back and leg seams. Beg at center of toe, join foot seam. With WS of work facing, thread elastic through every K st on first and every other row of ribbing at waist edge.

Shirt
Using No. 3 needles cast on 64sts for lower edge of back.
Work 5 rows garter st.
Beg with a K row, proceed in stockinette st until work measures 6in from beg, ending with a P row.
Inc one st at each end of next and

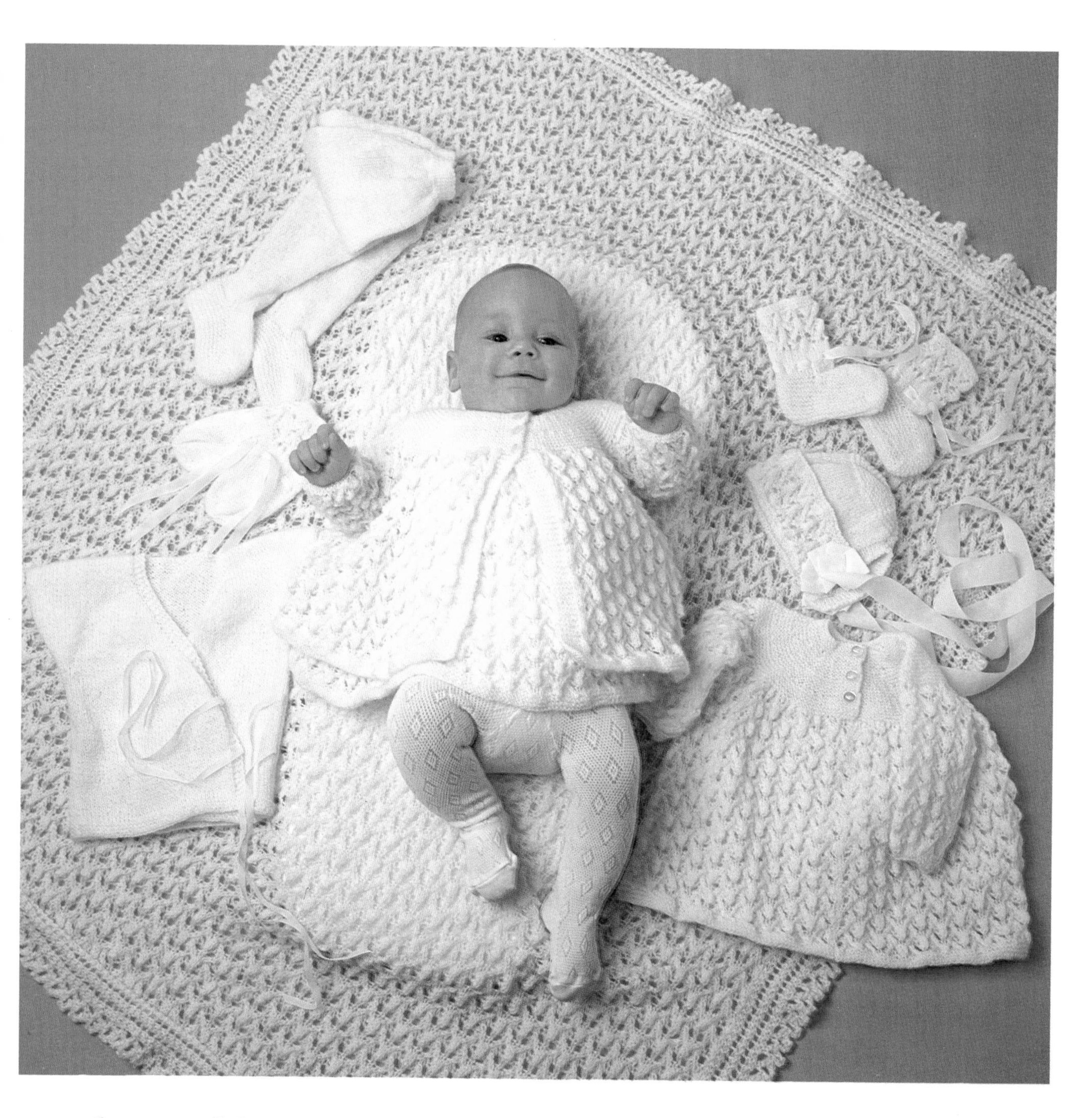

every other row until there are 72sts, ending with a P row.
Shape sleeves
Cast on 10sts at beg of next 2 rows. 92sts.
Next row K to end.
Next row K4, P to last 4sts, K4.
Rep last 2 rows until work measures 10in from beg, ending with a K row.
Next row K4, P29, K26, P29, K4.
Next row K to end.
Rep last 2 rows twice.
Divide for neck
Next row K4, P29, K4, turn and leave rem sts on holder.
Next row K4, inc in next st, K to end.
Next row K4, P to last 4sts, K4.
Cont in this way inc one st at front edge inside border on 11th row, then on every alternate row until sleeve edge measures 7in, ending at side edge. Bind off 10sts at beg of next row for sleeve. Continue to inc at front edge as before, at the same time dec one st at armhole edge on next and every alternate row 4 times in all. Keeping armhole edge straight, continue to inc at front edge until there are 45sts. Continue without shaping, keeping front border correct, until work measures

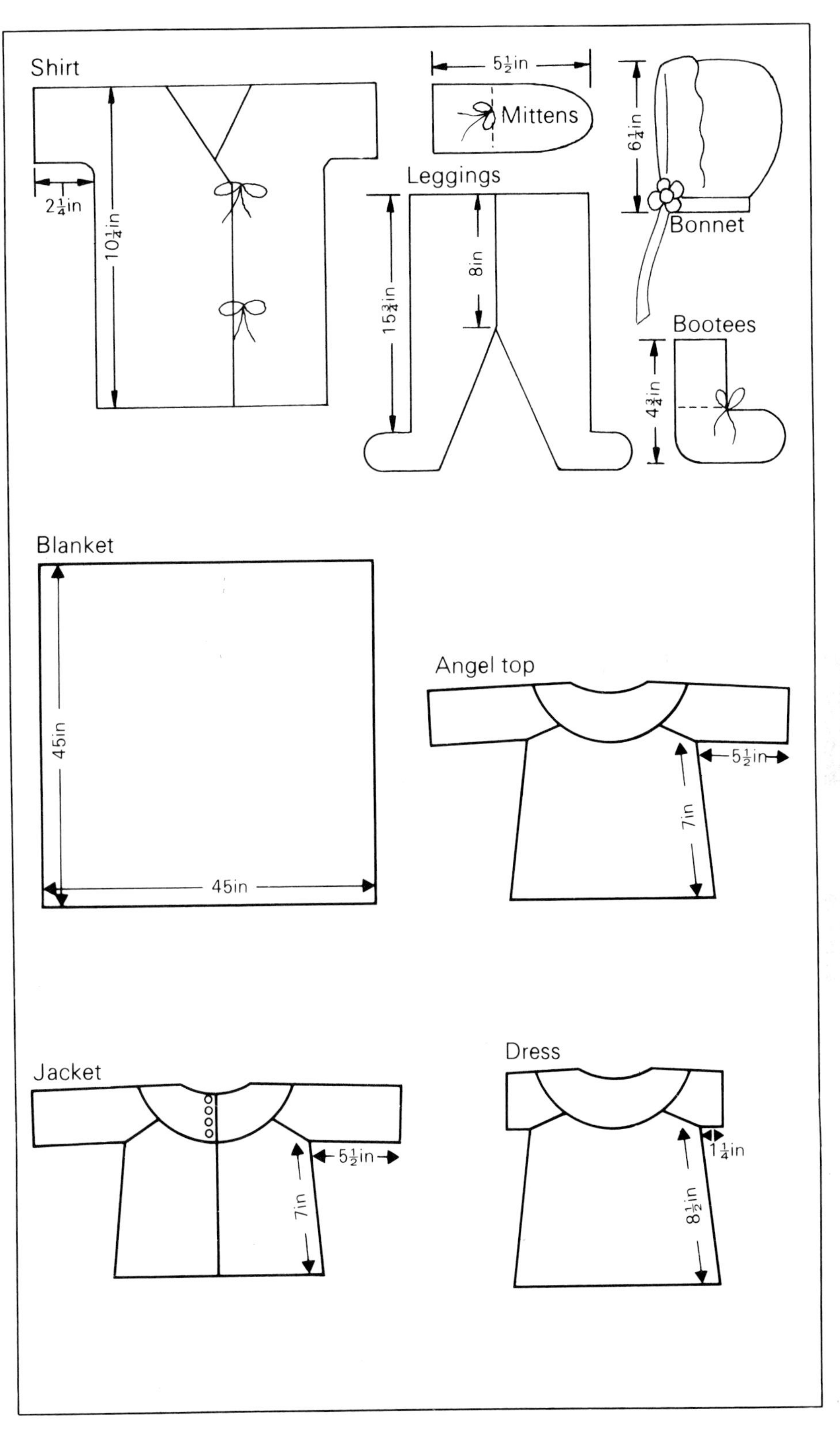

same as back to top of waistband, ending with a K row. Work 4 rows garter st. Bind off.
With WS of work facing, rejoin yarn to rem sts, bind off 18sts for center neck, work to end of row. Complete to match first side, reversing shaping.

To finish
Join side and sleeve seams. Overlap right front over left front and sew on ribbons to last shaping and 2in below.

Bonnet

Using No. 3 needles cast on 87sts.

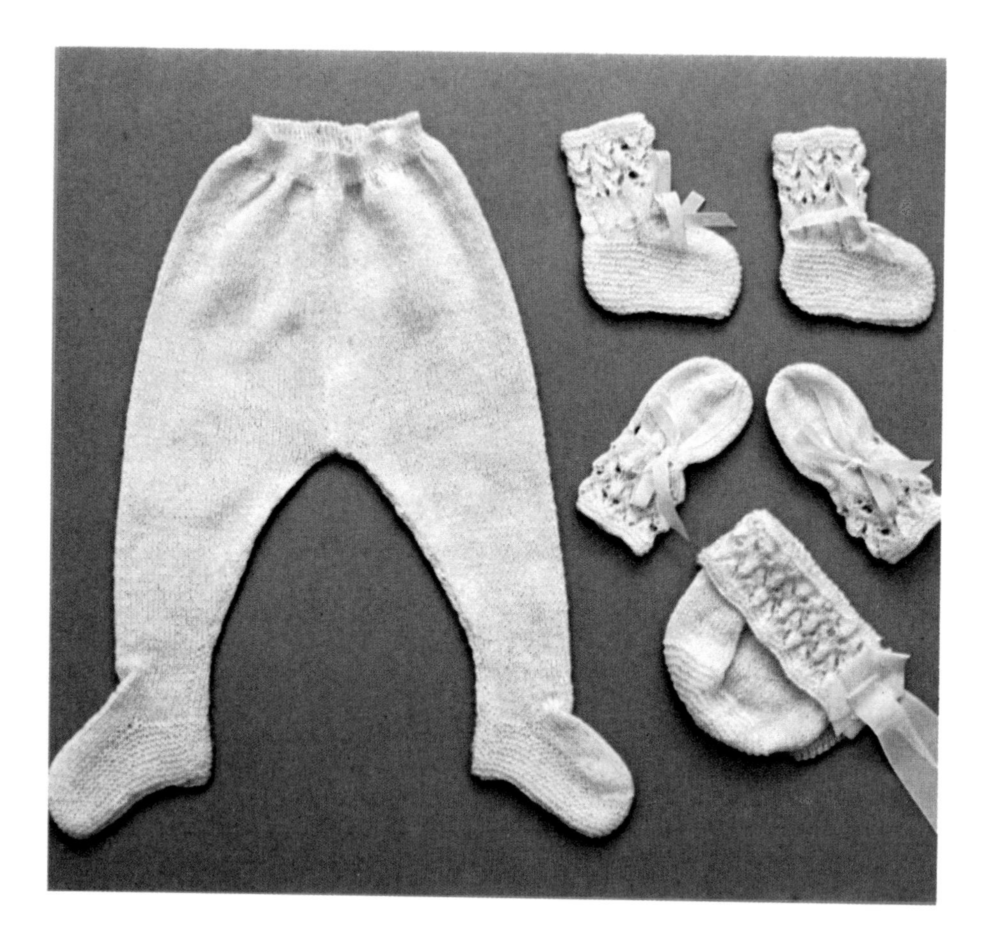

Work 4 rows garter st. Begin patt.
1st row K2, *sl 1, K1, psso, K3, yo, K1, yo, K3, K2 tog, K1, rep from * to last st, K1.
2nd row P2, *P2 tog, P2, yo, P3, yo, P2, P2 tog, tbl, P1, rep from * to last st, P1.
3rd row K2, *sl 1, K1, psso, K1, yo, K5, yo, K1, K2 tog, K1, rep from * to last st, K1.
4th row P2, *yo, P2 tog, P7, P2 tog tbl, yo, P1, rep from * to last st, P1.
5th row K2, *yo, K3, K2 tog, K1, sl 1, K1, psso, K3, yo, K1, rep from * to last st. K1.
6th row P3, *yo, P2, P2 tog tbl, P1, P2 tog, P2, yo, P3, rep from * to end.
7th row K4, * yo, K1, K2 tog, K1, sl 11, K1, psso, K1, yo, K5, rep from * to end but finish last rep K4 instead of K5.
8th row P5, *P2 tog tbl, yo, P1, yo, P2 tog, P7, rep from * to end but finish last rep P5 instead of P7.
These 8 rows form the patt. Rep them once more. Work 4 rows garter st.
1st rib row K1, (P1, K1) to end.
2nd rib row P1, (K1, P1) to end.
Rep these 2 rows 3 times, then work 1st rib row again.

Beg with a K row, proceed in stockinette st until work measures 6¼in from beg, ending with a P row and inc 3sts evenly across last row.
Work 4 rows garter st.
Shape for crown
1st row *K7, K2 tog, rep from * to end. 80sts.
2nd and every alternate row K to end.
3rd row *K6, K2 tog, rep from * to end. 70sts.
5th row *K5, K2 tog, rep from * to end. 60sts.
Continue dec in this way until 10sts rem. Cut off yarn, thread through rem sts, draw up and secure.

To finish
Join back seam to beg of shaping.
Turn back brim.
Neck edge Using No. 2 needles and with RS of work facing, pick up 81sts around neck, working through double thickness at brim.
Beg with 2nd rib row, work 6 rows.
Bind off.
Make 2 ribbon rosettes, leaving sufficient ribbon free to tie under the chin. Finally, sew one to each side of bonnet.

Bootees

**Using No. 3 needles, cast on 39sts. Work 5 rows garter st.
Work 16 rows patt as given for bonnet. Beg with a K row, work 6 rows stockinette st, inc one st at end of last row. 40sts.
Next row *K2, yo, K2 tog, rep from * to end.
Next row P to end.**
Next row K7, (K2 tog, K9) 3 times.
Next row P to end.
Divide for instep
1st row K24, turn.
2nd row P11, turn.
Work 20 rows stockinette st on these 11sts for instep. Cut off yarn. With RS of work facing, pick up 14sts along side of instep, K across instep sts, pick up 14sts along other side of instep and K across 13sts on left-hand needle. 65sts.
Work 15 rows garter st.
Shape foot
1st row K2 tog, K25, K2 tog, K7, K2 tog, K25, K2 tog.
2nd and every alternate row K to end.
3rd row K2 tog, K24, K2 tog, K5, K2 tog, K24, K2 tog.
5th row K2 tog, K23, K2 tog, K3, K2 tog, K23, K2 tog.
7th row K2 tog, K22, K2 tog, K1, K2 tog, K22, K2 tog.
8th row K to end. Bind off loosely.

To finish
Join foot and leg seams. Thread ribbon through eyelet holes and tie with a bow at center front.

Mittens

Work as given for bootees from ** to **. Continue in stockinette st Until work measures $2\frac{3}{8}$in from eyelet hole row.

Shape top
1st row *K2, K2 tog, rep from * to end.
2nd row P to end.
3rd row *K1, K2 tog, rep from * to end.
4th row P to end.
5th row *K2 tog, rep from * to end.
Cut off yarn, thread end through stitches, draw up tightly and secure.

To finish
Join seams. Thread ribbon through eyelet holes and tie with a bow at center front.

Blanket
Using No. 6 needles cast on 243sts. Beg patt.
1st row K2, *sl 1, K1, psso, K3, yo, K1, yo, K3, K2 tog, K1, rep from * to last st, K1.
2nd row P2, *P2 tog, P2, yo, P3, yo, P2, P2 tog tbl, P1 rep from * to last st, P1.
3rd row K2, *sl 1, K1, psso, K1, yo, K5, yo, K1, K2 tog, K1, rep from * to last st, K1.
4th row P2, *yo, P2 tog, P7, P2 tog tbl, yo, P1, rep from * to last st. P1.
5th row K2, *yo, K3, K2 tog, K1, sl 1, K1, psso, K3, yo, K1, rep from * to last st. K1.
6th row P3, *yo, P2, P2 tog tbl, P1, P2 tog, P2, yo, P3, rep from * to end.
7th row K4, *yo, K1, K2 tog, K1,

Technique tip

Shaping the instep
To shape the instep on leggings or bootees you need to divide the stitches into three groups. The center group of stitches is for the instep, and the groups on either side are for the two sides of the foot. The stitches left unworked are kept on the needles while you complete the center instep section: when this is completed, you knit across all the stitches including stitches picked up along the sides of the instep section.
The pattern will tell you how many stitches to work and how many to leave unworked. You begin by knitting across the stitches for one side of the foot and across those for the instep. Leave the group for the other side unworked, and turn the work. Work across the instep section to the group of stitches for the other side of the foot. Turn the work. Leave these unworked on the right-hand needle. The drawing shows the work at this stage (with two instep stitches knitted together, as instructed in pattern), ready for completion of instep.

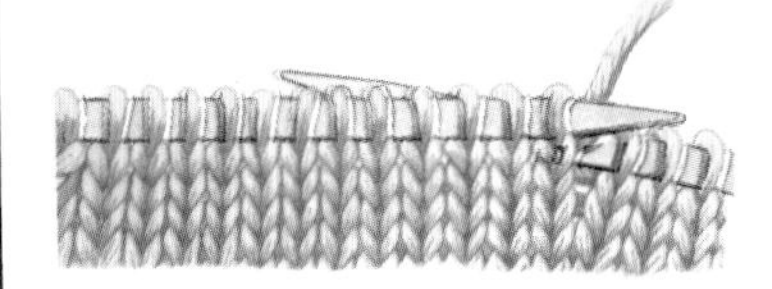

When the instep has been worked to the required length (WS facing), cut off the yarn. Turn the work. Rejoin the yarn at the left edge of the unworked stitches on the right-hand needle. Pick up the specified number of stitches along the right edge of the instep section; knit the instep stitches from the left-hand needle: pick up and knit the given number of stitches along the left side of the instep; finally, knit the remaining group of stitches from the left-hand needle. The diagram shows the sequence of picking up stitches for the foot.
You will now have on your right-hand needle all the stitches required for the foot.

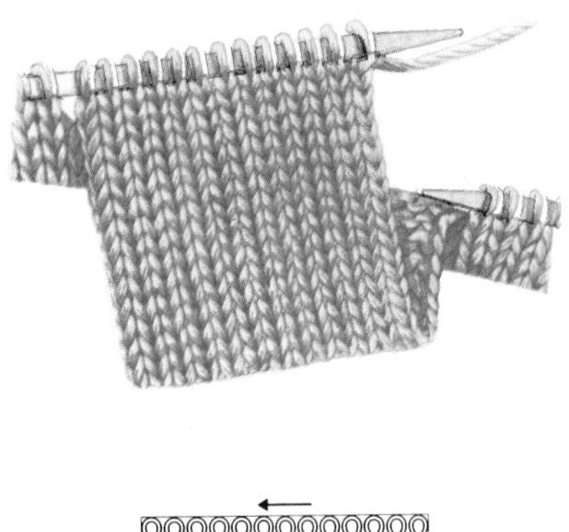

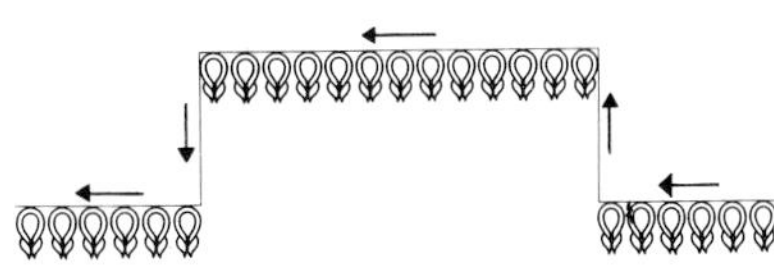

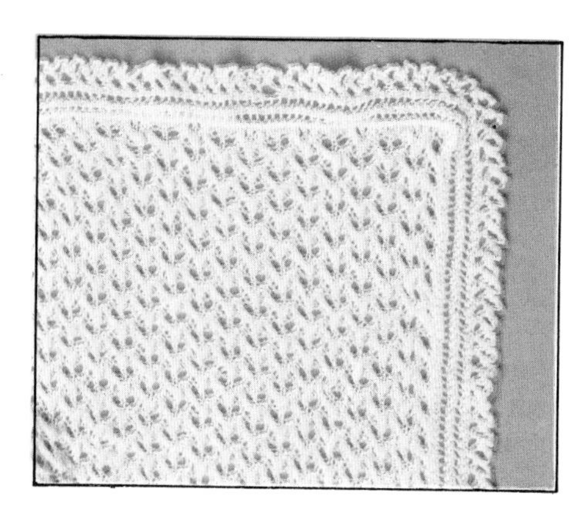

sl 1, K1, psso, K1, yo, K5, rep from * to end but finish last rep K4 instead of K5.
8th row P5, *P2 tog tbl, yo, P1, yo, P2 tog, P7, rep from * to end but finish last rep P5 instead of P7.
These 8 rows form the patt. Cont in patt until the 8th row of the 41st patt has been worked. Bind off.

Edging
Using No. 6 needles cast on 11sts. K one row. Begin patt.
1st row K3, (yo, sl 1, K1, psso, K1) twice, (yo) twice, K1, (yo) twice, K1, 15sts.
2nd row (K2, P1) 4 times, K3, (note that on this row each double yo is worked as 2sts, the first being knitted and the second being purled). 15sts.
3rd row K3, yo, sl 1, K1, psso, K1, yo, sl 1, K1, psso, K7, 15sts.
4th row Bind off 4sts, K4, P1, K2, P1, K3, 11sts.
These 4 rows form patt. Cont in patt until edging fits around outer edge of main piece, allowing an extra 1½in at corners. End with a 4th row. Bind off.

To finish
Join cast-on and bound-off edges of edging together. Sew edging to main piece, easing it in at corners. Roll in a damp cloth. Then lay flat, pat into shape and leave to dry.

Dress

Using No. 3 needles cast on 243sts and work in one piece to underarm. Work 7 rows garter st. Proceed in patt as for blanket until work measures 8½in from beg. End with an 8th row.
Divide for armholes
Next row Patt 63, bind off 2sts, patt until there are 113sts on right-hand needle after bound-off group, bind off 2sts, patt to end.
Keeping patt correct, dec one st at armhole edge on next 7 rows. 56sts. Cut off yarn and leave sts on holder. With WS of work facing, rejoin yarn to front sts, keeping patt correct dec one st at each end of next 7 rows, 99sts. Cut off yarn and leave sts on holder.
With WS of work facing, rejoin yarn to rem sts and complete to match right back, reversing shaping. Do not cut off yarn but leave sts on holder.

Sleeves
Using No. 1 needles cast on 49sts. Work 3 rows garter st.
Next row K4, *inc in next st, K2, rep from * to last 3sts, K3, 51sts. Change to No. 3 needles. Work 8 rows patt, inc one st at end of last row, 52sts.
Shape top
Keeping patt correct, bind off 2sts at beg of next 2 rows, then dec one st at each end of next 5 rows, 38sts. Work one row. Cut off yarn and leave sts on holder.
Yoke
Using No. 2 needles and with RS facing, work across sts on holders as foll:
Next row K6, (K2 tog) 25 times across left back; K2 tog, K34, K2 tog across left sleeve; K4, (K2 tog) 45 times, K5 across front: K2 tog, K34, K2 tog across right sleeve; (K2 tog) 27 times, K2 across right back; turn: cast on 6sts for underflap. 192sts. Work 11 rows garter st.
Next row (buttonhole row) K1, K2 tog, yo, K3, *K1, K2 tog, rep from * to last 6sts, K6, 132sts.
Work 11 rows garter st.
Next row (buttonhole row) K1, K2 tog, yo, K3, *K1, K2 tog, rep from * to last 6sts, K6, 92sts.

Technique tip

Working a yoke
The angel top, dress and jacket in this collection have a yoke that is worked in one piece. This is very common in babies' garments, as it eliminates the need for bulky seams. In these garments the main piece is worked in one to the top of the skirt. The work is then divided, and the armhole shaping is worked on each piece.
The stitches are then left on holders to be worked on at a later stage.
The sleeves are knitted next and left on holders, then all the stitches are knitted from the holders in the appropriate order, depending on the pattern. To shape the yoke, you decrease stitches across a number of rows. The decreases are worked across the row to give an even shape and should be spaced evenly so that they form an attractive feature of the garment rather than looking haphazard.

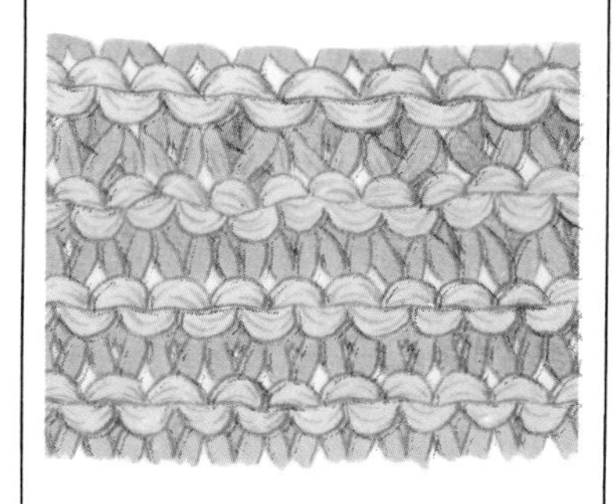

Work 7 rows garter st.
Next row K7, *K2 tog, K1, rep from * to last 7sts, K7, 66sts.
Next 2 rows K11, turn sl 1, K to end.
Next 2 rows K22, turn, sl 1, K to end. K one row across all sts.
Next 2 rows K11, turn, sl 1, K to end.
Next 2 rows K22, turn, sl 1, K to end. Change to No. 1 needles. Work 5 rows garter st making buttonhole as before at beg of 3rd row. Bind off.
To finish
Join sleeve and underarm seams. Join back to underflap. Sew down underflap. Sew on buttons.

Angel top

Work as for dress until skirt measures 7in then work armholes.

Sleeves
Using No. 1 needles cast on 32sts. Work 3 rows garter st.
Next row K6, *inc in next st, rep from * to last 7sts, K7, 51sts. Change to No. 3 needles. Proceed in patt until work measures 5½in, ending with an 8th row (inc one st in last row). 52sts.
Shape top
Keeping patt correct, bind off 2 sts at beg of next 2 rows, then dec one st at each end of next 5 rows. 38sts. Work one row. Cut off yarn and leave sts on holder.

Jacket

Using No. 3 needles cast on 243sts and work in one piece to underarm. Work 7 rows garter st. Proceed in patt working 6sts at each end on every row in garter st until work measures 7in from beg. End with an 8th row.
Divide for armholes
Next row K6, patt 57, bind off 2, patt until there are 113sts on right-hand needle after bound-off group, bind off 2, pat to last 6sts, K6.
Complete left front first. Keeping patt and garter st border correct, dec one st at armhole edge on next 7 rows. 56sts. Cut off yarn and leave sts on holder.
With WS of work facing, rejoin yarn to back sts and keeping patt correct dec one st at each end of next 7 rows. 99sts. Cut off yarn and leave sts on holder. With WS of work facing, rejoin yarn to right front sts and complete to match left front reversing shaping. Do not cut off yarn but leave sts on holder.

Sleeves
Work as given for sleeves of angel top.

Yoke
Using No. 2 needles and with RS of work facing, work across all sts on holders as foll:
Next row K1, K2tog, yo, K3, (K2 tog) 23 times, K4 across right front, K2 tog, K34, K2 tog across right sleeve, K4, (K2 tog) 45 times, K5 across back, K2 tog, K34, K2 tog across left sleeve, K4, (K2 tog) 23 times, K6 across left front. 192sts.
Work 11 rows garter st.
Next row (buttonhole row) K1, K2 tog, yo, K3, *K1, K2 tog, rep from * to last 6sts. K6. 132sts.
Work 11 rows garter st.
Next row (buttonhole row) K1, K2 tog, yo, K3, *K1, K2 tog, rep from * to last 6sts. K6. 92sts.
Work 7 rows garter st.
Next row K7, *K2 tog, K1, rep from * to last 7sts. K7. 66sts.
Next 2 rows K to last 11sts, turn, sl 1, K to last 11sts, turn.
Next 2 rows Sl 1, K to last 18sts, turn, sl 1, K to last 18sts, turn.
Next row Sl 1, K to end of row.
Change to No. 1 needles. Work 5 rows garter st making buttonhole as before at beg of 3rd row.
Bind off loosely.

To finish
Join sleeve and underarm seams.
Sew on buttons.

TRADITIONAL CHOICE

Size
46in square.

Materials
16oz of a sport yarn
1 pair of No. 6 needles

Gauge
1 patt rep (18sts) to 4in on No. 6 needles.

Technique tips

The lace pattern
Knitting lace patterns involves increasing stitches by one of the methods of decorative increasing – in this pattern the method is bringing the yarn forward and over the needle (yo) before knitting the next stitch to increase a stitch and make a hole. The increased stitches – say three in each pattern repeat across the row – must be compensated for by decreasing an equal number immediately or in the next row. The first method is to bring the yarn forward and slip the next stitch from the left-hand to the right-hand needle. Knit the next stitch; then, with the left needle, pass the slipped stitch over the knitted one, as shown. This decrease compensates for the increase made when bringing the yarn forward and over the needle. The abbreviation for this process is: "yo, sl 1, K1, psso."

In this pattern you will more often use the second method of making a hole: bring the yarn forward and over the needle to make an extra stitch, and knit the next stitch from the left-hand needle.

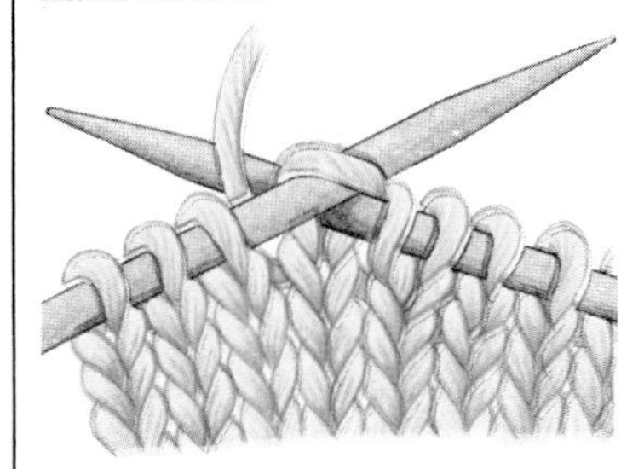

On the next row, work the extra (yo) stitch along with the next stitch to decrease one stitch, and end with the same number of stitches you started with.

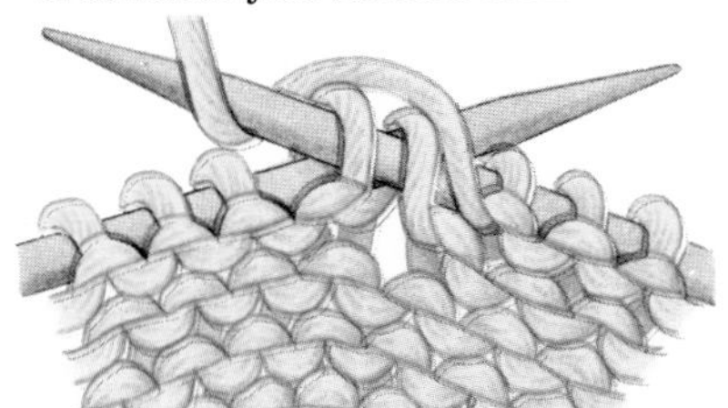

Blanket center
Cast on 217sts. Begin patt noting that sts are added on right side (RS) rows and reduced to the original number on wrong side (WS) rows.
1st row (RS) K2, *yo, K1, yo, sl 1, K1, psso, K9, K2 tog, yo, K1, yo, K3, rep from * to end, but finish last rep K2 instead of K3, 241sts.
2nd row P5, *P2 tog, P7, P2 tog through back of loops (tbl), P9, rep from * to end, but finish last rep P5 instead of P9. 217sts.
3rd row K2, yo, K3, yo, sl 1, K1, psso, K5, K2 tog, *(yo, K3) 3 times, yo, sl 1, K1, psso, K5, K2 tog, rep from * to last 5sts, yo, K3, yo, K2. 241sts.
4th row P7, *P2 tog, P3, P2 tog tbl, P13, rep from * to end, but finish last rep P7. 217sts.
5th row K2, *yo, K5, yo, sl 1, K1, psso, K1, K2 tog, yo, K5, yo, K3, rep from * to end, but finish last rep K2. 241sts.
6th row P9, *P3 tog, P17, rep from * to end, but finish last rep P9. 217sts.
7th row K5, *K2 tog, yo, K1, yo, K3, yo, K1, yo, sl 1, K1, psso, K9, rep from * to end, but finish last rep K5. 241sts.
8th row P4, *P2 tog tbl, P9, P2 tog, P7, rep from * to end, but finish last rep P4. 217sts.
9th row K3, *K2 tog, (yo, K3) 3 times, yo, sl 1, K1, psso, K5, rep from * to end, but finish last rep K3. 241 sts.
10th row P2, *P2 tog tbl, P13, P2 tog, P3, rep from * to end, but finish last rep P2. 217sts.
11th row K1, *K2 tog, yo, K5, yo, K3, yo, K5, yo, sl 1, K1, psso, K1, rep from * to end. 241sts.
12th row P2 tog, *P17, P3 tog, rep from * to end, but finish last rep P2 tog. 217sts. These 12 rows form the patt. Rep them 23 times. Bind off.

Edging
Cast on 9sts, K1 row and P1 row. Beg patt.
1st row (RS) Sl 1, K2, K2, yo, K2 tog tbl, K2 tbl, pick up loop lying between sts and K tbl – called M1 –, K2 tbl. 10sts.
2nd row K2 tbl, P1, P2 tbl, K2 tog tbl, P1, 10sts.
3rd row Sl 1, K2, yo, K2 tog tbl, K3 tbl, M1, K2 tbl. 11sts.
4th row K2 tbl, P1, P3 tbl, K2, yo, K2 tog tbl, P1. 11sts.
5th row Sl 1, K2, yo, K2 tog tbl, K4 tbl, M1, K2 tbl. 12sts.
6th row K2 tbl, P1, P4 tbl, K2, yo, K2 tog tbl, P1. 12sts.
7th row Sl 1, K2, yo, K2 tog tbl, K5 tbl, M1, K2 tbl. 13sts.
8th row K2 tbl, P1, P5 tbl, K2, yo, K2 tog tbl, P1. 13sts.
9th row Sl 1, K2, yo, K2 tog tbl, K6 tbl, M1, K2 tbl. 14sts.
10th row K2 tbl, P1, P6 tbl, K2, yo, K2 tog tbl, P1. 14sts.
11th row Sl 1, K2, yo, K2 tog tbl, K7 tbl, M1, K2 tbl. 15sts.
12th row K2 tbl, P1, P7 tbl, K2, yo, K2 tog tbl, P1. 15sts.
13th row Sl 1, K2, yo, K2 tog tbl, K10 tbl. 15sts.
14th row K10 tbl, K2, yo, K2 tog tbl, P1. 15sts.
15th row As 13th row.
16th row Bind off 6, K1 tbl, P1, P1 tbl, K2, yo, K2 tog tbl, P1. 9sts.
These 16 rows form the patt. Rep them until edging fits outer edge of blanket center allowing an extra $1\frac{1}{2}$in at each corner, ending with a 16th row. Bind off.

To finish
Join cast-on and bound-off edges of edging together. Sew edging to main piece easing it in at corners. Finish using the method for lace blankets and shawls.

Finishing method for lace blanket or shawl
This type of blanket does not require pressing on completion; instead it is dampened and stretched. First roll it in a damp cloth, then spread it on a sheet on the floor and pin opposite diagonal corners. Pin along the sides, placing a pin through each point of lace border. Keep taut and square until completely dry.

DAISY SUNDRESS

Sizes
To fit 16[20]in chest.
Length from top of bib, 11½[12¾]in.
Note *Directions for the larger size are in brackets []; where there is only one set of figures it applies to both sizes.*

Materials
4[5] × 1oz balls of a sport yarn in main color (A)
1[2] balls of contrasting color (B)
1 pair each Nos. 2 and 3 knitting needles
Size C crochet hook
2 small buttons

Gauge
28sts to 4in in stockinette st on No. 3 needles.

Sundress

Back

Using No. 3 needles and A, cast on 93[103]sts. Work 4 rows garter st. Beg with a K row, work 8 rows stockinette st.
Next row K6, (P1, K9) 8[9] times, P1, K6. Work 8 rows stockinette st, dec one st at each end of first row. Work 3 rows garter st. Beg patt.
1st row P to end.
2nd row K4, *P3, K7, rep from * ending with K4.
3rd row P4, *K3, P7, rep from * ending with P4.
4th row As 2nd.
5th row P to end.
6th row K to end.
7th row K2, *P7, K3, rep from * ending with K2.
8th row P2, *K7, P3, rep from * ending with P2.
9th row As 7th.
10th row K to end.
Rep last 10 rows, dec one st at each end of first and every foll 10th row until 83[91]sts rem. Cont straight until work measures 7[8]in from beg. Change to No. 2 needles.**

Next row K1, *P1, K1, rep from * to end.
Next row P1, *K1, P1, rep from * to end.
Rep last 2 rows twice. Cut off A and join in B. Work 1 row P1, K1 rib. Bind off in ribbing.

Front

Work as given for back to **.
Next row Rib 13[15], patt 57[61], rib 13[15].
Rep last row 5 times more. Join in B.
Next row Using B, rib 13[15], using A, patt 57[61], using B, rib 13[15].
Divide for bib
Next row Using B, bind off 13[15]sts, using A, patt 57[61], using B, bind off 13[15]. Change to No. 3 needles. Keeping a garter st border of 2sts at each end of every row, cont in patt for 3¾[4]in, dec one st at each end of 7th and every foll 8th row. Work 3 rows garter st. Bind off.

Pocket

Using No. 3 needles and A, cast on 16sts. Work 4 rows garter st. Keeping a garter st border of 2sts at each end of every row, work 2in stockinette st. Work 4 rows garter st. Bind off.

Straps (make 2)

Using No. 2 needles and A, cast on 70[75]sts. Work 3 rows garter st.
Next row K3, yo, K2 tog, K to end. Work 3 rows garter st. Bind off.

To finish

Press under a dry cloth with a cool iron. Join side seams.
Edging Using crochet hook, B and with RS facing, work in sc all around hem. Join with a sl st into first st.
Next round *3ch, sl st into same st at base of ch, sl st into each of next 2sts, rep from * to end.
Work edging around bib and straps. Using P sts as a guide, use B to embroider daisies around hem and on pocket. Sew pocket to center of bib. Sew on straps, with buttonholes at back. Sew on buttons. Press seams.

Hat

Crown

Using No. 3 needles and A, cast on 83sts. Work 8 rows garter st. Beg

with a K row, work 4 rows stockinette st.
Next row K6, (P1, K9) 7 times, P1, K6. Work 8 rows stockinette st. Work 9 rows garter st, dec one st at end of last row.

Shape top

1st row K1, (K2 tog tbl, K16, K2 tog) 4 times, K1, K5 rows.
7th row K1, (K2 tog tbl, K14, K2 tog) 4 times, K1.
K 3 rows.
11th row K1, (K2 tog tbl, K12, K2 tog) 4 times, K1.
K 1 row.
13th row K1, (K2 tog tbl, K10, K2 tog) 4 times, K1.
Cont to dec in this way on every alternate row until row "K1, (K2 tog tbl, K2 tog) 4 times, K1" has been worked. Cut off yarn, draw through rem sts and fasten off.

Brim

Using No. 3 needles and A, cast on 11sts.
****1st and 2nd rows** Sl 1, K10.
3rd row Sl 1, K3, turn.
4th row K4.
5th row Sl 1, K4, turn.
6th row K5.
7th row Sl 1, K5, turn.
8th row K6.
9th row Sl 1, K10.
Work backward from 8th to 3rd row. ** Rep from ** to ** until band fits loosely all around crown. Bind off.

To finish

Join seam at back of crown. Sew brim to crown loosely. Using B, work crochet edging as for dress all around brim. Embroider daisies around crown.

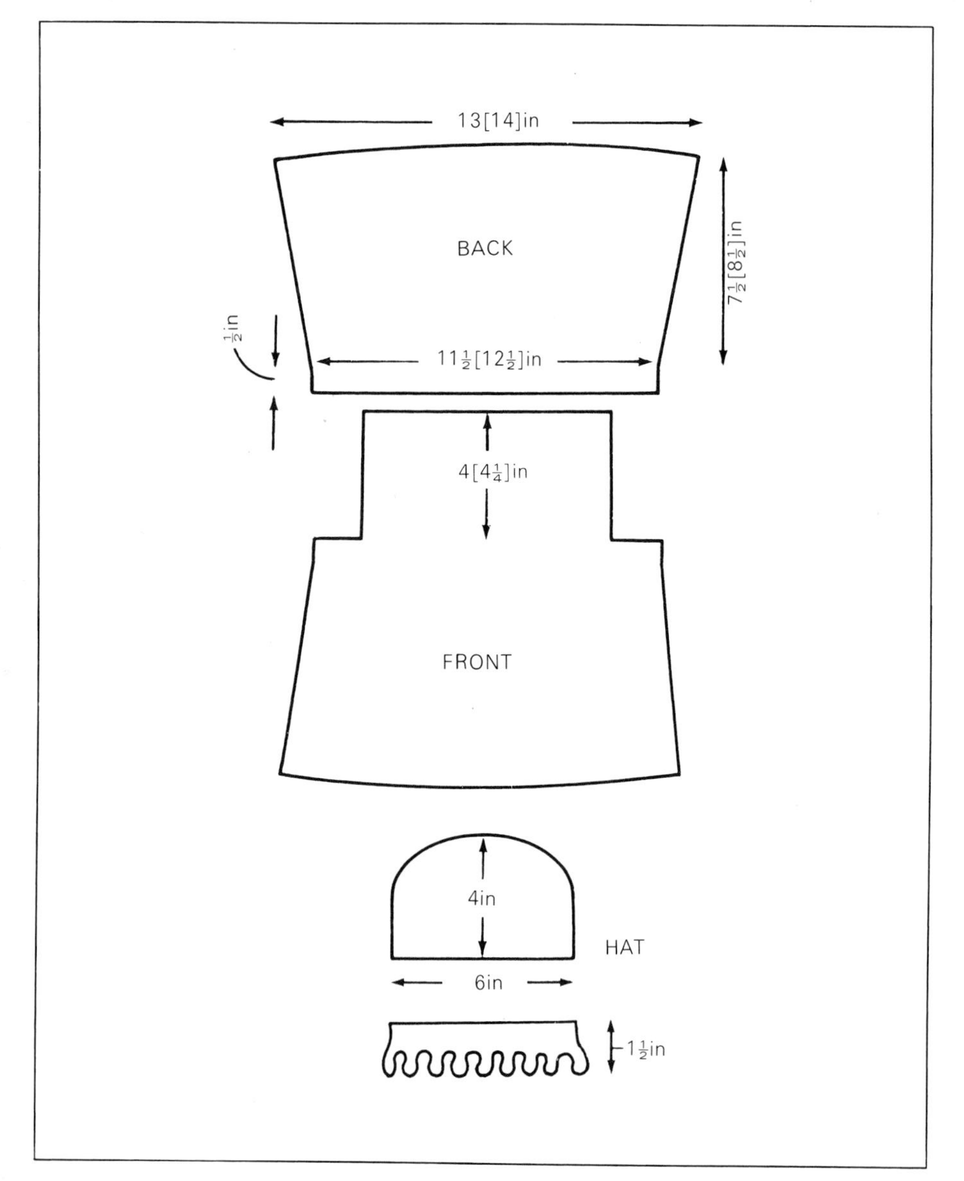

CUTE SUIT

Sizes
Sweater *To fit 18[20:22]in chest.*
Length, 11[$12\frac{1}{4}$:13]in.
Sleeve seam, $8\frac{1}{2}$[$9\frac{1}{2}$:$10\frac{1}{4}$]in.
Pants *Inner leg seam, 8[$9\frac{1}{2}$:11]in.*
Waist to crotch, $8\frac{1}{2}$[9:$9\frac{1}{2}$]in.
Shoes *Back of heel to toe, $4\frac{3}{4}$[5:$5\frac{1}{2}$]in.*

Note *Directions for larger sizes are in brackets []; where there is only one set of figures it applies to all sizes.*

Materials
Sport yarn:
Sweater *4[4:5]oz in main color (A)*
1oz each in 3 contrasting colors (B, C and D)

Pants and shoes *4[5:5]oz in main color (A)*
1 pair No. 3 (long) knitting needles
1 pair No. 2 knitting needles
6 buttons for sweater
Waist length plus seam allowance of $\frac{1}{2}$in-wide elastic for pants

Gauge
28sts and 36 rows to 4in on No. 3 needles.

Sweater

Front

Using No. 2 needles and A, cast on 68[76:84]sts. Work 10 rows in K1, P1 ribbing, inc one st at end of last row. 69[77:85]sts. Change to No. 3 needles. Beg with a K row, work 6[8:10] rows stockinette st. Beg first row of motifs. At beg of each motif cut 1yd each in B and C from ball and use these lengths for each motif, so that the yarn is not stranded across back of work.
1st row K9[11:13]A, (4A, 3B, 13[15:17]A) 3 times.
2nd row P9[11:13]A, (3A, 5B, 12[14:16]A) 3 times.
3rd row K9[11:13]A, (2A, 7B, 11[13:15]A) 3 times.
4th row P9[11:13]A, (1A, 9B, 10[12:14]A) 3 times.
5th row K9[11:13]A, (1A, 9B, 10[12:14]A) 3 times.
6th row P9[11:12]A, (11B, 9[11:13]A) 3 times.
Join on D.
7th and 8th rows K with D.
Cut off D.
9th row K9[11:13]A, (11C, 9[11:13]A) 3 times.
10th row P9[11:13]A, (1A, 9C, 10[12:14]A) 3 times.
11th row K9[11:13]A, (1A, 9C, 10[12:14]A) 3 times.
12th row P9[11:13]A, (2A, 7C, 11[13:15]A) 3 times.
13th row K9[11:13]A, (3A, 5C, 12[14:16]A) 3 times.
14th row P9[11:13]A, (4A, 3C, 13[15:17]A) 3 times.
Beg with a K row and using A, work 6[8:10] rows stockinette st.
Beg second row of motifs.
1st row K23[26:29]A, (3B, 17[19:21]A) twice, 6[7:8]A.
Work motifs as before, on sts as set, then beg with a K row and using A, cast on 40sts at beg of next 2 rows and 20[13:16]sts at beg of foll 2[4:4] rows. 189[209:229]sts.
Next row K to end.
Next row K8[10:12], P to last 8[10:12]sts, K8[10:12].
For 3rd size only, rep last 2 rows.

All sizes
Beg third row of motifs.
1st row K9[11:13]A, (4A, 3B, 13[15:17]A) 9 times.
Keeping the 8[10:12]sts at each end in garter st, work motifs as before on sts as set. Beg with a K row and using A, work 6[8:10] rows stockinette st with garter st borders.
Beg fourth row of motifs.
1st row K23[26:29]A, (3B, 17[19:21]A) 8 times, 6[7:8]A.
Keeping the 8[10:12]sts at each end in garter st, work motifs as before on sts as set. Cont with A only, work 2 rows.
Next row Bind off 20, K until there are 44[50:56]sts on right-hand needle, P1, (K1, P1) 30[34:38] times, K 64[70:76].
Working center 61[69:77]sts in ribbing as set, bind off 20sts at beg of next 3 rows. 109[129:149]sts.
Buttonhole row Bind off 8[10:12], work until there are 17[24:27]sts on right-hand needle, rib 1[3:2], (K2 tog, yo, rib 3[3:4]sts) 3 times, rib 32[36:41], (yo, K2 tog, rib 3[3:4]sts) twice, yo, K2 tog, rib 1[3:2], rib to end.
Keeping ribbing correct, bind off 8[10:12]sts at beg of next 5 rows.
Bind off in ribbing.

Back

Work as given for front, omitting buttonholes and do not bind off.
Shoulder plackets
Next row Rib 16[18:20], bind off 29[33:37], rib to end.
Work 8 rows in K1, P1 ribbing on each set of rem 16[18:20]sts. Bind off in ribbing.

To finish

Press lightly. Join sleeve and

shoulder seam, then sew edge of placket at side edge behind front neck ribbing. Join side and underarm seams. Sew on buttons.

Pants

Front

Right leg Using No. 2 needles and A, cast on 20[22:24]sts.
Work in K1, P1 ribbing for 2in.
Next row Rib 4, (work twice into next st, rib 1) to end. 28[31:34]sts.
Change to No. 3 needles. Beg with a K row, cont in stockinette st, inc one st at each end of 5th and every foll 8th row until there are 38[41:44]sts. Cont straight until work measures 8[9½:11]in; end with a P row. Cut off yarn and leave sts on a spare needle.
Left leg Work as given for right leg, but do not cut off yarn.
Next row K to end, turn and cast on 10, turn again and onto same

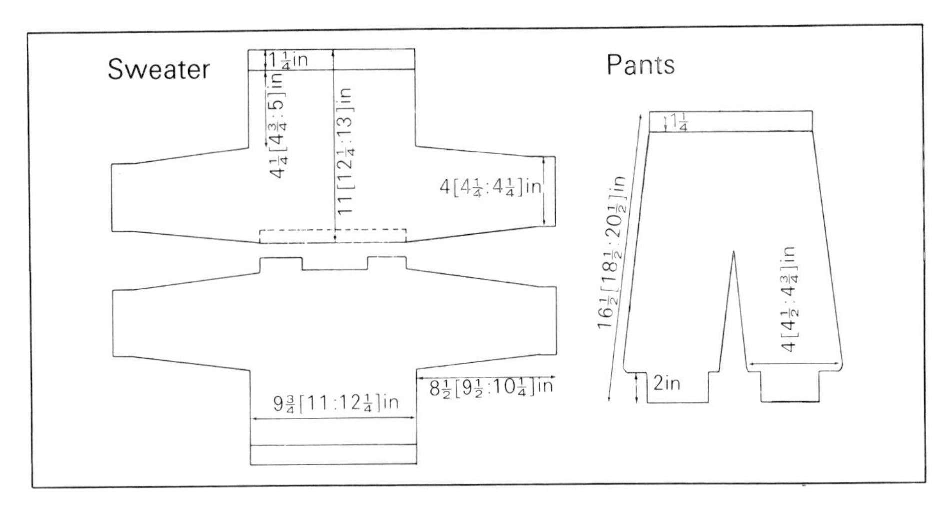

needle K the sts of right leg. 86[92:98]sts.

Shape crotch

Next row P to end.

Next row K37[40:43], sl 1, K1, psso, K8, K2 tog, K37[40:43].

Next row P to end.

Next row K37[40:43], sl 1, K1, psso, K6, K2 tog, K37[40:43].

Cont to dec in this way on every foll alternate row until 76[82:88]sts rem. Cont straight until work measures 7¼[7¾:8¼]in from beg of crotch; end with a P row. Change to No. 2 needles. Work in K1, P1 ribbing for 1¼in. Bind off.

Back

Work as given for front until 1 row less has been worked to beg of waist ribbing.

Shape back

Next 2 rows Work to last 8sts, turn.

Next 2 rows Work to last 16sts, turn.

Next 2 rows Work to last 24sts, turn.

Next 2 rows Work to last 32sts, turn.

Next row P to end.

Change to No. 2 needles. Work in K1, P1 ribbing for 1¼in. Bind off.

To finish

Press lightly. Join side and inner leg seams. Work herringbone casing over elastic on wrong side of waist ribbing.

Shoes (alike)

Using No. 2 needles and A, cast on 40[44:48]sts.

Work 28 rows in K1, P1 ribbing.

Eyelet hole row (K1, yo, K2 tog, P1) to end.

Rib 3 rows. Change to No. 3 needles.

Divide for instep

1st row K25[27:29], turn.

2nd row K10, turn.

K22[26:30] rows on these 10sts. K 4 rows, dec one st at each end of 1st, 3rd and 4th of these rows. Cut off yarn and leave rem 4sts on a holder. With RS facing and using right-hand needle pick up and K 26[30:34]sts along side of foot, K 4sts from holder, pick up and K 26[30:34]sts along other side of foot, then K sts from left-hand needle. 86[98:110]sts.

1st row P15[17:19], (K1, P1) 28[32:36] times, P15[17:19].

2nd row K15[17:19], (K1, P1) 28[32:36] times, K15[17:19].

Rep these 2 rows 4 times more.

11th row P15[17:19], (P2 tog) 28[32:36] times, P15[17:19]. 58[66:74]sts.

Shape for sole

1st row K6, K2 tog tbl, K17[21:25], K2 tog, K4, K2 tog tbl, K17[21:25], K2 tog, K6. 54[62:70]sts.

2nd row P.

3rd row K6, K2 tog tbl, K15[19:23], K2 tog, K4, K2 tog tbl, K15[19:23], K2 tog, K6. 50[58:66]sts.

4th row P.

5th row K6, K2 tog tbl, K13[17:21], K2 tog, K4, K2 tog tbl, K13[17:21], K2 tog, K6. 46[54:62]sts.

6th row P. Bind off.

To finish

Do not press. Join center back and sole seam. Press seam. Using 4 strands of yarn tog, make a twisted cord. Thread cord through eyelet holes to tie at center front.

JUNIOR JUMPSUITS

Sizes
Tops *To fit 22[24:26:28]in chest.*
Length, $15\frac{1}{2}[16\frac{1}{2}:17\frac{3}{4}:19]$in.
Sleeve seam, $10[10\frac{1}{2}:11\frac{1}{4}:12]$in.
Pants *Waist to crotch (front), $7[8:8\frac{1}{2}:9\frac{1}{2}]$in.*
Inside leg, $12[13\frac{1}{2}:15:16\frac{1}{2}]$in.
Note *Directions for larger sizes are in brackets []; where there is only one set of figures it applies to all sizes.*

Materials
Sport yarn:
V-neck top *6[7:7:8] × 1oz balls in main color (A)*
1[1:2:2] × 1oz balls in contrasting color (B)
Zipped top *6[7:7:8] × 1oz balls in main color (A)*
1[1:2:2] × 1oz balls in contrasting color (B)
Pants *6[7:7:8] × 1oz balls in main color (A)*
1 pair each Nos. 2 and 4 knitting needles
1 set of four No. 2 double-pointed knitting needles
12[14:16:16]in open-ended zipper
1yd narrow elastic for pants

Gauge
24sts and 36 rows to 4in in stockinette st on No. 4 needles.

V-neck top

Back
Using No. 2 needles and A, cast on 75[81:87:93]sts and beg with a K row work 8 rows stockinette st. Place a marker at each end of last row to mark hemline. Change to No. 4 needles and cont in stockinette st for $15\frac{1}{2}[16\frac{1}{2}:17\frac{3}{4}:19]$in from markers; end with a P row.

Shape shoulders
Bind off 6[6:7:7]sts at beg of next 4 rows, then 6[7:7:8]sts at beg of next 4 rows. Cut off yarn and leave rem 27[29:31:33]sts on a holder for neck.

Front
Work as for back until work measures $8\frac{3}{4}[9\frac{1}{2}:10\frac{1}{4}:11]$in from markers; end with a P row.

Divide for neck
1st row K37[40:43:46], turn and leave rem sts on a spare needle.
2nd row P to end.
3rd row K to last 3sts, sl 1, K1, psso, K1. Cont to dec at neck edge on every 4th row until 24[26:28:30]sts rem, then cont straight until work measures same as back to shoulders; end with a P row.

Shape shoulder
Bind off 6[6:7:7]sts at beg of next and foll alternate row, then 6[7:7:8]sts at beg of foll 2 alternate rows. Return to sts on spare needle; sl first st onto safety pin for front neck, rejoin yarn to next st and K to end of row.
Next row P to end.
Next row K1, K2 tog, K to end.
Cont to match left side, reversing shaping.

Sleeves
Using No. 2 needles and B, cast on 33[35:37:39]sts.
1st row K1, *P1, K1, rep from * to end.
2nd row P1, *K1, P1, rep from * to end. Rep these 2 rows for $1\frac{1}{2}$in; end with 2nd row. Cut off B. Change to

No. 4 needles and join in A.
Next row K twice into each st to end. 66[70:74:78]sts.
Beg with a P row, cont in stockinette st until work measures 9[9½:10¼:11]in; end with a P row.
Cut off A, join in B and cont in stockinette st for 1in. Bind off.

Neckband
Join shoulder seams. Using set of four No. 2 needles, B and with RS facing, K back neck sts, pick up and K 51[53:55:57]sts down left front neck, K center front st from safety pin, pick up and K 51[53:55:57]sts up right front neck.
130[136:142:148]sts.
Next round Work in K1, P1 ribbing to within 2sts of center front, sl 1, K1, psso, K1, K2 tog, rib to end.
Rep this round 6 times more. Bind off in ribbing, dec at center front as before.

To finish
Set in sleeves, placing center of sleeves to shoulder seams. Join side and sleeve seams. Fold up hem at lower edge and sl st in position.
Make twisted or crochet cord in B and thread through hem.

Zipped top

Back
Work as for V-neck top until work measures 10[10¾:11½:12¼]in from markers; end with a P row.
Shape armholes
Bind off 3sts at beg of next 2 rows, then work 2 rows without shaping.
Next row K1, K2 tog, K to last 3sts, sl 1, K1, psso, K1.
Next row P to end.
Rep the last 2 rows until 25[27:29:31]sts rem; end with a P row. Bind off.

Left front
Using No. 2 needles and A, cast on 37[40:43:46]sts and work as for back to armholes; end with a P row.
Shape armhole
Bind off 3sts at beg of next row, then work 3 rows without shaping.
Next row K1, K2 tog, K to end.
Rep the last 2 rows until 20[21:23:24]sts rem; end with a K row.
Shape neck
Bind off 4[5:5:6]sts at beg of next row.
Next row K1, K2 tog, K to last 3sts, sl 1, K1, psso, K1.
Next row P to end.
Rep the last 2 rows 5[5:6:6] times more. 4sts.
Cont to dec at armhole edge on alternate rows twice, then bind off rem sts.

Right front
Work to match left front, reversing shaping.

Sleeves
Work as for sleeves of V neck top until work measures 9[9½:10¼:11]in; then cont in A until work measures 10[10½:11¼:12]in; end with a P row.
Mark each end of last row, then work 4 more rows.
Shape top
Next row K1, K2 tog, K to last 3sts, sl 1, K1, psso, K1.
Next row P to end.
Rep the last 2 rows until 36sts rem; end with a P row.
Next row K1, K2 tog, K13, K2 tog, sl 1, K1, psso, K13, sl 1, K1, psso, K1.
Cont to dec in center of every 6th row twice, and at same time cont to dec at each end of every other row until 14sts rem; end with a P row. Bind off.

Collar
With RS facing, using No. 2 needles and B, pick up and K 81[87:93:99]sts around neck.
Next row K2, (P1, K1) 27[29:31:33] times, P1, turn.
Next row (K1, P1) 16[17:18:19] times, K1, turn.
Next row (P1, K1) 18[19:20:21] times, P1, turn.
Next row (K1, P1) 20[21:22:23] times, K1, turn.
Cont in this way, working 4 more sts on each row until the row rib 73[75:85:87] turn has been worked.
Next row Rib to last 2sts, K2.
Now work across all sts.
Next row K2, rib to last 2sts, K2.
Rep last row until collar measures 2¼[2¼:2¾:2¾]in from beg measured at front edge. Bind off in ribbing.

Left front pocket
Using No. 4 needles and A, bind off 26[26:28:28]sts. *Beg with a K row, work 4 rows stockinette st. Join in B and work 2 rows garter st.

Technique tip

Making a twisted cord
This is a simple form of trimming that is ideal for ties, drawstrings and belts. Strands of yarn are twisted together to form a cord, the number varying according to the thickness of yarn used.

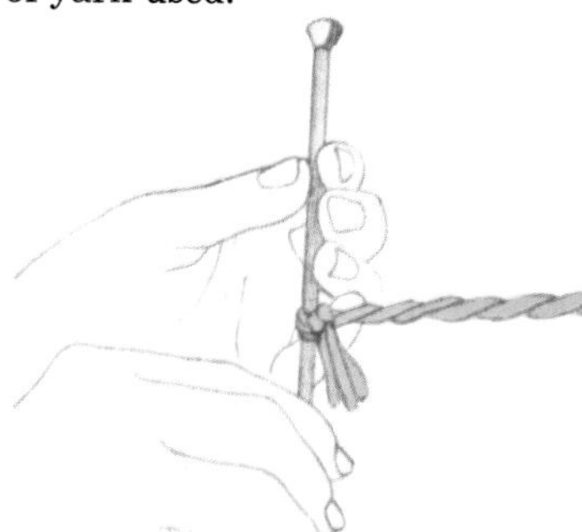

The strands of yarn should be three times the length of the finished cord. Tie a knot about ¾in from each end. Insert a knitting needle through knots, and with the help of a friend, twist the needles in a clockwise direction.

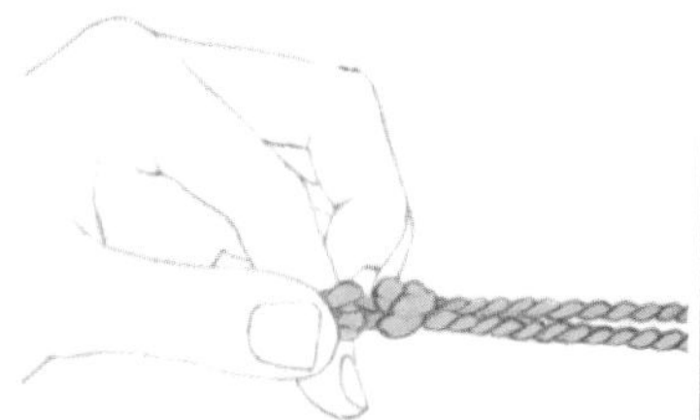

Continue to turn the needles until strands are tightly twisted.
Keeping the strands taut, fold them in half at center. Without letting go of the ends, remove the needles and knot the two ends together.

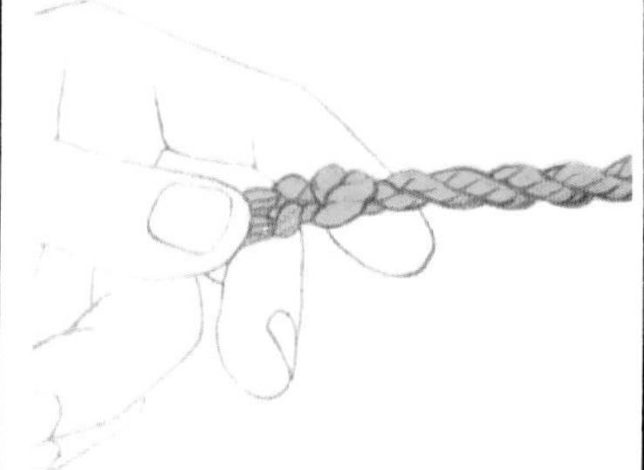

Hold the knot and shake the cord, letting the cord twist back on itself. Undo the original knots and even out the yarn in the tassel. If the cord is to be used as a tie, sew the folded end to the garment; if the cord is to be used as a drawstring or belt, knot the other end of the cord and cut the fold to make a tassel.

Change to A.* Rep from * to * 3 times, then rep first 2 rows again. Cont in patt dec one st at beg of next and every foll 4th row until 21sts rem; end with a WS row. Bind off.

Right front pocket
Work to match left front pocket, reversing shaping.

Front edges (alike)
Using No. 2 needles, A and with RS facing pick up and K 80[86:92:98]sts along front edge between hemline marker and neck edge.

To finish
Join raglan seams, sewing last 4 rows of sleeve seams to bound-off sts at armholes. Join side and sleeve seams. Fold up hem at lower edge and hem in position. Sew in zipper. Sew on pockets. Make twisted or crochet cord in B and thread through hem.

Pants

Right leg
Using No. 2 needles and A, cast on 90[96:102:108]sts and beg with a K row work 8 rows stockinette st. Mark end of last row for hemline. Change to No. 4 needles and cont in stockinette st until work measures 12[13½:15:16½]in from markers; end with a P row. Adjust length here if required.

Shape crotch
Bind off 4sts at beg of next row, then 2sts at beg of next 3 rows.
Next row K1, K2 tog, K to last 3sts, sl 1, K1, psso, K1.
Next row P to end.
Next row K1, K2 tog, K to end.
Next row P to end.
Cont to dec at front edge on every other row 1[2:3:4] times and at same time cont to dec at back edge on every 4th row until 70[74:78:82]sts rem. Cont straight until work measures 7[8:8½:9½]in from beg of crotch; end with a K row.

Shape back
1st row P35[40:45:50], turn.
2nd and every foll alternate row K to end.
3rd row P28[32:36:40], turn.
5th row P21[24:27:30], turn.
Cont to work 7[8:9:10]sts less on alternate rows twice, then P across all sts. Change to No. 2 needles and work 8 rows. Bind off.

Left leg
Work to match right leg, reversing all shaping.

To finish
Do not press. Join back, front and leg seams. Fold up hems and sl st in place. Turn last 8 rows at waist to WS and sl st in place. Thread elastic through hems at waist and ankles.

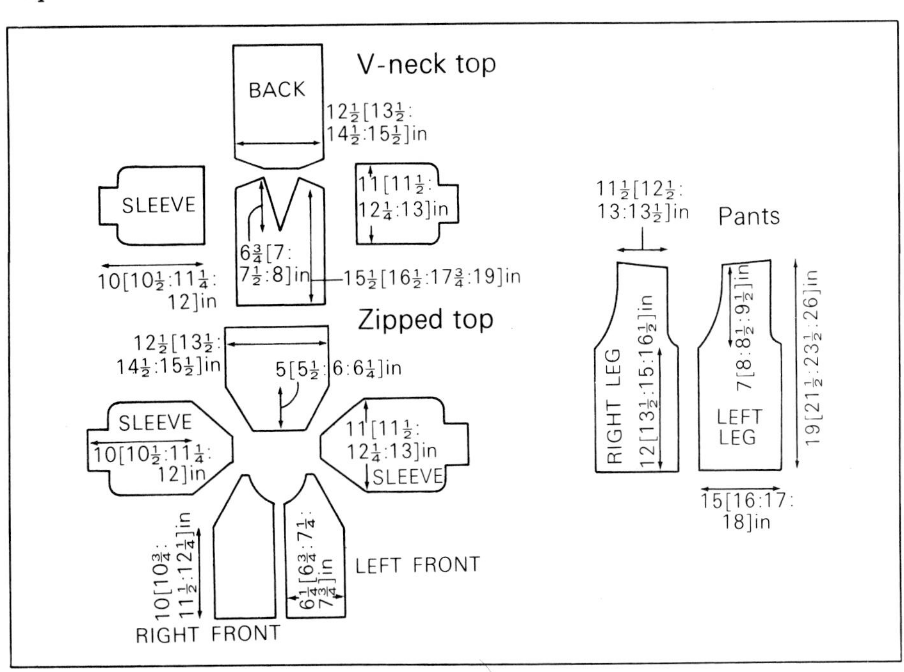

SUNNY DAY DRESSES

Sizes
To fit 20[22:24]in chest.
Length to shoulder, 15½[17:18½]in.
Note *Directions for larger sizes are in brackets []; where there is only one set of figures it applies to all sizes.*

Materials
Sport yarn:
Dress with striped hem
5[5:6] × 1oz balls in main shade (A)
2 balls in contrasting color (B)
Dress with pocket *5[5:6] × 1oz balls in main shade (A)*
2 balls in contrasting color (B)
Striped dress *2[3:3] × 1oz balls in main shade (A) for hem*
1[2:2] balls each in contrasting colors, (B, C and D)
1 pair each Nos. 2 and 3 knitting needles
1 pair No. 00 knitting needles for dress with striped hem

Gauge
26sts and 34 rows to 4in in stockinette st on No. 3 needles.

Dress with striped hem

Front
Using No. 2 needles and A, cast on 130[142:154]sts. Beg with K row, work 7 rows stockinette st; end with K row.
Next row K to end to form hemline. Change to No. 3 needles. Beg with a K row, work 6 rows stockinette st.
Next row (hem row) *K one st from needle tog with one loop from cast-on edge, rep from * to end.
Beg with P row, work 3 rows stockinette st. Join in B. Cont in stockinette st, work in stripe sequence of 6 rows B, 6A, 4B, 4A and 2B. Cut off B. Using A throughout, cont in stockinette st until work measures 7[7½:8]in from hemline; end with K row.
Shape bodice
Next row *P2 tog, rep from * to end. 65[71:77]sts.
Next row K1, *P1, K1, rep from * to end.
Next row P1, *K1, P1, rep from * to end. Rep last 2 rows until work measures 11[12:13]in from hemline. Bind off loosely in ribbing.

Back
Work as for front.

Short strap
Using No. 2 needles and B, cast on 15sts.
1st row (RS) K2, *P1, K1, rep from * to last st, K1.
2nd row K1, *P1, K1, rep from * to end. Rep last 2 rows for 10[11:12]in. Bind off.
Long strap
Using No. 2 needles and B, cast on 3sts.
1st row (RS) P1, K1, P1.
2nd row K into front and back of first st – called inc 1 – P1, inc 1.
3rd row Inc 1, P1, K1, P1, inc 1.
4th row Inc 1, (P1, K1) twice, P1, inc 1.

5th row Inc 1, (P1, K1) 3 times, P1, inc 1.
6th row Inc 1, (P1, K1) 4 times, P1, inc 1.
7th row Inc 1, (P1, K1) 5 times, P1, inc 1. 15sts.
8th row K1, *P1, K1, rep from * to last st, K1.
9th row K2, *P1, K1, rep from * to last st, K1.
Rep last 2 rows for 14½[16:16½]in from point. Bind off.

Flower motif
Using No. 00 needles and A, cast on 2sts.
1st row K1, K into front and back of next st – so inc 1.
2nd row K3.
3rd row K2, inc 1.
4th row K4.
5th row K3, inc 1.
6th–9th rows K5.
10th row Bind off one st, K to end.
11th row K to end.
12th–15th rows Rep 10th and 11th rows twice.
16th row Bind off one st. Using right-hand needle, pick up and K one st between first and 2nd picot points, bind off one st and transfer rem st to left-hand needle.
Rep 16 rows 4 times, joining each petal in same way. Fasten off. Sew into circle to form flower.

To finish
Press under damp cloth with warm iron. Join sides. Place short strap on left shoulder, sewing ½in at each end to inside of top. Place long strap, sewing ½in of straight end to inside of back bodice with point just below waist. Catch long strap in position at top of front bodice and waist. Using B, sew flower motif to strap at waist, making one French knot at base of each petal and one in center. Press seams.

Dress with pocket

Front and back
Work as for front and back of dress with striped hem, omitting stripes and changing to B before shaping bodice.

Pocket
Using No. 3 needles and B, cast on 15sts. Beg with K row, work 2in stockinette st; end with K row.
Change to No. 2 needles.

Next row K to end to mark fold line. Beg with a K row work 6 rows stockinette st. Bind off.

To finish
Press under damp cloth with warm iron. Sew on pockets. Join side seams.
Straps For double straps cut 12 strands of color A, each 20in long. Braid tog, using 4 strands in each section. Cut in half, knot ends and sew to outside edge of front and back bodice.

Striped dress

Front
Using No. 2 needles and A, cast on 120[142:156]sts. Beg with K row, work 7 rows stockinette st; end with K row.
Next row K to end to mark

hemline. Change to No. 3 needles. Beg with a K row, work 4 rows stockinette st. Join in B and work 2 rows stockinette st.
Next row (hem row) *K one st from needle tog with one loop from cast-on edge, rep from * to end.
P1 row using B. Join in C. Cont in stockinette st and stripe sequence of 4 rows each C, D, A and B until work measures 7[7½:8]in from hemline, ending with 3rd row of any stripe.
Shape bodice
Next row P0[0:1], *P2 tog, rep from * to last 0[0:1]sts, P0[0:1]. 65[71:79]sts. Keeping color sequence correct, work 2 rows in each color as foll:
Next row K to end.
Next row P1, *K1, P1, rep from * to end. Rep last 2 rows until work measures 11[12:13]in from hemline; end with stripe in C. Bind off loosely in ribbing.

Back
Work as for front.

Straps (make 2)
Using No. 2 needles and D, cast on 9sts. Rib 20in for short strap of dress with striped hem. Bind off.

To finish
Press under damp cloth with warm iron. Join sides. Position straps on front bodice, sewing ½in at end to inside of bodice. Press seams.

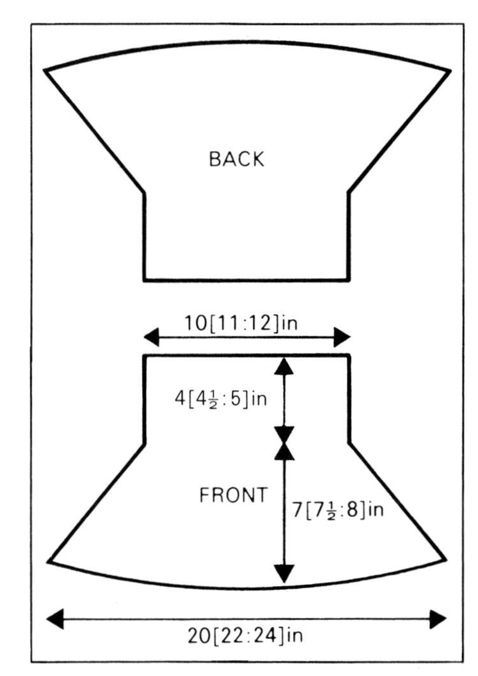

GOOD NEWS CABLE

Sizes
Sleeveless sweater *To fit 22[24:26:28]in chest.*
Length, 13[14½:16:17½]in.
Tunic *To fit chest sizes as above.*
Length, 17[19:20½:22]in.
Note *Directions for larger sizes are in brackets []; where there is only one set of figures this applies to all sizes.*

Materials
Sleeveless sweater *2[4:4:4]oz of a sport yarn in a dark color (A)*
2oz in a light color (B)
Tunic *4[4:4:6]oz of sport yarn in a dark color (A)*
2[4:4:4]oz in a light color (B)
1 pair each Nos. 4 and 7 knitting needles
1 cable needle (cn)

Gauge
21sts and 26 rows to 4in in stockinette st on No. 7 needles.

Tunic

Back

**Using No. 4 needles and A, cast on 28[30:33:35]sts, join in B and cast on 28[30:33:35]sts.
Next row K28[30:33:35]B, 28[30:33:35]A, twisting yarn at front of work when changing color to avoid a hole. Work further 6 rows garter st, twisting yarn on WS of work.
Next row Keeping colors correct,

K9[5:5:7], pick up loop between needles and work into back – M1 – (K13[10:11:8], M1) to last 8[5:6:7]sts, K to end. 60[66:72:78]sts.
Change to No. 7 needles.
Next row With B, K3, P21[24:27:30], K2, P4; with A, P4, K2, P21[24:27:30], K3. Keeping 3sts at each end in garter st, beg with 1st patt row, cont in patt as for sweater until back measures 4in at center from beg. Taking garter st at each end into stockinette st, cont in patt until back measures 12[13½:14:16]in at center from beg; end with WS row.** Shape armholes as for sweater, then cont straight until back measures 17[19:20½:22]in at center from beg; end with WS row. Shape shoulders as for sweater.

Front
Work as for back of tunic from ** to **. Shape armholes as for sweater, cont straight until front measures 14[15¾:17¼:19¼]in at center from beg; end with WS row. Shape neck and shoulders as for sweater.

Neck and armhole borders
Work as for sweater.

Belt
Using No. 4 needles and A, cast on 9sts.
1st row (RS) K2, (P1, K1) to last st, K1.
2nd row K1, (P1, K1) to end. Rep for 2 rows until belt measures 34[36:38:40]in. Bind off in ribbing.

To finish
Join side seams from top of garter st borders. Press seams.

Sleeveless sweater

Back
**Using No. 4 needles and A, cast on 56[60:66:70]sts and work in K1, P1 ribbing for 2in.
Next row Rib 9[5:5:7], pick up loop between needles and work into back – called make one or M1 – (rib 13[10:11:8], M1) to last 8[5:6:7]sts, rib to end. 60[66:72:78]sts. Change to No. 7 needles.
Next row K30[33:36:39] A, join in B, K30[33:36:39]B.
Next row With B, P24[27:30:33], K2, P4, then with A, P4, K2, P24[27:30:33]. Twist yarns when changing color to avoid a hole. Beg patt.
1st row (RS) With A, K24[27:30:33], P2, K4, then with B, K4, P2, K24[27:30:33].
2nd row With B, P24[27:30:33], K2, P4, then with A, P4, K2, P24[27:30:33].
3rd-6th rows 1st and 2nd rows twice.
7th row With A, K24[27:30:33], P2, sl next 4 sts in A onto cn and leave at front, with B, K4, join in 2nd ball of A, using 2nd ball of A, K4sts from cn, join in 2nd ball of B, with 2nd ball of B, P2, K24[27:30:33].
8th row With B, P24[27:30:33], K2, with A, P4, with B, P4, with A, K2, P24[27:30:33].
9th row With A, K24[27:30:33], P2, with B, K4, with A, K4, with B, P2. K24[27:30:33].
10th-19th rows Work 8th and 9th rows 5 times.
20th row As 8th row.
21st row With A, K24[27:30:33], P2, sl next 4sts in B onto cn and leave at front, with A, K4, with B, K4sts from cn, with B, P2, K24[27:30:33]. Cut off extra balls of A and B.
22nd row As 2nd row.
23rd-28th row Work first and 2nd rows 3 times. These 28 rows form patt. Cont in patt until work measures 8[9:10:11]in at center from beg; end with WS row.
Shape armholes
Bind off 6sts at beg of next 2 rows. Dec one st at each end of every row until 44[50:56:62]sts rem, at each end of every alternate row until 38[42:46:50]sts rem. **Cont straight until work measures 13[14½:16:17½]in at center from beg; end with WS row.
Shape shoulders
Bind off 3[4:4:5]sts at beg of next 2 rows and 4[4:5:5]sts at beg of foll 2. Put rem 24[26:28:30]sts on holder.

Front
Work as for back from ** to ** reversing colors – working B for A and A for B throughout. Cont straight until front measures 10[11½:13:14½]in at center from beg; end with WS row.
Divide for neck
Next row K11[12:13:14], turn and leave rem sts on spare needle.

Finish this side first. Dec one st at neck edge on next and foll 3 alternate rows. 7[8:9:10]sts. Cont straight until front is same length as back up to beg of shoulder; end with WS row.

Shape shoulder

Bind off 3[4:4:5]sts at beg of next row. Work 1 row. Bind off. Return to sts on spare needle, sl next 16[18:20:22]sts on holder, join yarn to next st and work to end of row. Match to first side.

Neck border

Join right shoulder seam. With RS facing and No. 4 needles and A, pick up and K 25sts along left front neck, K sts from holder, pick up and K 25sts along right front, K back sts from holder. 90[94:98:102]sts. Work in K1, P1 ribbing for $\frac{3}{4}$in. Bind off in ribbing.

Armhole borders (alike)

Join left shoulder and neck border seam. With RS facing, using No. 4 needles and A, pick up and K 70[76:82:88]sts around armhole. Work 6 rows in K1, P1 ribbing. Bind off in ribbing.

To finish

Join side seams. Press seams.

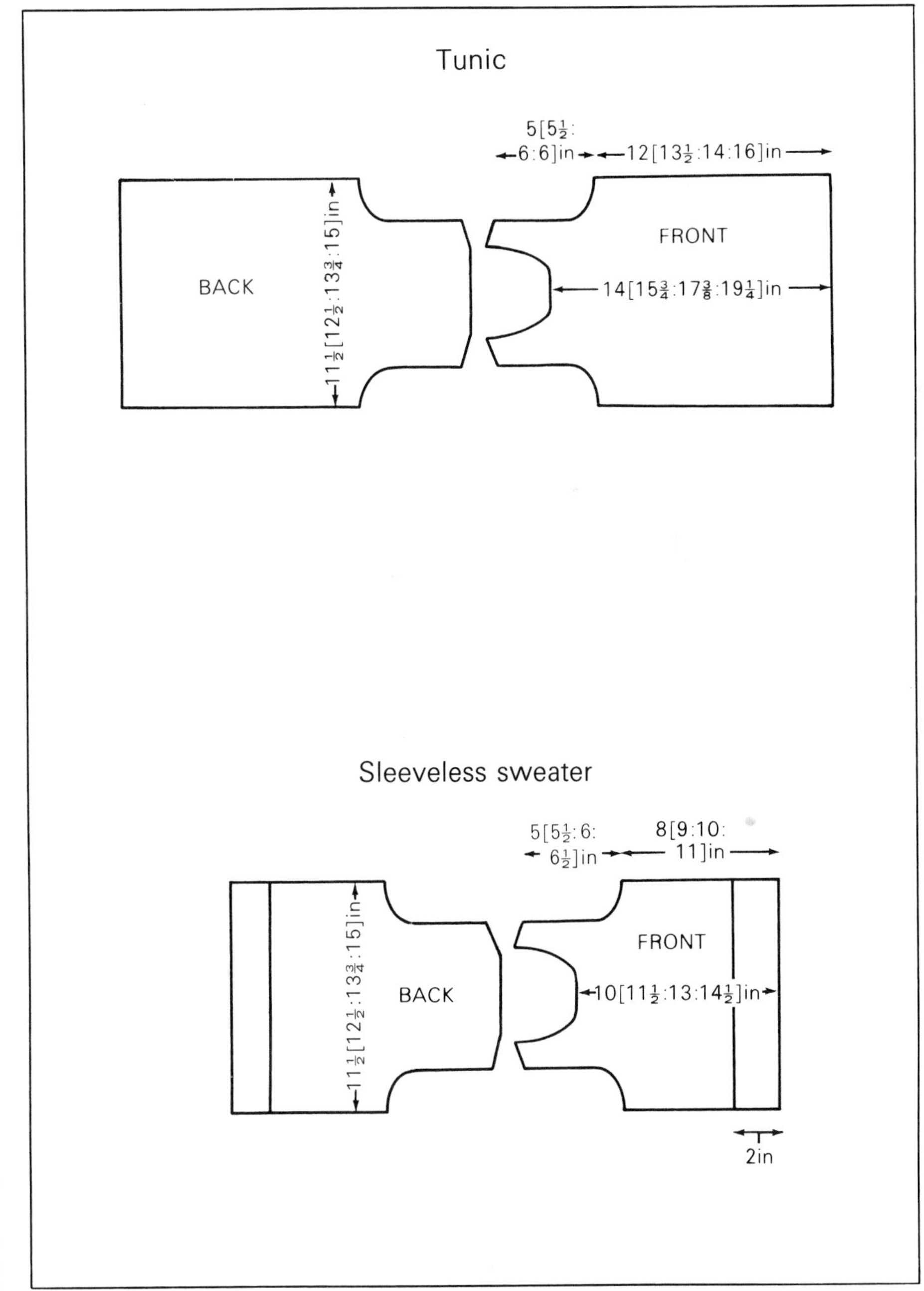

KIDS' STUFF

Sizes
To fit 22[24:26:28]in chest.
Length, 13½[15:16½:18]in.
Sleeve seam, 10[11½:13:15]in.
Note *Directions for larger sizes are in brackets []; where there is only one set of figures it applies to all sizes.*

Materials
Knitting worsted:
Fair Isle *5[5:6:6]oz in pink [A]*
2oz in red (B)
1oz in white (C)
Narrow stripes *2[2:3:3]oz in cream (A)*
2oz in each of red (B), blue (C) and mustard (D)
Wide stripes *3[3:4:4]oz in blue (A)*
2oz in each of green (B), pink (C) and mustard (D)
Seed stitch *7[7:8:8]oz in a random color (A)*
1 pair each Nos. 4 and 5 knitting needles

Gauge
24sts and 32 rows to 4in in stockinette st on No. 5 needles.
22sts and 36 rows to 4in in seed st on No. 5 needles.

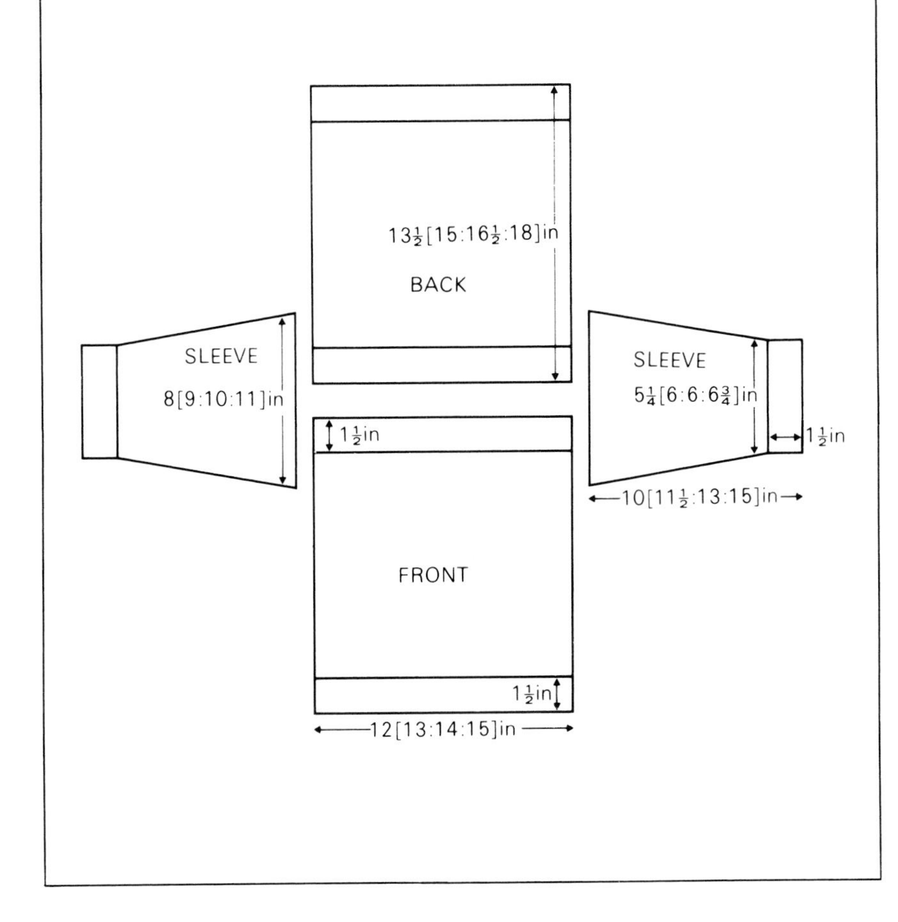

Fair Isle

Back and front

With A, K1 row and P1 row. Beg patt.
1st row K3[1:3:1]A, *1B, 3A, rep from * to last st, 1B.
2nd row P with A.
3rd row K1[3:1:3]A, *1B, 3A, rep from * to last 3sts, 1B, 2A.
4th row P with A.
These 4 rows form patt. Rep them 9[11:13:15] times, then the first 2 rows 1[0:1:0] times.

Yoke

1st and 2nd rows K with B.
3rd row K with C.
4th row P with C.
5th and 6th rows K with B.
7th row K with A.
8th row P0[3:2:1]A, *3A, 1C, 4A, rep from * to last 0[3:2:1]sts, 0[3:2:1]A.
9th row K0[3:2:1]A, *3A, 3C, 2A, rep from * to last 0[3:2:1]sts, 0[3:2:1]A.
10th row P0[3:2:1]A, *1A, 5C, 2A, rep from * to last 0[3:2:1]sts, 0[3:2:1]A.
11th row K0[3:2:1]A, *1A, 7C, rep from * to last 0[3:2:1]sts, 0[3:2:1]A.
12th row As 10th.
13th row As 9th.
14th row As 8th.
15th row As 7th.
16th row P with A.
17th-23rd rows As 1st-7th.
24th row P0[3:2:1]A, *3A, 1B, 4A, rep from * to last 0[3:2:1]sts, 0[3:2:1]A.
25th row K0[3:2:1]A, *3A, 1B, 1A, 1B, 2A, rep from * to last 0[3:2:1]sts, 0[3:2:1]A.
26th row P with A.
27th row K1[4:3:2]A, *7A, 1B, rep from * to last 7[10:9:8]sts, 7[10:9:8]A.
28th row P6[9:8:7]A, *1B, 1A, 1B, 5A, rep from * to last 2[5:4:3]sts, 2[5:4:3]A.
29th row K with A.
30th and 31st rows As 24th and 25th.
32nd row P with A.

Sleeves

1st row *K3A, 1B, rep from * to end.
2nd row P with A.
3rd row 1A, 1B, *3A, 1B, rep from * to last 2sts, 2A.
4th row P with A.
Rep these 4 rows throughout, working extra sts into patt.

Narrow stripes

Using stockinette st throughout, work in stripes of 6 rows C, 6 rows D, 6 rows B and 6 rows A.

Wide stripes

Back and front

Using stockinette st throughout, when work measures 4½[6:7½:9]in work 16 rows in B, 16 rows in C and 16 rows in D.

Sleeves

When work measures 2½[4:5½:7½]in work in stripes as for back and front.

Seed stitch

1st row *K1, P1, rep from * to end.
2nd row *P1, K1, rep from * to end.

Basic sweater

Back and front (alike)

With No. 4 needles and A, cast on 72[78:84:90]sts.
1st ribbing row K1, *P2, K2, rep

from * to last 3sts, P2, K1.
2nd ribbing row P1, *K2, P2, rep from * to last 3sts, K2, P1.
Rep these 2 rows 5 times.
Change to No. 5 needles.
Cont in patt of your choice until work measures 9[10:11:12]in; end with a WS row.
Mark each end of last row with a colored thread to denote beg of armholes.
Cont in patt until work measures 12[13½:15:16½]in; end with a RS row.
Beg with a 2nd ribbing row and with A, work 11 rows ribbing.
Bind off in ribbing.

Sleeves
With No. 4 needles and A, cast on 32[36:36:40]sts. Work 2 ribbing rows of back and front 6 times.
Change to No. 5 needles. Cont in patt, inc one st at each end of 3rd and every foll 4th row until there are 48[54:60:66]sts. Cont straight until work measures 10[11½:13:15]in. Bind off.

To finish
Join shoulder seams for 2½[2½:3¼:3¼]in. Sew bound-off edge of sleeves to armholes between markers. Join side and sleeve seams.

CANDY CARDIGAN

Sizes
To fit 26[28:30]in chest.
Length, $17\frac{1}{2}$[19:$20\frac{1}{4}$]in.
Sleeve seam, 13[14:15]in.
Note *Directions for larger sizes are in brackets []; where there is only one set of figures it applies to all sizes.*

Materials
9[9:10] × 1oz balls of a medium-weight mohair in main shade, (A)
1[1:2] balls each of contrasting colors, (B and C)
1 pair each Nos. 7 and 9 knitting needles
6 buttons

Gauge
14sts and 18 rows to 4in in stockinette st on No. 9 needles.

Back
Using No. 7 needles and A, cast on 49[53:57]sts.
1st row K1, *P1, K1, rep from * to end.
2nd row P1, *K1, P1, rep from * to end. Rep last 2 rows for 2in; end with a 2nd row. Change to No. 9 needles. Beg with a K row, work 4 rows stockinette st.
5th row K4[6:8], *using B, (K1, P1, K1, P1, K1) all into next st, turn, K5, turn, P5, turn, K5, turn, P2 tog, P3 tog, sl these 2sts back onto left-hand needle, then using A, K2 tog tbl, cut off contrasting color – called make a bobble (MB) –, K9A, rep from * 3 times. MB in B, K4[5:8]A.
Work 11 rows stockinette st.
17th row K9[11:13], *MB in C, K9A, rep from * twice more, MB in C, K9[11:13]A.
Work 11 rows stockinette st. Rep last 24 rows until work measures 12[13:14]in from beg; end with a P row.
Shape raglan armholes
Keeping patt correct, bind off 3sts at beg of next 2 rows.
Next row K1, sl 1, K1, psso, K to last 3sts, K2 tog, K1.
Next row P to end.
Rep last 2 rows (working bobbles as before) until 19[21:23]sts rem, ending with a P row. Bind off.

Left front
Using No. 7 needles and A, cast on 29[31:33]sts. Rib 2in as for back, ending with a 2nd row and inc one st at end of last row. 30[32:34]sts.
Change to No. 9 needles.
Next row K24[26:28], turn and leave rem 6sts on a holder.
Work 3 rows stockinette st.
5th row K4[6:8], *MB in B, K9A, rep from * once more.
Work 11 rows stockinette st.
17th row K9[11:13], MB in C, K9A, MB in C, K4A. Cont in patt until work matches back to underarm, ending with a P row.
Shape raglan armhole
Bind off 3sts at beg of next row.
Next row P to end.
Next row K1, sl 1, K1, psso, K to end. Rep last 2 rows until 14[15:16]sts rem, ending with a K row.
Shape neck
Bind off 3[4:5]sts at beg of next row.
Next row K1, sl 1, K1, psso, K to last 2sts, K2 tog.
Next row P to end.
Rep last 2 rows 3 times. 3sts.
Next row K1, sl 1, K1, psso. Bind off rem 2sts.

Right front
Using No. 7 needles and A, cast on 29[31:33]sts. Rib 1in as for back; end with a 2nd row.
Next row K1, K2 tog tbl, yo, rib to end.
Rib until work measures 2in from beg, ending with a 2nd row and inc one st at beg of last row. 30[32:34]sts.
Next row Rib 6 and leave these sts on a holder, change to No. 9 needles and K to end.
Work 3 rows stockinette st.
Next row *K9A, MB in B, rep from * once more, K4[6:8]A.
Work 11 rows stockinette st.

Next row K4A, MB in C, K9A, MB in C, K9[11:13]A.
Complete to match left front, reversing all shaping.

Sleeves
Using No. 7 needles and A, cast on 25[27:29]sts. Rib 2in as for back; end with a 2nd row. Change to No. 9 needles.
Next row K4[5:6], *pick up loop lying between needles and K tbl – called make 1 (M1) – K2, rep from * to last 3[4:5]sts, M1, K to end. 35[37:39]sts.
Work 7 rows stockinette st.
9th row K2[3:4], *MB in B, K9A, rep from * twice, MB in B, K2[3:4]A.
Work 11 rows stockinette st.
21st row K7[8:9], *MB in C, K9A, rep from * once more, MB in C, K7[8:9]A. Cont in patt until sleeve measures 13[14:15]in; end with same patt row as back at underarm.
Shape raglan top
Bind off 3sts at beg of next 2 rows. Dec as for back raglan shaping until 5sts rem; end with a P row. Bind off.

Collar
Using No. 7 needles and A, cast on 159[165:171]sts. Rib 4 rows as for back. Change to No. 9 needles.
Next row (K1, P1) twice, K to last 4 sts, (P1, K1) twice.
Next row (P1, K1) twice, P to last 4sts, (K1, P1) twice.
Rep last 2 rows for 2¾in, ending with a WS row.
Next row Rib 4, (K1, K2 tog) to last 5sts, K1, rib 4. 109[113:117]sts. Work 3 rows.
Next row Rib 4, (K2 tog) to last 5sts, K1, rib 4. Bind off.

Left front band
Sl sts from holder onto No. 7 needles, inc one st at inside edge. Cont in ribbing until band, slightly stretched, fits to neck edge. Bind off. Sew band in position and mark position of buttonholes, first in waistband to correspond with buttonhole already worked, last to come 4 rows below neck edge, with 4 more evenly spaced between.

Right front band
Work to match left front band, making buttonholes as before to correspond with markers.

To finish
Join raglan seams, then join side and sleeve seams. Sew on bands, then sew on collar beg and ending ½in from front edge. Sew on buttons.

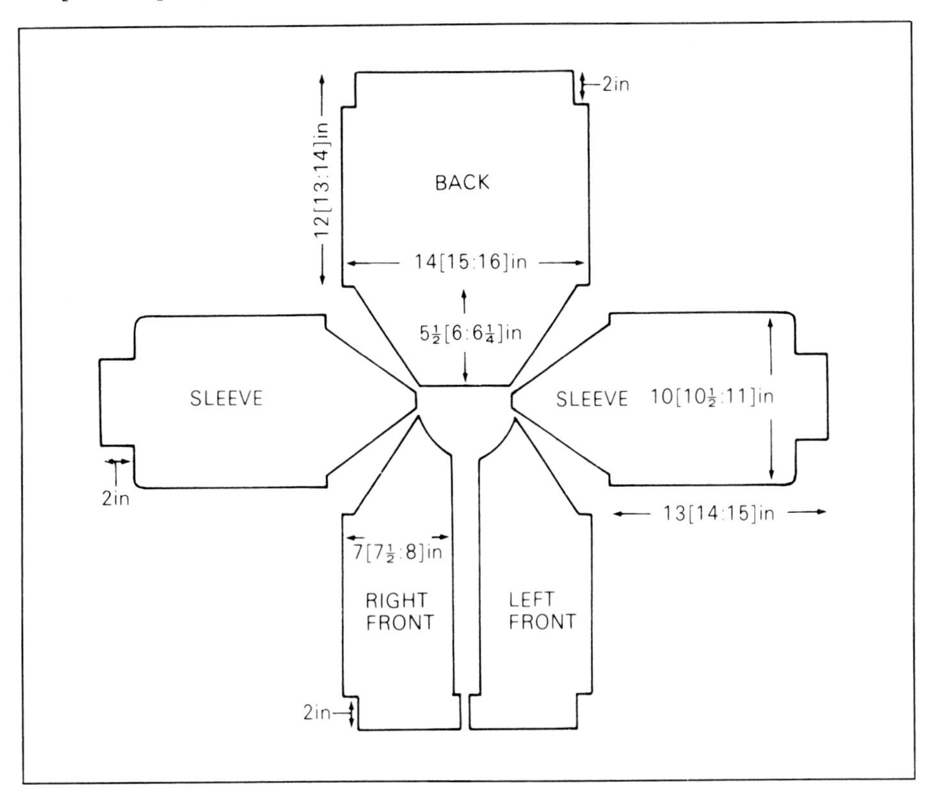

TASTY TURTLENECK

Sizes
To fit 32[34:36:38]in bust.
Length, 22½[22½:24:24]in.
Sleeve seam, 17[17:18:18]in.
Note *Directions for larger sizes are in brackets []; where there is only one set of figures it applies to all sizes.*

Materials
16[18:20:22]oz of a knitting worsted
1 pair each Nos. 8 and 10 knitting needles
1 set of four No. 7 double-pointed needles

Gauge
14sts and 18 rows to 4in in patt on No. 10 needles, using yarn double.
Note *Yarn is used double throughout.*

Back
Using No. 8 needles and yarn double, cast on 58[62:62:70]sts.
1st ribbing row (K2, P2) to last 2sts, K2.
2nd ribbing row (P2, K2) to last 2sts, P2. Rep these 2 rows for 2½in, end with 2nd row; for 1st and 4th sizes dec one st at end of last row and for 2nd and 3rd sizes inc one st at end of last row.
All sizes 57[63:63:69]sts. Change to No. 10 needles. Beg patt.
1st row (RS) K1, *K1, yo, K2 tog tbl, K1, K2 tog, yo, rep from * to last 2sts, K2.
2nd row K1, P2, *yo, P3 tog, yo, P3, rep from * to end, finishing last rep P2, K1.
3rd row K to end.
4th row K1, *P1, P2, tog tbl, yo, P1, yo, P2 tog, rep from * to last 2sts, P1, K1.
5th row K1, K2 tog, *yo, K3, yo, K3 tog, rep from * to last 6sts, yo, K3, yo, K2 tog tbl, K1.
6th row P to end.
These 6 rows form patt. Cont in patt until work measures 15[15:15½:15½]in from beg; end with WS row. Place marker at each end of last row for beg of armholes.
Cont in patt until work measures 7½[7½:8½:8½]in from markers; end with WS row.
Next row Work 20sts for shoulder, bind off next 17[23:23:29]sts for neck, work to end for shoulder.
Next row Bind off first 20sts, cut off yarn. Rejoin yarn to neck edge of rem sts, bind off these sts.

Front
Using No. 8 needles and yarn double, cast on 62[62:70:70]sts.
Work 2 ribbing rows for 2½in; end with 2nd row; for 1st and 2nd sizes inc one st at end of last row and for 3rd and 4th sizes dec one st at end of last row. All sizes 63[63:69:69]sts.
Change to No. 10 needles. Cont in patt as for back until work measures 15[15:15½:15½]in from beg; end with WS row. Place marker at each end of last row for beg of armholes. Cont in patt until work measures 5[5:5½:5½]in from markers; end with WS row.
Divide for neck
Next row Patt 25, turn and leave rem sts on spare needle. Dec one st at neck edge on next 5 rows. Cont in patt until work measures 7½[7½:8½:8½]in from marker, end at side edge. Bind off. With RS facing join yarn to inner end of sts on spare needle, bind off 13[13:19:19]sts, patt to end of row. Complete to match first side.

Sleeves
Using No. 8 needles and yarn double, cast on 30[30:34:34]sts.
Work 2 ribbing rows for 3in, end with 1st row.
Inc row P1[1:2:2], P twice into each of next 27[27:29:29]sts, P2[2:3:3]. 57[57:63:63]sts.
Change to No. 10 needles. Work in patt as for back until work measures 17[17:18:18]in. Bind off.

Turtleneck collar
Join shoulders. With RS facing, using 3 needles of set and yarn double, pick up and K 68[72:80:84]sts around neck. Work in rounds of K2, P2 ribbing for 7[7:8:8]in. Bind off in ribbing.

To finish
Sew sleeves to armholes. Join side and sleeve seams. Press seams lightly.

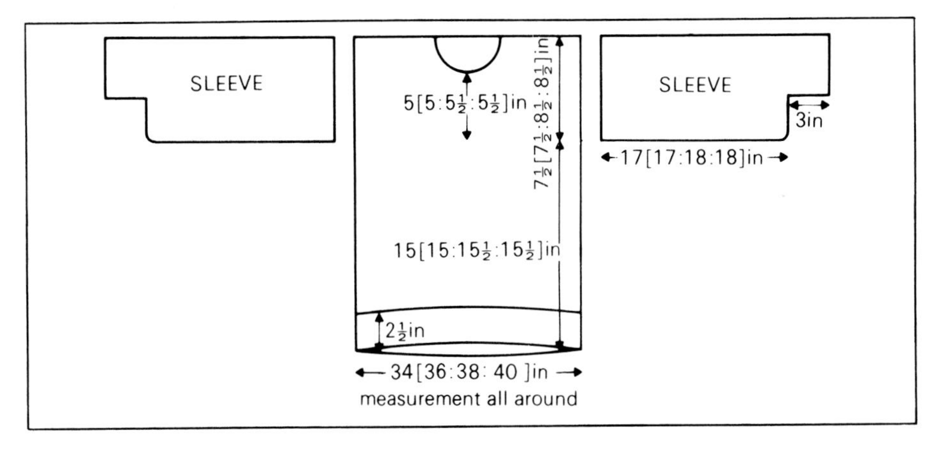

BEADED BEAUTY

Back
*Using No. 2 needles cast on 104[112:120]sts. Work 4 rows K1, P1 ribbing. Beg with a K row, cont in stockinette st, dec one st at each end of 3rd and every foll 4th row until 94[102:102]sts rem. Cont straight until work measures 3¼in; end with a P row. Now inc one st at each end of 7th and every foll 6th row until there are 120[126:134]sts. Cont straight until work measures 15in; end with a P row.
Shape armholes
Bind off 8sts at beg of next 2 rows. Dec one st at each end of every foll alternate row until 88[90:94]sts rem. Cont straight until armhole measures 4¼[4¾:5]in; end with a P row.*
Divide for back opening
Next row K43[44:46], turn and leave rem sts on a spare needle. Cont on first set of sts until armhole measures 7[7½:8]in; end at armhole edge.
Shape shoulder
Bind off 7sts at beg of next and foll 2 alternate rows and 5[5:7]sts at beg of foll alternate row. Work 1 row. Bind off. Rejoin yarn to inner end of sts on spare needle, bind off 2sts and K to end of row. Complete to match first side.

Front
Work as given for back from * to *.
Divide for neck
Next row K44[45:47], turn and leave rem sts on a spare needle.
Next row K1, P to end.
Next row K.
Next row K1, P to end.
Rep last 2 rows 6 times.
Next row K to last 5sts, (K2 tog) twice, K1.
Next row K1, P to end.
Next row K.
Next row K1, P to end.
Rep last 4 rows once.
Next row K to last 5sts, (K2 tog) twice, K1.
Next row K1, P to end.
Next row Bind off 7, K to end.
Next row K1, P to end.
Next row Bind off 7, K to last 5sts. (K2 tog) twice, K1.
Next row K1, P to end.
Next row Bind off 7. K to end.
Next row K1, P to end.
Next row Bind off 5[6:7], K to end. 10[11:11]sts.
Next row K1, P to end.
Next row K.
Rep last 2 rows until band fits from shoulder, along back neck edge to back neck opening, ending with a WS row. Bind off. Rejoin yarn to inner end of sts on spare needle.
Next row K.
Next row P to last st, K1.

Sizes
To fit 32[34:36]in bust.
Length, 22[22½:23]in.
Sleeve seam, 17[17½:18]in.
Note *Directions for larger sizes are in brackets []; where there is only one set of figures it applies to all sizes.*

Materials
10[10:11]oz of a lightweight mohair
1 pair No. 2 knitting needles
4in lightweight zipper
Sequins and beads for decoration

Gauge
28sts and 36 rows to 4in in stockinette st.

Rep last 2 rows 7 times more.
Next row K1, (sl 1, K1, psso) twice, K to end.
Next row P to last st, K1.
Next row K.
Next row P to last st, K1.
Rep last 4 rows once more.
Next row K1, (sl 1, K1, psso) twice. K to end.
Next row P to last st, K1.
Next row K.
Next row Bind off 7, P to last st, K1.
Next row K1, (sl 1, K1, psso) twice, K to end.
Next row Bind off 7, P to last st, K1.
Next row K.
Rep last 2 rows once.
Next row Bind off 5[5:7], P to last st, K1, 10[11:11]sts.
Next row K.
Next row P to last st, K1.
Rep last 2 rows until band fits from shoulder, along back neck edge to back neck opening, end with a WS row. Bind off.

Sleeves
Using No. 2 needles cast on 50[52:54]sts. Work 4 rows K1, P1 ribbing.
Beg with a K row, cont in stockinette st, inc one st at each end of 9th and every foll 8th[8th:7th] row until there are 84[88:92]sts. Cont straight, until work measures 17[17½:18]in; end with a P row.
Shape top
Bind off 8sts at beg of next 2 rows. Dec one st at each end of every row until 54[58:62]sts rem. Work 26[28:32] rows straight. Now dec one st at each end of next and every foll alternate row until 40[44:48]sts rem, then each end of every row until 28sts rem.
Bind off.

To finish
Join shoulder seams. Sew back neck band to neck edge. With RS facing, using No. 2 needles pick up and K 62sts evenly along back neck opening. Bind off.
Set in sleeves, gathering sleeve head to form "puff". Join side and sleeve seams.
Sew in zipper.

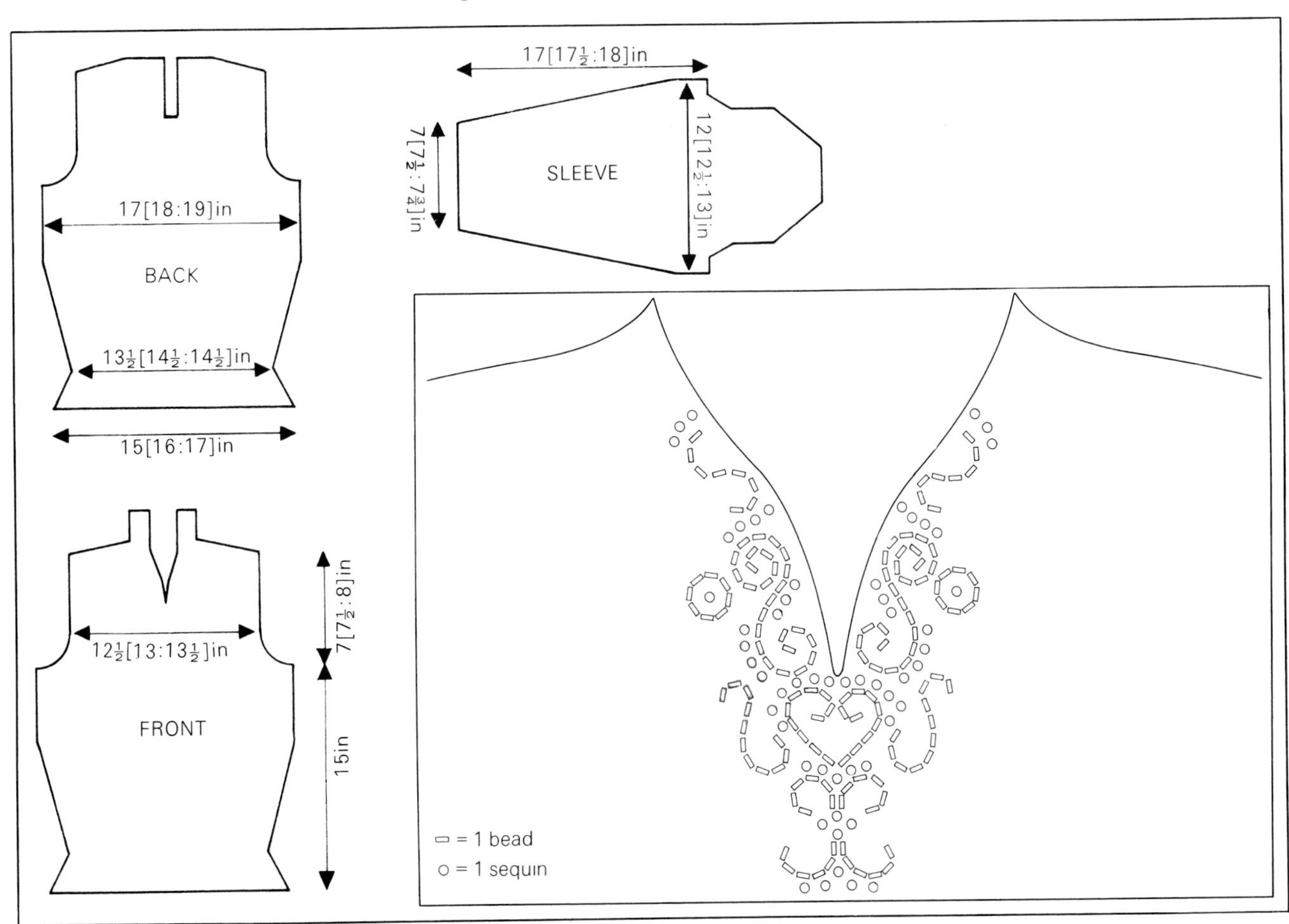

COUNTRY CASUAL

Sizes
To fit 32[34:36]in bust.
Length $24\frac{1}{2}$in.
Sleeve seam, $15\frac{3}{4}$in.
Note *The figures in brackets [] refer to the 2nd and 3rd sizes respectively.*

Materials
16[18:20]oz of a mohair-type knitting worsted
1 pair No. 9 knitting needles
No. 9 circular needle
Cable needle

Gauge
13sts and 26 rows to 4in in garter st on No. 9 needles.

Front
Using No. 9 needles cast on 72sts and work from side edge to side edge. Cont in garter st until work measures $6\frac{1}{4}[6\frac{3}{4}:7\frac{1}{8}]$in from beg.
Shape neck
Bind off 3sts at beg of next and every other row 10 times, ending at neck edge, 42sts. Cast on 3sts at beg of next and every other row 10 times. 72sts. Cont in garter st until work measures $18[19:19\frac{3}{4}]$in from beg. Bind off.
Back
Using No. 9 needles cast on 72sts and work from side edge to side edge. Cont in garter st until back measures same as front. Bind off.
Cable panels
Join shoulder seams.
Left side Using No. 9 needles cast on 10sts.
1st row (RS) P2, K6, P2.
2nd row K2, P6, K2.
3rd-4th rows As 1st-2nd.
5th row P2, sl next 3sts onto cable needle and leave at front of work, K3, then K 3sts from cable needle – called C6F –, P2.
6th row As 2nd.
7th-8th rows As 1st-2nd.
These 8 rows form patt. Rep them until strip fits from lower edge of front to shoulder and down to lower

Technique tip

Working a cable panel
Cable patterns are often used to add textural interest to a garment. On this sweater a simple cable pattern is worked separately and sewed to the side edges of the back and front. Two stitches in reverse stockinette stitch at each side of the cable emphasize its shape and texture. To work a panel of cable that crosses from right to left: On the row on which the cable is to be crossed, purl the first two stitches, and then slip the next three stitches onto a cable needle and leave them at the front of the work.

Knit the next three stitches, then knit the stitches from the cable needle. This is called "cable 6 front." Finally, purl the last two stitches.

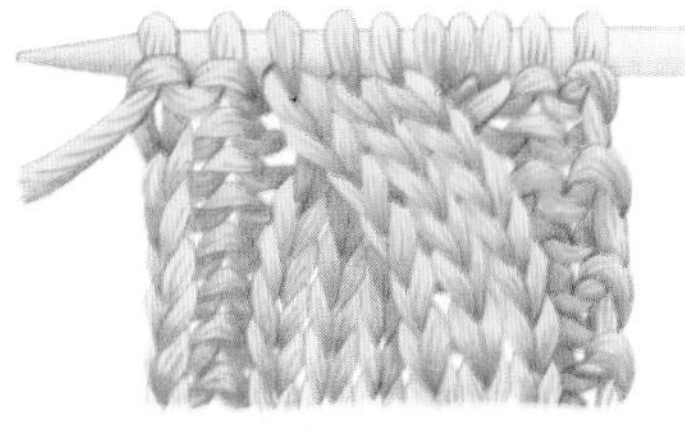

To work a panel of cable that crosses from left to right: Purl the first two stitches, then slip the next three stitches onto a cable needle and leave them at the back of the work.

Knit the next three stitches, then knit the stitches from the cable needle. This is called "cable 6 back." Finally, purl the last two stitches.

edge of back, end with an 8th patt row. Bind off.
Right side Work in same way as left side, reversing position of cable as follows:
5th row P2, sl 3sts onto cable needle and leave at back of work, K3, then K3sts from cable needle – called C6B –, P2. Sew panels in position along side edges of front and back.

Sleeves
Using No. 9 needles cast on 31sts.
1st row (RS) K1, *P1, K1, rep from * to end.
2nd row P1, *K1, P1, rep from * to end. Rep these two rows for 3in, end with a 2nd row. Cont in garter st, inc one st at each end of every 3rd row until there are 79sts. Cont without shaping until sleeve measures 15$\frac{3}{4}$in from beg, end with a WS row. Bind off.

To finish
Do not press. Mark position for sleeves 13in down from shoulders on back and front. Sew sleeve top in position. Join side and sleeve seams.
Lower border Using No. 9 circular needle and with RS of work facing, pick up and knit one st from each garter st ridge and 16sts along cable panels at sides – the total number of sts should be even. Work 3in in rounds of K1, P1 ribbing. Bind off loosely in ribbing.

Neckband Using No. 9 circular needle and with RS of work facing, beg at left shoulder and pick up and K 40sts down left front neck, one st at center of V (mark this with a loop of colored thread), 40sts up right front neck and 25sts across back neck. 106sts.
Next round (K1, P1) to within 3sts of marked center st, P3 tog, K center st, P3 tog through back loop, (K1, P1) to end. Rep last round 5 times. Bind off in rib, dec as before at each side of center.

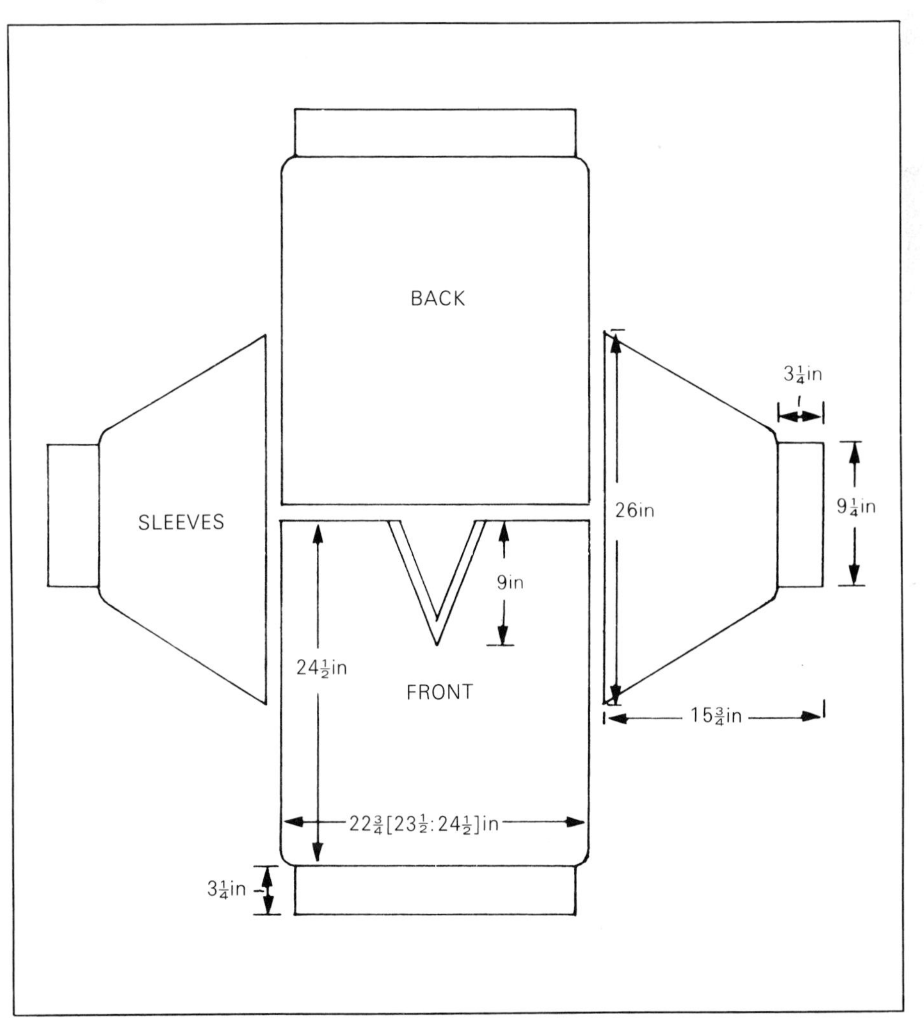

ALL SQUARE

Sizes
To fit 32[34:36:38]in bust.
Length, 26in.
Sleeve seam, 22in.
Note *Directions for larger sizes are in brackets [ ]; where there is only one set of figures it applies to all sizes.*

Materials
6[7:7:7]oz of a medium-weight mohair in main color (A)
5[5:6:6]oz in first contrasting color (B)
5[5:6:6]oz in first contrasting color (C)
6oz in 3rd contrasting color (D)
1 pair each Nos. 6, 8 and 10 knitting needles

Gauge
16sts to 4in in stockinette st using No. 8 needles.

Back
**Using No. 6 needles and A, cast on 66[70:74:78]sts.
1st ribbing row K2, *P2, K2, rep from * to end of row.
2nd ribbing row P2, *K2, P2, rep from * to end.
Rep these 2 rows for 4in: end with first ribbing row.
Next row Rib 7[9:10:12], (pick up loop lying between sts and work into back of it – called M1 – rib 17[17:18:18]sts) 3 times, M1, rib 8[10:10:12]sts. 70[74:78:82]sts.
Change to No. 8 needles. Twisting yarn when changing color to avoid a hole, cont in stockinette st as foll:
1st row K21[23:25:27]sts in B, 3 in A and 46[48:50:52] in C.
2nd row P46[48:50:52]sts in C, 3 in A and 21[23:25:27] in B.
Rep these 2 rows until work measures 11½in from beg; end with WS row. Cut off all colors. Join on A; beg with a K row, work 4 rows stockinette st.
Next row K46[48:50:52] in D, 3 in A and 21[23:25:27] in B.
Next row P21[23:25:27] in B, 3 in A and 46[48:50:52] in D.
Rep the last 2 rows until work measures 17¼in from beg; end with WS row. Cut off all colors. Join on A; beg with a K row, work 4 rows stockinette st.
Next row K21[23:25:27] in C, 3 in A and 46[48:50:52] in D.
Next row P46[48:50:52] in D, 3 in A and 21[23:25:27] in C.**
Rep last 2 rows until work measures 26in from beg; end with WS row.
Shape shoulders
Cont in colors as set, bind off 6[7:8:9]sts at beg of next 2 rows and 6sts at beg of foll 6 rows.
Cut off yarn and leave rem 22[24:26:28]sts on a holder.

Front
Work as for back from ** to **. Rep last 2 rows until work measures 23½in from beg; end with WS row.
Divide for neck
Cont in colors as set, work thus:
Next row Work 27[28:29:30], K2 tog, turn and complete this side first. Dec one st at neck edge on every row until 24[25:26:27]sts rem. Cont without shaping until work measures same as back to shoulder shaping, ending at armhole edge.
Shape shoulder
Bind off 6[7:8:9]sts at beg of next row and 6sts at beg of foll 3 alternate rows. Return to rem sts and place center 12[14:16:18]sts on a holder. Rejoin D to rem sts at neck edge, K2 tog, work to end of row. Complete to match first side, reversing shaping.

Technique tip

Using separate balls of yarn in a row

When you knit blocks of color across a row you will need to twist the yarns around each other when you change color; otherwise, you will make a hole in the knitting. In the sweater we have used three colors in each row, and these should be changed as described below.

To change color on a knit row: after you have knitted the required number of stitches using the first color, hold this color to the left at the back of the work; then pick up the second color and bring it across to the right at the back of the work, under and over the top of the first color.

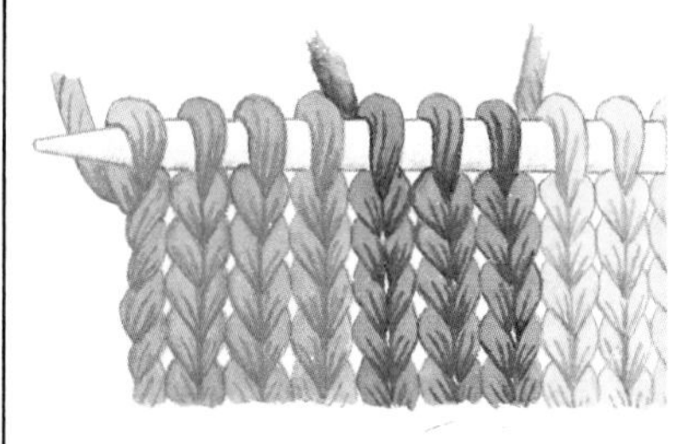

Knit the required number of stitches using the second color. Hold this color to the left, pick up the third color and bring it across to the right at the back of the work, under and over the top of the second color; knit to the end of the row.

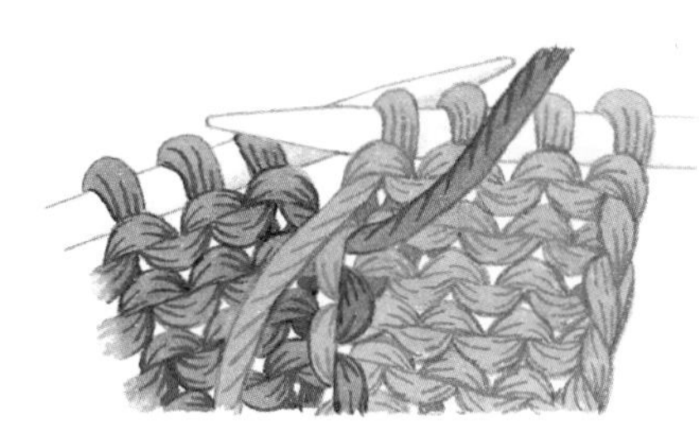

To change color on a purl row: after purling the required number of stitches using the third color, hold this color across to the left at the front of the work; then pick up second color and bring it across to the right at the front of the work, under and over the top of the third color.

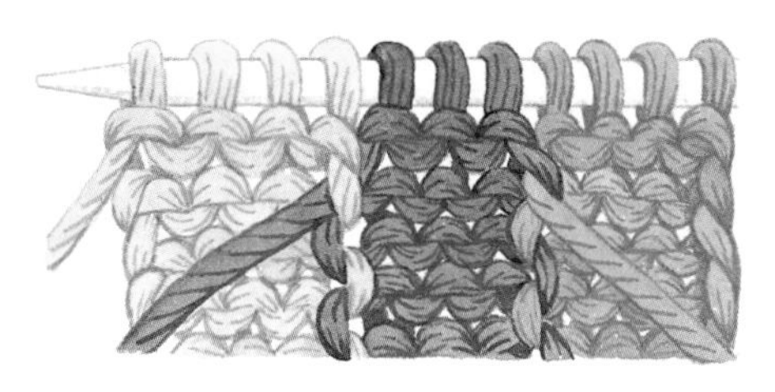

Purl the required number of stitches using the second color. Hold the second color across to the left at the front of the work. Pick up the first color and bring it across to the right at the front of the work, under and over the top of the second color; purl to the end of the row.

Left sleeve

Using No. 6 needles and A, cast on 46sts. Work 2 ribbing rows of back for 4in; end with first ribbing row.

Next row Rib 4, (M1, rib 1) 36 times, rib 2. 78sts.

Change to No. 8 needles. Twisting yarn when changing color to avoid a hole, cont in stockinette st as foll:

1st row K25 in B, 3 in A and 50 in C.

2nd row P50 in C, 3 in A and 25 in B.

Rep these 2 rows until work measures 9in from beg; end with WS row.

Cut off all colors. Join on A, beg with a K row, work 4 rows stockinette st.

Next row K50 in D, 3 in A and 25 in B.

Next row P25 in B, 3 in A and 50 in D. Rep these 2 rows until work measures $16\frac{1}{4}$in from beg; end with WS row. Cut off all colors. Join on A; beg with a K row, work 4 rows

stockinette st.
Next row K25 in C, 3 in A and 50 in D.
Next row P50 in D, 3 in A and 25 in C. Rep these 2 rows until work measures 22in from beg; end with WS row. Bind off loosely.

Right sleeve
Using No. 6 needles and A, cast on 46sts. Work 2 ribbing rows of back for 4in; end with first ribbing row.
Next row Rib 4, (M1, rib 1) 36 times, rib 2. 78sts.
Change to No. 8 needles. Twisting yarn when changing color to avoid a hole, cont in stockinette st as foll:
1st row K50 in B, 3 in A and 25 in C.
2nd row P25 in C, 3 in A and 50 in B. Rep these 2 rows until work measures 9in from beg; end with WS row. Cut off all colors. Join on A; beg with a K row, work 4 rows stockinette st.
Next row K25 in D, 3 in A and 50 in B.
Next row P50 in B, 3 in A and 25 in D. Rep these 2 rows until work measures 16$\frac{1}{4}$in from beg; end with WS row. Cut off all colors. Join on A; beg with a K row, work 4 rows stockinette st.
Next row K50 in C, 3 in A, 25 in D.
Next row P25 in D, 3 in A and 50 in C. Rep these 2 rows until work measures 22in from beg; end with WS row. Bind off loosely.

Collar
Join right shoulder seam. With WS of work facing, using No. 6 needles and A, pick up and K 21sts down left side of neck, K sts from holder, pick up and K 21sts up right side of neck, then K back neck sts from holder. 76[80:84:88]sts.
Next row K7[9:10:2]sts, (M1, K3[3:3:4]sts) 21 times, M1, K6[8:11:2]. 98[102:106:110]sts. Beg with ribbing row 2, rib as for back until collar measures 2$\frac{1}{4}$in. Change to No. 8 needles and cont in ribbing until collar measures 5$\frac{1}{4}$in. Change to No. 10 needles and cont in ribbing until collar measures 7$\frac{1}{2}$in. Bind off very loosely in ribbing.

To finish
Do not block. Join left shoulder and collar seams. Mark center of bound-off edge of sleeves with a pin, match pin to shoulder seam, then sew sleeves to back and front. Join side and sleeve seams.

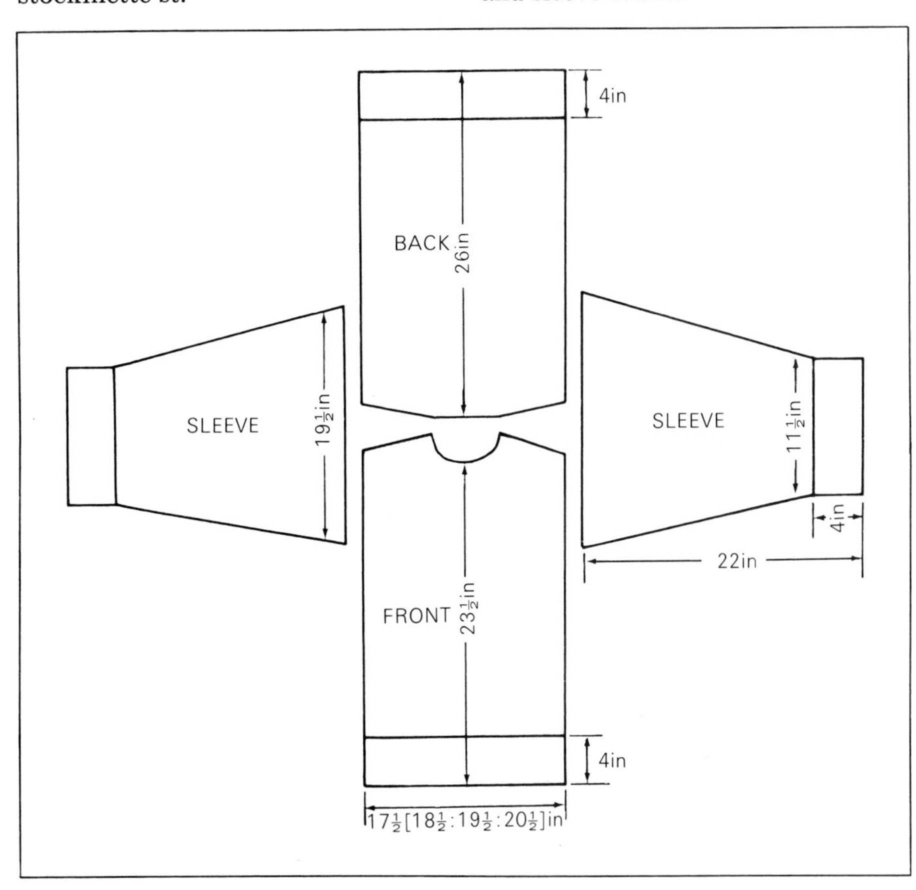

CITY VEST

Back
Using No. 3 needles and A, cast on 129[135:143:151:159]sts.
1st row K1, *P1, K1, rep from * to end.
2nd row P1, *K1, P1, rep from * to end.
These 2 rows form ribbing patt and are rep throughout. Cont until work measures 3in from beg. Mark each end of last row. Change to No. 2 needles and work a further 2in in rib. Mark each end of last row. Change to No. 3 needles. Cont in ribbing until work measures 12in from beg. Mark each end of last row with a colored thread to denote beg of armhole. Cont in ribbing until armholes measure 8$\frac{1}{4}$[8$\frac{1}{2}$:8$\frac{3}{4}$:9:9$\frac{1}{4}$]in.
Shape shoulders
Bind off in ribbing.
8[8:8:9:9]sts at beg of next 6 rows and 7[8:10:10:12]sts at beg of foll 4 rows. Bind off rem 53[55:55:57:57]sts.

Left front
Using No. 3 needles and A, cast on 58[62:66:70:74]sts. Work 7 rows K1, P1 ribbing. P 1 row. Beg patt. Slip st. with yarn at back on K rows and at front on P rows.
1st row (RS) Using B, K1, *sl 2, K4, rep from * to last 3[1:5:3:1]sts, sl 2, K1[K1:sl 2, K3:sl 2, K1:K1].
2nd row Using B, P all knitted sts and sl all slipped sts in previous row.
3rd row Using C, K3, *sl 2, K4, rep from * to last 1[5:3:1:5]sts, K1[sl 2, K3:sl 2, K1:K1:sl 2, K3].
4th row Using C, as 2nd.
5th row Using D, K1, *K4, sl 2, rep from * to last 3[1:5:3:1]sts, K3[1:5:3:1].
6th row Using D, as 2nd.
7th and 8th rows Using A, as 1st and 2nd.
9th and 10th rows Using B, as 3rd and 4th.
11th and 12th rows Using C, as 5th and 6th.
13th and 14th rows Using D, as 1st and 2nd.
15th and 16th rows Using A, as 3rd and 4th.
17th and 18th rows Using B, as 5th and 6th.
19th and 20th rows Using C, as 1st and 2nd.
21st and 22nd rows Using D, as 3rd and 4th.
23rd and 24th rows Using A, as 5th and 6th.
These 24 rows form patt and are repeated throughout. Cont in patt until work measures 3in. Mark side edge of last row with a colored thread. Change to No. 2 needles. Work 2in in patt. Mark side edge of last row. Change to No. 3 needles. Cont in patt until front matches back to armhole. Mark both ends of last row.
Shape front edge
Keeping patt correct, dec one st at front edge on next and every 4th row until 38[40:44:47:51]sts rem. Cont without shaping until front matches back to shoulder, ending at

Sizes
To fit 32[34:36:38:40]in bust.
Length, 21$\frac{1}{4}$[21$\frac{1}{2}$:21$\frac{3}{4}$:22:22$\frac{1}{4}$]in.
Note *Directions for the larger sizes are in brackets []; where there is only one set of figures it applies to all sizes.*

Materials
7[7:8:8:9]oz of a fingering yarn in main shade (A)
1[1:2:2:2]oz each of contrasting colors (B, C and D)
1 pair each Nos. 2 and 3 knitting needles
5 buttons
Slide buckle, $\frac{3}{4}$in wide

Gauge
30sts to 4in over sl st patt on No. 3 needles.
30sts and 39 rows to 4in over ribbing, when slightly stretched, on No. 3 needles.

side edge.

Shape shoulder
Bind off 8[8:8:9:9]sts at beg of next and foll 2 alternate rows and 7[8:10:10:12]sts at beg of foll alternate row. Work 1 row. Bind off.

Right front
Work as for left front, reversing shaping.

Right front band and collar
Using No. 2 needles and A, cast on 12 sts. Work ½in K1, P1, ribbing.
1st buttonhole row Rib 4, bind off 3sts, rib to end.
2nd buttonhole row Rib to end, casting on 3sts over those bound off in previous row. Cont in ribbing, working a further 4 buttonholes at intervals of 2¾in. Cont in ribbing, inc one st at inside edge of next and every alternate row until there are 30sts, then on every 3rd row until there are 36sts. Cont straight until collar measures 12¼[12¾:13:13½:13¾]in from last buttonhole. Bind off in ribbing.

Left front band and collar
Work as for right front band and collar, omitting buttonholes and reversing shaping.

Belt (make 2)
Using No. 2 needles and A, cast on 12sts. Work 9½[10:10½:11:11½]in K1, P1 ribbing. Bind off in ribbing.

Armbands (alike)
Join shoulder seams. Using No. 2 needles, A and with RS of work facing, pick up and K 128[134:140:146:152]sts between colored markers. Work 8 rows K1, P1 ribbing. Bind off in ribbing.

To finish
Press fronts only on WS with warm iron over damp cloth. Join side seams, setting belt between waist markers at sides. Join center back of collar. Sew on front bands and collar, matching beg of collar shaping to colored markers at start of front edge shaping. Press seams. Sew on buttons. Sew on buckle.

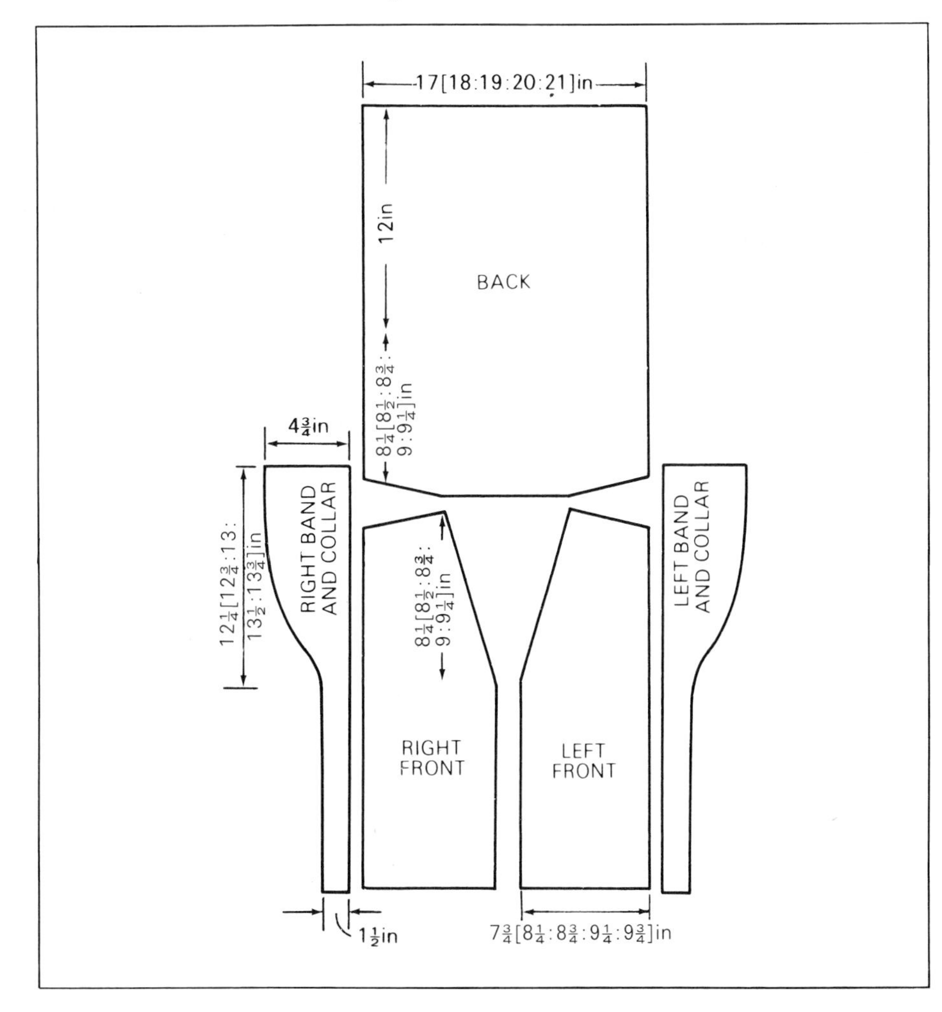

TYROLEAN CARDIGAN

Back
Using No. 3 needles and B, cast on 132[142:152:162]sts. **K2 rows. Cut off B and join in A. Beg bud patt.
1st row (WS) P to end.
2nd row K8, *(K1, yo, K1, yo, K1) all into next st, K9, rep from * ending with K3 instead of K9.
3rd row P3, *P5 winding yarn twice around needle for each st, P9, rep from * ending with P8.
4th row K8, *keeping yarn at back, sl 5 dropping extra loops, K9, rep from * ending with K3.
5th row P3, *keeping yarn at front, sl 5, P9, rep from * ending with P8.
6th row K8, *sl next 3sts tog knitwise, K2 tog, pass slipped sts all over K2 tog, K9, rep from * ending with K3.
7th row P to end.
8th row K3, *(K1, yo, K1, yo, K1) all into next st, K9, rep from * ending with K8.
9th row P8, *P5 winding yarn twice around needle for each st, P9, rep from * ending with P3.
10th row K3, *keeping yarn at back, sl 5 dropping extra loops, K9, rep from * ending with K8.
11th row P8, *keeping yarn at front, sl 5, P9, rep from * ending with P3.
12th row K3, *sl next 3sts tog knitwise, K2 tog, pass slipped sts all over K2 tog, K9, rep from * ending with K8.
These 12 rows form patt. Rep them twice **.
Next row P2[6:3:0], *P2 tog. P7[6:6:6], rep from * 13[15:17:19] times, P2 tog, P2[6:3:0]. 117[125:133:141]sts.
Next row K1, *P1, K1, rep from * to end.
Next row P1, *K1, P1, rep from * to end.
Cont in ribbing until work measures $8\frac{1}{2}[8\frac{1}{2}:9:9]$in from beg of ribbing.
Shape armholes
Bind off 7sts at beg of next 2 rows. Dec one st at each end of every row until 89[97:105:113]sts rem. Cont straight until armholes measure $7[7:7\frac{1}{2}:7\frac{1}{2}]$in.
Shape shoulders
Bind off 8sts at beg of next 6 rows and 5[7:9:11]sts at beg of foll 2 rows. Bind off rem 31[35:39:43]sts.
Left front
Using No. 3 needles and B, cast on 82[82:92:92]sts. Work from ** to ** as given for back.
Next row P4[4:3:0], *P2 tog, P4[7:4:7], rep from * 11[7:13:9] times, P2 tog, P4[4:3:0]. 69[73:77:81]sts.
Beg ribbing and flower border panel.
1st row (RS) (K1, P1) 12[13:14:15] times, K13A, (P1, K1) 16[17:18:19] times.
2nd row Rib 32[34:36:38], P13A, rib 24[26:28:30].
3rd row Rib 24[26:28:30], K13B, rib 32[34:36:38].
4th row Rib 32[34:36:38], K5B, K3 winding yarn 3 times around needle for each st, K5B, cut off B, rib 24[26:28:30].
5th row Rib 24[26:28:30], K1, sl 1 with yarn at back, K3, sl 3 dropping extra loops, K3, sl 1, K1, rib to end.
6th row Rib 32[34:36:38], P1, sl 1 with yarn in front, P3, sl 3, P3, sl 1, P1, rib to end.
7th row Rib 24[26:28:30], K5, sl 3 with yarn at back, K5, rib to end.
8th row Rib 32[34:36:38], P5, sl 3 with yarn in front, P5, rib to end.
9th row Rib 24[26:28:30], K3, sl 2 with yarn at back, drop next st off needle at front of work, replace 2 slipped sts onto left-hand needle, pick up dropped st and K it, K3, drop next st off needle at front of work, K2, pick up dropped st and K

Sizes
To fit 32[34:36:38]in bust.
Length to shoulder, $19\frac{1}{2}[19\frac{1}{2}:20\frac{1}{2}:20\frac{1}{2}]$in.
Sleeve seam, $17[18:18:18\frac{1}{2}]$in.
Note *Directions for larger sizes are in brackets []; where there is only one set of figures it applies to all sizes.*

Materials
15[15:16:16]oz of a sport yarn in main color (A)
2oz each in contrasting colors (B and C)
1 pair No. 3 knitting needles
Cable needle
5 buttons

Gauge
28sts and 36 rows to 4in in stockinette st on No. 3 needles.

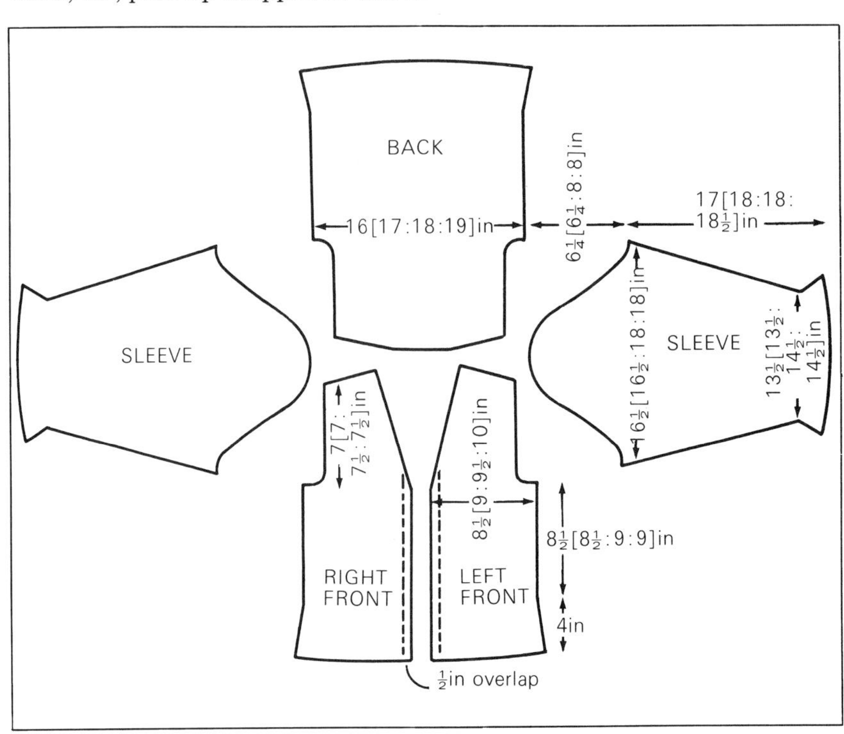

it, K3, rib to end.
10th row Rib 32[34:36:38], P3 in A, (P1, K1, P1 all into next st in C, sl 2) twice, P1, K1, P1 all into next st in C, P3A, rib to end.
11th row Rib 24[26:28:30] in A, K3, (make bobble in C as foll: P3, turn and K3, turn and sl 1, K2 tog, psso, K2A) twice, make bobble in C, K3A, cut off C, rib to end.
12th row Rib 32[34:36:38], P13 working into back of bobble sts, rib to end.
13th row As 1st.
14th row As 2nd.
These 14 rows form patt. Cont in patt until work measures $7\frac{1}{2}$[$7\frac{1}{2}$:8:8]in from beg of ribbing; end with a RS row. Dec one st at beg of next and every foll alternate row until work measures $8\frac{1}{2}$[$8\frac{1}{2}$:9:9]in from beg of ribbing; end with a WS row.
Shape armhole
Bind off 7sts at beg of next row. Cont to dec one st at front edge as before, dec one st at armhole edge on next 7 rows. Dec at front edge only until 29[31:33:35]sts rem. Cont straight until armhole measures

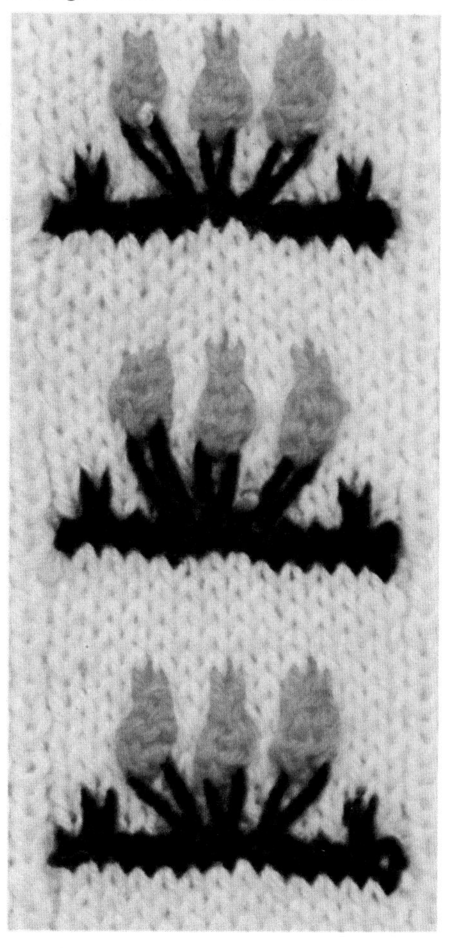

7[7:$7\frac{1}{2}$:$7\frac{1}{2}$]in; end with a WS row.
Shape shoulder
Bind off at beg of next and foll alternate rows 8sts 3 times. Work 1 row. Bind off rem 5[7:9:11]sts.

Right front
Work as for left front, reversing shaping and position of ribbing and flower border panel as foll:
1st row (K1, P1) 16[17:18:19] times, K13A, (P1, K1) 12[13:14:15] times. Patt 3 more rows.
Next row (buttonhole row) Rib 3, bind off 2sts, patt to end.
Next row Patt to end, casting on 2sts over those bound off in previous row. Make 4 more buttonholes $1\frac{3}{4}$in apart.

Sleeves
Using No. 3 needles and B, cast on 82[82:92:92]sts. K2 rows. Cut off B and join in A. Work 19 rows bud patt as given for back.
Next row K1[1:5:5], *K2 tog, K11[11:6:6], rep from * 5[5:9:9] times, K2 tog, K1[1:5:5]. 75[75:81:81]sts.
Beg first row with P1, cont in K1, P1 ribbing, inc one st at each end of every 10th[10th:8th:8th] row until there are 91[91:101:101]sts. Cont straight until sleeve measures $11\frac{1}{2}$[12:12:12]in from beg of ribbing, end with a WS row and inc one st at end of last row. 92[92:102:102]sts.
Work $3\frac{1}{2}$[4:4:$4\frac{1}{2}$]in in bud patt; end with a WS row.
Shape top
Bind off 7sts at beg of next 2 rows. Dec one st at each end of every foll 4th row 5 times in all, then at each end of every foll alternate row until 27sts rem. Bind off.

To finish
Press under damp cloth with warm iron, omitting ribbing. Join shoulder seams. Set in sleeves, gathering around top 8in to fit along shoulder edge. Join side and sleeve seams.
Border Using No. 3 needles, B and with RS facing, pick up and K80[80:84:84]sts along right front edge to shaping, 70[70:74:74]sts along shaped front edge and 15[17:19:21]sts to center back neck. Bind off knitwise on WS. Work similar border on left side. Press seams and border. Sew on buttons.

RASPBERRY RIPPLE

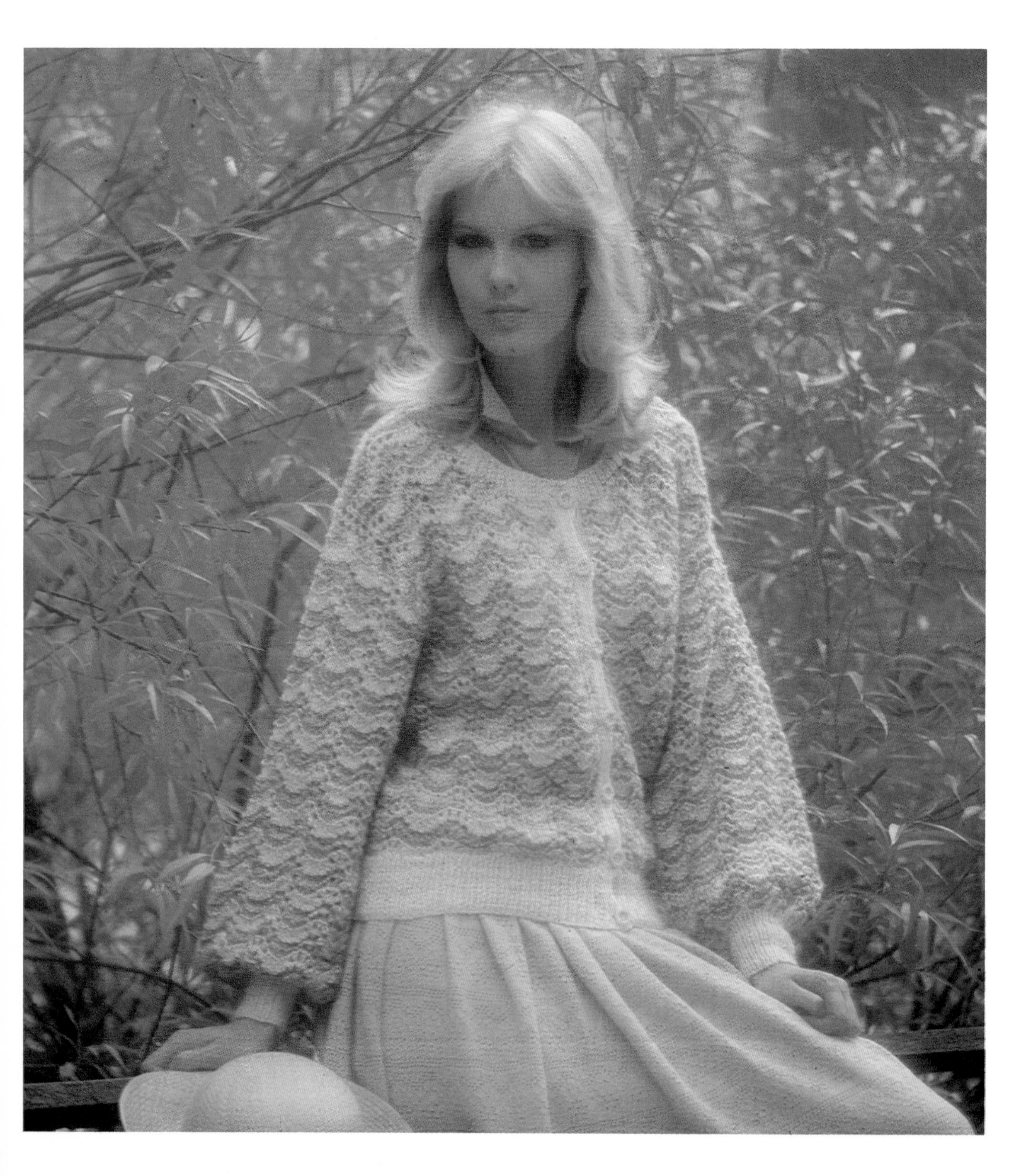

Sizes
To fit 32–34[36–38]in bust.
Length, 22[23]in.
Sleeve seam, 18in.
Note *Directions for larger size are in brackets []; where there is only one set of figures it applies to both sizes.*

Materials
8oz of a lightweight mohair in main color (A)
6oz in each of 2 contrasting colors (B and C)
1 pair each Nos. 3 and 5 knitting needles
7 buttons

Gauge
22sts and 30 rows to 4in pattern on No. 5 needles.

Back
Using No. 3 needles and A, cast on 96[108]sts, work K1, P1 ribbing for 3in.
Inc row Rib 10, pick up horizontal loop lying between needles and work into back of it – called make 1 or M1 –, *rib 7[8], M1, rep from * to last 9[10]sts, rib to end. 108[120]sts.
Change to No. 5 needles. Joining on colors as required, beg patt.
1st row (RS) With A, K to end.
2nd row With A, P to end.
3rd row With A, *(K2 tog tbl) twice, (yo, K1) 4 times, (K2 tog tbl) twice, rep from * to end.
4th row With B, K to end.
5th-7th rows As 1st-3rd rows but use B instead of A.
8th row With C, K to end.
9th-11th rows As 1st-3rd rows but use C instead of A.
12th row With A, K to end.
These 12 rows form patt.
Cont in patt until work measures 13in; end with a WS row. Place a marker at each end of last row.
Cont in patt until work measures 22[23]in; end with a WS row.
Shape shoulders
Bind off 10[11]sts at beg of next 6 rows. Cut off yarn and leave rem 48[54]sts on a holder.

Left front
**Using No. 3 needles and A, cast on 48[54]sts and work in K1, P1 ribbing for 3in.
Inc row Rib 6[10], M1, *rib 6[7], M1, rep from * to last 6[9]sts, rib to end. 55[60]sts.
Change to No. 5 needles. Joining on colors as required, beg patt.**
1st size only
1st row (RS) With A, K to end.
2nd row With A, P to end.
3rd row With A, *(K2 tog tbl) twice, (yo, K1) 4 times, (K2 tog tbl) twice, rep from * to last 7sts, (K2 tog tbl) twice, (yo, K1) twice, K1.
4th row With B, K to end.
5th-7th rows As 1st-3rd rows but use B instead of A.
8th row With C, K to end.
9th-11th rows As 1st-3rd rows but use C instead of A.
12th row With A, K to end.
These 12 rows form patt.
2nd size only
1st row (RS) With A, K to end.
2nd row With A, P to end.
3rd row With A, *(K2 tog tbl) twice, (yo, K1) 4 times, (K2 tog tbl) twice, rep from * to end.
4th row With B, K to end.
5th-7th rows As 1st-3rd rows but use B instead of A.
8th row With C, K to end.
9th-11th rows As 1st-3rd rows but use C instead of A.
12th row With A, K to end.
These 12 rows form patt.

Both sizes
Cont in patt until work measures 13in; end with a WS row. Place a marker at end of last row. Cont in patt until work measures 18[19]in; end with a WS row.
Shape neck
Next row Patt to last 12sts, turn and leave these 12sts on a safety pin. Keeping patt correct, dec one st at neck edge on every foll alternate row until 30[35]sts rem.
Cont straight until front is same length as back to shoulders; end at side edge.
Shape shoulder
Bind off 10[11]sts at beg of next and foll alternate row. Work 1 row.
Bind off.

Right front
Work as for left front from ** to **.
1st size only
1st row (RS) With A, K to end.
2nd row With A, P to end.
3rd row With A, K1, (K1, yo) twice, (K2 tog tbl) twice, * (K2 tog tbl) twice, (yo, K1) 4 times, (K2 tog tbl) twice, rep from * to end.
4th row With B, K to end.
5th-7th rows As 1st-3rd rows but use B instead of A.
8th row With C, K to end.
9th-11th rows As 1st-3rd rows but use C instead of A.
12th row With A, K to end.
These 12 rows form patt.
2nd size only
1st row (RS) With A, K to end.
2nd row With A, P to end.
3rd row With A, *(K2 tog tbl) twice, (yo, K1) 4 times, (K2 tog tbl) twice, rep from * to end.
4th row With B, K to end.
5th-7th rows As 1st-3rd rows but use B instead of A.
8th row With C, K to end.
9th-11th rows As 1st-3rd rows but use C instead of A.
12th row With A, K to end.
These 12 rows form patt.

Both sizes
Complete to match left front, reversing shapings and mark beg of row instead of end.

Sleeves
Using No. 3 needles and A, cast on 46[48]sts and work in K1, P1 ribbing for 3in.
Inc row *Rib 1, M1, rep from * to last st, rib 1. 91[95]sts.
Next row P5[11], inc in next st, (P4[2], inc in next st) 16[24] times, P5[11], 108[120]sts.
Cont in patt as for back until work measures 18in; end with a WS row.
Bind off.

Neck border
Join shoulder seams. With RS facing using No. 3 needles and A, K 12sts from right front, pick up and K 30[32]sts up right side of neck, K the sts from holder dec one st at center, pick up and K 30[32]sts down left side of neck, then K 12sts from left front, 131 [141]sts.
Next row P1, (K1, P1) to end.
Next row K1, (P1, K1) to end.
Rep these 2 rows for 1in.
Bind off in ribbing.

Button border
Using No. 3 needles and A, cast on 7sts.
1st rib row (RS) K2, (P1, K1) twice, K1.
2nd rib row (K1, P1) 3 times, K1.
Rep these 2 rows until border, slightly stretched, fits up left front to top of neck border. Bind off in ribbing. Mark 7 button positions on this border, the first ½in from cast-on edge, the last ½in from bound-off edge and the others evenly spaced between.

Buttonhole border
Work as for button border but make buttonholes to correspond with markers as foll:
Buttonhole row (RS) Rib 3, yo, P2 tog, rib 2.

To finish
Do not press. Set in sleeves between markers, then join side and sleeve seams. Sew on the borders and buttons.

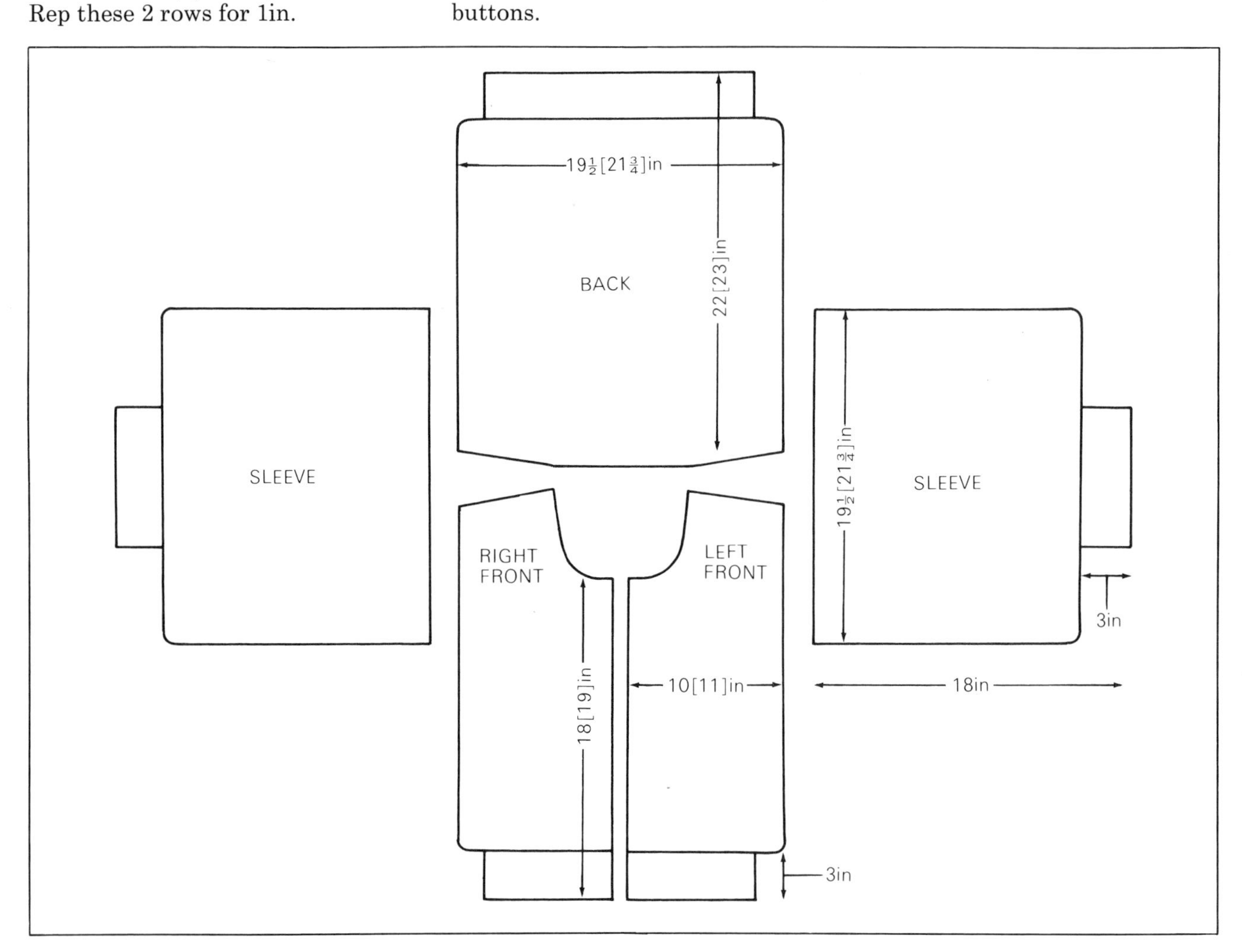

QUILTED JACKET

Sizes
To fit 32–34in bust.
Length, 23in.

Materials
18oz of a knitting worsted
1 pair No. 7 knitting needles
1½yd of padding
1½yd of lining fabric
Matching thread

Gauge
1 diamond measures 5¾in wide by 4½in deep with yarn used double and before quilting.
Note *Yarn is used double throughout.*

Back and fronts (worked in one piece). Using No. 7 needles and yarn double, cast on 73sts for lower edge of back. Beg patt.
1st row (RS) K3, P1, *K8, work K1, P1 and K1 all into next st, turn P3, turn K3, then pass 2nd and 3rd sts over 1st – called make bobble or MBK –, K3, MBK, K8, P1, rep from * to last 3sts, P3.
2nd row P2, K1, P1, K1, *P19, K1, P1, K1, rep from * to last 2sts, P2.
3rd row K1, P1, K1, *K2, P1, K8, MBK, K8, P1, K1, rep from * to last 4sts, K2, P1, K1.
4th row K1, P3, *P2, K1, P15, K1, P3, rep from * to last 3sts, P2, K1.
5th row K3, *K4, P1, K13, P1, K3, rep from * to last 4sts, K4.
6th row P4, *P4, K1, P11, K1, P5, rep from * to last 3sts, P3.
7th row K3, *K6, P1, K9, P1, K5, rep from * to last 4sts, K4.
8th row P4, *P6, K1, P7, K1, P7, rep from * to last 3sts, P3.
9th row K3, *K8, P1, K5, P1, K7, rep from * to last 4sts, K4.
10th row P3, then P1, K1 and P1 all into next st, turn K3, turn P3, then pass 2nd and 3rd sts over 1st and place bobble at front of work – called make bobble purl or MBP –, *P8, K1, P3, K1, P8, MBP, rep from * to last 3sts, P3.
11th row K3, *K10, P1, K1, P1, K9, rep from * to last 4sts, K4.
12th row P1, MBP, P2, *P1, MBP, P8, K1, P8, MBP, P2, rep from * to last 3sts, P1, MBP, P1.
13th-22nd rows Work 11th-2nd rows in this reverse order.
These 22 rows form the patt.
Cont in patt until work measures 15in; end with a WS row.

Shape for sleeves
Keeping patt correct, cast on 4sts at beg of next 2 rows. 81sts.
Cont straight until work measures 24in; end with a WS row.
Divide for fronts
Next row Patt across first 29sts, bind off next 23sts, patt to end.
Cont on last set of sts for left front.
Patt 10 rows, then inc one st at front edge on next 7 rows.
Cast on 5sts at beg of next row. 41sts. Cont straight until work measures 9in from beg of front, ending at armhole edge.
Shape for sleeve
Bind off 4sts at beg of next row.
Cont straight until work measures 24in from beg of front. Bind off.
Return to rem set of 29sts and cont on these sts for right front, working to match left front, reversing shaping.

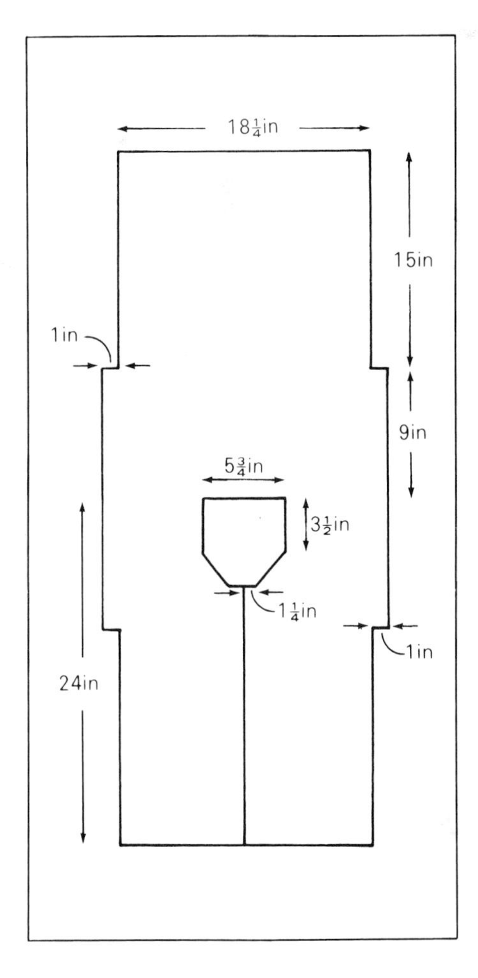

Technique tip

To quilt knitted fabric
Place padding between lining and knitting, with right side of knitting uppermost.

Machine- or hand-sew along lines of diamonds using matching sewing thread and sewing through all three thicknesses to form quilting.

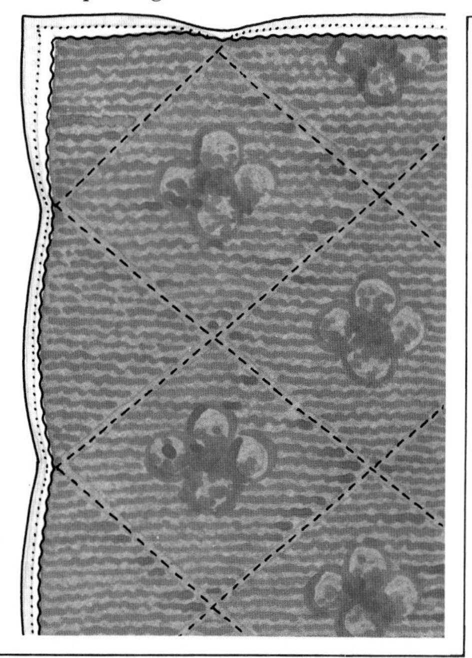

When the fabric has been quilted, join the side seams. Now finish the side seams with strips of lining fabric cut on the bias or use $\frac{3}{4}$in-wide bias binding.

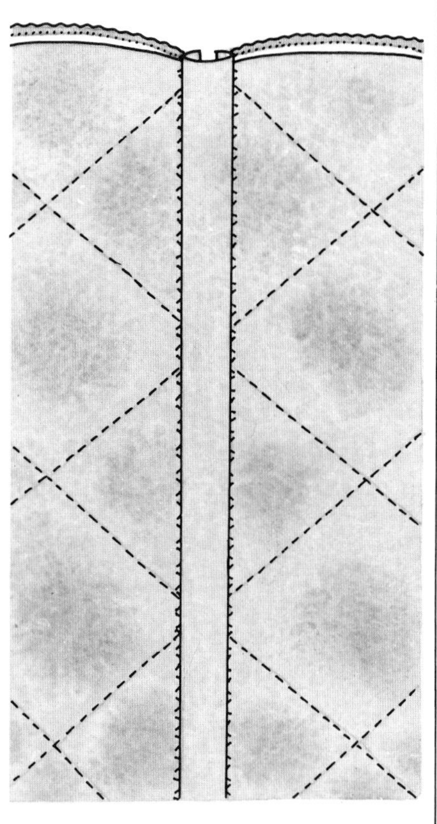

Cut $1\frac{1}{2}$in-wide strips for length of each seam. Turn under $\frac{1}{2}$in along each edge and tack in place. Sew strip over seam to cover raw edges.

Bindings
Using No. 7 needles and yarn double cast on 8sts. Cont in stockinette st until work, when slightly stretched, fits all around outer edge. Bind off.
Using No. 7 needles and yarn double, cast on 8sts. Cont in stockinette st until work, when slightly stretched, fits all around armhole. Bind off.

To finish
Do not press. Using knitting as a pattern, cut out padding and lining, with $\frac{1}{2}$in seam allowance along side seam and underarm seam only. Quilt, either by hand or machine, along diamond lines. Sew on bindings, covering all raw edges. Bind seams with lining.

SET FOR SUCCESS

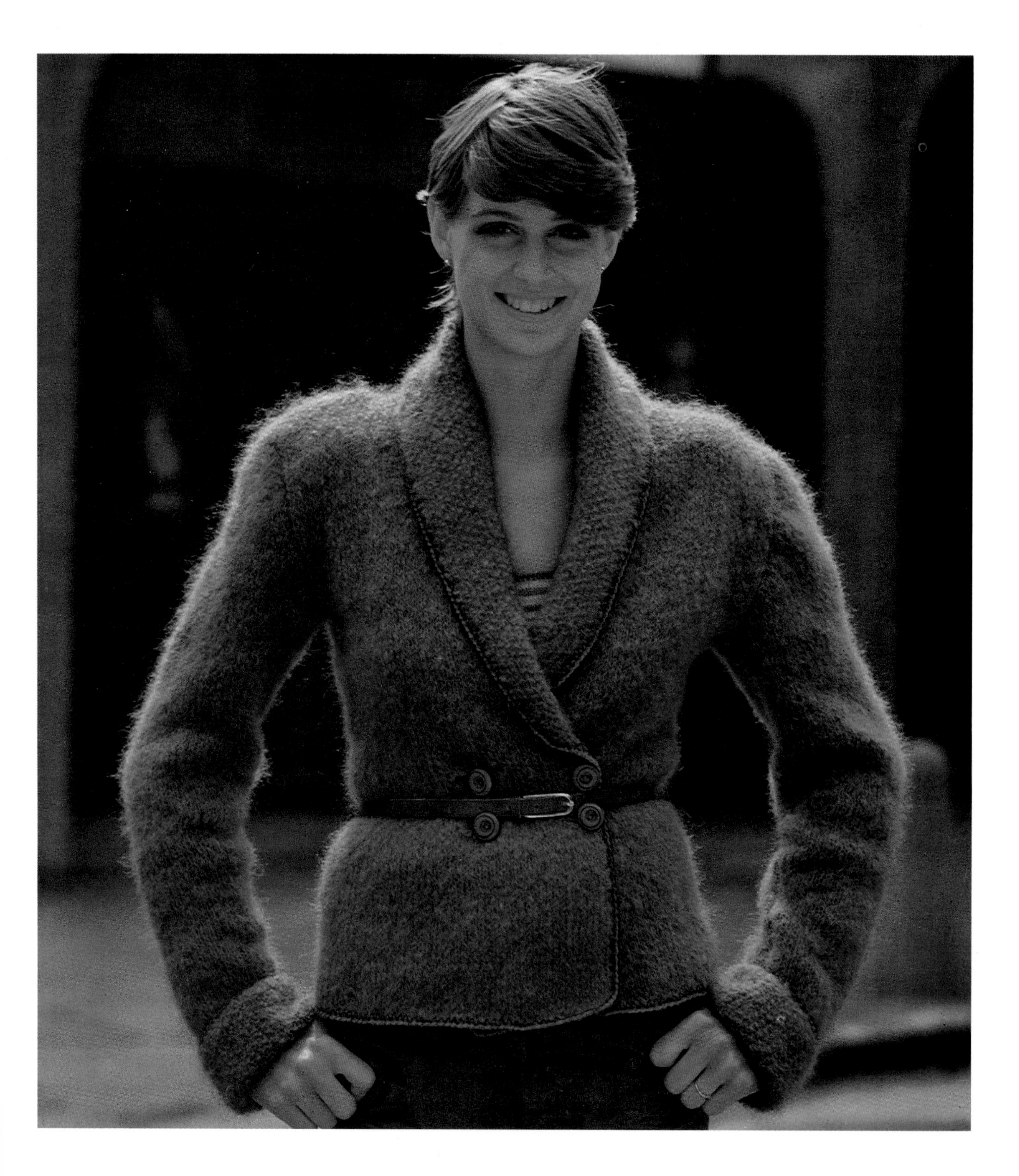

Sizes
To fit 32[34:36:38]in bust.
Jacket *Length, 22[23:23$\frac{3}{4}$:24$\frac{3}{4}$]in.*
Sleeve, 18[18$\frac{1}{2}$:18$\frac{3}{4}$:19$\frac{1}{4}$]in.
Body tube *Length, 12$\frac{1}{2}$[13$\frac{1}{2}$:14$\frac{1}{2}$:15$\frac{1}{2}$]in.*
Note *Directions for larger sizes are in brackets []; where there is only one set of figures it applies to all sizes.*

Materials
Jacket *15[16:17:19]oz of a medium-weight mohair*
1oz of a fingering yarn in contrasting color (B) for trimming
1 pair No. 6 knitting needles
Size C crochet hook
4 buttons
1 pair shoulder pads
Body tube *4[4:4:6]oz of a fingering yarn in main color (A)*
2oz in each of 2 contrasting colors (B and C)
1 pair each Nos. 2 and 3 knitting needles
Size C crochet hook

Gauge
17sts and 22 rows to 4in in stockinette st on No. 6 needles with mohair.
30sts and 40 rows to 4in in stockinette st on No. 2 needles with fingering yarn.

Jacket

Back

Using No. 6 needles and A, cast on 77[81:85:89]sts. Beg with a K row, work 8[8:8:10] rows stockinette st.
1st dec row K5[7:9:11], *K2 tog, K14, rep from * 3 times, K2 tog, K6[8:10:12]. Work 9[9:9:11] rows.
2nd dec row K5[7:9:11], *K2 tog, K13, rep from * 3 times, K2 tog, K5[7:9:11]. Work 9[9:9:11] rows.
3rd dec row K5[7:9:11], *K2 tog, K12, rep from * 3 times, K2 tog, K4[6:8:10]. Work 9[9:9:11] rows.
4th dec row K5[7:9:11], *K2 tog, K11, rep from * 3 times, K2 tog, K3[5:7:9]. 57[61:65:69]sts.
Cont straight until work measures 6$\frac{1}{2}$[7:7$\frac{1}{2}$:8]in; end with a P row. Mark each end of last row. Work 18 rows.
1st inc row K4[6:8:10] *pick up running thread between sts with left needle and knit it tbl – called puk – K7, rep from * 6 times, puk, K4[6:8:10]. Work 19 rows.
2nd inc row K4[6:8:10] *puk, K8, rep from * 7 times, puk, K5[7:9:11]. 73[77:81:85]sts.
Cont straight until back measures 14$\frac{1}{2}$[15:15$\frac{1}{2}$:16]in; end with a P row.

Shape armholes
Bind off 6sts at beg of next 2 rows. 61[65:69:73]sts. Cont in stockinette st until armhole measures 4$\frac{1}{4}$[4$\frac{3}{4}$:5:5$\frac{1}{2}$]in; end with a P row. Beg seed st.
Patt row *P1, K1, rep from * to end. Cont in seed st for 3$\frac{1}{4}$in; end with a WS row.

Shape shoulders
Bind off 8[8:9:10]sts at beg of next 2 rows and 8[9:10:11]sts at beg of foll 2 rows. Bind off.

Right front

Using No. 6 needles and A, cast on 51[54:57:60]sts. Beg with a K row, work 8[8:8:10] rows stockinette st.
1st dec row K25, K2 tog, K14, K2 tog, K8[11:14:17]. Work 9[9:9:11] rows.
2nd dec row K25, K2 tog, K13, K2 tog, K7[10:13:16]. Work 9[9:9:11] rows.
3rd dec row K25, K2 tog, K12, K2 tog, K6[9:12:15]. Work 5[7:9:5] rows.
1st buttonhole row K2, bind off 4, K until there are 13sts on right-hand needle after bound-off group, bind off 4, K to end.
2nd buttonhole row P to end, casting on 4sts over those bound off on previous row. Work 2[0:0:4] rows.
4th dec row K25, K2 tog, K11, K2 tog, K5 [8:11:14]. 43[46:49:51]sts.
Cont straight until work measures 6$\frac{1}{2}$[7:7$\frac{1}{2}$:8]in; end with a P row. Mark each end of last row. Work 4 rows.
1st buttonhole row K2, bind off 4, K until there are 13sts on right-hand needle after bound-off group, bind off 4, K to end.
2nd buttonhole row P to end, casting on 4sts over those bound off on previous row. Work 12 rows stockinette st, decreasing one st at front edge on 9th and 12th of these rows.
Inc row K21, *puk, K7, rep from * twice, puk, K4[7:10:13].
Work 19 more rows, dec one st at front edge on 2nd and every foll 3rd row.
Inc row K2 tog, K13, *puk, K8, rep from * twice, puk, K5[8:11:14].
Cont to shape front edge on every 3rd row until work measures same as back to armhole shaping, ending at side edge.

Shape armhole
Bind off 6sts at beg of next row. Cont in stockinette st, dec at front edge until armhole measures 4$\frac{1}{4}$[4$\frac{3}{4}$:5:5$\frac{1}{2}$]in; end with a P row. Work in seed st as for back for 3$\frac{1}{4}$in, dec at front edge until 16[17:19:21]sts rem; end at armhole edge.

Shape shoulder
Bind off 8[8:9:10]sts at beg of next row. Work 1 row. Bind off.

Left front

As for right front, reversing all shapings, and omitting both sets of buttonholes.

Sleeves

Using No. 6 needles and A, cast on 43sts and work 4in in seed st. Cont in stockinette st, work 22 rows. Inc one st at each end of next and every 9th row 9 times in all. 61sts. Cont straight until sleeve measures 22[22$\frac{1}{2}$:22$\frac{3}{4}$:23$\frac{1}{4}$]in; end with a P row.

Shape top
Bind off 3sts at beg of next 2 rows and 2 sts at beg of foll 2 rows. Dec

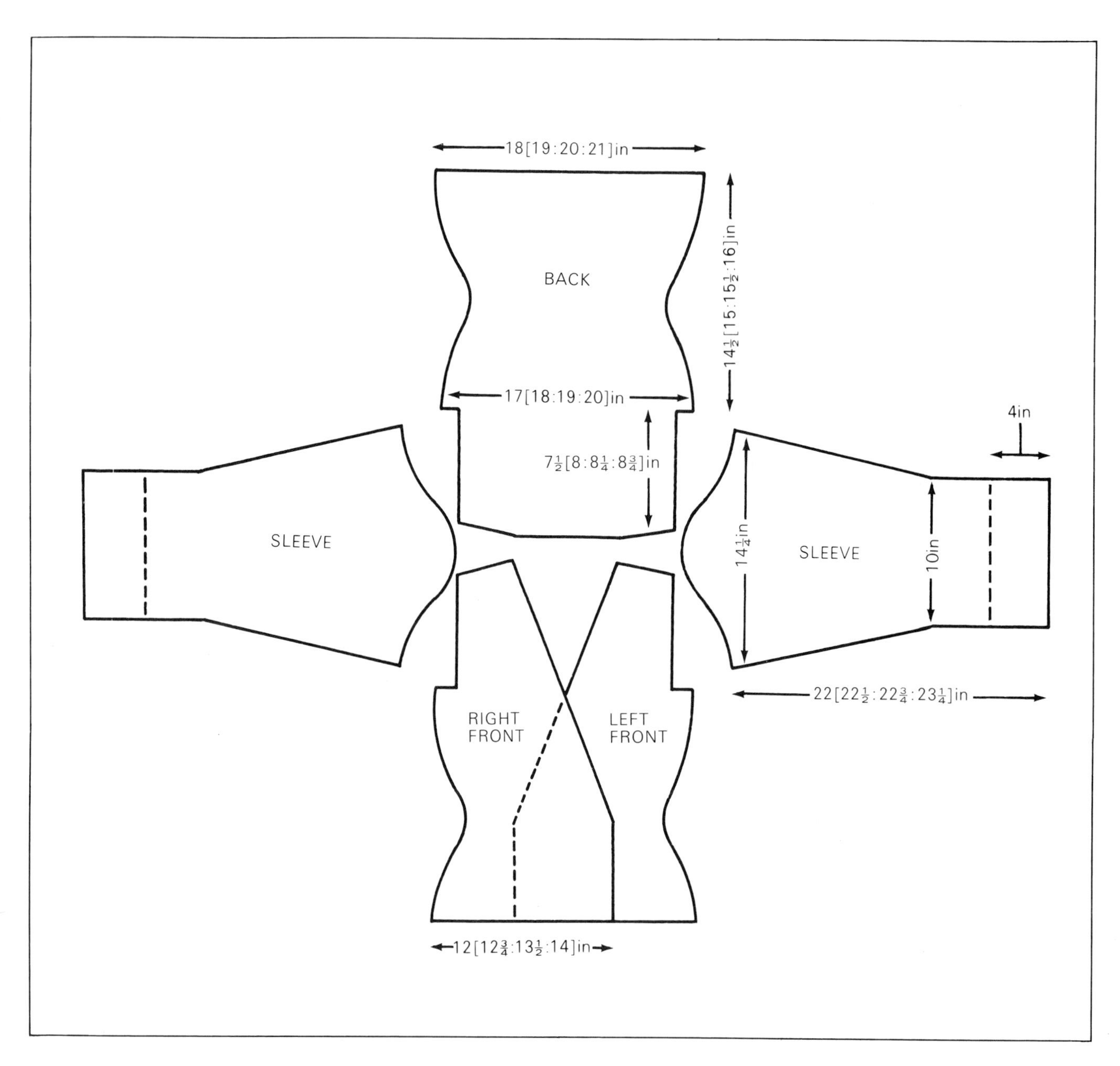

one st at each end of next and every foll alternate row 14 times in all. Bind off 4sts at beg of next 4 rows. Bind off.

Lapels and collar
Using No. 6 needles and A, cast on 3sts and work in seed st for 3 rows. Inc one st at each end of next row, then cont in seed st, inc one st at end of 3rd row and at this same edge on every foll 3rd row until there are 30[30:33:33]sts. Cont straight until collar measures 15[15¼:15¾:16¼]in; end at straight edge. Mark each end of last row. Cont in seed st for a further 3[3:3¼:3¼]in; end at straight edge. Bind off. Work another piece reversing all shapings.

Shoulder facings (make 2)
Using No. 6 needles and A, cast on 23sts. Cont in stockinette st, dec one st at each end of every alternate row until 1st rem. Bind off.

To finish
Join shoulder seams. Set in sleeves. Join side and sleeve seams. Sew on lapels and collar from marked row at front edge, matching shoulder seam to marked row on collar. Fold 4in of seed st to RS to form cuff. Sew on buttons. Using crochet hook and B, work crab st (sc worked from left to right) edging around outer

edge. Finish cuffs in same way. Sew in shoulder pads and baste facings over them.

Body tube

Back and front (alike)
Using No. 2 needles and A, cast on 113[121:129:137]sts.
1st ribbing row *K1, P1, rep from * to last st, K1.
2nd ribbing row *P1, K1, rep from * to last st, P1.
Rep these two rows for $1\frac{1}{2}$in.
Change to No. 3 needles. Cont in stockinette st working in stripes of 4 rows A, 2 rows B, 4 rows A and 2 rows C.
Rep stripe sequence 9[10:10:11] times in all, then work 4[4:10:10] rows more in sequence, so ending 4 rows A. Bind off in A.

To finish
Join side seams. Using crochet hook and B, work crab st edging around top edge.

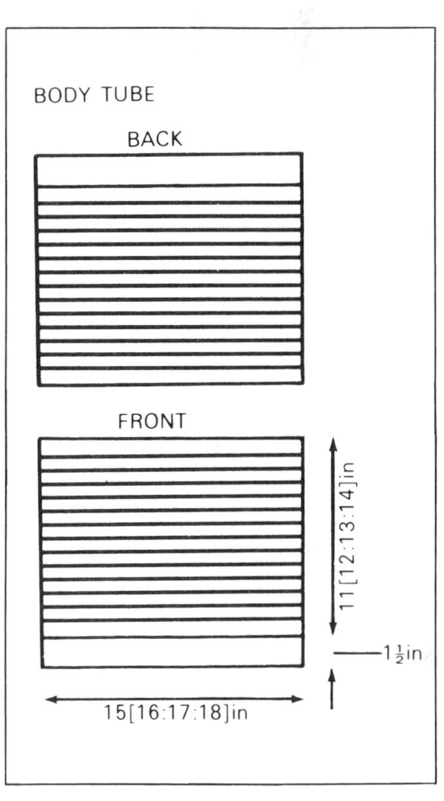

COFFEE WITH CREAM

Sizes
To fit 32–34[36–38:40–42]in.
Length to shoulder, 26[28:30]in.
Sleeve seam, 16½[17½:18½]in.
Note *Directions for larger sizes are in brackets []; where there is only one set of figures it applies to all sizes.*

Materials
11[12:13]oz of a medium-weight mohair in main color (A)
4oz in contrasting color (B)
2oz in contrasting color (C)
1 pair each Nos 5, 6 and 8 knitting needles
18[20:22]in zipper

Gauge
16sts and 22 rows to 4 in in stockinette st worked on No. 6 needles.

Back
Using No. 6 needles and B, cast on 76[84:91]sts. Beg with a K row, work 5 rows stockinette st.
Next row K to form hemline.
Change to No. 5 needles. Beg with a K row cont in stockinette st, working in patt and stranding yarns not in use across back of work, as foll:
1st row With B, K to end.
2nd row With B, P to end.
3rd row K4 B[8B:4B], *1C, 4B, 2C, 2B, 2C, 4B, rep from * to last 12[16:12]sts, 1C, 4B, 2C, 2B, 2C, 1B[5B:1B].
4th row P1B[5B:1B], *2C, 2B, 2C, 3B, 3C, 3B, rep from * to last 0[4:0]sts, 0B[4B:0B].
5th row K2B[6B:2B], *2C, 1B, 2C, 3B, 4C, 3B, rep from * to last 14[18:14]sts, 2C, 1B, 2C, 3B, 4C, 2B[6B:2B].
6th row P3B[7B:3B], *2C, 3B, rep from * to last 3[7:3]sts, 2C, 1B[5B:1B].
7th row K1B[5B:1B], *2C, 3B, rep from * to last 5[9:5]sts, 2C, 3B[7B:3B].
8th row P2B[6B:2B], *4C, 3B, 2C, 1B, 2C, 3B, rep from * to last 14[18:14]sts, 4C, 3B, 2C, 1B, 2C, 2B[6B:2B].
9th row K3B[7B:3B], *3C, 3B, 2C, 2B, 2C, 3B, rep from * to last 13[17:13]sts, 3C, 3B, 2C, 2B, 2C, 1B[5B:1B].
10th row P1B[5B:1B], *2C, 2B, 2C, 4B, 1C, 4B, rep from * to last 0[4:0]sts, 0B[4B:0B].
11th row As 1st.
12th row As 2nd.
13th row K26B[30B:26B], *1C, 4B, 2C, 2B, 2C, 4B, rep from * to last 5[9:5]sts, 1C, 4B[8B:4B].
14th row P3B[7B:3B], *3C, 3B, 2C, 2B, 2C, 3B, rep from * to last 28[32:28]sts, 3C, 25B[29B:25B].
15th row K24B[28B:24B], *2C, 1B, 2C, 3B, 4C, 3B, rep from * to last 7[11:7]sts, 2C, 1B, 2C, 2B[6B:2B].
16th row P1B[5B:1B], *2C, 3B, rep from * to last 20[24:20]sts, 20B[24B:20B].
17th row K23B[27B:23B], *2C, 3B, rep from * to last 3[7:3]sts, 2C, 1B[5B:1B].
18th row P2B[6B:2B], *2C, 1B, 2C, 3B, 4C, 3B, rep from * to last 29[33:29]sts, 2C, 1B, 2C, 24B[28B:24B].
19th row K25B[29B:25B], *3C, 3B, 2C, 2B, 2C, 3B, rep from * to last 6[10:6]sts, 3C, 3B[7B:3B].
20th row P4B[8B:4B], *1C, 4B, 2C, 2B, 2C, 4B, rep from * to last 27[31:27]sts, 1C, 26B[30B:26B].
21st row As 1st.
22nd row As 2nd.
23rd row K49B[53B:49B], (1C, 4B, 2C, 2B, 2C, 4B) 1[1:2] times, 1C, 4B, 2C, 2B, 2C, 1B[5B:1B].
24th row P1B[5B:1B], (2C, 2B, 2C, 3B, 3C, 3B) 2[2:3] times, 45B[49B:45B].
25th row K47B[51B:47B], (2C, 1B, 2C, 3B, 4C, 3B) 1[1:2] times, 2C, 1B, 2C, 3B, 4C, 2B[6B:2B].
26th row P3B[7B:3B], (2C, 3B) 6[6:9] times, 43B[47B:43B].
27th row K46B[49B:46B], (2C, 3B) 6[6:9] times, 0B[5B:0B].
28th row P2B[6B:2B], (4C, 3B, 2C, 1B, 2C, 3B) 2[2:3] times, 44 B[48B:44B].
29th row K48B[52B:48B], (3C, 3B, 2C, 2B, 2C, 3B) 1[1:2] times, 3C, 3B, 2C, 2B, 2C, 1B[5B:1B].
30th row P1B[5B:1B], (2C, 2B, 2C, 4B, 1C, 4B) 2[2:3] times, 45B[49B:45B].
31st row As 1st.
32nd row As 2nd.
These 32 rows complete patt panel. Break off B and C. Join in A.
Change to No. 6 needles. Beg with a K row cont in stockinette st, dec one st at each end of next and every foll 6th row until 70[78:85]sts rem.
Cont straight until work measures 16[17:18]in from hemline; end with a P row.
Change to No. 5 needles. Break off A. Join in B. Cont in stockinette st, working in patt as foll:
1st row With B, K to end.
2nd row With B, P to end.
3rd row K2B[6B:2B], (2C, 2B, 2C, 4B, 1C, 4B) 4[4:5] times, 2C, 2B, 2C, 2B[6B:2B].
4th row P2B[6B:2B], (2C, 2B, 2C, 3B, 3C, 3B) 4[4:5] times, 2C, 2B, 2C, 2B[6B:2B].
5th row K3B[7B:3B], (4C, 3B, 2C, 1B, 2C, 3B) 4[4:5] times, 4C, 3B[7B:3B].
6th row P4B[8B:4B], (2C, 3B) 13[13:16] times, 1B[5B:1B].
7th row As 6th row, but K instead of P.
8th row As 5th row, but P instead of K.
9th row As 4th row, but K instead of P.

10th row As 3rd row, but P instead of K.
11th row As 1st.
12th row As 2nd.
These 12 rows complete patt panel. Break off B and C. Join in A. Change to No. 6 needles. Beg with a K row, work 2 rows stockinette st.

Shape armholes
Bind off 2[3:4]sts at beg of next 2 rows. Dec one st at each end of next and every row until 52[58:63]sts rem. Cont straight until work measures 26[28:30]in from hemline; end with a P row.

Shape shoulders
Bind off at beg of next and every row 5[5:6]sts twice and 5[6:6]sts 4 times. Leave rem 22[24:27]sts on holder.

Front
Using No. 6 needles and B, cast on 76[84:91]sts. Work as given for back until 32 rows of patt panel have been completed. Break off B and C. Join in A. Change to No. 6 needles.

Divide for opening
Next row K2 tog, K33[37:40]sts, turn and leave rem sts on holder. Beg with a K row, cont in stockinette st on these sts for left front, dec one st at side edge on every foll 6th row 2[2:1] times more. 32[36:40]sts. Cont straight until front matches back to next patt panel; end with a P row. Break off A. Join in B. Change to No. 5 needles. Beg patt.
1st and 2nd sizes only
1st row With B, K to end.
2nd row With B, P to end.
3rd row K2B[6B:], (2C, 2B, 2C, 4B, 1C, 4B) twice.
4th row *P3B, 3C, 3B, 2C, 2B, 2C, rep from * once more, 2B[6B].
5th row K3B[7B], *4C, 3B, 2C, 1B, 2C, *, 3B, rep from * to * once, 2B.
6th row P1B, *2C, 3B, rep from * 4 times, 2C, 4B[8B].
7th row K4B[8B], *2C, 3B, rep from * 4 times, 2C, 1B.
8th row P2B, *2C, 1B, 2C, 3B, 4C, *, 3B, rep from * to * once, 3B[7B].
9th row K2B[6B], *2C, 2B, 2C, 3B, 3C, 3B, rep from * once.
10th row *P4B, 1C, 4B, 2C, 2B, 2C, rep from * once, 2B[6B].
11th row As 1st.
12th row As 2nd.
3rd size only
Work as given for back panel, working figures in parentheses twice instead of 5 times except on 6th row, where figures in paren will be worked 7 times instead of 16.

All sizes
Break off B and C. Join in A. Change to No. 6 needles. Beg with a K row, work 2 rows stockinette st.
Shape armhole
Bind off 2[3:4]sts at beg of next row. P1 row. Dec one st at armhole edge on next and every row until 23[26:29]sts rem. Cont without shaping until front measures 1½in less than back to shoulder; end with a P row.
Shape neck
Next row K16[18:19]sts, K2 tog, K1, turn and leave rem sts on holder.
Next row P to end.
Next row K to last 3sts, K2 tog, K1. Cont dec in this way on foll 2 alternate rows. 15[17:18]sts. P1 row.
Shape shoulder
Bind off at beg of next and foll alternate rows 5[5:6]sts once and 5[6:6]sts twice. Using No. 6 needles, A and with RS of work facing, rejoin yarn to rem sts at beg of opening, bind off first 6[6:7]sts, K to last 2sts, K2 tog. Work to match first side to patt panel. Break off A. Join in B. Change to No. 5 needles.
1st and 2nd sizes only
1st row With B, K to end.
2nd row With B, P to end.
3rd row *K4B, 1C, 4B, 2C, 2B, 2C, rep from * once, 2B[6B].
4th row P2B[6B], *2C, 2B, 2C, 3B, 3C, 3B, rep from * once.
Complete as given for left front band in patt as set, reversing each row.
3rd size only
Work as given for left front patt panel.
All sizes
Complete as given for left front, reversing shaping and working sl 1, K1, psso, at neck shaping, instead of K2 tog.

Sleeves
Using No. 8 needles and A, cast on 37[39:41]sts.
1st row K1, *P1, K1, rep from * to end.
2nd row P1, *K1, P1, rep from * to end.
Rep these 2 rows until work measures 3in from beg; end with a 2nd row. Change to No. 6 needles. Beg with a K row cont in stockinette st, inc one st at each end of next and every foll 6th row until there are 55[59:63]sts. Cont without shaping until sleeve measures 14[15:16]in; end with a P row. Break off A. Join in B. Change to No. 5 needles. Beg patt panel.
1st row With B, K to end.
2nd row With B, P to end.
3rd row K2B[4B:6B], *2C, 2B, 2C, 4B, 1C, 4B, rep from * twice, 2C, 2B, 2C, 2B[4B:6B].
4th row P2B[4B:6B], *2C, 2B, 2C, 3B, 3C, 3B, rep from * twice, 2C, 2B, 2C, 2B[4B:6B].
5th row K3B[5B:7B], *4C, 3B, 2C, 1B, 2C, 3B, rep from * twice, 4C, 3B[5B:7B].
6th row P4B[6B:8B], *2C, 3B, rep from * 9 times, 1B[3B:5B].
7th row As 6th row, but K instead of P.
8th row As 5th row, but P instead of K.

9th row As 4th row, but K instead of P.
10th row As 3rd row, but P instead of K.
11th row As 1st.
12th row As 2nd.
These 12 rows complete patt panel. Break off B and C. Join in A. Change to No. 6 needles. Beg with a K row work 2 rows stockinette st.

Shape top

Bind off 2[3:4]sts at beg of next 2 rows. Dec one st at each end of next and every foll 4th row until 47sts rem. Dec one st at each end of every foll alternate row until 27sts rem, then dec one st at each end of every row until 11sts rem. Bind off.

Neckband

Join shoulder seams. Using No. 8 needles, A and with RS of work facing, K across 4[5:7]sts of right front neck on holder, pick up and K 14sts up right front neck, K across 22[24:27]sts of back neck on holder, pick up and K 14sts down left front neck and K across 4[5:7]sts of left front neck on holder. 58[62:69]sts. Work 9 rows K1, P1 ribbing as given for sleeves, inc one st at center back neck on 1st and 2nd sizes only on first row. Bind off in ribbing.

Right front band

Using No. 8 needles, A and with RS of work facing, pick up and K 91[101:111]sts evenly up front edge to top of neckband. Work 3 rows K1, P1 ribbing as for sleeves. Bind off in ribbing.

Left front band

Work as for right front band.

Hood

Using No. 8 needles and A, cast on 97[103:109]sts. Work 6 rows K1, P1 ribbing as for sleeves. Change to No. 6 needles.

Shape head

Next row K to last 4sts, turn.
Next row P to last 4sts, turn.
Next row K to end.
Next row P to end.
Rep last 4 rows 9[10:11] times.
Next row Bind off 32[34:36]sts, K until there are 33[35:37]sts on right-hand needle, bind off rem 32[34:36]sts.
With WS of work facing, rejoin yarn to center sts. Cont in stockinette st for a further 8[8½:9]in on these sts; end with a P row.
Next row K1, *K2 tog, rep from * to end.
Next row P to end. Bind off.

To finish

Press under a damp cloth with a warm iron. Set in sleeves. Join side and sleeve seams. Join back seams of hood. Sew hood to neckband, beg and ending at edge of front opening. Sew in zipper. Press seams.

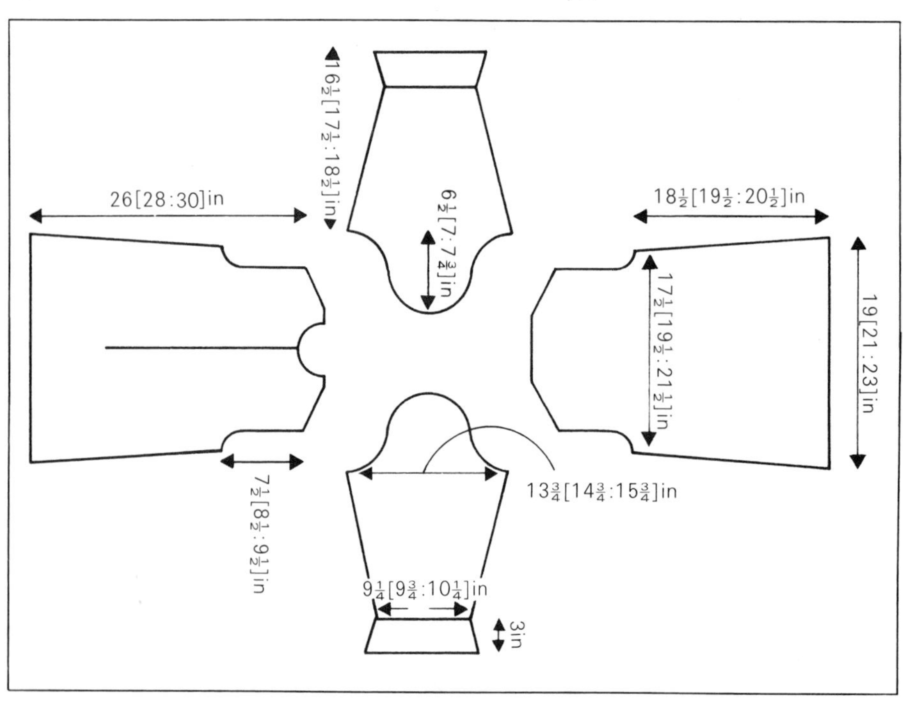

COUNTRY GIRL

Sizes
Skirt *To fit 34–38in hips. Length, 27in.*
Shawl *50in by 21in.*

Materials
Sport yarn:
Skirt *9oz in main color (A)*
1oz in contrasting color (B)
Waist length of 1in wide elastic
Shawl *In main color (A)*
1oz in contrasting color (B)
1 pair No. 5 needles
Ribbon if required

Gauge
24sts and 28 rows to 4in in stockinette on No. 5 needles.

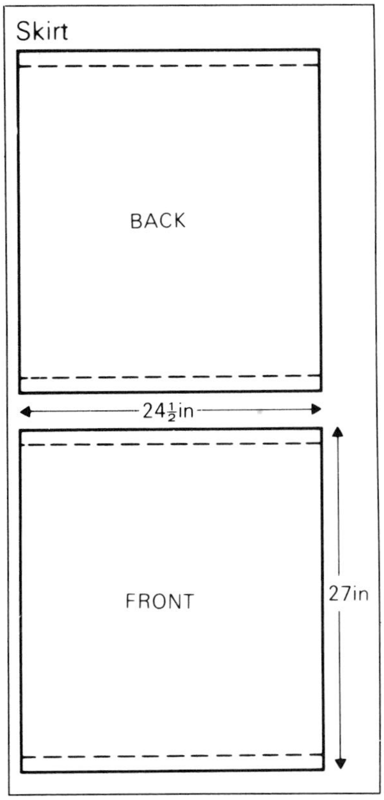

Skirt
BACK
24½in
FRONT
27in

Skirt

Back

Using No. 5 needles and B, cast on 150sts. **Beg with a K row, work 6 rows stockinette st.
Next row (hem row) K1, *yo, K2 tog, rep from * to last st, K1.
P1 row and K1 row. Cut off B and join in A.**
Work 5 more rows stockinette st.
Beg patt.
1st row (RS) K to end.
2nd and foll alternate rows P to end.
3rd row *K4, yo, K2 tog, rep from * to end.
5th row K to end.
7th row K2, *yo, K2 tog, K4, rep from * ending last rep with K2 instead of K4.
8th row P to end.
These 8 rows form patt. Rep throughout until work measures 8in less than length required. Cont in stockinette st until work measures 28in from hem row; end with P row. Cut off A and join in B. K 1 row and P 1 row.
Next row (waist row) K1, *yo, K2 tog, rep from * to last st, K1. Beg with P row, work 9 rows stockinette st. Bind off.

Front

Work as given for back.

To finish

Press under a damp cloth with a warm iron. Join side seams. Fold hem to WS and sew in position. Fold waistband to WS and sew in position, leaving opening to insert elastic. Sew up opening after inserting elastic. Press seams. Thread through ribbons.

Shawl

Using No. 5 needles and B, cast on 303sts. Work as for skirt back from ** to **. Beg patt and shape as foll:
1st row (RS) K2 tog, K to last 2sts, K2 tog.
2nd and foll alt rows P2 tog, P to last 2 sts, P2 tog.
3rd row K2 tog, yo, K2 tog, *K4, yo, K2 tog, rep from * to last 7sts, K3, K2 tog, yo, K2 tog.
5th row As 1st.
7th row K2 tog, K5, *yo, K2 tog, K4, rep from * to last 2sts, K2 tog.
9th row As 1st.
11th row K2 tog, K4, *yo, K2 tog, K4, rep from * to last 7 sts, yo, K2 tog, K3, K2 tog.
13th row As 1st.
15th row K2 tog, K3, *yo, K2 tog, K4, rep from * to last 6sts, yo, K2 tog, K2, K2 tog.
16th row As 2nd.
Beg with a K row, cont in stockinette st, dec one st at each end of every row until 3sts rem.
Bind off.

Edging

Using No. 5 needles, B and with RS facing, pick up and K 154sts along one diagonal edge. P 1 row.
Next row (picot row) K1, *yo, K2 tog, rep from * to last st, K1. P 1 row and K 1 row.
Bind off.
Complete other diagonal edge in the same way.

To finish

Press as given for skirt. Fold all edges to WS along picots and sew in position. Thread through ribbons as required.

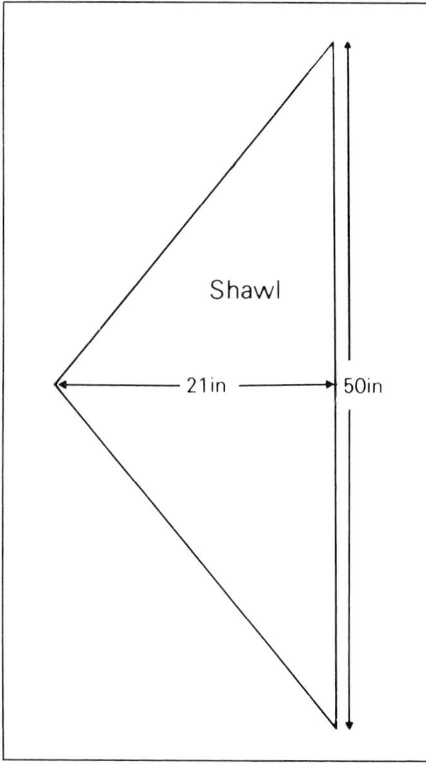
Shawl
21in
50in

CHIC CITY SUIT

Sizes
Jacket *To fit 34[36:38]in bust.*
Length, 25¼[26:26¾]in.
Sleeve seam, 17[17¼:17¾]in.
Skirt *To fit hips 36[38:40]in.*
Length, 28in or adjusted.
Note *Directions for larger sizes are in brackets []; where there is only one set of figures it applies to all sizes.*

Materials
41[43:45]oz of a knitting worsted
1 pair each Nos. 3 and 5 knitting needles
1 pair of shoulder pads for jacket
A waist length of ¾in-wide elastic for skirt.

Gauge
24sts and 28 rows to 4in in patt on No. 5 needles.

Jacket

Right front

Using No. 5 needles cast on 62[64:66]sts. Work in garter st for 1¼in. Beg patt.

1st row (RS) K.

2nd row P1, *K1, P1, rep from * to last 5sts, K5 for front border.

These 2 rows form patt. Cont in patt dec one st at end of every foll 10th row 4 times in all. 58[60:62]sts. Cont 5-st garter st border at front edge, cont in patt until work measures 8¼in; end at front edge.

Next row K6, patt to end.

Keeping 6sts at front edge in garter st, work 1[5:5] rows. Taking 1 more st into garter st border on next and every foll 6th row, at same time inc one st at front edge on next and every foll 5th row until there are 70[72:75]sts, work 3[3:0] rows; end at side edge.

Shape armhole

Keeping patt correct and shaping collar as set, bind off 3sts at beg of next row and 2sts at beg of foll alternate row. Dec one st at armhole edge on every foll alternate row 7 times in all. 62[64:66]sts. Keeping armhole edge straight cont to shape collar until there are 69[71:73]sts.

Cont straight until armhole measures 8¼[8¾:9]in; end at armhole edge.

Shape shoulder

Bind off 21[23:25]sts at beg of next row, then cont in garter st on rem 48sts of collar for 3¼[3¼:3½]in. Bind off.

Left front

Work as given for right front reversing all shaping and working patt rows thus:

1st row (RS) K.

2nd row K5 for border, P1, *K1, P1, rep from * to end.

Back

Using No. 5 needles cast on 111[117:123]sts. Work in garter st for 1¼in. Beg patt.

1st row (RS) K.

2nd row P1, *K1, rep from * to end.

These 2 rows form patt. Cont in patt, dec one st at each end of every foll 10th row 4 times in all. 103[109:115]sts. Cont straight until work measures same as fronts to beg of armhole; end with a WS row.

Shape armholes

Bind off 3sts at beg of next 2 rows and 2sts at beg of foll 2 rows. Dec one st at each end of every foll alternate row 7 times. 79[85:91]sts. Cont straight until armhole measures 8¼[8¾:9]in; end with a WS row.

Shape shoulders

Bind off 21[23:25]sts at beg of next 2 rows. Bind off.

Sleeves

Using No. 5 needles cast on

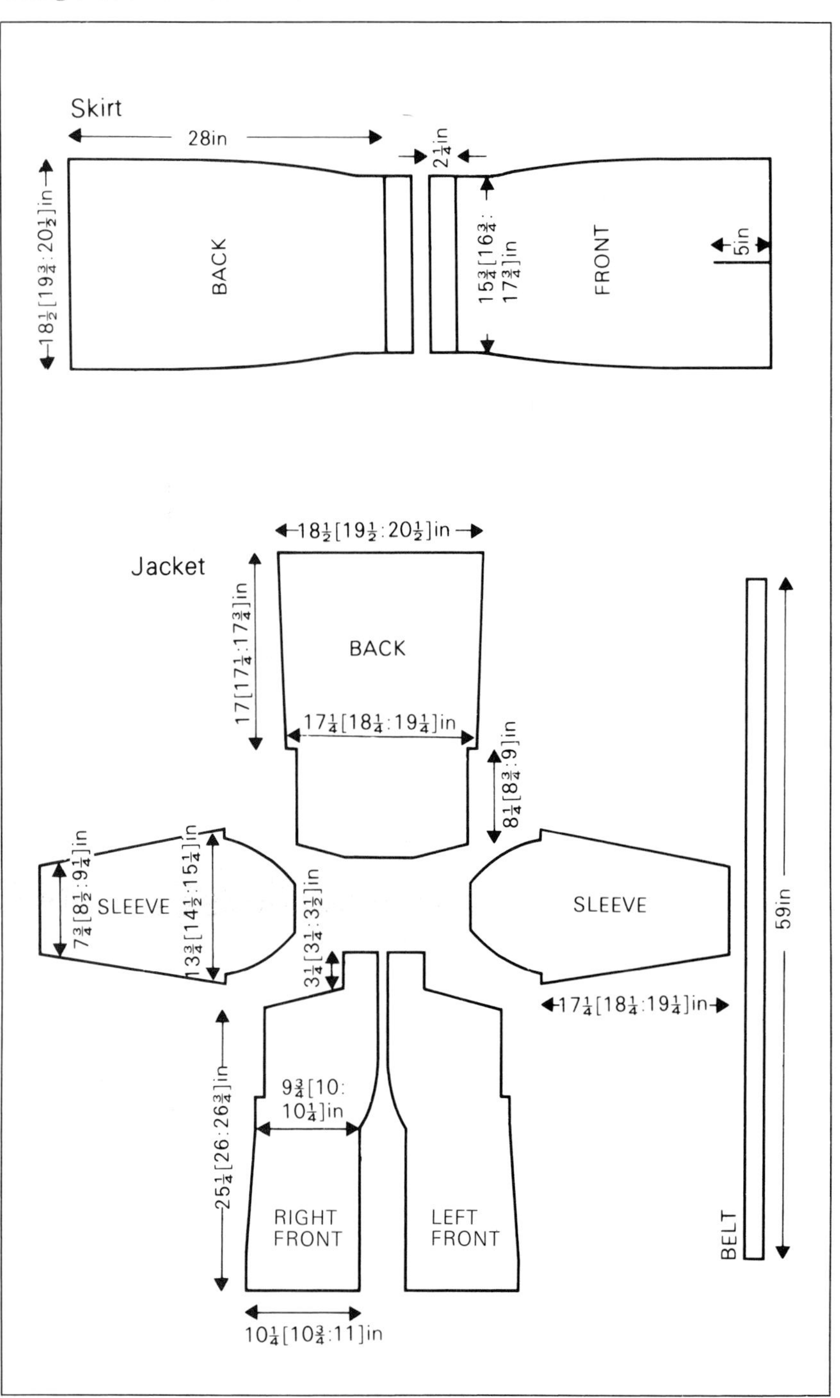

47[51:55]sts. Work in garter st for $1\frac{1}{4}$in. Cont in patt as for back, inc one st at each end of every foll 5th[5th:6th] row until there are 83[87:91]sts. Cont straight until work measures 17[$17\frac{1}{4}$:$17\frac{3}{4}$]in; end with a WS row.

Shape top

Bind off 3sts at beg of next 2 rows and 2sts at beg of foll 2 rows. Dec one st at each end of next and every foll alternate row 13[14:15] times in all, then bind off 2sts at beg of next 8 rows. Bind off.

Belt

Using No. 5 needles cast on 10sts and work in garter st for 59in. Bind off.

Shoulder pad facings (make 2)

Using No. 5 needles cast on 31sts. Cont in stockinette st, dec one st at each end of every other row until one st rem. Bind off.

To finish

Join shoulder and collar seams. Set in sleeves, then join side and sleeve seams. Join collar to back neck edge. Sew in shoulder pads and facings.

Skirt

Front

Using No. 5 needles cast on 55[59:61]sts. Work in garter st for $1\frac{1}{4}$in. Beg patt.

1st row (RS) K.

2nd row K5 for vent border, *K1, P1, rep from * to end.

Rep these 2 rows until work measures 5in; end with a WS row. Cut off yarn and leave sts on a spare needle. Using No. 5 needles cast on 55[59:61]sts. Work in garter st for $1\frac{1}{4}$in. Beg patt.

1st row (RS) K.

2nd row *P1, K1, rep from * to last 5sts, K5 for vent border.

Rep these 2 rows until work measures 5in; end with a WS row.

Next row Work to end, turn and cast on one st, then work across sts of first piece. 111[117:123]sts.

Cont in patt, working 11sts at center of row in garter st as set for a further $1\frac{1}{4}$in; end with a WS row. Cont in patt, omitting garter st at center until work measures $19\frac{1}{4}$in; end with a WS row. (Adjust length here if required.) **Dec one st at each end of next and every foll 5th row 9 times in all. 93[101:105]sts. Cont straight until work measures 28in; end with a WS row. Change to No. 3 needles.

1st rib row *K1, P1, rep from * to last st, K1.

2nd rib row *P1, K1, rep from * to last st, P1.

Rep these 2 rows for $2\frac{1}{4}$in. Bind off in ribbing.**

Back

Using No. 5 needles cast on 111[119:123]sts. Work in garter st for $1\frac{1}{4}$in. Beg patt.

1st row (RS) K.

2nd row P1, *K1, P1, rep from * to end. These 2 rows form patt. Cont in patt until work measures $19\frac{1}{4}$in; end with a WS row. (Adjust length here if required.) Complete to match front from ** to **.

To finish

Join side seams. Fold ribbing in half to WS and slipstitch in position leaving an opening for elastic. Insert elastic, then slipstitch opening.

BEACHCOMBER

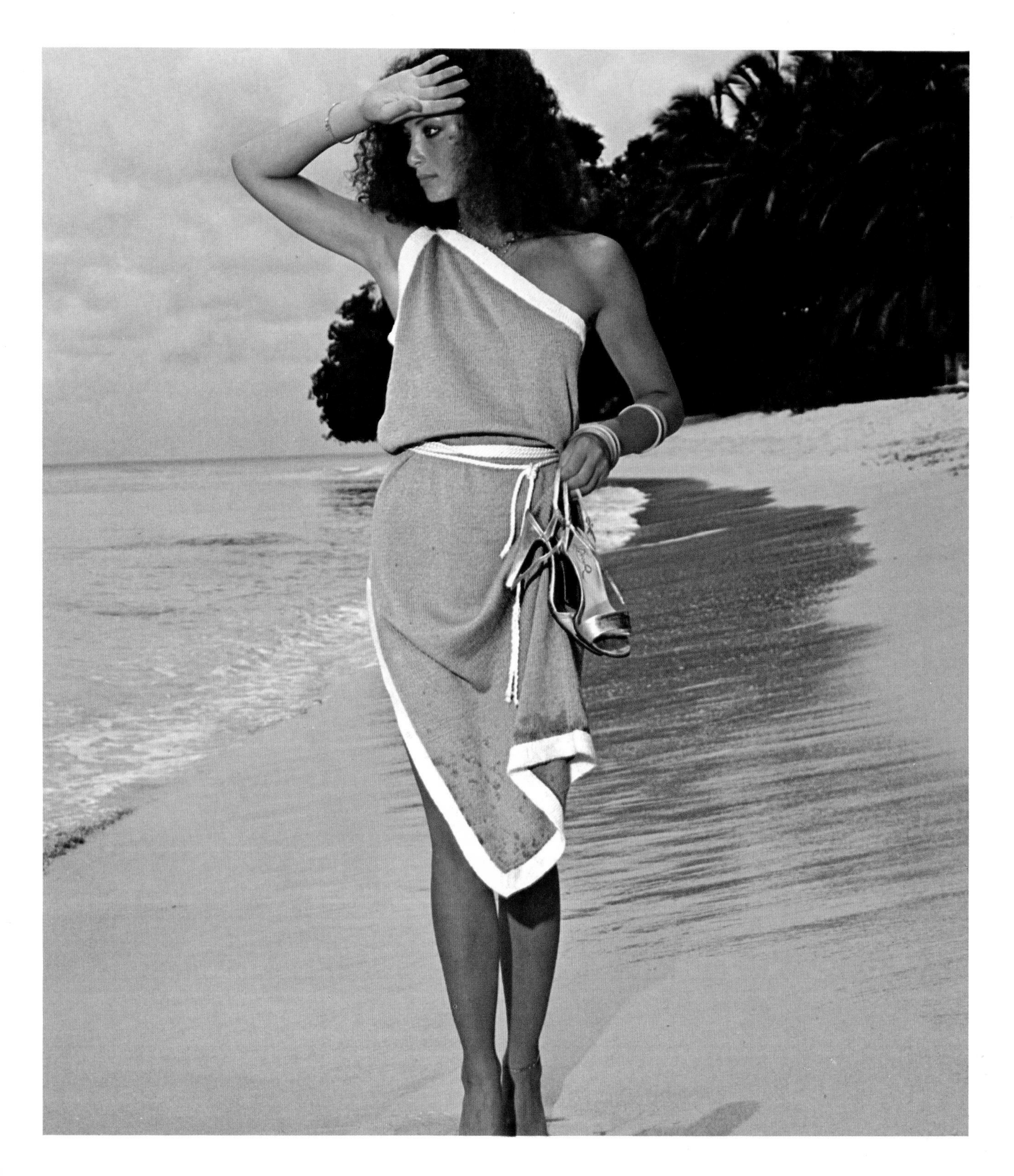

Sizes
To fit 32[34:36:38]in bust.
Length when hanging,
46[48:50:52]in.
Note *Directions for larger sizes are in brackets []; where there is only one set of figures it applies to all sizes.*

Materials
14[15:15:16]oz of a sport yarn in main color (A)
3[3:4:4]oz in contrasting color (B)
1 pair each Nos. 2 and 3 knitting needles
3¼yd of cord for tie (optional)

Gauge
28sts and 36 rows to 4in in stockinette st on No. 3 needles.

Front
Using No. 3 needles and A, cast on 114[121:128:135]sts. Beg with a K row, cont in stockinette st until work measures 19¾[20½:21¼:22]in: end with a P row.
Cast on 6sts at beg of next row. 120[127:134:141]sts.
Dec one st at each end of next and every foll 50th row 5 times in all. Cont straight until work measures 37¾[39¼:41:42½]in: end with a P row. Bind off 3sts at beg of next row, 8[8:10:11]sts at beg of next row, 2sts at beg of next row and 7[8:10:10]sts at beg of foll row. Now dec one st at beg of next row and bind off 2sts at beg of foll row. Dec one st at beg of next row and every foll alternate row 29[31:32:34] times in all and *at same time* dec one st at end on next and every foll row 56[60:62:66] times in all.
Next row K2 tog, K1, K2 tog. Fasten off.

Back
Work as for front reversing shaping.

Edgings
Using No. 2 needles and B, cast on 9sts and work in garter st until strip fits along lower edge.
Next 2 rows K1, turn and K1.
Next 2 rows K2, turn and K2.
Next 2 rows K3, turn and K3.
Cont in this way until all sts are worked, then cont in garter st until strip fits along side edge to top of vent. Bind off. Work another piece in the same way. Using No. 2 needles and B, cast on 9sts and work in garter st until strip fits along shoulder edge from side seam to point. Cut off yarn and leave sts on a holder. Using No. 2 needles and B, cast on 9sts and work in garter st until strip fits along short edge.
Next row K to end, then K the sts of first strip. 18sts.
Cont in garter st, dec one st at each end of next and every foll 4th row until 9sts rem. Cont without shaping until strip measures 13¾in from last dec, for strap. Bind off. Work other edging and strap in the same way.

To finish
Join side seams, leaving vent open. Sew edgings in position. Tie straps at shoulder.

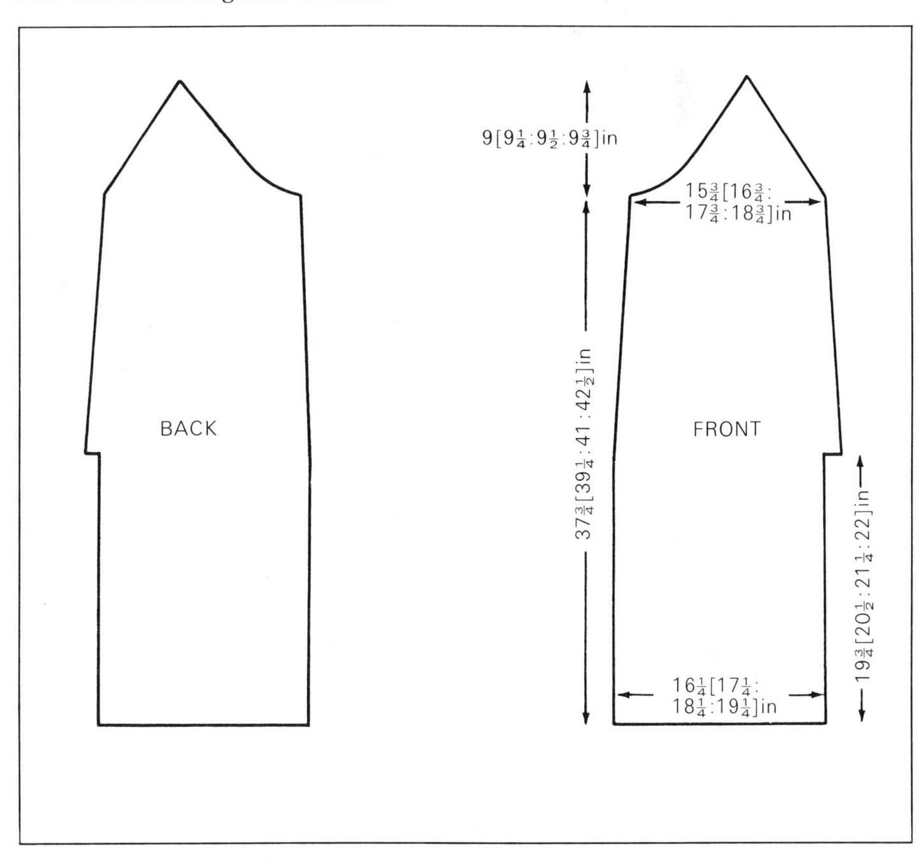

SIZZLING SUN TOPS

Beaded tube

Size

To fit 32–34in bust.
Length to underarm, 15¼in.

Materials

6oz sport yarn
1 pair No. 3 knitting needles
32 bugle beads
32 tiny beads

Gauge

44sts and 34 rows to 4in in ribbing on No. 3 needles.

Top with contrasting borders

Sizes

To fit 32[34:36:38]in bust.
Length to underarm, 13¾[13¾:14:14]in.

Materials

2[2:3:3]oz sport yarn in main color (A)
1[1:2:2] balls of contrasting color (B)
1 pair each Nos. 2 and 3 knitting needles

Gauge

25 sts and 35 rows to 4in in stockinette st on No. 3 needles.

Beaded tube

Using No. 3 needles cast on 232sts. Work 20in K2, P2 rib. Bind off in ribbing.

Straps (make 2)
Using No. 3 needles cast on 10sts.
1st row (RS) K2, *P2, K2, rep from * to end.
2nd row P2, *K2, P2, rep from * to end. Rep last 2 rows for 10in. Bind off in ribbing.

To finish
Join back seam, reversing it for 4¾in at top to turn back. Sew on bugle beads in groups of 4 on K sts of ribbing, with 2 rows between each bead of group. Attach 1st bead 8sts from back seam and 12 rows from bottom edge of folded-down top. With 3 stripes of K ribbing between each group of 4 bugles, sew 1st bead of 2nd group of 4 bugles 6 rows up from last bead of 1st group. Rep these 2 groups 3 times more. Fasten each bead at foot with tiny bead. Sew on straps ½in from top edge.

Top with contrasting borders

Front
**Using No. 2 needles and B, cast

on 88[94:102:108]sts.
1st row P1[2:2:1], K2, *P2, K2, rep from * to last 1[2:2:1]sts, P1[2:2:1].
2nd row K1[2:2:1], P2, *K2, P2, rep from * to last 1[2:2:1]sts, K1[2:2:1]. Rep last 2 rows for $3\frac{1}{2}$in; end with a 1st row. Cut off B. Join in A. Change to No. 3 needles.
Next row P3[6:5:8]. P into front and back of next st, *P8[8:9:9], P into front and back of next st, rep from * to last 3[6:6:9]sts, P to end. 98[104:112:118]sts. Cont in reverse stockinette st until work measures $12\frac{1}{4}[12\frac{1}{4}:12\frac{1}{2}:12\frac{1}{2}]$in; end with a K row.**

Shape top
1st row P to last 6[6:7:7]sts, turn.
2nd row Sl 1, K to last 6[6:7:7]sts, turn.
3rd row Sl 1, P to last 12[12:14:14]sts, turn.
4th row Sl 1, K to last 12[12:14:14]sts, turn. Cont to work 6[6:7:7]sts less on alternate rows in this way until 24[24:28:28]sts are left unworked at each side. Cut off yarn. Sl rem 24[24:28:28]sts onto same needle.

Border
Using No. 2 needles, B and with RS of work facing, cont as foll:
1st row K6[6:7:7], pick up loop lying between needles and K tog with next st – called (M1) K2 tog – (K5[5:6:6], (M1) K2 tog) 3 times, K49[55:55:61], *(M1) K2 tog, K5[5:6:6], rep from * to end.
2nd row K2[1:1:2], P2, *K2, P2, rep from * to last 2[1:1:2]sts, K2[1:1:2].
3rd row P2[1:1:2], K2, *P2, K2, rep from * to last 2[1:1:2]sts, P2[1:1:2]. Rep 2nd and 3rd rows 6 times. Bind off in ribbing.

Back
Work as for front from ** to **. Cut off A. Join in B.

Border
Using No. 2 needles and B, K1 row. Work 14 rows ribbing as for front border. Bind off in ribbing. Join side seams.

Ribbed top with shaped detail

Back
**Using No. 2 needles cast on 115[121:129:137]sts.
1st row K1, *P1, K1, rep from * to end.
2nd row P1, *K1, P1, rep from * to end. Rep last 2 rows for 2in; end with a 1st row.
Next row Rib 29[20:21:34], pick up loop lying between needles and K tbl – called make 1 (M1) –, (rib 57[40:43:68], M1) 1[2:2:1] times, rib to end. 117[124:132:139]sts. Change to No. 3 needles. Beg patt.
1st row (RS) P0[1:0:1], *P2, K1, P1, K1, rep from * to last 2[3:2:3]sts, P2[3:2:3].
2nd row K0[1:0:1] *K2, P2, rep from * to last 2[3:2:3]sts, K2[3:2:3]. The last 2 rows form patt. Cont in patt until work measures $12\frac{1}{2}[13:13\frac{1}{2}:13\frac{3}{4}]$in; end with a 2nd row and inc 0[1:1:0]st at center of last row. 117[125:133:139]sts. ** Change to No. 2 needles. Work 15 rows K1, P1 ribbing. Bind off in ribbing.

Front
Work as for back from ** to **. Change to No. 2 needles. Work 3 rows K1, P1 ribbing.
Next row Rib 58[62:66:69], M1, rib to end. 118[126:134:140]sts.
Insert a marker at each end of last row.

Ribbed top with shaped detail

Sizes
As for top with contrasting borders.
Length at center front $13[13\frac{1}{4}:14:14\frac{1}{4}]$in.

Materials
3[3:4:4] × 2oz balls sport yarn
1 pair each Nos. 2 and 3 knitting needles
Length of narrow elastic

Gauge
30sts and 38 rows to 4in in stockinette st on No. 3 needles.

Crossover top

Sizes
As for top with contrasting borders.
Length, $19\frac{1}{2}[20:20\frac{3}{4}:21]$in.

Materials
4[4:5:5] × 2oz balls of sport yarn in main color (A)
1[1:2:2] balls each in contrasting colors (B and C)
1 pair each Nos. 2 and 3 knitting needles

Gauge
25sts and 35 rows to 4in in stockinette st on No. 3 needles.
Note *Directions for larger sizes are in brackets []; where there is only one set of figures it applies to all sizes.*

Technique tip

Elastic casing

Cut a length of narrow elastic to fit snugly around the top of the bust, allowing ½in to overlap. Stitch elastic into a circle, securing the ends with a few strong stitches. Divide circle into four equal parts and mark with pins.

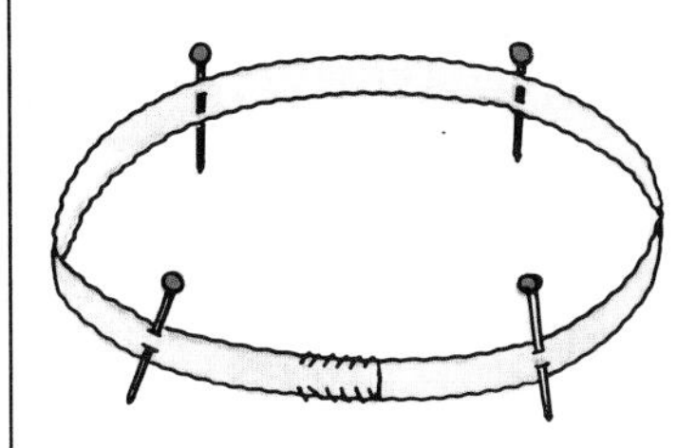

Divide the knitting into quarters, around upper edge at casing position and mark the four points with pins. Pin the elastic into position matching the quarter section pins on the elastic with those on the knitting. Stretch the elastic slightly to fit.

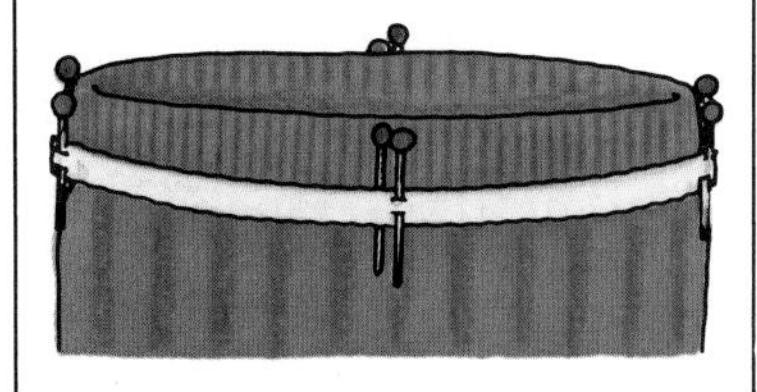

Thread a blunt needle with a strand of matching yarn. (Here contrasting for clarity.) Secure yarn at casing position at left-hand side seam of knitting. Work a herringbone stitch from left to right encasing the elastic as you work. Take care to distribute the knitting evenly and finish off thread securely.

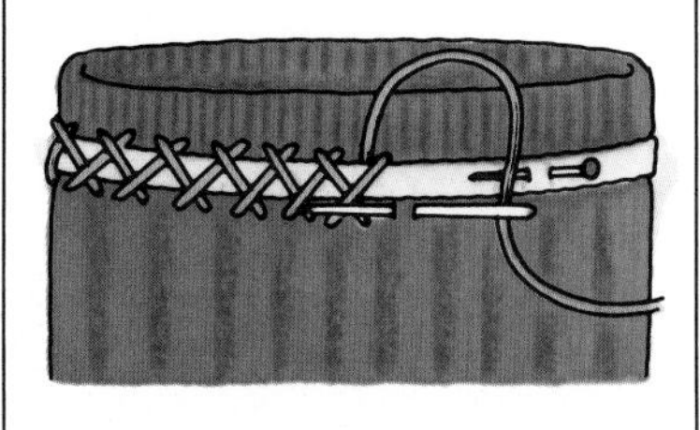

Shape left front flap
Next row Rib 59[63:67:70], turn and leave rem sts on a spare needle.
***Work 10 rows ribbing on these sts.
Next row Rib 49[52:55:59], turn.
Next row Sl 1, rib to end.
Next row Rib 39[41:44:46], turn.
Next row Sl 1, rib to end.
Next row Rib 29[30:33:34], turn.
Next row Sl 1, rib to end.
Next row Rib 9[10:11:11], turn.
Next row Sl 1, rib to end.
Bind off in ribbing.***
Shape right front flap
Using No. 2 needles and with RS of work facing, rejoin yarn and rib to end. Work 1 row. Complete as for left front flap from *** to ***.

To finish
Do not press. Join side seams. Cut elastic to fit just above bust and join into a ring. Work herringbone casing over elastic on inside at level of markers.

Crossover top

Left front
**Using No. 2 needles and A, cast on 99[105:111:119]sts.
1st row K1, *P1, K1, rep from * to end.
2nd row P1, *K1, P1, rep from * to end. Rep last 2 rows 6 times, then work 1st row again.
Next row Rib 11[10:11:13], pick up loop lying between needles and K tbl – called make 1 (M1) –, (rib 19[21:22:23], M1 4 times, rib to end. 104[110:116:124]sts. **
Change to No. 3 needles. Beg with a K row, cont in stockinette st and stripe patt of 6 rows A, 2 rows A, 6 rows A and 6 rows C, *at the same time* shape front edge by dec one st at beg of every alternate row until 57[63:69:77]sts rem; end with a P row.
Shape armhole
Cont to shape at front edge as before, work armhole as foll:
Next row Bind off 3 sts, K to end.
Next row P2 tog, P to end.
Dec one st at armhole edge on next 5[7:5:7] rows, then on foll 5[5:9:9] alternate rows, *at the same time* cont to dec at front edge as before until 37[39:40:45]sts rem.
Keeping armhole edge straight, dec one st at front edge only as before until 19[20:20:22]sts rem.
Cont without shaping until armhole measures 7[7½:8¼:8½]in; end with a P row.
Shape shoulders
Bind off 10[10:10:11]sts at beg of next row. Work 1 row. Bind off 9[10:10:11]sts.

Right front
Using No. 2 needles and A, cast on 99[105:111:119]sts.
Work 7 rows ribbing as for back waistband.
Next row *(buttonhole row)* Rib 2, bind off 3, rib 89[95:101:109], bind off 3, rib to end.
Next row Rib to end, casting on 3sts over those bound off in previous row.
Work a further 6 rows ribbing.
Complete to match left front, reversing shaping.

Back
Work as for left front from ** to **. Change to No. 3 needles. Beg with a K row, cont in stockinette st and stripe patt until back matches front to underarm, ending with a P row.
Shape armholes
Bind off 3sts at beg of next 2 rows. Dec one st at each end of every row until 88[90:100:104]sts rem, then at each end of every foll alternate row until 78[80:82:86]sts rem.
Cont without shaping until back matches front to shoulder, ending with a P row.
Shape shoulders
Bind off 10[10:10:11]sts at beg of next 2 rows and 9[10:10:11]sts at beg of foll 2 rows. Bind off rem 40[40:44:44]sts.

Front border
Join shoulder seams. Using No. 2 needles and C, cast on 4sts. Work in garter st until strip, slightly stretched, fits up left front, around back neck and down right front to lower edge. Bind off.

Armhole borders
Using No. 2 needles and B, cast on 4sts. Work in garter st until strip, slightly stretched, fits armhole.

To finish
Do not press. Sew on front and armhole borders. Join side seams. Sew on buttons.

FAIR ISLE CLASSIC

Sizes
To fit 36–38[40–42]in chest.
Length, 26[26½]in.

Note *Directions for larger size are in brackets []; where there is only one set of figures it applies to both sizes.*

Materials
8oz of a sport yarn in main color
2oz in each of 3 contrasting colors (A, B and C)
1oz in contrasting color (D)
1 pair each Nos. 2 and 3 knitting needles

Gauge
28sts and 36 rows to 4in in Fair Isle patt worked on No. 3 needles.

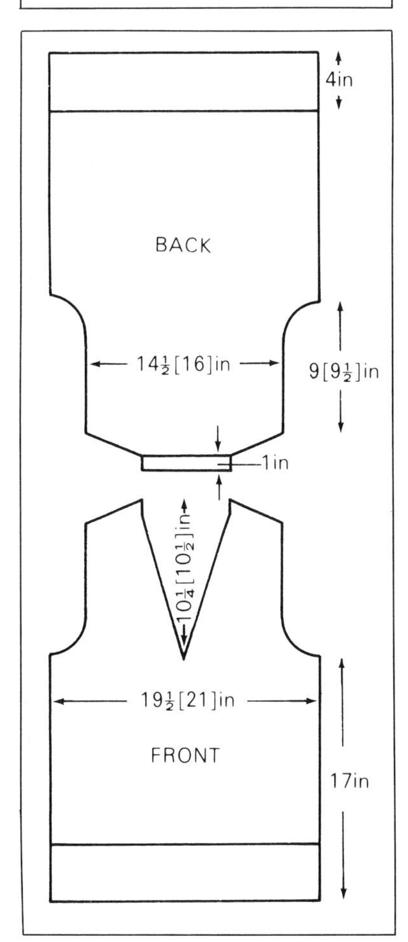

Back
Using No. 2 needles and main color, cast on 136[148]sts.
1st ribbing row K1, (P2, K2) to last 3sts, P2, K1.
2nd ribbing row P1, (K2, P2) to last 3sts, K2, P1.
Rep these 2 rows for 4in; end with a 2nd ribbing row. Change to No. 3 needles. Reading RS rows from right to left and WS rows from left to right, cont in stockinette st, working Fair Isle patt from chart until work measures 17in; end with a WS row.
Shape armholes
Bind off 6sts at beg of next 2 rows, 4sts at beg of next 2 rows, 3sts at beg of next 2 rows, 2sts at beg of next 2 rows and 1st at beg of foll 4[6] rows. 102[112]sts.
Cont in patt straight until armhole measures 9[9½]in; end with a WS row.
Shape shoulders
Bind off 6[7]sts at beg of next 10 rows. 42sts.
Change to No. 2 needles and cont in main color only.
1st ribbing row K2, (P2, K2) to end.
2nd ribbing row P2, (K2, P2) to end.
Rep 2 ribbing rows for 1in; end with a 2nd ribbing row. Bind off in ribbing.

Front
Work as for back until work measures 2 rows less than back at beg of armhole.
Divide for neck and shape armhole
Next row Patt 68[74], turn and leave rem sts on a spare needle. Complete this side of neck first.
Patt 1 row.
Bind off 6sts at beg of next row, 4sts at beg of foll alternate row, 3sts at beg of foll alternate row, 2sts at beg of foll alternate row and 1st at beg of foll 2[3] alternate rows, *at same time* dec one st at neck edge on every 4th row until 30[35]sts rem.
Cont straight until armhole measures 9in; end at armhole edge.
Shape shoulder
Bind off 6[7]sts at beg of next and foll 3 alternate rows. Work 1 row. Bind off.
With RS facing, join yarn to inner end of sts on spare needle and patt to end of row. Patt 2 rows.
Complete to match first side reversing shaping.

Neckband
With RS facing, using No. 2 needles join on main color and pick up and K 74[78]sts evenly along one side of front neck. Beg with 2nd ribbing row, rib as for back neckband for 1in; end with a 2nd ribbing row. Bind off in ribbing. Finish other side of neck in same way.

Armhole borders (alike)
Join shoulder seams. With RS facing, using No. 2 needles and main color, pick up and K 134[138]sts evenly along armhole edge.
Beg with 2nd ribbing row, rib as for back neckband for 1in; end with a 2nd ribbing row. Bind off in ribbing.

To finish
Join side seams. Sew neckband to center front neck, lapping left over right.

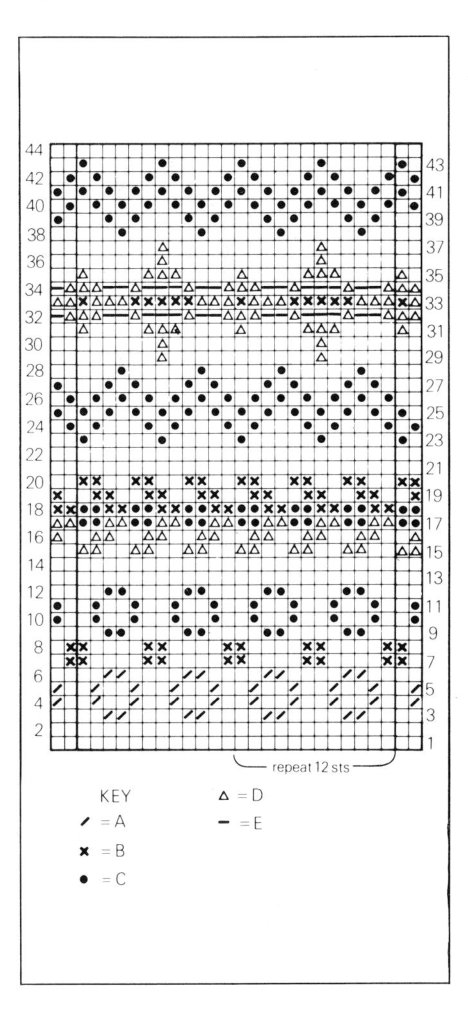

FISHERMAN'S FAVORITE

Sizes
To fit 38[40:42]in chest.
Length, 26[$26\frac{1}{4}$:$26\frac{3}{4}$]in.
Sleeve seam, 18in.
Note *Directions for the larger sizes are in brackets []; where there is only one set of figures it applies to all sizes.*

Materials
12[13:13] × 2oz balls of a knitting worsted in main color (A)
Small amounts of 5 contrasting colors as shown on chart
1 pair each Nos. 2 and 5 needles
9 buttons

Gauge
22sts and 30 rows to 4in in stockinette st worked on No. 5 needles.

Back
Using No. 2 needles and main color, cast on 113[119:125]sts.
1st row K2, *P1, K1, rep from * to last st, K1.
2nd row *K1, P1, rep from * to last st, K1.
Rep last 2 rows for $3\frac{1}{2}$in; end with a 2nd row. Change to No. 5 needles.
Beg with a K row, work 24 rows stockinette st.
Use small, separate balls of yarn for each section of patt and twist yarns tog when changing color to avoid making a hole, beg motif from chart.
1st row K48[51:54]A, 18 in 1st contrasting color, 47[50:53]A.
After motif is complete, cont in stockinette st and main color only until work measures $15\frac{3}{4}$in from beg; end with a P row.
Shape raglan armholes
Bind off 3sts at beg of next 2 rows.
3rd row K2, sl 1, K1, psso, K to last 4sts, K2 tog, K2.
4th row P2, P2 tog, P to last 4sts, P2 tog tbl, P2.

Rep last 2 rows 1[2:3] times.
Next row As 3rd.
Next row P to end.
Rep last 2 rows until 27[27:29]sts rem; end with a P row. Bind off.

Left front
Using No. 2 needles and main color, cast on 55[57:61]sts. Rib 3½in as for back, ending with a 2nd row and dec one st at end of last row on 1st and 3rd sizes only. 54[57:60]sts. Change to No. 5 needles. Beg with a K row, work 14 rows stockinette st.
Make pocket
Next row K18[21:24]sts, turn and cast on 25sts for pocket lining, leaving rem sts on a spare needle. Work 41 rows on these 43[46:49]sts.
Next row K18[21:24]sts, bind off rem sts.
Cut off yarn and leave sts on a spare needle. Rejoin yarn to sts on first spare needle and work 43 rows; end with a K row.
Next row P to end, then P across sts on spare needle.
Cont in stockinette st until front measures same as back to armholes; end with a P row.

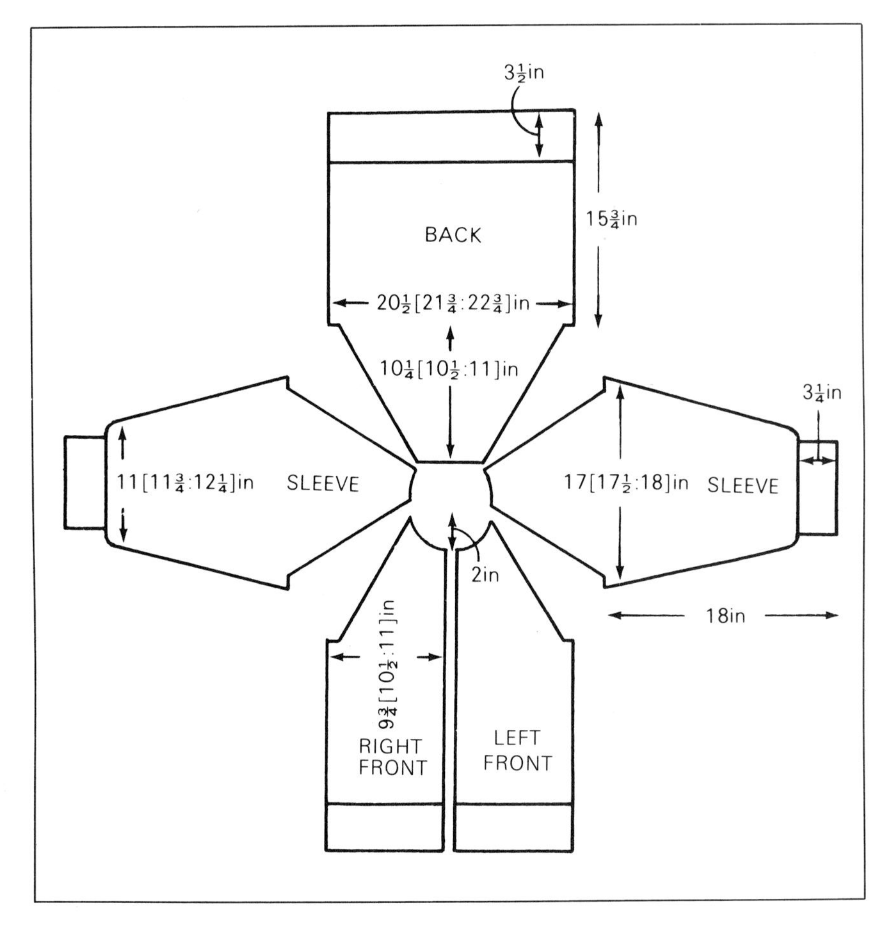

Shape raglan armhole
1st row Bind off 3sts, K to end.
2nd row P to end.
3rd row K2, sl 1, K1, psso, K to end.
4th row P to last 4sts, P2 tog tbl, P2.
Rep 3rd and 4th rows 1[2:3] times.
Next row As 3rd.
Next row P to end.
Rep last 2 rows until 21[21:22]sts rem; end with a P row.
Shape neck
Next row K2, sl 1, K1, psso, K to last 3[3:4]sts, bind off these sts. Cut off yarn. Turn work and rejoin yarn at neck edge. Cont to shape raglan on alternate rows as before, *at the same time* dec one st at neck edge on next 5 rows, then 4 foll alternate rows. K tog 2 rem sts. Fasten off.
Pocket border
Using No. 2 needles and with RS facing, pick up and K 39sts evenly along edge of pocket opening.
1st row *K1, P1, rep from * to last st, K1.
2nd row K2, *P1, K1, rep from * to last st, K1.
Rep last 2 rows 3 times. Bind off.

Right front
Work as for left front from ** to **, but dec at beg instead of at end of last row of ribbing.
Make pocket
Next row K36sts, turn and leave rem sts on a spare needle.
Work 42 rows on these sts; end with a K row. Cut off yarn and leave sts on a spare needle.
Cast on 25sts for pocket lining, then using same needle K across sts on first spare needle. Work 41 more rows; end with a P row.
Next row Bind off 25sts, K to end.
Next row P to end, then P across sts on spare needle.
Cont in stockinette st until front measures same as left front to armholes, end with K row.
Shape raglan armhole
1st row Bind off 3sts, P to end.
2nd row K to last 4sts, K2 tog, K2.
3rd row P2, P2 tog, P to end.
Rep 2nd and 3rd rows 1[2:3] times.
Next row As 2nd.
Next row P to end.
Rep last 2 rows until 21[21:22]sts rem; end with a P row.
Shape neck
Next row Bind off 3[3:4]sts, K to last 4sts, K2 tog, K2.

Complete to match left front, including pocket border.

Left sleeve
**Using No. 2 needles and main color, cast on 59[61:63]sts. Rib 3¼in as for back; end with a 2nd row. Change to No. 5 needles.
Next row K to end, inc 2[4:4]sts evenly across row. 61[65:67]sts. Beg with a P row, work 3 rows stockinette st. Cont in stockinette st, inc one st at each end of next and every foll 8th row until there are 83[87:89]sts. Cont straight until sleeve measures 15½in from beg; end with a P row. Inc one st at each end of next and every foll 4th row until there are 93[97:99]sts. Work 3 rows.
Shape top
Bind off 3sts at beg of next 2 rows.
3rd row K2, sl 1, K1, psso, K to last 4sts, K2 tog, K2.
4th row P to end. Rep last 2 rows until 17sts rem; end with a P row.**
Shape neck
Next row K2, sl 1, K1, psso, K to last 7sts, bind off these sts. Cut off yarn.
Turn work and rejoin yarn to rem sts at neck edge. Cont shaping raglan as before, *at the same time* dec one st at neck edge on next 5 rows. K2 tog. Fasten off.

Right sleeve
Work as for left sleeve from ** to **.
Shape neck
Next row Bind off 7sts, K to last 4sts, K2 tog, K2.
Complete to match left sleeve.
Buttonhole border
Using No. 2 needles and main color, cast on 15sts.
1st row K2, *P1, K1, rep from * to last st, K1.
2nd row *K1, P1, rep from * to last st, K1.
Work 2 more rows ribbing.
1st buttonhole row Rib 6, bind off 3sts, rib to end.
2nd buttonhole row Rib to end, casting on 3sts over those bound off in previous row.
Rib 23 rows. Rep last 25 rows until there are 8 buttonholes. Rib 18 more rows. Bind off in ribbing.

Button border
Work to match buttonhole border, omitting buttonholes.

Neck border
Using No. 2 needles and main color, cast on 15sts. Work 17¾[17¾:18]in ribbing, when slightly stretched, as for buttonhole border; end with a WS row. Make buttonhole in next 2 rows, then rib 6 rows.
Next row Sl 1, K1, psso, rib to last 2 sts, K2 tog.
Rep last row 5 times more. K tog rem 3sts. Fasten off.

To finish
Press each piece lightly according to directions on yarn label. Join raglan seams. Join side and sleeve seams. Sew on pocket linings, pocket borders and neck border. Sew on buttons.

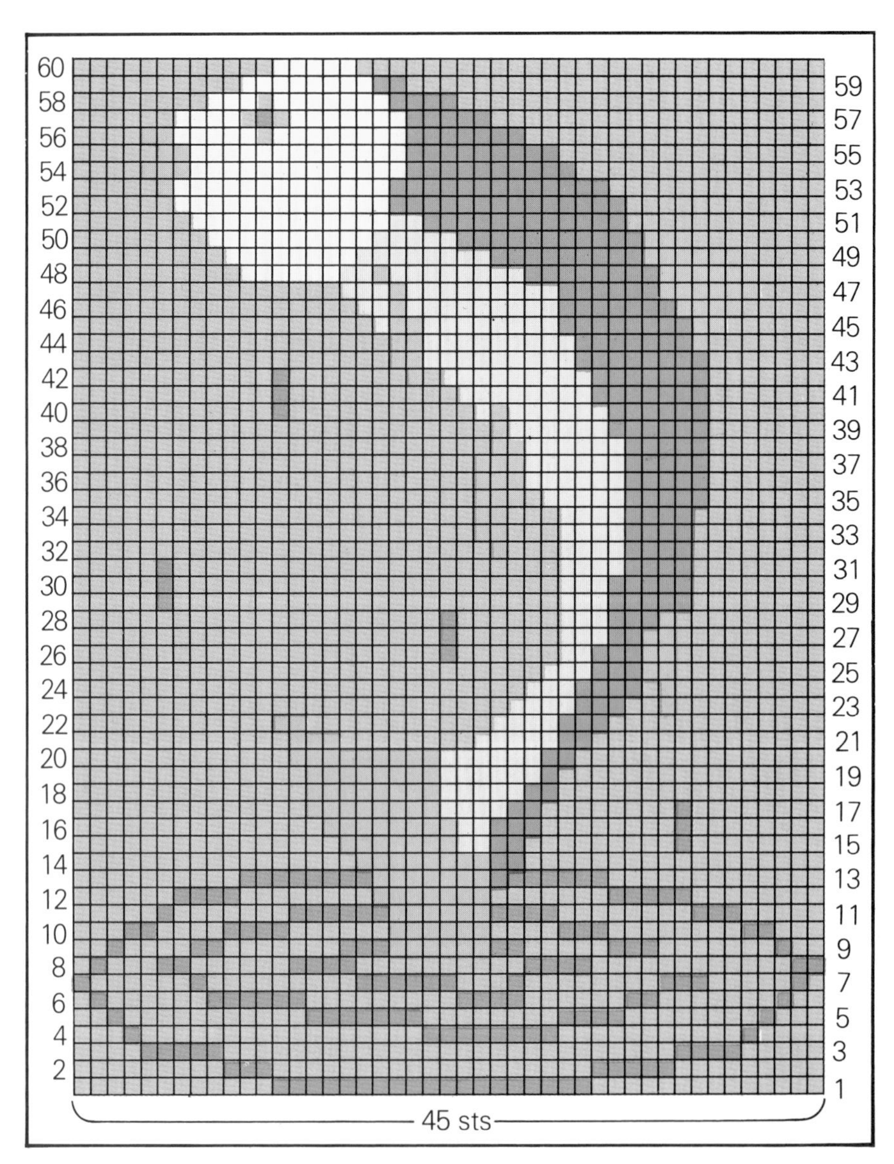

MAN ABOUT TOWN

Back
**Using No. 2 needles cast on 102[112:112]sts and work in K1, P1 ribbing for 2½in.
Dec row Rib 7[8:6], K2 tog, *rib 7[6:6], K2 tog, rep from * to last 3[6:2]sts, rib to end. 91[99:107]sts.
Change to No. 4 needles. Beg ribbing patt.
1st row K.
2nd row (RS) K1, *K1, K next st inserting needle into st one row below – called knit one below or K1 b – rep from * to last 2sts, K2.
3rd row K1, *K1b, rep from * to end.
The last 2 rows form patt. Cont in patt until work measures 18in from beg; end with WS row.
Shape armholes
Bind off 3sts at beg of next 2 rows and 2sts at beg of foll 2 rows. 81[89:97]sts. ** Cont straight until armhole measures 8¼[8½:9]in; end with WS row.
Shape shoulders
Bind off 3sts at beg of next 12 rows and 4sts at beg of foll 0[2:4] rows.
Shape neck
Next row Bind off 4, work until there are 12sts on right-hand needle, turn and leave rem 29sts on a spare needle.
Next row Bind off 8, work to end. Bind off. Rejoin yarn to inner end of sts on spare needle, bind off 13, work to end.
Complete to match first side.

Front
Work as for back from ** to **.
Cont straight until work measures ¾[1¼:1½]in from beg of armhole; end with WS row.
Divide neck
Next row Patt 37[41:45], turn and leave rem sts on a spare needle. Cont on first set of sts until armhole measures 4[4½:4¾]in; end at armhole edge.
Shape neck
Dec one st at neck edge on next and every foll 4th row 8 times in all. Place a marker at neck edge on last row. Dec one st at neck edge on foll 6th row 3 times in all. Cont straight until armhole measures 8¼[8½:9]in; end at armhole edge.
Shape shoulder
Bind off 3sts at beg of next and foll 6 alternate rows and 4sts at beg of foll 1[2:3] alternate rows. Work 1 row. Bind off. Rejoin yarn to inner end of sts on spare needle, bind off 7, patt to end. Complete to match first side, reversing shaping.

Sleeves
Using No. 2 needles cast on 52[56:60]sts and work in K1, P1 ribbing for 1½in, but inc one st at beg of last row. 53[57:61]sts.
Change to No. 4 needles. Cont in ribbing patt as for back, but inc one st at each end of every foll 12th row until there are 77[81:85]sts. Cont straight until work measures 19¼in from beg; end with WS row.
Shape top
Bind off 5sts at beg of next 2 rows, 4sts at beg of foll 2 rows, 3sts at beg of foll 4 rows, 2 sts at beg of foll 0[2:4] rows, one st at beg of foll 20 rows, 2sts at beg of foll 2 rows and 3 sts at beg of foll 2 rows. Bind off.

Collar
Using No. 2 needles cast on 10sts.
Next row K2, inc in next st to form P1 K1 *P1, K1, rep from * to last 4 sts, P1, inc in next st to form K1, P1, K2.
Next row P2, rib to last 2sts, P2.
Cont in ribbing inc at each end of

Sizes
To fit 36[38:40]in chest.
Length, 26¼[26½:27]in.
Sleeve seam, 19¼in.
Note *Directions for larger sizes are in brackets []; where there is only one set of figures it applies to all sizes.*

Materials
10[11:12] × 2oz balls of a knitting worsted
1 pair each Nos. 2, 4 and 5 needles

Gauge
19st and 44 rows to 4in in ribbing patt on No. 4 needles.

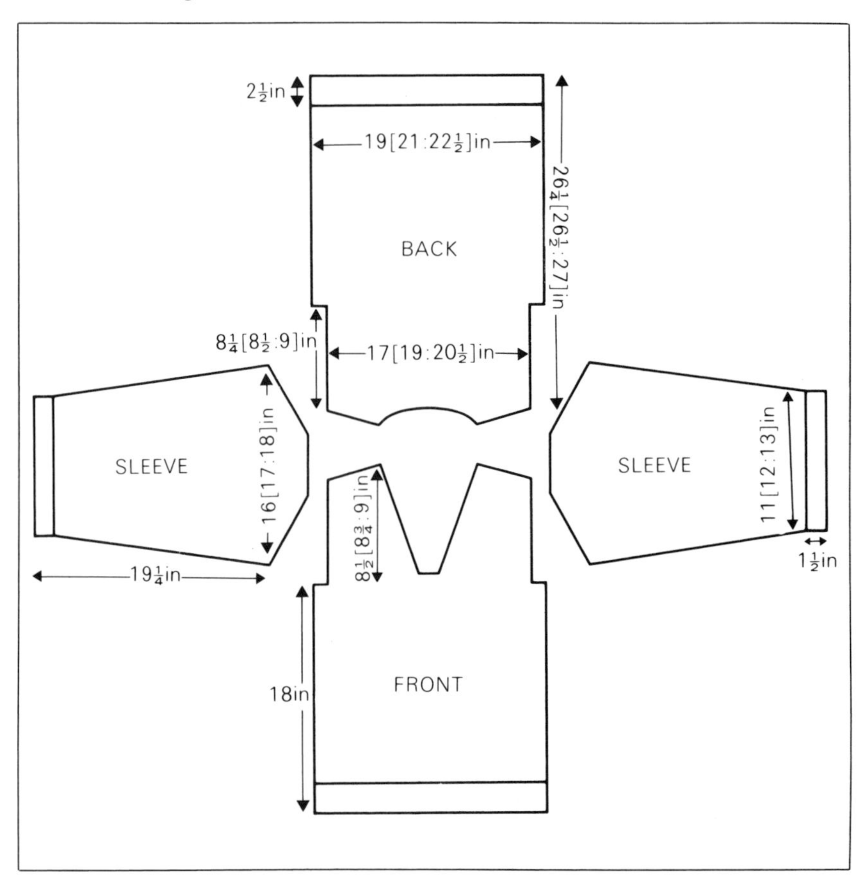

Technique tip

Knitting into stitch below

This method is often used in ribbing patterns to produce a highly textured fabric.

Insert right-hand needle into center of next stitch on left-hand needle *but* one row below. Knit the stitch in the usual way, drawing right-hand needle point through center of same stitch. Drop the loop from the left-hand needle.

The finished fabric here comprises a simple knit one, knit one below repeat, known as "fisherman's ribbing."

next and every foll alternate row 3 times more. Work 1 row.
Change to No. 4 needles and cont to inc on next and every foll alternate row 4 times in all. Work 1 row.
Change to No. 5 needles and cont to inc on next and every foll alternate row 4 times in all. 129sts. Work 9 rows straight.
Next row Rib 1, sl 1, rib 1, psso, rib to last 3sts, work 2 tog, rib 1.
Next row P2, rib to last 2sts, P2.
Cont in rib dec at each end of next and every foll alternate row 3 times more. Change to No. 4 needles and cont to dec on every alternate row 4 times. Change to No. 2 needles and cont to dec on every alternate row 4 times. 105sts. Work 1 row. Bind off.

Front bands
Using No. 2 needles cast on 41sts.
1st row K2, *K1, P1, rep from * to last 3sts, K1, K2 tog.
2nd row Bind off 1, rib to last 3 sts, P3.
Rep these 2 rows 11 times.
17sts. Work 15 rows ribbing as set.
Bind off. Work another band to match, reversing shaping.

To finish
Join shoulder seams. Set in sleeves, then join side and sleeve seams. Sew front bands to opening up to markers. Sew collar around neck edge and to top of bands. Fold collar in half to WS and slipstitch in position.

TWO'S COMPANY

Sizes
To fit 36[38:40:42]in chest.
Pullover *Length, 24[24:25½:25½]in.*
Jacket *Length, 29[29:29½:29½]in.*
Sleeve seam, 19in.
Note *Directions for larger sizes are in brackets []; where there is only one set of figures it applies to all sizes.*

Materials
Pullover *11[11:11:13]oz of a fingering yarn in main color (A)*
4oz in each of 2 contrasting colors (B and C)
1 pair each Nos. 2, 3 and 4 knitting needles
Jacket *18[20:20:22]oz of a knitting worsted in main color (A)*
13[15:15:15]oz in 1st contrasting color (B)
11[11:11:13]oz in 2nd contrasting color (C)
1 pair each Nos. 5, 6 and 7 knitting needles
6 buttons

Gauge
Pullover *28sts and 32 rows to 4in in main patt using No. 4 needles.*
Jacket *18sts and 22 rows to 4in in stockinette st using No. 7 needles.*

Pullover

Back

Using No. 2 needles and A, cast on 134[142:150:158]sts.
1st ribbing row P2, (K2, P2) to end.
2nd ribbing row K2, (P2, K2) to end.
Rep these 2 rows for 4in; end with a 2nd ribbing row and dec one st at end of last row. 133[141:149:157]sts.
Change to No. 4 needles. Join on B. Beg main patt.
1st row (RS) K with A.
2nd row P with A.
3rd row K1 A, (1B, 3A) to end.
4th row P with A.
5th row K with A.
6th row P1A, (1B, 3A) to end.
These 6 rows form patt. Cont in patt until work measures 15[15:15½:15½]in; end with a WS row.

Shape armholes
Keeping patt correct, bind off 8sts at beg of next 2 rows. Dec one st at each end of next and every foll alternate row until 109[113:117:121]sts rem. Cont straight until armhole measures 4[4:4¾:4¾]in; end with a 2nd or 4th row.*
Yoke
Change to No. 3 needles and work in garter st, working in stripes of 2 rows C and 2 rows B until armhole measures 9[9:10:10]in; end WS row.
Shape shoulders
Bind off 11[11:12:12]sts at beg of next 4 rows and 11[12:11:12]sts at beg of foll 2 rows. Cut off yarn and leave rem 43[45:47:49]sts on a holder.

Front

Work as for back to *.

Yoke
Change to No. 3 needles and work in garter st, working in stripes of 2 rows C and 2 rows B until armhole measures 7[7:8:8]in; end WS row.
Divide for neck
Next row K38[39:40:41], turn and leave rem sts on a spare needle. Complete left side of neck first. Dec one st at neck edge on every row until 33[34:35:36]sts rem. Cont straight until armhole measures 9[9:10:10]in; end at armhole edge.
Shape shoulder
Bind off 11[11:12:12]sts at beg of next and foll alternate row. Work 1 row. Bind off. Return to sts that were left. With RS facing place next 33[35:37:39]sts on a holder, join yarn to next st and K to end of row. Complete to match first side, reversing shaping.

Neckband

Join right shoulder seam. With RS facing, using No. 2 needles join A to top of left front neck and pick up and K 21sts from left front neck, K sts from holder, pick up and K 21sts from right front neck, then K back neck sts from holder. 118[122:126:130]sts. Beg with a 2nd ribbing row, rib as for back for 2in. Bind off in ribbing.

Armhole borders (alike)

Join left shoulder and neckband seam. With RS facing, using No. 2 needles and A, pick up and K 142[142:150:150]sts evenly along armhole edge. Beg with a 2nd ribbing row, rib as for back for 1in. Bind off in ribbing.

To finish

Press according to instructions on ball band. Join side seams. Double neckband to WS and slipstitch in position.

Jacket

Back

Using No. 5 needles and A, cast on 90[94:98:102]sts.
1st ribbing row P2, (K2, P2) to end.
2nd ribbing row K2, (P2, K2) to end.
Rep these 2 rows for 4in; end with a 2nd ribbing row and dec one st at end of last row. 89[93:97:101]sts.
Change to No. 7 needles. Beg garter st patt.
1st and 2nd rows K with B.
3rd and 4th rows K with C.
5th and 6th rows K with B.
These 6 rows form garter st patt.
Beg spotted patt.
1st row K with A.
2nd row P with A.
3rd row K2A, 1C, (3A, 1C) to last 2sts, 2A.
4th row P with A.
5th row K with A.
6th row P (1C, 3A) to last st, 1C.
These 6 rows form spotted patt. Rep them three times more. With A, K 1 row and P 1 row. Work 6 rows of

garter st patt once and 6 rows of spotted patt 3 times. With A, K 1 row and P 1 row. Now work 6 rows of garter st patt again. Beg bobble patt.

1st-4th rows With C, work in stockinette st.

5th row K4[6:8:2]C, (with B, work K1, P1, K1, P1 and K1 all into next st, turn, P5, turn, K5, turn P5, turn K5, then pass 4th, 3rd, 2nd and 1st sts over 5th st – bobble made or MB –, K7C) to last 5[7:9:3]sts, MB with B, K4[6:8:2]C.

6th-10th rows With C, work in stockinette st.

11th row K8[2:4:6], (MB with B, K7C) to last 9[3:5:7]sts, MB with B,

K8[2:4:6]C.
12th-16th rows With C, work in stockinette st.
17th row As 5th row.
18th-22nd rows With C, work in stockinette st.
These 22 rows form the bobble patt.
Shape armholes
Working in garter st patt, bind off 4sts at beg of next 2 rows. Dec one st at each end of next and foll alternate rows. Work 1 row. Working in spotted patt, dec one st at each end of next and every foll alternate rows. Work 1 row. rem. Cont straight until the 3rd spotted patt rep has been worked. With A, K 1 row and P 1 row. Working in garter st patt, dec one st at each end of every row. 61[65:69:73]sts. With C, bind off.

Pocket linings (make 2)
Using No. 7 needles and A cast on 20sts. Work 32 rows stockinette st; end with a P row. Cut off yarn and leave sts on a holder.

Left front
Using No. 5 needles and A, cast on 46[46:50:50]sts.
Rib as for back for 4in; end with a 2nd ribbing row and dec one st at end of last row on 1st and 3rd sizes and inc one st at end of last row on 2nd and 4th sizes. 45[47:49:51]sts. Change to No. 7 needles. Work garter st patt as for back. Beg spotted patt.
1st row K with A.
2nd row P with A.
3rd row K2A, 1C, (3A, 1C) to last 2[0:2:0]sts, 2[0:2:0]A.
4th row P with A.
5th row K with A.
6th row P0[2:0:2]A, 1C, (3A, 1C) to end.
These 6 rows form spotted patt. Rep them twice. With A, K 1 row and P 1 row. Work 6 rows garter st patt.
Divide for pocket
Next row K12[13:14:15]A, with B, bind off 20, K13[14:15:16]A.
Next row P13[14:15:16]A, P the sts of one pocket lining, P to end of row.
Cont in spotted patt until the 3rd spotted patt rep has been worked. With A, K 1 row and P 1 row. Work garter st patt. Work bobble patt as for back but work bobble rows thus:
5th row K4[6:8:2]C, MB with B, (K7C, MB with B) to end.
11th row K8[2:4:6]C, MB with B, (K7C, MB with B) to last 4sts, K4B.
Shape armhole
Working in garter st patt, bind off 4sts at beg of next row. Dec one st at beg of foll 2 alternate rows. Work 1 row. Working in spotted patt, dec one st at beg of next and every foll alternate row until 37[49:41:43]sts rem. Cont without shaping until the 3rd spotted patt rep has been worked. With A, K 1 row and P 1 row. Working in garter st patt, dec one st at armhole edge on every row. 31[33:35:37]sts. With C, bind off.

Right front
Work as for left front, reversing shaping and reading patt rows from end to beg.

Left sleeve
Using No. 5 needles and A, cast on 34[34:38:38]sts. Work ribbing rows 1 and 2 of back for 4in; end with a 2nd ribbing row and for 1st and 2nd sizes only inc one st at end of last row. Join on B.
Next row With B, K0[0:2:2], (K twice in next st) to last st, K1. 69[69:73:73]sts.
K1 row B, 2 rows C and 2 rows B.
Work spotted patt as for back 3 times. With A, K1 row and P1 row. Work garter st patt as for back.
Rep from * to * once. Now work bobble patt as for back following 2nd[2nd:3rd:3rd] size.
Shape top
Working in garter st patt, bind off 4sts at beg of next 2 rows. Work 4 rows. Working in spotted patt, dec one st at each end of next and every foll alternate row until 37[37:41:41]sts rem. Work 1 row. Now with A, K 1 row and P 1 row dec one st at each end of first row. 35[35:39:39]sts.
Saddle shoulder extension
Cont straight working in stripes of 2 rows B and 2 rows C until saddle shoulder extension measures 5[5$\frac{3}{4}$:6:6$\frac{1}{2}$]in; end with a RS row.
Shape neck
Cont in stripes, bind off 18[18:20:20]sts at beg of next row. Cont in stripes for a further 2$\frac{3}{4}$[2$\frac{3}{4}$:3:3]in for back neck; end with a WS row.
Bind off.

Right sleeve
Work as given for left sleeve reversing neck shaping.

Collar
Join bound-off edge of sleeves tog for center back. Join saddle shoulder extensions to top of fronts, leaving 12[12:13:13]sts free at front edge. With RS facing, join B to right front neck and using No. 5 needles pick up and K 12[13:13:14]sts from right front neck, 18[18:20:20]sts from sleeve, 24[26:26:28]sts across back neck, 18[18:20:20]sts from sleeve and 12[13:13:14]sts from left front neck. 84[88:92:96]sts.
1st ribbing row K2, (P2, K2) to end.
2nd ribbing row K1, P1, (K2, P2) to last 2sts, P1, K1.
Rep these 2 rows for 2in. Change to No. 6 needles and work a further 2in. Change to No. 7 needles and cont in ribbing until collar measures 6in from beg. Bind off loosely in ribbing.

Button border
Using No. 5 needles and B, cast on 6sts. Work in garter st until band, slightly stretched, fits along front edge to neck. Bind off.
Sew on border. Mark 6 button positions on this border, the first ½in from lower edge and the others level with the bands of garter st patt.

Buttonhole border
Work as for button border but make buttonholes to correspond with markers as foll:
1st buttonhole row K2, bind off 2, K2.
2nd buttonhole row K2, cast on 2, K2.

To finish
Press spotted patt only. Join top edge of back to saddle shoulder extensions. Sew sleeves to armholes, then join side and sleeve seams. Sew down pocket linings. Sew on buttonhole border and buttons.

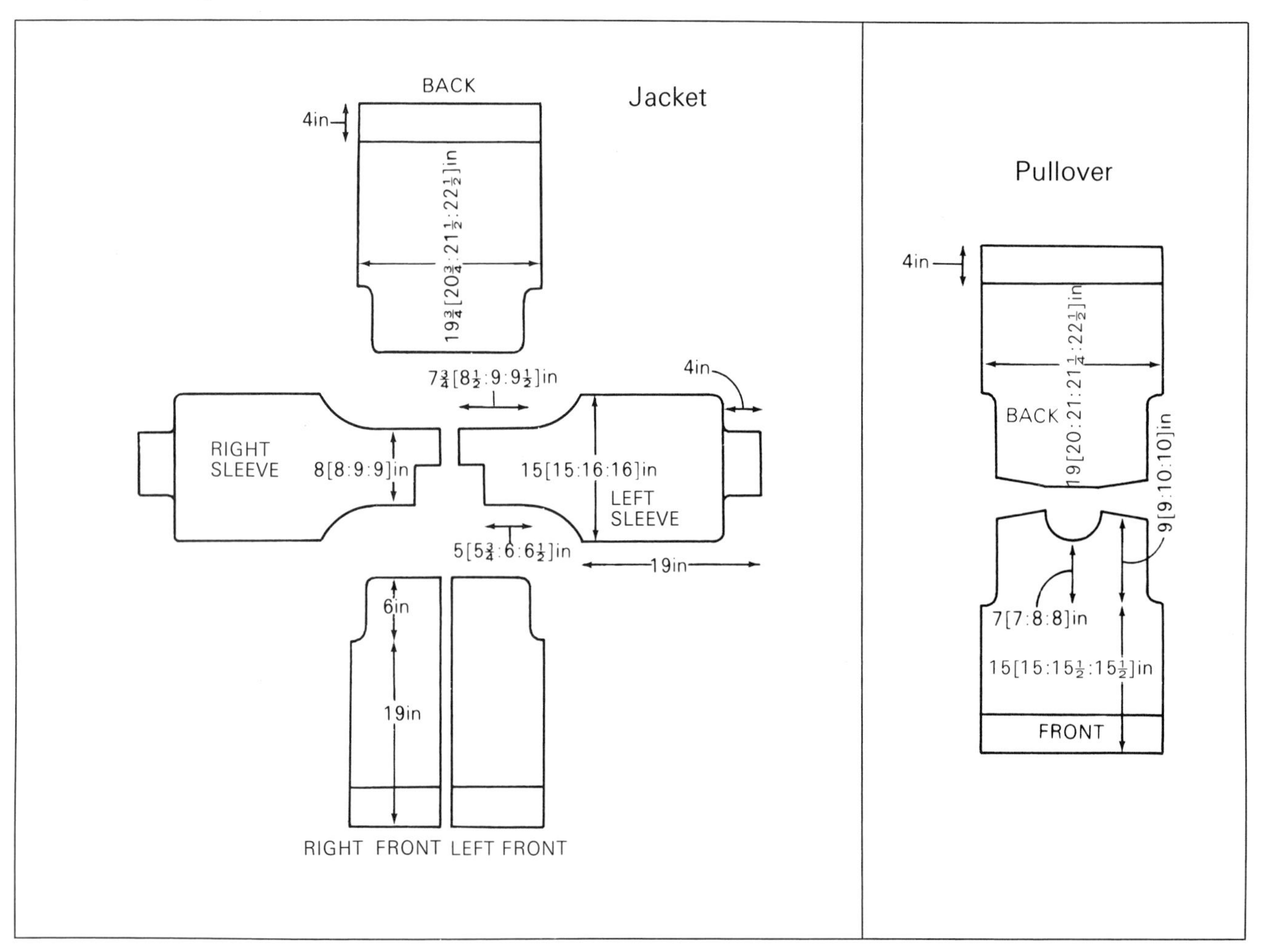

ANGORA CLASSICS

Sizes
To fit 32[34:36:38:40:42:44]in bust/chest.
Length, 25½[26:26½:27½:28:28½:28¾]in.
Sleeve seam, 16½[17:17½:17¾:18:18½:19]in.
Note *Directions for larger sizes are in brackets []; where there is only one set of figures this applies to all sizes.*

Materials
9[10:10:11:12:12:13]oz of a lightweight angora
1 pair each Nos. 3 and 5 knitting needles
Set of four No. 3 double-pointed needles
Beads as required

Gauge
24sts and 30 rows to 4in in stockinette st on No. 5 needles.

Back
Using No. 3 needles cast on 105[111:117:123:129:135:141]sts. Work 2in of K1, P1 ribbing, inc one st at each end of last row. 107[113:119:125:131:137:143]sts. Change to No. 5 needles. Beg with a K row, cont in stockinette st until work measures $17\frac{1}{2}$[$17\frac{3}{4}$:18:$18\frac{1}{2}$:$18\frac{1}{2}$:$18\frac{1}{2}$:$18\frac{1}{2}$]in or length required; end with a P row.

Shape armholes
Bind off 5sts at beg of next 2 rows, then 2sts at beg of foll 2[2:2:4:4:4:6] rows. Dec one st at each end of next and foll 4[5:6:6:7:8:8] alternate rows. 83[87:91:93:97:101:103]sts. Cont straight until armholes measure 8[$8\frac{1}{4}$:$8\frac{1}{2}$:9:$9\frac{1}{2}$:10:$10\frac{1}{4}$]in; end with a P row.

Shape shoulders
Bind off 5[5:6:6:6:7:7]sts at beg of next 6 rows, then 5[6:5:5:7:5:5]sts at beg of foll 2 rows. Leave rem 43[45:45:47:47:49:51]sts on a holder.

Front
Work as for back to armhole shaping; end with a P row.

Shape armhole and divide for neck
Next row Bind off 5. K until there are 48[51:54:57:60:63:66]sts on right-hand needle, turn and leave

rem sts on a spare needle.
Complete left side of neck first.
Next row P2 tog, work to end.
Cont to shape armhole to match back *at the same time* dec one st at neck edge on every 3rd row until 20[21:23:23:25:26:26]sts rem
Cont straight until armhole measures same as back to shoulder, end at armhole edge.

Shape shoulder
Bind off 5[5:6:6:6:7:7]sts at beg of next and foll 2 alternate rows. Work

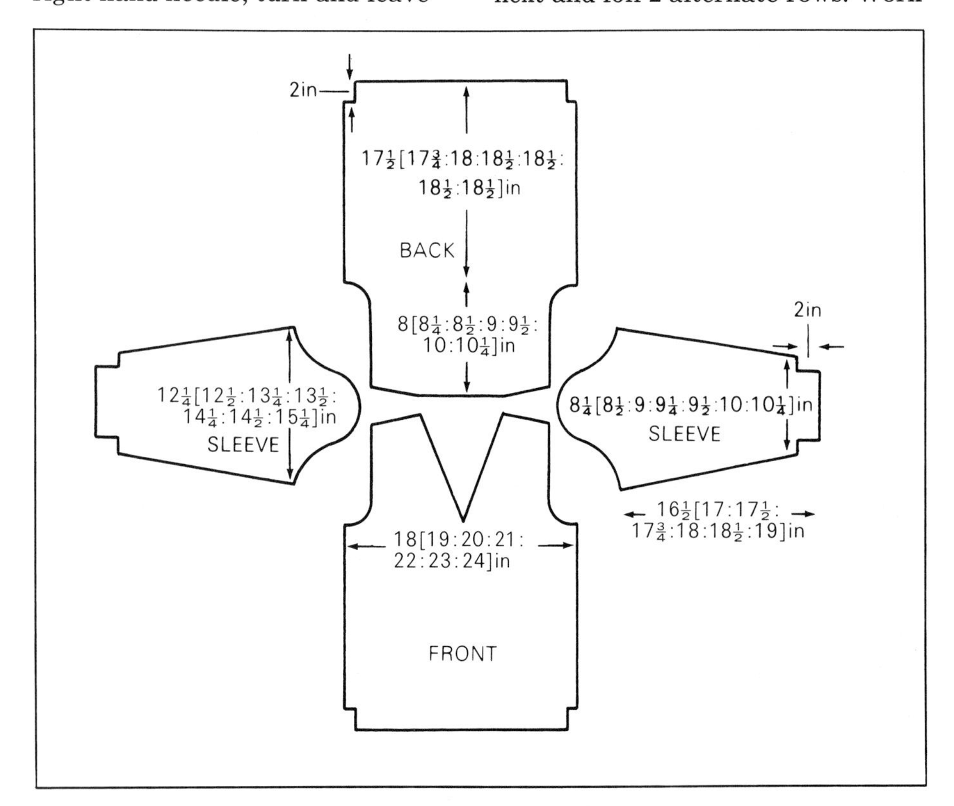

1 row. Bind off rem 5[6:5:5:7:5:5]sts. With RS of work facing, return to sts on spare needle and sl first st onto safety pin for neck, rejoin yarn to next st and K to end.
Next row Bind off 5, P to last 2 sts, P2 tog.
Complete to match first side.

Sleeves
Using No. 3 needles cast on 43[45:47:49:51:53:55]sts. Work 2in K1, P1 ribbing, inc 6sts evenly across last row.
49[51:53:55:57:59:61]sts. Change to No. 5 needles. Beg with a K row, cont in stockinette st, inc one st at each end of 9th and every foll 8th row until there are 73[75:79:81:85:87:91]sts. Cont straight until sleeve measures $16\frac{1}{2}$[17:$17\frac{1}{2}$:$17\frac{3}{4}$:18:$18\frac{1}{2}$:19]in or length required; end with a P row.

Shape top
Bind off 5sts at beg of next 2 rows. Dec one st at each end of next and foll 14[15:16:17:18:19:20] alternate rows, ending with a P row.
Bind off 2sts at beg of next 6 rows, then 3sts at beg of foll 4 rows. Bind off rem 9[9:11:11:13:13:15]sts.

Neckband
Join shoulder seams. Using set of four No. 3 needles and with RS of work facing, K across back neck sts, pick up and K 55[57:60:62:65:67:70]sts down left front neck, K center front st from safety pin, then pick up and K 55[57:59:62:65:67:70]sts up right front neck.
Next round Work in K1, P1 ribbing to 2sts before center front st, K2 tog, P1, sl 1, K1, psso, rib to end.
Rep last round 7 times. Bind off in ribbing, dec at center front as before.

To finish
Do not press. Set in sleeves. Join side and sleeve seams. Sew on beads.

BOUCLÉ FOR TWO

Sizes
To fit 32[34:36:38:40:42]in bust/chest.
Length, 26[26:26:28:28:28½]in.
Sleeve seam, 19[19:19:20½:21:21½]in.

Note *Directions for larger sizes are in brackets []; where there is only one set of figures it applies to all sizes.*

Materials
6[7:7:8:9:9] × 2oz balls of a medium-weight bouclé in main color (A)
3[3:3:3:4:4] balls in a contrasting color (B)
1 pair each Nos. 3, 5 and 7 needles

Gauge
20sts to 4in in patt on No. 7 needles.

Back
**Using No. 3 needles and A, cast on 74[78:82:86:90:94]sts.
1st ribbing row K2, *P2, K2, rep from * to end.
2nd ribbing row P2, *K2, P2, rep from * to end. Rep these 2 rows for 4in; end with 2nd ribbing row.

Change to No. 7 needles.
Next row K11[4:6:8:10:12], *inc in next st, K2[3:3:3:3:3], rep from * 16 times, inc in next st, K to end. 92[96:100:104:108:112]sts.
Next row P to end.
Join on B. Beg patt.
1st row (RS) Using B, K3, *wyib (with yarn in back) sl2 P-wise, K2, rep from * to last st, K1.
2nd row Using B, P3, *sl2 P-wise, P2, rep from * to last st, P1.
3rd row Using A, K to end.
4th row Using A, P to end.
5th row Using B, K1, wyib sl2 P-wise, *K2, wyib sl2 P-wise, rep from * to last st, K1.
6th row Using B, P1, sl2 P-wise, *P2, sl2 P-wise, rep from * to last st, P1.
7th row Using A, K to end.
8th row Using A, P to end.
These 8 rows form patt. Mark each end of last row to denote beg of pocket. Cont in patt until work measures 10[10:10:11:11:11]in; end with WS row.
Mark each end of last row to denote end of pocket opening. ** Cont in patt until work measures 26[26:26:28:28:28½]in; end with 2nd or 6th patt row.

Shape shoulders
Bind off 34[34:36:38:40:42]sts at beg of next 2 rows. Cut off yarn and leave rem 24[28:28:28:28:28]sts on a holder.

Front
Work as for back from ** to **. Cont in patt until work measures 15½[15½:15½:17:17:17]in; end with WS row.
Divide for neck
Patt 45[47:49:51:53:55], turn and leave rem sts on a spare needle. Complete this side of neck first. Work 1 row. Dec one st at neck edge on next row, then on every foll 4th row until 34[34:36:38:40:42]sts rem. Cont straight until work measures 26[26:26:28:28:28½]in; end at side edge. Bind off. Return to rem sts on spare needle. With RS facing slip next 2sts onto a safety pin; join yarn to next st and patt to end of row. Complete to match first side, reversing shaping.

Sleeves
Using No. 3 needles and A, cast on 42[46:46:50:50:54]sts.
Rep the 2 ribbing rows of back for 4in; end with 2nd ribbing row.

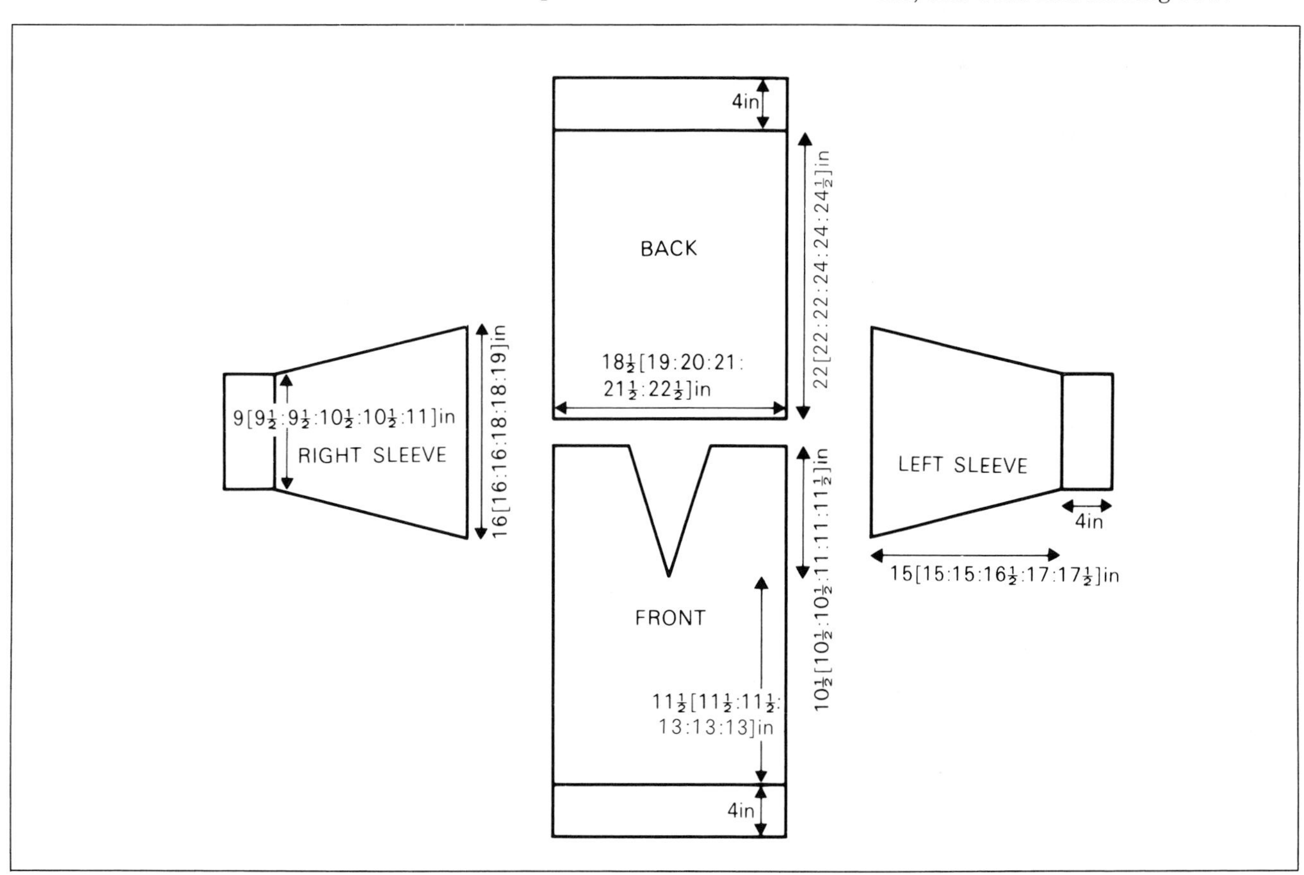

Change to No. 7 needles.
Next row K to end, but inc one st at each end. 44[48:48:52:52:56]sts.
Next row P to end.
Join on B. Cont in patt as for back and working extra sts into patt where possible, inc one st at each end of 9th row and every foll 4th row until there are 80[80:80:90:90:94]sts. Cont straight until work measures 19[19:19:20½:21:21½]in; end with an 8th row. Bind off very loosely.

Neckband
Join right shoulder seam. Using No. 3 needles and A and with RS facing pick up and K 56[56:56:64:64:68]sts evenly along left front neck; place a marker on right-hand needle, K 2sts from safety pin; place another marker on right-hand needle, pick up and K 56[56:56:64:64:68]sts along right front neck, then K back neck sts from holder. 138[142:142:158:158:166]sts.
1st ribbing row (WS) K2, (P2, K2) to within 2sts of marker, K2tog tbl, sl marker, P2, sl marker, K2tog, K2, (P2, K2) to end.
2nd ribbing row Rib to within 2sts of marker, work 2tog tbl, sl marker, rib 2, sl marker, work 2tog, rib to end.
Rep last row 5 times. Bind off loosely in ribbing, dec at center front neck as before.

Pocket linings (alike)
Using No. 5 needles and A, with RS of back facing, pick up and K 27sts evenly between markers. Beg with P row, work 35 rows stockinette st. Bind off.

Pocket facings (alike)
Using No. 5 needles and A, with RS of front facing, pick up and K 27sts evenly between markers. Beg with P row, work 7 rows stockinette st. Bind off.

To finish
Fold pocket facings on front to WS and slipstitch in place. Join left shoulder and neckband seams. Mark center of bound-off edge of each sleeve. Pin to shoulder seam, sew sleeves to back and front. Join sleeve seams. Join side seams either side of pocket openings. Slip stitch pocket linings in place.

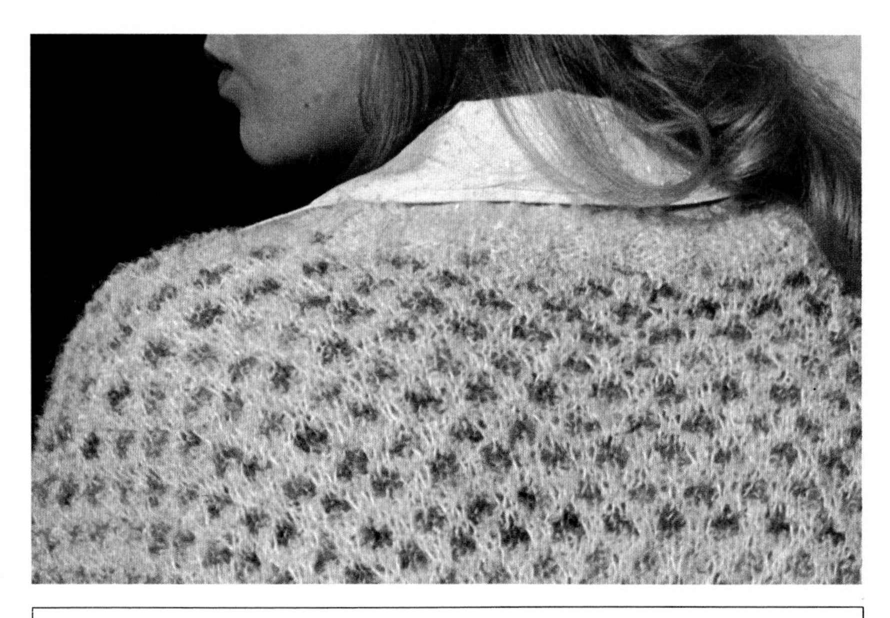

Technique tip

In the pattern used for the bouclé sweaters you do not have to use two colors in one row as in colorwork knitting. The effect is produced by slipping stitches. When slipping the stitches you must keep the yarn on the wrong side of the work.
Before you begin the pattern you will need to work at least one row in the main color. Then join on the contrasting color for the first row of the pattern.

Using the contrasting color, knit the first stitches. Then, keeping the yarn at the back of the work slip the next 2 stitches purlwise and then knit the next 2 stitches. You will see that the 2 slipped stitches are in the main color and the contrasting color passes across the back. Continue to slip 2 stitches and knit 2 stitches to the end of the row. Knit the last stitch.

To work the second row, using the contrasting color, purl the first 3 stitches, slip the next 2 stitches purlwise, then purl the next 2 stitches. The contrasting color will pass across the front of the 2 slipped stitches. Using the main color, knit one row and purl one row.

To alternate the 2-color pattern, using the contrasting color knit the first stitch, then keeping the yarn at the back of the work slip the next 2 stitches purlwise, then knit the next 2 stitches.

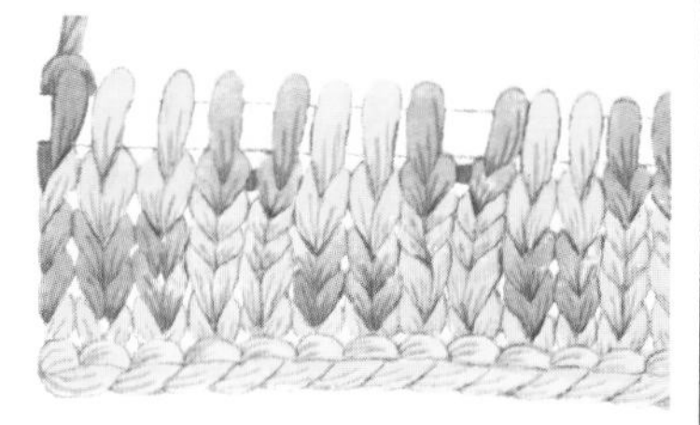

Continue to the end of the row, knitting the last stitch. On the next row purl the first stitch, then slip the next 2 stitches purlwise, then purl the next 2 stitches.
Continue to the end of the row, purling the last stitch.
Using main color, knit one row and purl one row.
These 8 rows form the pattern and are repeated throughout.

SKI SLOPE SWEATERS

Back
Using No. 4 needles and A, cast on 70[74:82:86:94]sts.
1st row K2, *P2, K2, rep from * to end.
2nd row P2, *K2, P2, rep from * to end.
Rep these 2 rows for 2½in; end with 2nd row and dec one st in center of last row. 69[73:81:85:93]sts. Change to No. 6 needles. ** Beg with K row, cont in stockinette st. Work 2 rows. Join in B. Work 4 rows patt from chart A. ** Cut off B. Cont in stockinette st with A until work measures 15½[15¾:16:16½:17]in; end with P row, *at same time* inc one st at each end of 1st row on 2nd and 4th sizes only. 69[75:81:87:93]sts.
Shape armholes and yoke
1st row Bind off 2, K until there are 27[29:31:34:36]sts on right-hand needle, turn.
2nd and foll alternate rows Sl 1, P to end.
3rd row K1, K2 tog, K19[21:23:25:27], turn.
5th row K1, K2 tog, K13[15:17:18:20], turn.
7th row K1, K2 tog, K7[9:11:11:13], turn.
9th row K1, K2 tog, K2[3:4:4:5]. Cut off yarn. Sl 30[33:36:39:42]sts onto right-hand needle, rejoin yarn and K to end. 29[31:33:36:38]sts.
2nd row Cast off 2, P until there are 27[29:31:34:37]sts on right-hand needle, turn.
3rd and foll alternate rows Sl 1, K to last 3sts, K2 tog tbl, K1.
4th row P21[23:25:27:29], turn.
6th row P15[17:19:20:22], turn.
8th row P9[11:13:13:15], turn.
9th row As 3rd. 57[63:69:75:81]sts.
10th row P across all sts. Cut off yarn and leave sts for time being.

Front
Work as given for back.

Sleeves
Using No. 4 needles and A, cast on 34[34:38:38:42]sts. Rib 2½in as for back; end with 2nd row and dec one st in center of last row. 33[33:37:37:41]sts. Change to No. 6 needles. Work from ** to ** as for back. Cut off B. Cont in stockinette st with A, inc one st at each end of next row on 2nd and 4th sizes only, then at each end of every foll 6th row on all sizes until there are 53[55:57:59:61]sts. Cont straight until sleeve measures 17[17½:17¾:18:18½]in; end with P row.
Shape top
Bind off 2sts at beg of next 2 rows.
Next row K1, K2 tog, K to last 3sts, K2 tog tbl, K1.
Next row P to end.
Rep last 2 rows 3 times more. 41[43:45:47:49]sts. Cut off yarn and leave sts for time being.

Yoke
Using No. 6 circular needle, A and with RS facing, beg at back and K across all sts on holders, K2 tog at each seam, then K to center back and start all rounds from here. 192[208:224:240:256]sts. K0[1:2:3:4] rounds, then cont in stockinette st and patt as follows:
1st round *1A, 1D, rep from * to end.
2nd round Work in D.
3rd round *1D, 1A, rep from * to end.
4th and 5th rounds Work in A.
6th-9th rounds Work from chart A.
10th round Work in A.
11th round Using A, *K6, K2 tog, rep from * to end. 168[182:196:210:224]sts.
12th-14th rounds As 1st-3rd rounds, using C instead of D.
15 and 16th rounds Work in A.
17th-27th rounds Work from chart B.

Sizes
To fit 32[36:38:40:44]in bust/chest.
Length, 26¼[26¾:27¼:28:29]in.
Sleeve seam, 17[17½:17¾:18:18½]in.
Note *Directions for larger sizes are in brackets []; where there is only one set of figures it applies to all sizes.*

Materials
12[13:14:15:16] × 2oz balls of a knitting worsted in main color (A)
1[1:2:2:3] balls in contrasting color (B)
1 ball in contrasting color (C)
1 ball in contrasting color (D)
1 pair each Nos. 4 and 6 knitting needles
No. 6 circular knitting needle
Set of four No. 4 double-pointed needles

Gauge
15sts and 22 rows to 4in in stockinette st on No. 6 needles.

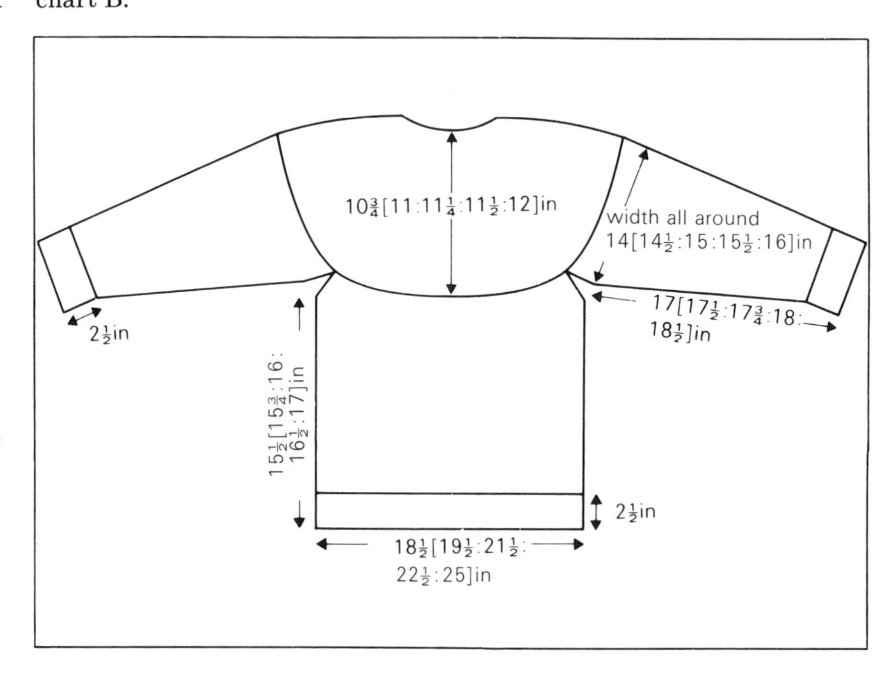

Chart A

X				X				X
X	X		X	X	X		X	X
	X	X	X		X	X	X	
		X				X		

end st for bottom of sleeves and sweater only

rep 4 sts

Chart B

			X	X				X	X				
			X	X	X		X	X	X				
X	X	X		X	X	X	X	X		X	X	X	
	X	X	X		X	X	X		X	X	X		
		X	X	X		X		X	X	X			X
X			X	X	X		X	X	X			X	X
		X	X	X		X		X	X	X			X
	X	X	X		X	X	X		X	X	X		
X	X	X		X	X	X	X	X		X	X	X	
			X	X	X		X	X	X				
			X	X				X	X				

rep 14 sts

Chart C

X				X				X	X
	X		X	X	X		X		
		X		X		X			
	X		X		X		X		
X	X	X		X		X	X	X	
	X		X		X		X		
		X		X		X			
	X		X	X	X		X		
X				X				X	X

rep 10 sts

□ (A) X (B)

28th round Work in A.
29th round Using A, *K5, K2 tog, rep from * to end. 144[156:168:180:192]sts.
30th-33rd rounds As 1st-3rd rounds.
34th round Work in A.
35th round Using A, *K4, K2 tog, rep from * to end. 120[130:140:150:160]sts.
36th-44th rounds Work from chart C.
45th round Work in A.
46th round Using A, *K3, K2 tog, rep from * to end. 96[104:112:120:128]sts.
47th-49th rounds As 12th-14th rounds.
50th round Work in A.
51st round Using A, *K2, K2 tog, rep from * to end. 72[75:78:81:84]sts.
Change to four No. 4 needles. Cont in K2, P2 ribbing, dec 0[3:2:1:0]sts in 1st round. 72[72:76:80:84]sts. Work $2\frac{1}{2}$in for crew neck or $6[6:6\frac{1}{2}:6\frac{1}{2}:7\frac{1}{2}]$in for turtleneck. Bind off loosely in ribbing using a larger needle.

To finish
Join underarm, sleeve and side seams. Press seams.

GUERNSEY GETAWAYS

Sizes
To fit 32[34:36:38:40:42]in bust/chest.
Length, 24[25:26:26½:27:28]in.
Underarm sleeve measurement, 18[18½:19:19½:20:20½]in.

Note *Directions for larger sizes are in brackets []; where there is only one set of figures it applies to all sizes.*

Materials
22[23:25:26:28:29] × 1oz balls of a knitting worsted
1 pair each Nos. 3 and 4 knitting needles
Nos. 3 and 4 circular needles
Set of four each Nos. 3 and 4 double-pointed needles
Cable needle

Gauge
24sts and 32 rows to 4in in stockinette st on No. 4 needles.

Back and front
Using No. 3 needles cast on 103[109:115:121:127:133]sts. Work 4in garter st; end with WS row. Cut off yarn and leave sts for time being. Work a second piece in same way, but do not cut off yarn. Using No. 3 circular needle K across 2nd piece to last st, K last st tog with first st of other piece, then K to last st of other piece, K last st tog with first st of first piece. 204[216:228:240:252:264]sts.
Next round *K2, P2, rep from * to end.
Rep last round once. K 2 rounds. Rep these 4 rounds once, then work first 2 rounds again. Change to No. 4 circular needle.
Next round Pick up loop lying between needles and K tbl – called make one or M1 – K102[108:114:120:126:132], M1, K102[108:114:120:126:132]. 2sts increased.
Next round K to end.
Next round *P1, K102[108:114:120:126:132], rep from * once.
Rep last 2 rounds until work measures 15in from beg.

Shape gusset
Next round *M1, K1, M1, K102[108:114:120:126:132], rep from * once more.
Next round K to end.
Next round *M1, K3, M1, K102[108:114:120:126:132], rep from * once. Cont to inc in this way at each side of both gussets on every other round until there are 238[250:262:274:286:298]sts; end with inc round.
Next round K17 and sl these sts onto a thread, K102[108:114:120:126:132], turn and cont on these sts for back.
Change to No. 3 needles. K 3 rows, dec one st in center of last row on 2nd size, inc one st in center on 3rd and 6th sizes and inc one st at each end on 5th size. 102[107:115:120:128:133]sts.
Change to No. 4 needles. Beg yoke patt.
1st row *P2, K6[6:10:10:14:14], P2, K1, M1, K2, M1, K1, P2, K10, P2, K5, P1, K5, P2 **, (P2, K3) 4[5:5:6:6:7] times, rep from ** back to *. 106[111:119:124:132:137]sts.
2nd row *K2, P6[6:10:10:14:14], K2, P6, K2, P10, K2, P5, K1, P5, K2 **, K1, (P3, K2) 3[4:4:5:5:6] times, P3,

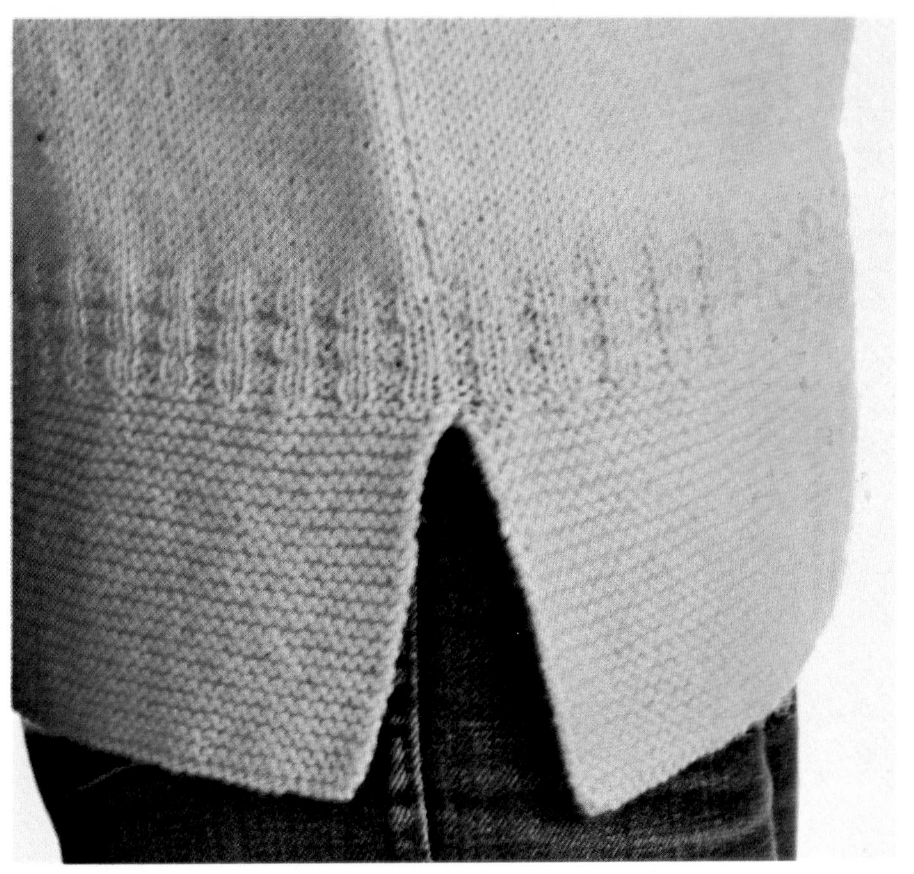

K1, rep from ** back to *.
3rd row *(P2, K2) 2[2:3:3:4:4] times, P2, sl next 3sts onto cable needle and leave at back of work, K3, then K the sts from cable needle – called cable 6 back or C6B –, P2, (K2, P2) 3 times, K4, P1, K1, P1, K4, P2 **, (K3, P2) 4[5:5:6:6:7] times, rep from ** back to * but work C6F (sl next 3sts onto cable needle and leave at front of work, K3, then K the sts from cable needle) instead of C6B.
4th row *(K2, P2) 2[2:3:3:4:4] times, K2, P6, K2, (P2, K2) 3 times, P4, K1, P1, K1, P4, K2 **, P1, (K2, P3) 3[4:4:5:5:6] times, K2, P2, rep from ** back to *.
5th row *P2, K6[6:10:10:14:14], P2, K6, P2, K10, P2, K3, (P1, K1) twice, P1, K3, P2 **, K1, (P2, K3) 3[4:4:5:5:6] times, P2, K2, rep from ** back to *.
6th row *K2, P6[6:10:10:14:14], K2, P6, K2, P10, K2, P3, (K1, P1) twice, K1, P3, K2 **, (P3, K2) 4[5:5:6:6:7] times, rep from ** back to *.
7th row *(P2, K2) 2[2:3:3:4:4] times, P2, K6, P2, (K2, P2) 3 times, K2, (P1, K1) 3 times, P1, K2, P2 **, P1, (K3, P2) 3[4:4:5:5:6] times, K3, P1, rep from ** back to *.
8th row *(K2, P2) 2[2:3:3:4:4] times, K2, P6, K2, (P2, K2) 3 times, P2, (K1, P1) 3 times, K1, P2, K2, **, (K2, P3) 4[5:5:6:6:7] times, rep from ** back to *.
9th row *P2, K6[6:10:10:14:14], P2, C6B, P2, K10, P2, K1, (P1, K1) 5 times, P2, **, K2, (P2, K3) 3[4:4:5:5:6] times, P2, K1, rep from ** back to * but work C6F instead of C6B.
10th row *K2, P6[6:10:10:14:14], K2, P6, K2, P10, K2, P1, (K1, P1) 5 times, K2 **, patt 20[25:25:30:30:35] as 8th row, rep from ** back to *.
11th row Patt 43[43:47:47:51:51] as 7th row, patt 20[25:25:30:30:35] as 7th row, patt to end as 7th row.
12th row Patt 43[43:47:47:51:51] as 8th row, patt 20[25:25:30:30:35] as 6th row, patt to end as 8th row.
13th row Patt 43[43:47:47:51:51] as 5th row, patt 20[25:25:30:30:35] as 5th row, patt to end as 5th row.
14th row Patt 43[43:47:47:51:51] as 6th row, patt 20[25:25:30:30:35] as 4th row, patt to end as 6th row.
15th row Patt 43[43:47:47:51:51] as 3rd row, patt 20[25:25:30:30:35] as 3rd row, patt to end as 3rd row.
16th row Patt 43[43:47:47:51:51] as 4th row, patt 20[25:25:30:30:35] as 2nd row, patt to end as 4th row.
Note that patt over center 20[25:25:30:30:35]sts repeats over 16 rows, with cables worked on every 6th row; rest of patt is repeated over 16 rows as given.
Cont in patt until work measures 24[25:26:26½:27:28]in from beg; end with WS row and then start shoulder shaping.
Next row Bind off 22[23:25:27:29:32], K to end.
Next row Bind off 22[23:25:27:29:32], P to end, inc one st on 2nd, 3rd and 6th sizes. 62[66:70:70:74:74]sts.
Change to No. 3 needles.
Next row K2, *P2, K2, rep from * to end.
Work 6 more rows in ribbing, dec one st at each end of every row.
Bind off loosely in ribbing.

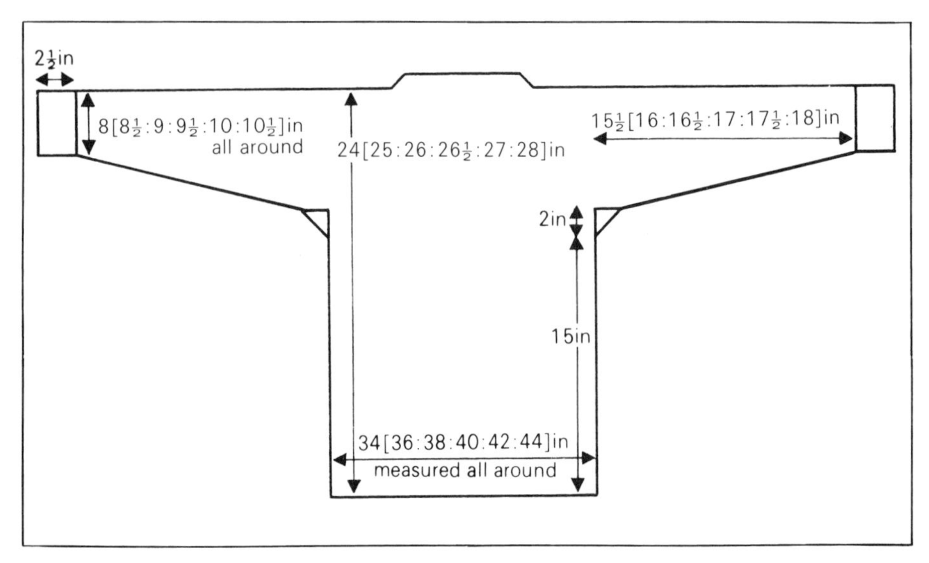

Return to sts that were left, sl first 17sts onto a thread, rejoin yarn and K to end. Complete to match back.

Sleeves
Join shoulder seams. Using set of four No. 4 needles and with RS facing, K across 17 gusset sts, pick up and K 85[90:95:100:105:110]sts around armhole.
1st round Sl 1, K1, psso, K13, K2 tog, (P2, K3) to end.
2nd round K15, P1, (K3, P2) to last 4sts, K3, P1.
3rd round Sl 1, K1, psso, K11, K2 tog, (K3, P2) to end.
4th round K15, (P2, K3) to last 3sts, P2, K1.
5th round Sl 1, K1, psso, K9, K2 tog, K1, (P2, K3) to last 4sts, P2, K2.
6th round K11, (P2, K3) to end.
7th round Sl 1, K1, psso, K7, K2 tog, P1, (K3, P2) to last 4sts, K3, P1.
8th round K9, (K3, P2) to end.
9th round Sl 1, K1, psso, K5, K2 tog, K2, P2, (K3, P2) to last st, K1.
10th round K7, patt to end as for 8th round.
11th round Sl 1, K1, psso, K3, K2 tog, patt to end as 7th round.
12th round K5, patt to end as 6th round.
13th round Sl 1, K1, psso, K1, K2 tog, patt to end as 5th round.
14th round K5, patt to end as 4th round.
15th round Sl 1, K2 tog, psso, patt to end as 3rd round.
86[91:96:101:106:111]sts.
16th round K1, patt to end as 2nd round.
17th round K1, patt to end as first round.
18th round K to end.
19th round P to end.
Rep 18th and 19th rounds once.
22nd round P1, K to end.
23rd round K to end.
Rep last 2 rounds throughout, dec one st at either side of seam st on next and every foll 6th round (i.e. P1, sl 1, K1, psso, K to last 2sts, K2 tog) until 48[51:54:57:60:63]sts rem.
Cont straight until sleeve seam measures 15½[16:16½:17:17½:18]in; end at end of round and inc one st at end of last round on 2nd and 6th sizes, dec 2sts on 3rd size and dec one st on 4th size.
48[52:52:56:60:64]sts.
To finish
Change to four No. 3 needles. Work K2, P2 ribbing for 2½in. Bind off loosely in ribbing.

SEASIDE SPECIALS

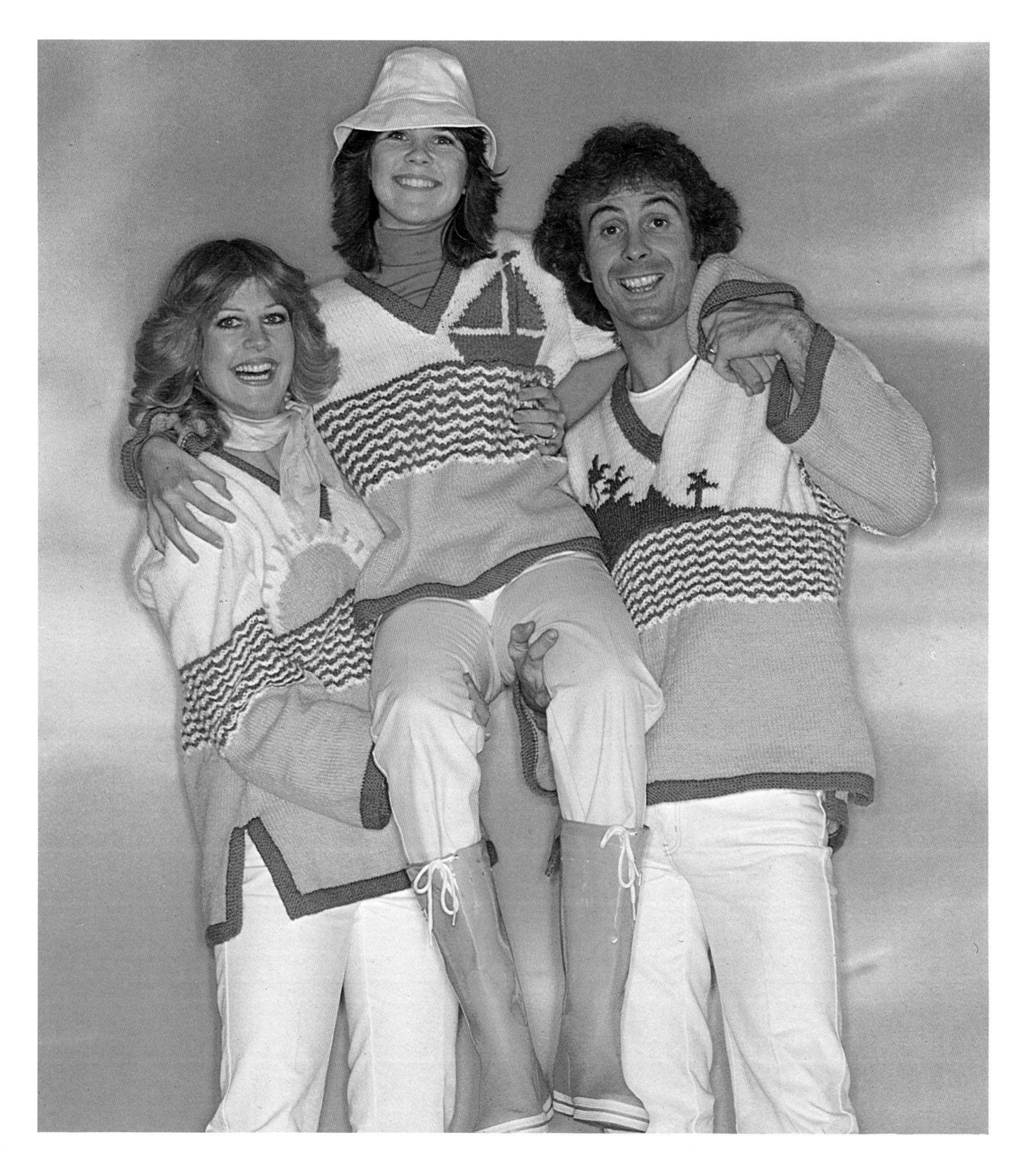

Sizes
To fit
26[28:30:32:34:36:38:40]in chest/bust.
Length,
20¾[23:24¾:26:27¼:27¼:28:28]in.
Sleeve seam,
13[15:16:17:17¼:17¼:18:18]in.
Note *Directions for larger sizes are in brackets []; where there is only one set of figures it applies to all sizes.*

Materials
Knitting worsted:
11[11:13:13:13:15:15:15]oz in white (A)
8[8:9:9:9:11:11:11]oz in yellow (B)
6[6:8:8:8:9:9:9]oz in blue (C)
2oz each in rust (D) for boat motif and in dark blue (E) for island motif
1 pair each Nos. 5 and 7 knitting needles

Gauge
18sts and 26 rows to 4in in stockinette st on No. 7 needles.

Back
**Using No. 5 needles and C, cast on 72[78:84:90:96:102:108:114]sts. K 10 rows. Change to No. 7 needles. Cut off C and join on B. Cont in stockinette st until work measures 6in from beg; end with P row. Cast on 4sts at beg of next 2 rows for top of slits.
80[86:92:98:104:110:116:122]sts.
Cont in stockinette st until work measures 7½[8½:9½:10¼:10½:11:11:11]in from beg; end with P row. Cut off B.
Joining on and cutting off colors as required, beg wave patt.
1st row With A, K1, *K2 tog, (K into front and back of next st) twice, K2 tog, rep from * to last st, K1.
2nd row With A, K to end.
3rd row With C, as 1st row.
4th row With C, P to end.
These 4 rows form the patt. Rep them 7 times more. Cut off C.**
Cont in stockinette st with A only, until work measures 14½[16¼:17½:18½:19:19:19½:19½]in from beg; end with P row.
Shape armholes
Bind off 3[3:4:4:4:5:5:5]sts at beg of next 2 rows. Dec one st at each end of next and every foll alternate row until 64[68:72:76:80:84:88:92]sts rem.
Cont straight until work measures 6¼[6¾:7¼:7½:8¼:8¼:8½:8½]in from beg of armhole; end with P row.
Shape shoulders
Bind off 7[7:8:8:9:9:10:10]sts at beg of next 4 rows and 6[8:7:9:8:10:9:11]sts at beg of foll 2 rows. Change to No. 5 needles and K 10 rows for neckband. Bind off.

Front
Work as for back from ** to **. Beg motif. Note that for 4th size you can choose either boat or sun motif and for 6th size you can choose either sun or island motif.
For 1st, 2nd, 3rd and 4th sizes, K10[13:15:18]A, 24D (as row 1 of boat chart), with A, K to end.
For 4th, 5th and 6th sizes, K50[53:55]A, 30B (as row 1 of sun chart), with A, K to end.
For 6th, 7th and 8th sizes, K28[34:40]A, 80E (as row 1 of island chart), with A, K to end.
Foll chart for design you are making, cont in stockinette st twisting yarns when changing color to avoid a hole, until work measures same as back to armhole; end with P row.

Shape armhole and divide for neck
Next row Cont to foll chart, bind off 3[3:4:4:4:5:5:5], K until there are 37[40:42:45:48:50:53:56]sts on right-hand needle, turn and leave rem sts on a spare needle. Complete left side of neck first. Work 1 row. Dec one st at armhole edge on next and every foll alternate row and at the same time dec one st at neck edge on next and every foll 4th row until 29[31:33:34:36:38:39:41]sts rem. Keeping armhole edge straight, cont to dec at front edge on every 4th row until 20[22:23:25:26:28:29:31]sts rem. Cont straight until front measures same as back up to shoulder; end with P row.
Shape shoulder
Bind off 7[7:8:8:9:9:10:10]sts at beg of next and foll alternate row. Work 1 row. Bind off. With RS facing rejoin yarn to inner end of sts on spare needle and K to end. Match first side, reversing shaping and completing motif.

Sleeves
Using No. 5 needles and C, cast on 68[74:74:80:80:86:86:86]sts. K 10 rows. Change to No. 7 needles. Cut off C and join on B. Cont in stockinette st until sleeve measures

Child's motif
x = rust
o = blue
□ = white

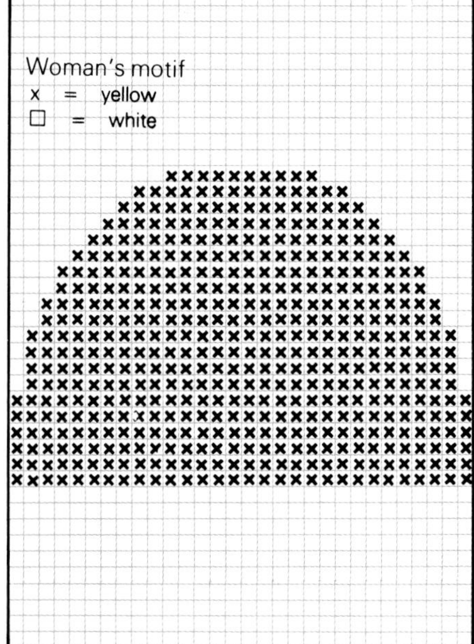
Woman's motif
x = yellow
□ = white

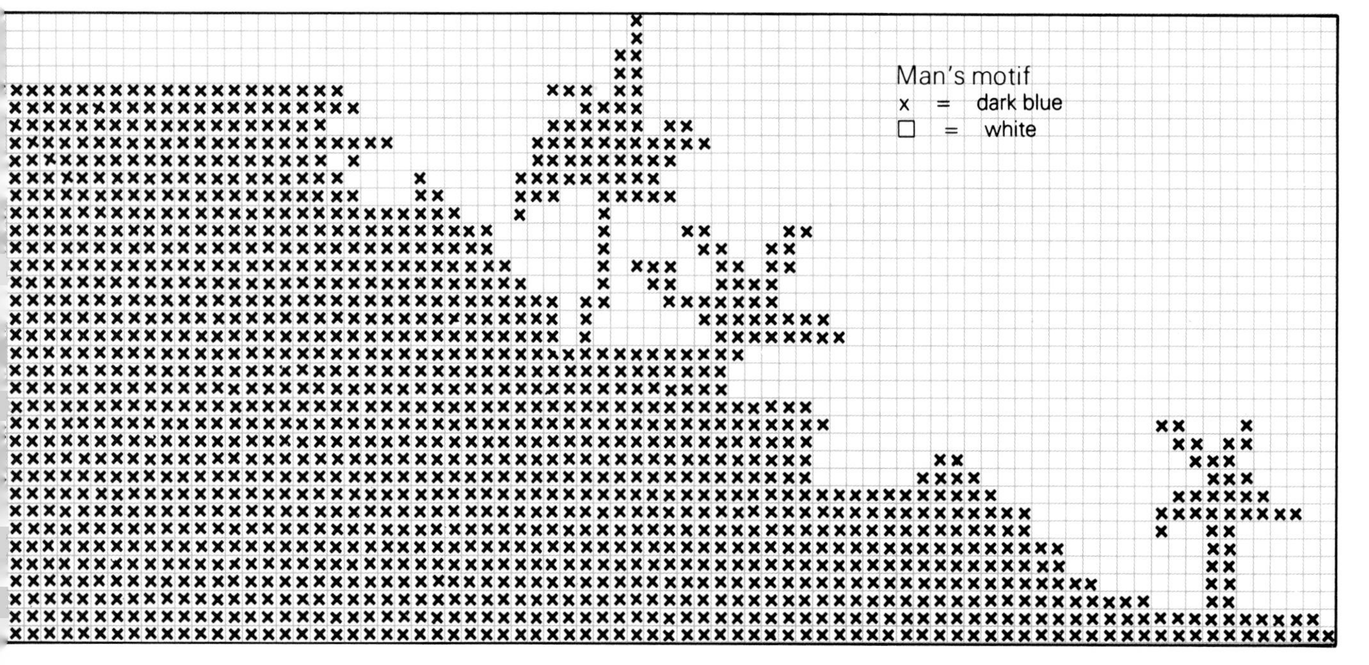
Man's motif
x = dark blue
□ = white

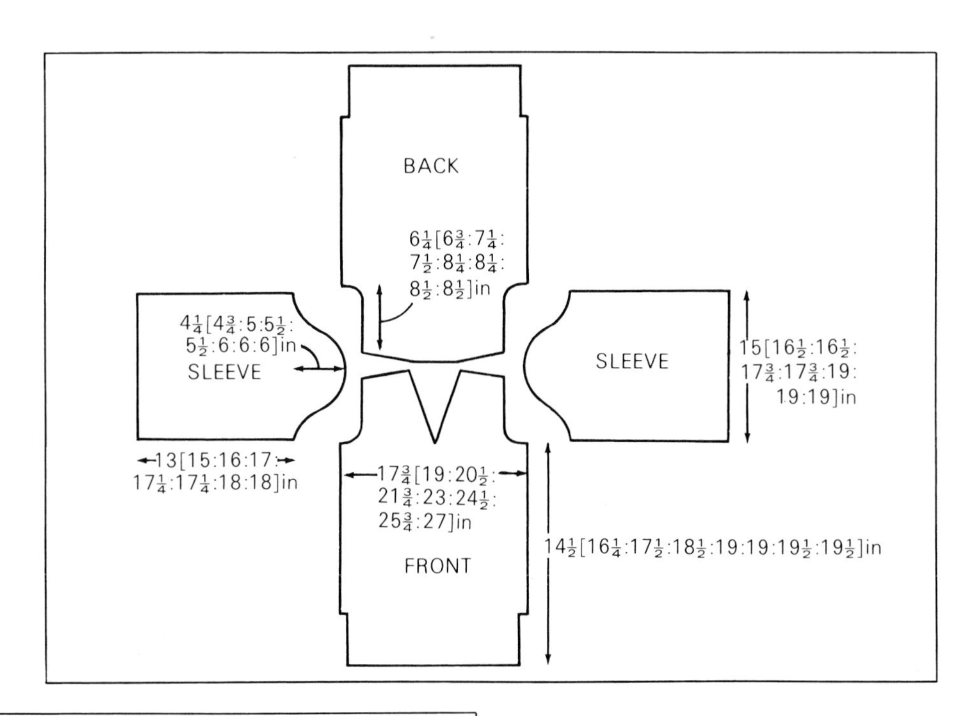

Technique tip

Side slits

Side slit openings are very popular on longer style sweaters and tunics as they allow a bit of extra movement.

Slits normally have a border which sits in rather than extends beyond the side seam.

To make a side slit in this way, first calculate the width of the back of the garment, then decide on the depth of the border to be worked. The combined depth of the borders should then be deducted from the width of the garment – for example, if you want your garment to measure 18in across the back and each border to measure 1¼in you will need to cast on stitches to produce 15½in in width. Calculate the number of stitches for this width, cast on the stitches required and knit until the slit depth has been reached. Cast on stitches at beginning of next 2 rows to give an extra 1¼in at each end – you will now have the total width of the back on the needles.

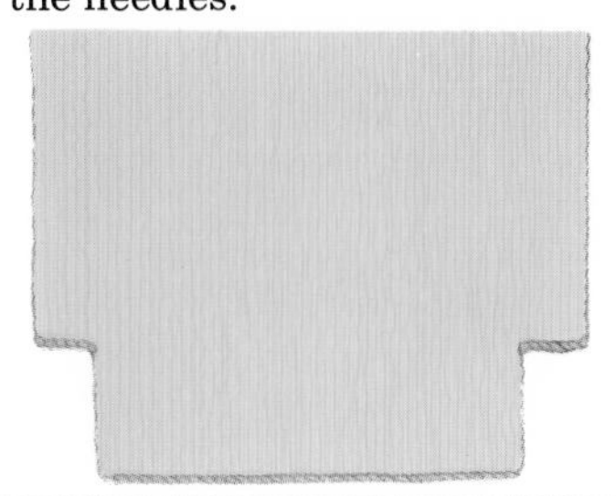

Complete your knitting, then work the borders.

The slit borders can either be knitted onto the main fabric or knitted separately and sewed on.

To knit onto the main fabric, pick up and knit stitches evenly along side of slit between group of stitches cast onto garment and lower edge. Knit for 1¼in, then bind off. Sew the top edge to cast-on group of stitches.

To knit separately, cast on stitches to produce 1¼in in width. Knit for depth of bind opening, then bind off. Sew border to side and top to slit opening.

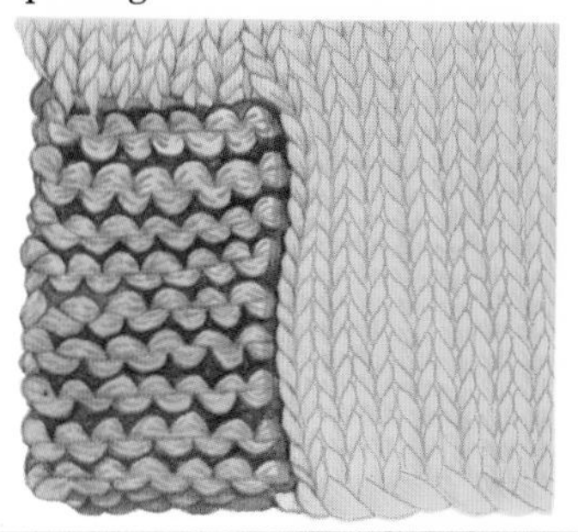

6[7½:7¾:9:9½:9½:9½:9½]in from beg; end with P row. Joining on and cutting off colors as required work 4 wave patt rows as for back 8 times. Cut off C. Cont in stockinette st with A only until sleeve measures 13[15:16:17:17¼:17¼:18:18]in from beg; end with P row.

Shape top

Bind off 3[3:4:4:4:5:5:5]sts at beg of next 2 rows. Dec one st at each end of next and every foll alternate row until 48[48:50:50:52:52:54:54]sts rem, then at each end of every row until 14[16:16:18:18:20:20:20]sts rem. Bind off.

Neckband

With RS facing, using No. 5 needles and C, pick up and K 36[38:40:40:42:42:44:44]sts evenly along left side of neck. K 9 rows. Bind off. Work along right neck in same way.

Slit borders (4 alike)

With RS facing, using No. 5 needles and C, pick up and K 30sts along side slit between lower edge and cast-on group. K 9 rows. Bind off.

To finish

Press with warm iron over damp cloth, omitting borders. Join shoulder seams. Set in sleeves. Join side and sleeve seams. Overlap neckband at front and sew in position. Swiss darn rays of sun.

FAMILY MITTENS

Adult's Fair Isle mittens

Size
Width around hand above thumb, 7in.

Note
Working in stockinette st and reading odd-numbered rows from right to left and even-numbered rows from left to right, work the 22sts of back of mitten in Fair Isle patt from chart. Where there is only 1 color in a row, work this color across palm; otherwise work the palm in main color. Cut off colors when not in use.

Materials
1 × 2oz ball of a sport yarn in each of 4 colors
1 pair each Nos. 2 and 4 knitting needles

Gauge
26sts to 4in in stockinette on No. 4 needles.

Adult's striped mittens

Size
Width around hand above thumb, 7in.

Materials
2 × 1oz balls of a knitting worsted in red
1 ball each of yellow, green, blue and white
1 pair No. 3 knitting needles

Gauge
26sts to 4in in garter st on No. 3 needles.

Adult's mittens with snowflake pattern

Size
Width around hand above thumb, 8¾in.

Materials
2 × 2oz balls of a sport yarn in main color
Small amount of contrasting color
1 pair each Nos. 3 and 5 knitting needles

Gauge
20sts to 4in in stockinette st on No. 5 needles.

Adult's Fair Isle mittens

Right-hand mitten

Using No. 2 needles and main color, cast on 44sts. Work 20 rows K1, P1 ribbing. Change to No. 4 needles. Working first 22sts from chart, work 2 rows stockinette st.

Shape thumb

1st inc row K22, inc in next st, K1, inc in next st, K19.
Work 3 rows without shaping.
2nd inc row K22, inc in next st, K3, inc in next st, K19.
Work 3 rows straight. Cont to inc in this way on next and every foll 4th row until there are 56sts. Work 1 row.

Divide for thumb

Next row K22sts from chart, using main color K15, turn and cast on 2sts.
Next row P16, turn and cast on 2sts.
Using main color, cont on these

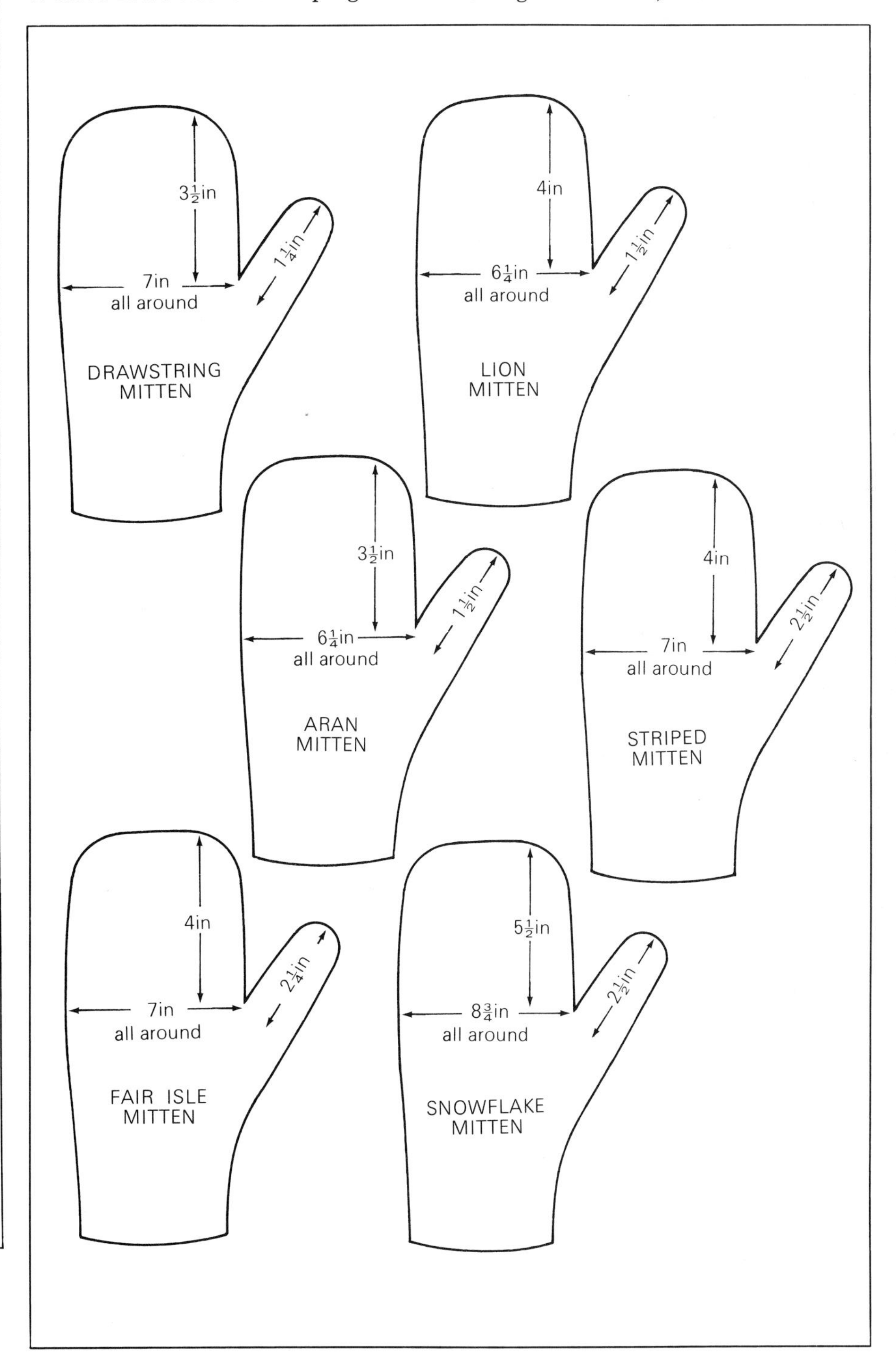

18sts for 2in; end with P row.

Shape top

1st row (K2 tog) 9 times.

2nd row P to end.

3rd row K1, (K2 tog) 4 times.

Cut off yarn leaving a long end; thread through rem sts, draw up and fasten off securely. Join thumb seam.

Using right-hand needle and main color, pick up 4sts from base of thumb, K to end of row. 46sts.

Working 22sts in Fair Isle from chart, cont straight until 48th row has been completed.

Shape top

Use main color only.

1st row K2, *sl 1, K1, psso, K16, K2 tog, K2, rep from * once.

2nd and every alternate row P to end.

3rd row K2, *sl 1, K1, psso, K14, K2 tog, K2, rep from * once.

5th row K2, *sl 1, K1, psso, K12, K2 tog, K2, rep from * once.

7th row K2, *sl 1, K1, psso, K10, K2 tog, K2, rep from * once.

8th row P to end.

Bind off. Join top and side seam.

Left-hand mitten

Work to match right-hand mitten, working last 22sts in patt from chart and reversing position of thumb as foll:

1st inc row K19, inc in next st, K1, inc in next st, K22.

Divide for thumb as foll:

Next row Using main color K34, turn and cast on 2sts.

Next row P16, turn and cast on 2sts.

Adult's striped mittens

Right-hand mitten

Using No. 3 needles and red, cast on 44sts. Work 20 rows K1, P1 ribbing. Cont in garter st and stripe sequence of 4 rows blue, 2 rows white, 4 green, 2 white, 4 yellow, 2 white, 4 red and 2 white. K 6 rows.

Shape thumb

1st inc row K22, inc in next st, K1, inc in next st, K19. K 5 rows.

2nd inc row K22, inc in next st, K3, inc in next st, K19.

Cont in this way, working 2sts more between increases, on every foll 6th row until there are 56sts. K 3 rows.

Divide for thumb

Next row K37, turn and cast on 2sts.

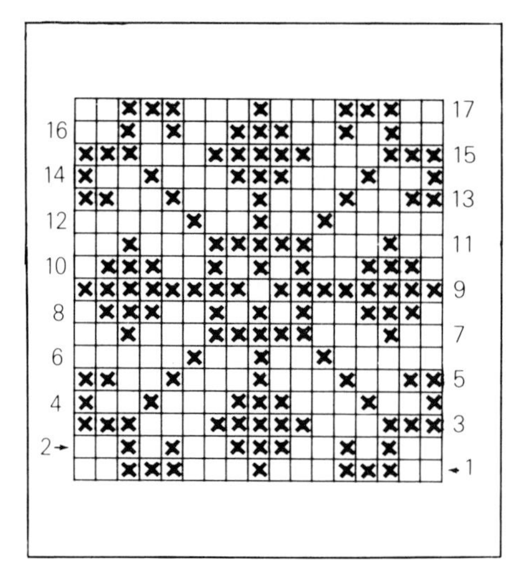

Next row K16, turn and cast on 2sts.

Cont on these 18sts in garter st and red only for 2½in.

Shape top

1st row K1, (K2, K2 tog) 4 times, K1.

2nd row K to end.

3rd row K1, (K2 tog) 6 times, K1.

Cut off yarn leaving a long end; thread through rem sts, draw up and fasten off securely. Join thumb seam.

Using right-hand needle and appropriate color, pick up and K 4sts from base of thumb, K to end of row. Work a further 4in in stripes; end with a WS row.

Shape top

1st row K2, *sl 1, K1, psso, K16, K2 tog, K2, rep from * once.

2nd and every alternate row K to end.

3rd row K2, *sl 1, K1, psso, K14, K2 tog, K2, rep from * once.

5th row K2, *sl 1, K1, psso, K12, K2 tog, K2, rep from * once.

7th row K2, *sl 1, K1, psso, K10, K2 tog, K2, rep from * once.

8th row K to end.

Bind off. Join top and side seam.

Left-hand mitten

Work to match right-hand mitten, reversing position of thumb as foll:

1st inc row K19, inc in next st, K1, inc in next st, K22.

2nd inc row K19, inc in next st, K3, inc in next st, K22.

Divide for thumb as foll:

Next row K34, turn and cast on 2sts.

Next row K16, turn and cast on 2sts.

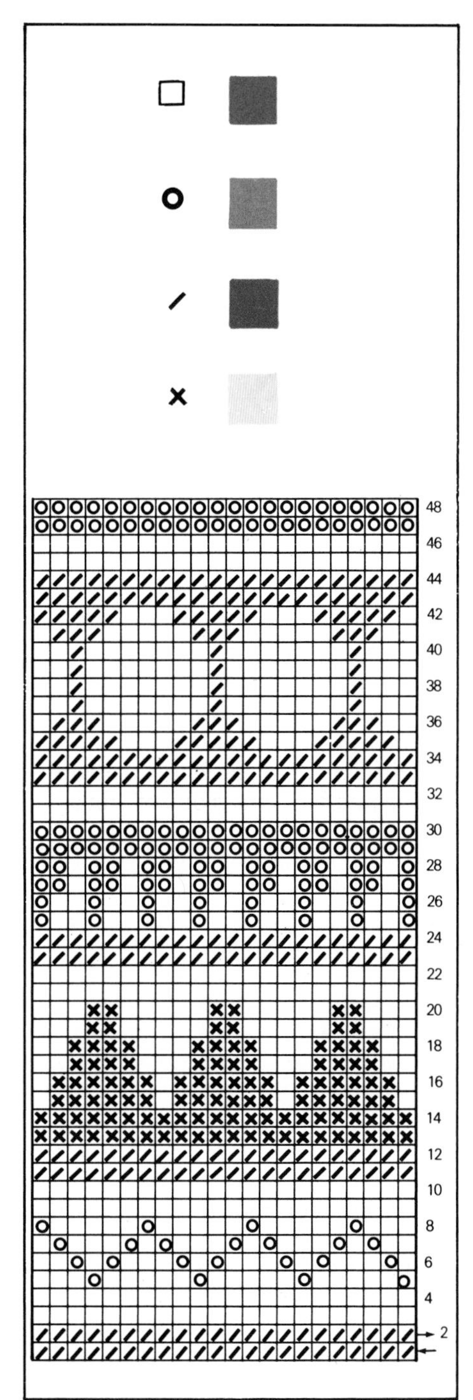

Adult's mittens with snowflake pattern

Right-hand mitten

Using No. 3 needles and main color (MC), cast on 37sts.

1st row K1, *P1, K1 rep from * to end.

2nd row P1, *K1, P1, rep from * to end.

Rep these 2 rows for 2in; end with a 1st row.

Next row (inc row) *Rib 4, inc in next st, rep from * 6 times, rib 2. 44sts. Change to No. 5 needles.

Shape thumb

1st row K24, pick up loop lying between needles and K tbl – called make 1 (M1) –, K1, M1, K19.

Work 3 rows stockinette st.

5th row K24, M1, K3, M1, K19.

Work 3 rows stockinette st.

9th row K24, M1, K5, M1, K19.

Work 3 rows stockinette st.

13th row K24, M1, K7, M1, K19.

14th row P to end.

Divide for thumb

Next row K34, turn and cast on 3sts.

Next row P14, turn.

Work 12 rows stockinette st on these 14sts.

Shape top

1st row *K1, K2 tog, rep from * 3 times, K2.

2nd row P to end.

3rd row K1, *K2 tog, rep from * 3 times, K1.

Cut off yarn leaving a long end; thread through rem sts, draw up and fasten off securely. Join thumb seam.

With right-hand needle, pick up and K 3sts from base of thumb, K to end of row. 44sts. P 1 row. Join in contrasting color (C). Beg snowflake patt.

1st row K5MC, 3C, 3MC, 1C, 3MC, 3C, using MC K to end.

2nd row P26MC, 1C, 1MC, 1C, 2MC, 3C, 2MC, 1C, 1MC, 1C, 5MC.

Cont in stockinette st and patt as set, beg row 3 of chart work 15 more rows. Using MC only, cont in stockinette st until work measures 4¾in from base of thumb; end with a P row.

Shape top

1st row K2, (sl 1, K1, psso, K15, K2 tog, K2) twice.

2nd and alternate rows P to end.

3rd row K2, (sl 1, K1, psso, K13, K2 tog, K2) twice.

5th row K2, (sl 1, K1, psso, K11, K2 tog, K2) twice.

7th row K2, (sl 1, K1, psso, K9, K2 tog, K2) twice.

8th row P to end.

Bind off. Join top and side seam.

Left-hand mitten

Work to match right-hand mitten, reversing position of thumb as foll:

1st row K19, M1, K1, M1, K24.

Divide for thumb as foll:

Next row K29, turn and cast on 3sts.

Next row P14, turn.

Child's mittens with drawstring

Right-hand mitten

Using No. 3 needles and A, cast on 34sts. Work 15 rows K1, P1 ribbing.
Next row (eyelet-hole row) K1, *yo, K2 tog, rep from * to last st, K1.
Change to No. 5 needles. Beg patt.
1st row *K1 tbl, P1, rep from * to end.
2nd row K to end.
These 2 rows form patt and are rep throughout. Work 2 more rows.

Shape thumb

1st inc row Patt 17, (P1, K1, P1) all into next st, K1, (P1, K1, P1) all into next st, patt 14. Patt 3 rows.
2nd inc row Patt 17, (P1, K1, P1) all into next st, patt 5, (P1, K1, P1) all into next st, patt 14. Patt 3 rows.
3rd inc row Patt 17, (P1, K1, P1) all into next st, patt 9, (P1, K1, P1) all into next st, patt 14. Patt 3 rows.

Divide for thumb

Next row Patt 31, turn and cast on 2sts.
Next row K14, turn and cast on 2sts.
Cont in patt on these 16sts for 1¼in; end with a WS row.

Shape top

Next row K2, (patt 2, work 2 tog) 3 times, patt 2.
Next row K to end.
Next row K1, (K2 tog) 6 times.
Cut off yarn leaving a long end; thread through rem sts, draw up and fasten off securely. Join thumb seam.
Using right-hand needle, pick up and K 4sts at base of thumb, patt to end of row. Work a further 3½in; end with a WS row.

Shape top

1st row *K2 tog, rep from * to end.
2nd row K1, *K2 tog, rep from * to end.
Cut off yarn leaving a long end; thread through rem sts, draw up and fasten off securely. Join side seam.

Left-hand mitten

Work to match right-hand mitten, reversing position of thumb as foll:
1st inc row Patt 14, (K1, P1, K1) all into next st, P1, (K1, P1, K1) all into next st, patt 17.
2nd inc row Patt 14, (K1, P1, K1) all into next st, patt 5, (K1, P1, K1) all into next st, patt 17.
3rd inc row Patt 14, (K1, P1, K1) all into next st, patt 9, (K1, P1, K1) all into next st, patt 17.
Divide for thumb as foll:
Next row Patt 28, turn and cast on 2sts.
Next row K14, turn and cast on 2sts.

To finish

Ties Using 4 strands of B tog, make 2 twisted cords 20in long. Thread through eyelet-hole row to tie at center back of mitten. Using remainder of B, make 4 pompons 2in in diameter and attach one to each end of each tie.

Child's Aran mittens

Cable panel (worked over 12sts)
1st row P2, K8, P2.
2nd row K2, P8, K2.
3rd and 4th rows As 1st and 2nd.
5th row P2, sl next 2sts onto cable needle and leave at back of work, K2, then K2 from cable needle – called C2B –, sl next 2sts onto cable needle and leave at front of work, K2, then K2 from cable needle – called C2F – P2.
6th row As 2nd.
7th and 8th rows As 1st and 2nd.
These 8 rows form patt and are repeated throughout.

Right-hand mitten

*Using No. 3 needles cast on 29sts.
1st row K1, *P1, K1, rep from * to end.
2nd row P1, *K1, P1, rep from * to end.
Rep these 2 rows for 2in; end with a 1st row.
Next row (inc row) Rib 2, *inc in next st, rib 7, rep from * twice, inc in next st, rib to end. 33sts.
Change to No. 5 needles.

Shape thumb

1st row K3, work 1st row cable panel, K2, pick up loop lying between needles and K tbl – called make 1 (M1) –, K2, M1, K14.
2nd row P to last 15sts, work 2nd row cable panel, P3.
3rd row K3, work 3rd row cable panel, K to end.
4th row P to last 15sts, work 4th row cable panel, P3.
5th row K3, work 5th row cable panel, K2, M1, K4, M1, K14.
These 5 rows set patt. Work a further 9 rows inc as set on 2 foll 4th rows. 41sts.

Child's mittens with drawstring

Size
Width around hand above thumb, 7in.

Materials
1 × 2oz ball of a sport yarn in main color (A)
1 ball of contrasting color (B) for drawstring and pompon
1 pair each Nos. 3 and 5 knitting needles

Gauge
22sts to 4in in patt on No. 5 needles.

Child's Aran mittens

Size
Width around hand above thumb, 6¼in.

Materials
1 × 2oz ball of a knitting worsted
1 pair each Nos. 3 and 5 knitting needles

Gauge
16sts to 4in in stockinette st on No. 5 needles.

Child's lion mittens

Size
Width around hand above thumb, 6¼in.

Materials
2 × 1oz of a knitting worsted in main color (A)
1 ball of contrasting color (B)
Scraps of black yarn for embroidery
4 buttons
1 pair each Nos. 3 and 5 knitting needles

Gauge
22sts and 24 rows to 4in in stockinette st on No. 5 needles.

Divide for thumb
Next row Patt 27sts, turn.
Next row P10, turn and cast on 2sts.
Work 8 rows stockinette st on these 12sts.
Shape top
Next row *K2 tog, rep from * to end.
Cut off yarn leaving a long end; thread through rem sts, draw up and fasten off. Join thumb seam. Using right-hand needle, pick up and K2sts from base of thumb, K to end of row. 33sts. Work further 3in in patt; end with WS row.*
Shape top
1st row K1, K2 tog tbl, K12, K2 tog, K2, K2 tog tbl, K9, K2 tog, K1.
2nd row P to end.
3rd row K1, K2 tog tbl, K10, K2 tog, K2, K2 tog tbl, K7, K2 tog, K1.
4th row P to end.
Bind off. Join top and side seam.

Left-hand mitten
Work to match right-hand mitten from * to *, reversing position of thumb as foll:
1st row K14, M1, K2, M1, K2, work cable panel 1st row, K3.
Divide for thumb as foll:
Next row K24, turn.
Next row P10, turn and cast on 2sts.

Shape top
1st row K1, K2 tog tbl, K9, K2 tog, K2, K2 tog tbl, K12, K2 tog, K1.
2nd row P to end.
3rd row K1, K2 tog tbl, K7, K2 tog, K2, K2 tog tbl, K10, K2 tog, K1.
4th row P to end.
Bind off. Join top and side seam.

Child's lion mittens

Right-hand mitten
Using No. 3 needles and A, cast on 32sts. Work 16 rows K1, P1 ribbing. Change to No. 5 needles. K1 row and P1 row.
Shape thumb
1st inc row K16, inc in next st, K1, inc in next st, K13.
Work 3 rows stockinette st.
2nd inc row K16, inc in next st, K3, inc in next st, K13.
Cont to inc in this way, working 2 more sts between increases, on every foll 4th row until there are 40sts. Work 3 rows stockinette st.
Divide for thumb
Next row K27, turn and cast on 2sts.
Next row P12, turn and cast on 2sts.
Work 1in stockinette st on these 14sts; end with P row.
Shape top
Next row K1, (K2, K2 tog) 3 times, K1.
Next row P to end.
Next row (K2 tog) 5 times, K1.
Cut off yarn leaving a long end; thread through rem sts, draw up and fasten off securely. Join thumb seam. Using right-hand needle pick up and K 4sts at base of thumb, K to end of row. Work a further 3¼in stockinette st; end with P row.
Shape top
1st row K2, *sl 1, K1, psso, K10, K2 tog, K2, rep from * once.
2nd and every alternate row P to end.
3rd row K2, *sl 1, K1, psso, K8, K2 tog, K2, rep from * once.
5th row K2, *sl 1, K1, psso, K6, K2 tog, K2, rep from * once.
7th row K2, *sl 1, K1, psso, K4, K2 tog, K2, rep from * once.
8th row P to end.
Bind off. Join top and side seam.

Left-hand mitten
Work to match right-hand mitten, reversing position of thumb as foll:
1st inc row K13, inc in next st, K1, inc in next st, K16.
2nd inc row K13, inc in next st, K3, inc in next st, K16.
Divide for thumb as foll:
Next row K24, turn and cast on 2sts.
Next row P12, turn and cast on 2sts.

To finish
Sew 2 buttons for eyes onto palm of mittens level with beg of top shaping.
Mane Cut 5in lengths of color B. Taking 2 strands tog each time, knot a pair of fringes through matching edge sts at back of hand and palm, beg about 8 rows below top shaping and cont all around to similar position on opposite side. Embroider nose and whiskers in black yarn as shown.
Tail Using 4 strands of B tog, make 2 twisted cords approx 4¾in long. Attach fold end to back of each mitten, then brush out knotted end.

GLOSSARY

bind off—Close off the knitting loops. See page 124 for working instructions.
blanket stitch—A simple looped embroidery stitch. When the loops are worked close together, it is known as buttonhole stitch. See page 17 for working instructions.
buttonhole stitch—A simple looped embroidery stitch. It is useful for reinforcing both knit and crocheted buttonholes. See page 119 for working instructions.
cast on—Make the required number of loops onto your knitting needle to form the foundation of the knitted fabric. See page 122 for working instructions.
continue straight—This phrase appears in knitting and crochet patterns. It means that you should continue working on the same number of stitches without increasing or decreasing stitches until told to do so.
crab stitch—A simple crochet stitch, usually used as an edging. To work crab stitch, make single crochet stitches into the top of the stitches of the previous row but work from left to right instead of from right to left (see page 48).
decreasing—Lessening the number of stitches in a row of knitting or crochet. See page 124 for how to work knitting decreases and page 13 for how to work crochet decreases.
fasten off—Break off the yarn and draw the end through the last loop on the needle or hook.
garter stitch—This knitting stitch is formed by knitting both right-side and wrong-side rows. For circular knitting, knit one row and purl one row alternately.
herringbone stitch—A simple crossed embroidery stitch. It is useful for attaching elastic to waistbands of knit or crocheted skirts or pants. See page 200 for working instructions.
increasing—Adding to the number of stitches in a row of crochet or knitting. See page 125 for how to make knitting increases and page 13 for how to make crochet increases.
knitting into the stitch below—A method for increasing the number of stitches. See page 208 for working instructions.
knitwise—Insert the needle into the stitch as if you were about to knit it. Also written K-wise.
knotted fringe—See page 89 for working instructions for this useful edging.
lazy daisy stitch—A looped embroidery stitch. For working instructions see page 17.
pick up and knit (or purl)—Knit (or purl) into the loops along the edge of the fabric. See page 125 for working instructions.
picot edging—See page 21 for the working instructions for this useful crochet border.
purlwise—Insert the needle into the stitch as if you were about to purl it. Also written P-wise.
reverse stockinette stitch—Also called "purl fabric". All right-side rows are purled and all wrong-side rows are knit.
slip stitch color patterns—A technique used to create colorwork stitches in knitting. See page 219 for working instructions.
splicing yarn—A method used to join on a new ball of yarn. For working instructions see page 12.
stem stitch—A flat embroidery stitch. See page 68 for working instructions.
stockinette stitch—Also known as "plain knitting". All right-side rows are knit and all wrong-side rows are purled.
surface crochet—Chain stitch (or single crochet) worked through the fabric. See page 112 for working instructions.
Tunisian crochet—Also called "Afghan crochet". See page 96 for working instructions.
twisted cord—A simple cord formed by twisting two or more strands of yarn around one another. See page 143 for working instructions.

approx	approximately
beg	begin(ning)
ch	chain(s)
cm	centimeter(s)
cont	continu(e)(ing)
dc	double crochet
dec	decreas(e)(ing)
dtr	double triple crochet
foll	follow(ing)
g	gram(s)
grp(s)	group(s)
hdc	half double crochet
in	inch(es)
inc	increas(e)(ing)
K	knit
m	meter(s)
mm	millimeter(s)
no(s)	numbers
oz	ounce(s)
P	purl
patt	pattern
psso	pass slipped stitch over
rem	remain(ing)
rep	repeat
RS	right side
sc	single crochet
sl	slip
sp(s)	space(s)
sl st	slip stitch
st(s)	stitch(es)
tbl	through back of loop(s)
tog	together
tr	triple crochet
tr tr	triple triple
WS	wrong side
wyib	with yarn in back
wyif	with yarn in front
yd	yard(s)
yo	yarn over (hook or needle)

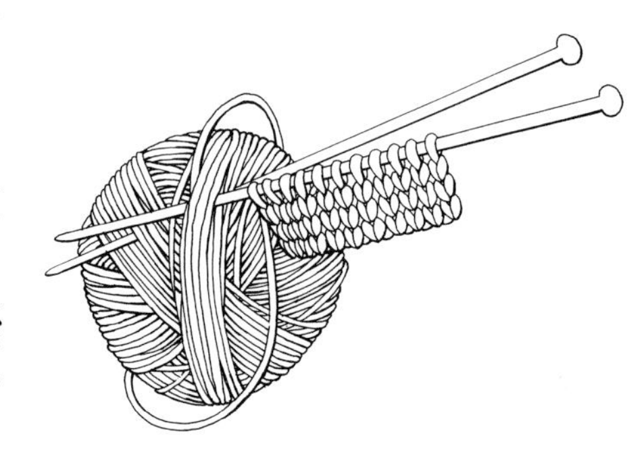

INDEX

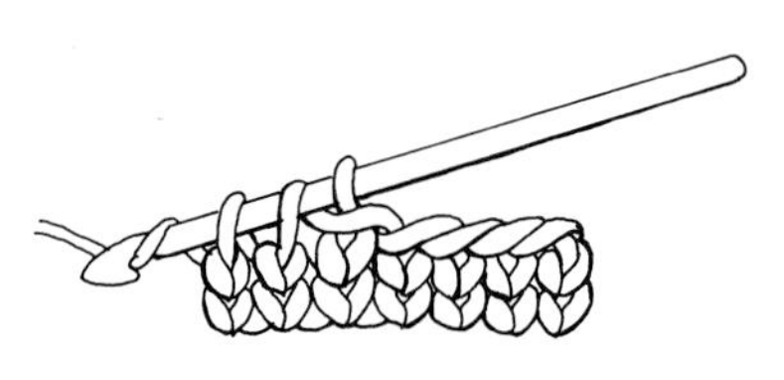

Photographers

Caroline Arber: 65
Belinda: 39, 153, 155, 156
Tony Boase: 31, 145, 146, 147, 197, 198, 199, 223, 226
Michael Boys: 15
David Bradfield: 25
Simon Butcher: 16, 19, 27, 34, 36
Roger Charity: 185
Rod Delroy: 49, 51, 86, 179, 209, 211, 214, 216
Ray Duns: 68, 169
Ross Greetham: 42
Chris Harvey: 181, 184, 206, 208(r), 220
Serge Krouglikoff: 46, 54, 73, 75, 88, 89, 90, 171, 227, 229
Tom Leighton: 105
Chris Lewis: 120
Vince Loden: 91
Sandra Lousada: 83
Stefano Massimo: 61, 161
Stuart McLeod: 23, 80/1, 135, 136, 172, 175
Kim Sayer: 8, 29, 30, 35, 57, 59, 113, 127, 131(b), 132, 133, 203
Jerry Tubby: 129, 130
Jean Claude Volpeliere: 70, 76, 195
Peter Waldman: 201
Gary Warren: 52, 163, 165, 166, 217, 219
Si Wells: 37, 107
Marcus Wilson-Smith: 95, 111
Victor Yuan: 67, 98/9, 103, 117, 139, 141, 142, 149, 150, 191(r), 192, 194, 231

Illustrators

Patricia Capon: 68, 69(r)
Terry Cheverton: 38(r)
Terry Evans: 17(r), 180, 200
Barbara Firth: 66(l)
John Hutchinson: 14, 17(l), 24, 26, 28, 32, 33(l), 53(l), 60, 62, 63, 77, 78, 79, 92, 97, 100, 101, 104, 106, 109(l), 114, 119(t), 128(t), 137, 144, 152, 158, 168, 170(b), 173, 177, 178, 183, 196, 202(l), 204, 213, 215, 229, 230(t), 232
Trevor Lawrence: 74
Brian Mayor: 20, 36, 41, 47, 56(r), 69(l), 71, 96(b), 110, 128(b), 154, 160, 190, 191(bl), 193, 207, 218, 222, 225
Andy Miles: 45, 66(r), 82, 84, 148(l), 189, 225
Coral Mula: 10–13, 21, 33(r), 38(l), 56(l), 72, 75, 89, 96(t), 109(r), 119(b), 123–125, 130, 131(c), 143, 164, 167, 208(l), 219

D1360877